The Far Beyond

The Far Beyond

BY WARWICK THOMPSON

David Ling Publishing Limited
PO Box 34601, Birkenhead
Auckland 0746, New Zealand
www.davidling.co.nz

ISBN 978-1-877378-27-0

First Published 2009

© Warwick Thompson 2009

The author has asserted his right to be
identified as the author of this work

This book is copyright. Apart from any
fair dealing for the purpose of private study,
research, criticism, or review as permitted
under the Copyright Act, no part may be
reproduced by any process without the
prior written permission of the Publisher.

The cover shows a detail from 'In The Kawara Gorge'
by William Mathew Hodgkins.
Reproduced by permission of the Alexander Turnbull Library, Wellington.

Typeset by Express Communications Limited
Printed in New Zealand

Dedicated to the memory of my great-grandfather and the many like him who voyaged to 'the far beyond'.

Although *The Far Beyond* refers to real events and actual historical figures, the work as a whole is fiction and the dialogue and characterisations of individuals are from the author's own imagination.

ONE

The 18th of March 1834 was not a good day for my father Hugh Fraser.

Even though my mother Catherine had successfully survived my birth that day, Father now had another body to feed, house and clothe and he had all the work that was available in the village of Melvich already. Another pregnancy so long after my two brothers were born could not have been met with unalloyed happiness by either of them, just renewed apprehension at the risks of childbirth and the burden of yet another life to sustain.

Above all else, the Highland Scots were known for their stoicism imprinted onto successive generations by centuries of oppression, hardship, and the harsh environment. No doubt that forbearance sustained my father and mother for the intervening months and beyond, and by then I had arrived and the inevitable expansion of the family had been accepted. At least we were all boys; boys could grow to be independent one day and perhaps help to support their parents when age eventually wearied them.

I don't have significant memories of my early years, just impressions like those that most of us carry deeply through life, particularly those that affected us physically. Above all, I remember the cold; a cold seemingly always present, that seeped up from the stone floor as if coming from the centre of the earth itself, or waiting patiently outside ready to pounce and surge through into the cottage whenever the door was opened. No doubt the stone walls did keep out the worst of it but they too were always cold to the touch even when logs blazed in the hearth and I soon learned the air was coldest next to them. Later, I could always tell a man who had been raised in a stone cottage by how far he kept away from the walls of a house.

My eldest brother Thomas died of consumption before a picture of him had even formed in my memory and so only my older brother Robert and I had to share the small room with a sloping roof at the back of the cottage. Because of the years between us, Robert was seemingly always big like my father, though tall and narrow in the shoulders, so that his clothes that were later passed on to me were too long in the arms and legs but tight around my chest.

We were never perpetually hungry that I can recall, unlike many Highland Scots young boys. There was ample porridge each morning and meat every night. My mother would knead dough on the big wooden table and bake squat loaves of bread in a great iron pot beside the fire. The sweet smell of cooking crust filled the room until I could barely contain my expectation. Then the lid would come off and the brown loaves would rest on the table to cool, taking forever, while I would clutch Mother's skirts with one small arm and stare longingly at the crust knowing that eventually she would break a piece off for me. My father and Robert would come in at night and Father, seeing the loaf already broken, would always say 'Catherine, you've been spoiling the boy again.'

The door of the cottage faced to the more sheltered south, up the glen to the mountains beyond. Not that we could see the highlands very often. The far north Sunderlandshire coast of Scotland is as one with the sea, ocean unbroken by land all the way north to the arctic ice and Melvich would drift in and out of fog for much of the time. Fog and ocean and sky would blend into a greyness without boundaries, hiding the mountains that you knew were the limits of the glen and one moment Melvich was a part of the land and next seemingly adrift in the grey sea itself. In winter, when fierce storms had roared in from the northeast and swept the land with snow, for a brief time the sky might clear and as the faint winter daylight returned in the middle of the day, the highlands would reappear, dominating our world with their size and whiteness. Such was the rarity of this sight that we would stop whatever was being done and stand to look, so that when again it vanished into the cloud we could carry the curve of the land rising up from the glen to the mountains, in our minds.

Across the stone-paved yard beyond the door, within a distance my mother could reach with a call, was the forge. My first and earliest memory is of following Father as he and Robert crossed the yard in the brightening morning light one summer into the sudden darkness of the stone building of the forge. I think by then I was probably about five or coming close to six. I still remember feeling the warmth as if being enveloped and wrapped by some invisible presence and being fascinated by the brightness of the fire that burned like a piece of the sun captured behind the stone hearth.

By winter of that year I too was making a daily journey across the yard through the heaped snow to watch Robert and my father at work in the forge. The small stone building with its earthen floor soon became an irresistible attraction for me and my mother had to become very insistent for me to stay in the cottage each morning and help her.

We would wash the dishes after porridge, clean down the table and sweep the floor with a straw whisk. The fire would be held in with fresh squares of peat to keep burning slowly until wood was added in the evening. My Mother would often sit in front of the spinning wheel and I learned to help tease and twist the greasy strands of raw wool for her to feed to the rotating wheel driven by her foot and then to wind the woven strand into a ball, round and round until my fingers slowed and hurt. Other days she would sit before the fire and knit this wool into the thick socks, shirts and jerkins that we wore, or mittens and caps that smelled forever of the wool grease that seemed never to wash away.

But the forge, not the cottage, was where I impatiently wanted to be. So eventually, mother would acknowledge my obvious fidgeting to leave and with her 'och John, be gone with you now' still in my ears I would be across the yard and into the low stone building.

It was such an impressive place of noise and heat and violence. Robert, being so much older than I, was already growing to a young man and worked all day helping my father. Using a small wooden handcart and shovel he would bring loads of coal from out in the yard to add to the heap in the corner by the furnace. Every so often this had to be lifted a shovel-full at a time and thrown deep into the fire to vanish instantly in the swirl of living flames. Then Robert would pump the two arms of the wood and leather bellows that blasted air into the furnace, forcing the yellow flame to change to a white intensity so bright that it seemed to burn into your eyes just to look at it.

My father, bare from the waist up and golden-brown from the light of the furnace will always be to me the biggest man I have ever known. Even now I can still see the huge yoke of his shoulders shining with sweat and patterned with lines of coaldust as his long thick-muscled arm swung the giant peening hammer lightly down on the anvil, showering sprays of sparks out across the earthen floor.

The forge and what was done there fascinated me. It wasn't just the physical violence. It was a magic place, where lumps of heavy black iron came alive, glowing on the anvil and spewing white-heated streams of stars in protest at being struck by the hammer. Then hissing and steaming in the quenching trough, before emerging in new shapes and forms of their own. It was as if the dragons my mother told me about in stories were themselves being tamed and formed here in this very room.

I longed to try shaping hot iron myself. I had no knowledge of what each strange shape that rose still steaming from the quenching trough clasped firmly in my father's tongs was for. Now I know well that each was a vital part and substance of village life; hinges for a gate or a door, harness parts for horses, the rims of carriage wheels, knives, fire and cooking tools, gardening implements, rivets, elbows, knees, fairleads, rowlocks, small stanchions and anchors all for boats. Each with a distinctive shape and for a different life of its own.

Soon I was allowed to try. Holding the glowing piece with small tongs in my left hand and lying it still on the anvil, I gently and then more strongly struck it with a hammer for the first time. As I watched and struck again and again it changed shape, more slowly and needing more force than I expected, but for an oversize seven-year-old I was quite strong enough to make a difference to it. I think that moment was the real beginning of my life. It is with me still.

From just beating pieces of white-hot iron with a hammer I quickly developed sufficient confidence to try recognisable physical shapes. Within weeks I had progressed to forming simple flanges for gate hinges and then to open buckle-frames for harnesses. My father watched with some surprise and then much encouragement when he saw that my capability with the hammer was already of some practical use and he often stood at my left shoulder, guiding my hammer with his years of experience. Even Robert gave me space on the anvil.

I spent a lot of my time in the forge making rivets and ship-nails – square-sided long tapering nails with a flat head – and after not much practise I could beat these out very quickly, filling several boxes each day. Horseshoes were another simple piece and I could work the metal into its curve, moving the piece with the tongs between hammer-blows left-then-right, left-then-right. These both became so easy to make that while I worked my mind would roam off into thinking where each ship nail and shoe would be used and imagining them travelling to some far-off place.

Each day I would find a moment to try forging some new piece and other than the limitation of my actual physical strength it seemed that the shapes would just flow out under the blows and taps of the hammer almost unconsciously. Once, a shipwright from the village collecting another box of ship-nails stood back against the wall to watch us work and called to my father 'Do y'ken Fraser, young John may be a mite but he has a sweet hammer in his hand and for his age he's no a wee laddie either.'

I remember my father walking back across the cobbled yard to the house one evening put his huge hand on my shoulder and said 'Robert's learning to be a good blacksmith but you John, I think you could become a true artist with the iron' and my shoulders lifted in pride at the unexpected praise. And later, he commented to my mother 'the boy's still a child, but he has a strong feeling for hot iron. The day will come when he's a better smithy than his brother.'

* * *

We stood on the hillside, backs turned against the wind and huddled together trying to form a common shelter against the sweeping shafts of rain. Women of Melvich clothed and hooded in black, men standing straight to help protect them from the cold, my father strongly between Robert and I with his great hands on each of our shoulders. A man whom I did not know was reading from a book but his words were being stolen by the wind. Before us was a hole in the ground, fresh earth and stones piled up behind, glistening in the rain - another scene seared like a burn onto the memories of childhood, to become a scar for life. My dear mother had died.

I had known for weeks before that she was sick. Coming back from the forge into the evening comfort and warmth of the cottage, the smell of hot food and the welcome hugs from my mother were so commonplace until one night we crossed the yard, opened the door, and she wasn't there. Instead, a woman from the village leaned over the iron stove and my father strode past with a mumbled greeting and through the doorway to their room. Our mother lay in bed and for days the sound of her coughing kept sounding in my ears even when she had stopped, or even against the ringing of my hammer on the anvil in the forge. We prepared and ate our own porridge in silence each morning and waited until a village woman would arrive before we would leave the house.

Then a day came when Father left Robert and I alone in the forge and with help from some village people, carried mother wrapped in heavy woollen blankets to a waiting dray. Robert and I stood together in the doorway of the forge, watching. The horse plodded over our cobbled yard, the wheels rumbled against the stones and the dray disappeared out through the gate and into the lane. It was the last time I saw her.

Now it seemed such a short time later and we were standing here on the hillside feeling so alone, listening to women crying and watching the man with no voice reading from a book. I had not been to this place before, yet dying was a commonplace event in Melvich and, like all the children of the village, I had come to know about it from the earliest time I could understand. Men went missing at sea, they drowned whilst fishing or had accidents with horses and equipment working the land; women died during or shortly after childbirth; children – like the brother I had never known – died from measles or chickenpox or other poxes from cuts; and everyone could die from the consumption and coughs that swept through Melvich with the fogs and winds from the North Sea. The small groups of people in dark clothes shuffling along behind a horse-drawn dray were a familiar sight in Halla Dale. And occasionally for the few better off who were buried in caskets, my father would make their brass or iron handles and cornices in our forge.

Then the man closed his book, a piper blew and squeezed his bagpipes and the huddled people began to sing a slow and low song together. The giant hand of my father gripped my shoulder so hard I struggled not to show the pain. I watched rivulets of rain carving their path through the heaped earth. Two men with shovels stepped forward trying not to slip on the sodden ground, dug soil and stones from the pile and began to fill in the open hole before us in the ground. Then almost as a group, we all turned to face into the rain and with heads down, shuffled off toward the gate in the low stone wall and back down the hill to Melvich.

That evening our cottage was filled with people, many of whom were strangers but all of whom would seek me out, put a hand on my head or shoulder and press me against them. The men drank whisky and the women put food on the table for us all. Finally they were gone and the house was still. Then it was back to a daily routine of stirring awake the embers of the fire, cooking and eating our morning porridge, waiting for a woman from the village to come, and listening to the silence. At evening, the woman would give us a dinner and then disappear into the night.

My father would rarely speak. He would sit or stand and for long periods stare into the fire, saying nothing to us, as if he had gone to another place and only left his body there in the room with Robert and I. In the forge, he would sometimes seem too tired to work, yet other times swing the penning hammers so hard the piece itself would shatter on the anvil, skidding chunks of bright red iron in every direction across the room as Robert and I leapt away in fright.

I can remember being in the cottage alone, creeping into my mother's room as if being watched and afraid of being discovered. I would open the wooden chest standing against the wall and take out a shawl or wrap she had knitted herself from wool we had probably spun together, and with uncontrollable childhood tears bury my face into it, breathing in her still-present distinctive smell that would envelop me and accentuate my loneliness still more, until sitting on the floor with my head against my knees and arms wrapped tightly against the wool, I would sob myself out.

We lived not as a family but as a man, a boy and a child existing and working together until one evening when we returned to the cottage, Mrs McCullough, the lady from the village, came from in front of the iron stove and handed my father a letter.

For some days after, he became very quiet and silent, working all day in the forge and saying almost nothing. At night after Mrs McCullough had left, he would sit in solitude, staring into the fire, saying nothing, until Robert and I would go to bed. Finally one morning as we crossed the yard from the house to the forge, he gripped my shoulder and suddenly said, 'John, we are going on a voyage soon. We are going to visit my sister – your aunt.'

He slowed as we got closer to the forge, Robert walking on ahead, holding me back with his tightly-gripping hand and turning me to face more toward himself. Like the day that my mother was laid to rest, I could feel the strength of emotion surging through his hand.

'I canna keep y'here. Y'still a bairn John and I canna look after ye. Robert is old enough to stay here and to work, but you're a mite wee laddie yet f'that. Y'auntie has agreed to take y'in and take care of ye. They have a big place, far away from here, but they can do for you what I canna. You can go to school, learn to read and write. You have cousins – boys near your own age – they all live in a big house with land around. I don't want it John, but it's no' right to keep y'here,' and suddenly releasing me, he walked into the forge.

More days passed. Father went to Port Skerra from Melvich with a horse and returned with two large wooden sea chests which were slowly packed with clothing, footwear and some bedding. Then came one morning, clear and calm, when Mrs McCullough arrived early to take Robert back to her cottage in the village and for my father and I to leave.

For me it was an adventure, going outside my normal surroundings and I was eager to see what was ahead. So leaving our home was not that important and the significance of it only came to me a long time later, when I would think back to our last moments closing the door, walking across the grey cobbles of the yard and out through the gate, father leading the horse carrying our two boxes and me striding along beside. We took the road to the port. With no bridges to cross the multitude of rivers and inlets along the north coast of Scotland there were also no roads, and all journeys began or ended at the port.

I had never been onto a boat before, I had only seen them from afar. From among the bustle of people crowded on the quay in Port Skerra, walking on to the boat was just an extension of the land and climbing down a narrow stairway into the darker spaces below was like the ladder to the loft above our forge. It was only when we pulled away from the quay and the space of water between us grew wider that our actually being with the boat was a reality. I watched the sail being hoisted and felt the boat lift and move like a live thing, absorbed in this new experience.

Out of the little port, the ocean surface was no longer calm and the boat took on a regular motion with the waves, Father and I standing by a rail and holding tightly to the ropes, watching waves surge up from under the bow and the whiter spray curling back onto the grey sea until it was almost dark.

Night was especially frightening. For a child accustomed to the solidity of a stone cottage which didn't move even the slightest when the winds of winter roared across the roof, being buried in darkness below the deck of the boat was as if I had been swallowed by huge animal. Amid a cacophony of new sounds, each filled with the unknown, the narrow wooden bed on which I huddled would not keep still and the rolling and pitching motion soon made me feel unwell. It was the same for my father too, and together we struggled grimly through an almost sleepless night.

When daylight returned, we emerged back on deck and, clutching the rail with a fresh wind blowing around us, we looked out toward a diffused grey horizon, and soon both of us felt better and more interested in our surroundings. Before long my apprehension decreased and I was enjoying watching the oncoming waves roll toward the dipping bow and feeling the lift as the crest swung past us in curls of froth and spray. A confidence developed that the boat was able to follow the contours of the windy ocean and that we would not be buried by each advancing wave.

During that second day as I learned to move against the motion of the boat and gained some stability, I could look up and watch the wind rippling across the grimy sails, listening to the sounds they made and the creaking of all the ropes when gusts would stretch the grimy canvas out. Thus I rapidly learned the origin and causes of many of the noises which had so frightened me during the night.

By the third day, I had decided that a boat was indeed like a huge animal, though one that men were controlling and we were riding. It was a whole new world of new experience – an ever-changing and fascinating one.

More days and nights passed. All too soon for me, land again appeared out of the greyness one morning. As we closed toward it, the sea smoothed, the sails sagged and flapped and we disturbed large flocks of birds which beat at the water with their wings and walked on the surface with their large feet and glided into the air as they escaped us. Closer to land I could see we were heading to the entrance of a port, much larger than Port Skerra we had left behind. Long columns of grey stone houses lined down the hillside in rows and a cluster of masts soon revealed many other boats ranged against a long quay. We had arrived at Larne, on the northeast coast of Ireland.

Two small boats came towards us and, after attaching lines, pulled us toward the timbered stone of the quay. Soon we were fast alongside and I watched from the rail as crowds of people surged around, a busy mass of shouting and movement. Holding tightly to my hand, Father pushed down the ramp from the boat and pulled me behind him through the noisy throng. We soon came to a large building fronting the quay. After our days on the boat, the ground itself seemed to be moving and I had difficulty walking straight. Inside, the building was quieter but still busy with people. He spoke for some time with men behind a long counter, then we moved to a calmer corner of the room and sat on a bench at a long table.

We waited. When I was almost asleep, a tall smiling young man approached us.

'Mr Fraser?' My father stood up. 'I am Arthur, your nephew, and this must be my cousin John? I've been waiting for you for many days, not knowing on which boat you would be arriving, but I was sent to await word of you and to fetch you home.'

We were outside again, moving away from the crowded quay and I looked closely at my new-found cousin as he and Father strode along. He was as tall as father but not as broad-shouldered, freckled faced and with reddish-coloured hair. A brown jacket of leather covered slightly rounded shoulders and he wore heavy leather boots. We arrived at stables and waited again for Arthur to appear, leading a horse pulling a small large-wheeled cart onto which we climbed.

We returned to the quay, which was less crowded and noisy now and, with the horse making a way for us through the surging crowd, came to our boat from which father collected our two large chests. Then we moved off the quay, down a stone-covered road past the town and out into the countryside. It was my first ride on a cart; the speed of the ground moving beneath us in a blur was initially quite frightening and I clung tightly to the iron rail beside me.

I was surprised how different the country was from my brown familiar land around Melvich. All around us was green: green grass, green hedges and trees covered all the rolling landscape. We travelled through small valleys, then alongside streams, crossing at times on raised stone bridges and passing large houses of grey stone. Our journey went through several villages where grey stone buildings with few windows loomed over both sides of the road, the steady 'clomp' of the horses' hooves echoing loudly as we rolled by. Other horses with carts of different shapes and sizes, many carrying loads, passed by us on the road and their riders would call and wave. Later in the day, the valley we were in became deeper and wider, with higher hills in the distance on either side, until finally we turned from the road into a narrow, winding, hedge-lined lane.

Around a corner and on our left stood another grey stone house, larger than most we had seen and set back from the lane behind a low stone wall. From a gate in the wall, a path lined with small dark trees led to a large closed door. 'This is home,' Arthur shouted as we passed by and turned left from the lane, past the end of the house and around left again into a walled and paved yard behind, scattering geese, ducks and fowls. Other stone buildings fronted onto the yard and we turned sharply in front of one.

People appeared from a doorway in the house as we climbed down stiffly from the cart. An enormous woman with long hair, almost as wide across as she was tall and calling, 'Hugh, Hugh' threw her arms around my father. Two other boys, both tall, one closer to my age, stood nearby, looking curiously at us. Father gripped me by the shoulder and pulled my forward.

'This is John, my son.'

The huge woman spoke directly to me in a strong loud voice, 'and I am your father's sister, your aunt Colina, and (turning toward them both), these boys are more of your cousins, Harry and George.' She reached out and pulled me to her, hugging me into her voluminous skirt. It smelled of peat smoke.

The next several days seemed to pass in a blur but, because I came to know it so well, the house and its surrounds are clear in my mind since that first day my new cousin George led me around it. After our small cottage in Melvich, I stared in amazement as we went into one large room after another, following my aunt who was so broad that she had to turn herself on an angle to go through each doorway.

From the rear door off the wide stone-cobbled yard we passed through an outer room with a sloping slate roof, stacked high at the back with peat sods and neatly-piled cut rounds of wood, through another doorway into a large kitchen in the centre of which was a great wooden table. A familiar warmth surrounded us as we entered. Along one wall was a wide shallow pit and hearth with a peat fire burning, smoke twisting up in places along its length into a cavernous stone chimney. Rising from the floor at the right of the fireplace and angled completely across it was a thick iron beam, similar to the beams I had seen on the boat being used to swing nets of boxes on and off the quayside, from which on a series of hooks dangled a variety of large blackened pots. A large wooden chair sat in the corner to the right of the fire where the iron beam was bedded in the floor.

Well to the left of the fireplace, another low open doorway showed light in a rear room which we passed by without entering before following my aunt around the long kitchen table and through another door at the end of the room. This was the front hall and in front of me towered the great wooden door which we had seen from the lane as we passed by the house when we first arrived. On the left, a wide stone stairway rose up to another level out of sight above us and on the right we followed my aunt through into a single room, larger than our whole cottage in Melvich, filled with tables and chairs and another high stone fireplace. Windows set deep into the two-foot thick outer walls lit the room and I stared in surprise at woven coverings on the floor, which to my further surprise, my aunt now walked upon.

Without stopping, she led my father and I, followed closely by George and Harry, back into the entry hall and up the stone stairs to the level above. From the top of the stairs, a wooden-floored narrow hall led off to the right with doorways on either side into rooms that faced either to the front or the rear of the house. We passed by one and through the next entered a square room with a roof sloping down toward a window looking out over the rear walled yard.

'This is your room, Hugh, during your stay,' she said to my father 'and then John can share it with young George.' It was a very different room from the one I had shared with my brother Robert.

At night, the house filled with men as my other cousins and my uncle returned home from working in the fields. I was in some awe with the size of these people I had never seen before. Although my father was one of the biggest men in Melvich, he didn't seem so big among my new relatives. My cousins were grown men whom I now knew as Charles, Alexander, Hugh and David, then Arthur who had met us at Larne and was almost a man, followed by younger Harry and then closer to my age, came George. My uncle, Malcolm Bruce, was a red-haired giant who towered over them all.

During those next days, I explored all our new surroundings, initially with the help of Harry and George. Behind the stone wall at the rear of the house, farmland stretched off into the distance. The stone-cobbled rear yard into which we had arrived was a long rectangle almost surrounded by buildings of various sizes connected with a high wall so that it appeared completely enclosed.

The two-level section of the house was mostly along its south side, falling to one level at the west end, making an L. This lower section of house, the rear door of which we had entered, was divided into three rooms; the rear entry hall closest to the main building, then a small room enclosing a low square stone structure topped with a wooden seat above a very deep hole, then at the end a much larger room for a wash-house. This stone-paved room, with several windows, had an enormous iron bath on legs along the back wall and at the right end a large copper bowl was mounted on top of a stone fireplace with chimney above. To either side on the floor squatted more and smaller copper bowls and wooden tables. Cut logs of wood were stacked neatly up to the sloping roof in the corner.

Outside the washhouse stood a large black iron pump, its long hinged handle almost at the height of my chest. Water buckets of various sizes surrounded its base. My cousins daily pumped this handle up and down in a long slow routine, filling buckets to carry to the house and for the animals across the yard.

A high stone wall joined the outer end of the washhouse, enclosing the end of the yard across to the northwest corner. A wooden door, divided across its middle into two sections, was set into this wall, which opened into a large orchard filled with apple, plum and walnut trees surrounded by a low stone wall to keep out animals.

Fronting onto the north side of the yard was another long narrow slate-roofed stone building, a byre, divided by internal walls into many bays. The front of each bay had wooden rails and a door. At the time of our arrival, most of these were empty, but one contained two large cows and a further two bays at the east end held a number of noisy pigs. Where the byre ended at the east was a recessed section of high wall which curved away in the corner to a large timber gate leading out to the farmland.

All along the west end of the yard was another two-level stone building, much narrower than the main house and not as high. This building had no windows but at regular spaces along both levels were small solid-wood doors, all closed. Several ladders were leaning against the wall reaching to the upper-level doors. In the corner between this building and the house was the walled entrance leading from the lane, through which we had come on our arrival.

That end of the house which at first I had thought was enclosed on the ground level, was actually open to the yard in two large bays. Each was sufficiently large to hold a cart or carriage, one completely enclosing the gig in which we had travelled from Larne with its shafts up to the roof, the other holding a much larger open carriage, its long curving shafts projecting out into the yard and resting on the paving stones.

We didn't venture far beyond the rear wall through the short lane leading out to the farmland but out there I could see cows, horses and sheep. Poultry wandered everywhere. Green fields spotted with trees stretched away as far as I could see in all directions.

My men-cousins were about the yard at times during the day, pumping and carrying water, bringing wood and peat-sods for the fires on a horse-drawn dray or piles of hay to feed to the animals in the byre. Each evening when my uncle and cousins finally returned to the house, we all gathered in the kitchen around the great wooden table. Seemingly all day my aunt had been working with food in the kitchen or sitting in the large wooden chair to the right of the fire as she tended to the iron pots hanging from the beam over the hot coals. Now the beam would be swung away, the pots lifted onto the table and with long-handled ladles, our plates were piled with potatoes and meat stews.

In a moment of silence, my uncle would recite a short grace the end of which signalled a pent-up rush to eat and to talk. Sitting beside my father, while our heads were bowed in silence for the grace, I peered through half-closed eyes at the ten of us around the table – a scene so different from the cottage we had left behind in Melvich. All around, my cousins were talking, mostly of things I did not understand and with words I did not know. There was also some laughing together and I even saw my father smiling at times, something I had only seen when my mother was alive and not since then.

At night, father and I shared George and Harry's upstairs room together. During the day, from early in the morning, he was gone from the house with all the other men to help in the fields and I wished that I too could go with him. A day after our arrival and every day after, both Harry and George left early each morning to go to school in villages nearby and so I was alone around the house and yard with my aunt. I would help carrying water or peat and wood for the fire, and collect potatoes and other vegetables from the outbuildings.

My aunt talked with me a lot, asking me many questions about Melvich, Robert, questions I couldn't answer about my other brother who died of the consumption, or questions about my mother which I didn't want to discuss. But quickly I felt that she was friendly to me and, in return, she would tell me of anything I asked about all that newly surrounded me.

Then just as I was becoming more familiar with my new surroundings and accustomed to all my new relations, I woke one morning to find my father still in our room sitting on the side of the bed, instead of having left early with the other men for the fields. He was already dressed. As I left the bed he reached out and clasped my shoulder firmly in his huge hand. Standing, I turned to face him, our eyes almost at the same level. He put his left hand on my other shoulder. Both his hands tightened in a familiar grip.

'Son, the day has come when I must leave you here. It is time to go back to Robert and our place in Melvich. I have to return to Belfast again now and wait there for a boat that can take me home. The journey back is much longer than the one that brought us here and I can tarry no longer. I must go.'

I felt a sudden hollowness forming inside me that made it hard to breathe.

'You will be looked after well here, of that I'm sure. Your uncle and aunt and your cousins will all take care of you. You can go to school, and quickly you'll be grown old enough to look after yourself. Then I'll come and fetch you back. We'll work together again, the three of us, and you'll become the artist with the hammer and iron that I know you can be.'

He looked away and released me.

A tightening band formed around my chest, squeezing my breath. I could say nothing, shocked by the unexpected suddenness of his words - another finality, another turmoil I would have to confront, aware again of the helplessness of being too young to change it. The enormity of his leaving me here, all alone, crushed down on me. The last of the pillars of my small life - my mother, my brother, our cottage and the forge, my confidence and security - being ripped away from me.

Out in the yard, my uncle had hitched a horse to the gig. Together, he and Father heaved up one of the two chests we had brought with us from our home, tying it in place with leather straps. My aunt and I waited in the early morning sun by the wall of the house. She put an arm across my shoulders. My uncle swung himself up onto the gig. My father strode across to us, kissed my aunt on the cheek, arms tightly around her. She broke away, tears falling on her face. Again he clasped me by the shoulders.

'Be a good boy for your aunt, John, until I come back for you.'

Something tightened around my throat. No words would come. Only tears. He turned quickly and climbed onto the gig. It sagged beneath such two large men. Perhaps it wouldn't go. My uncle shook the reins. The horse wheeled to the right. The gig rolled over the cobbles. It turned past the end of the house toward the lane.

I pulled away from my aunt and ran in the rear door of the house, through the kitchen, and into the front hall. I swung up the iron bar of the latch on the wooden door, pulled it open, ran down the stone steps and along the path through yew trees to the front gate. I burst out the gate into the lane. But the gig had already passed.

I stood there in the middle of the lane, hand half raised to wave goodbye. The horse trotted quickly away, my father and my uncle shoulder to shoulder, their backs toward me. Smallness and loneliness swept over me. I shouted, sure to this day that my father could hear me. But he didn't look back, he sat facing firmly away, and the gig reached a corner in the lane, and then disappeared from sight.

It was the last time I've ever seen him. My crushing despair, standing there alone, hot tears rushing down my face, gasping to breathe, comes back to me still. I was eight years old. Though he said he would come back for me, he never did: and though I've promised myself many times I'd return to my home on the north coast of Scotland, nor yet have I.

TWO

Life in the great stone house on the farm settled into a routine.

George moved back into the upstairs room with me after my father had left and because we were closer in age, we soon became good friends.

Living on the farm was different in every way from my former life in Melvich. Just being constantly surrounded by animals, their smell and muck, would alone have taken some adjustment, but my living place was also filled with people, many large and grown-up people.

Very quickly I was absorbed into the daily and weekly flow. The greater patterns were set by the seasons – an influence that had not significantly affected my previous life, but which now determined so much of all that we did. I had arrived in Ireland in the late summer which I soon learned was the peak of outside activity around the farm.

My men-cousins at that time were away from the house most of each day, working in the fields. Although there were cows to be milked and other animals to be moved or fed, the main activity was the growing of potatoes and other vegetables. In the fields farthest away from the house, lay row upon evenly-spaced row of green potato tops, each separated by a strip of brown earth. The crumbly sandy soil had to be constantly tilled to remove weeds and to be heaped up against the mounds of flourishing green tops to protect the growing tubers in the ground from sunlight. This was a continual long labour for my uncle and cousins, whose slowly moving stooped forms could be seen most days dotted among the rows.

Cows brought to timbered stalls at the rear of the byre were daily milked by hand into buckets which were emptied into large cone-shaped urns. Using a large ladle on a shaft, David or Arthur (who seemed to look after the cows) would skim off the thicker cream from the milk in these urns and transfer it to a single urn which was then carried to the house.

Each day, several of these milk-urns (with most of their cream removed) were collected by a man driving a trap who left empty urns standing in their place for the next day.

Through a low doorway off the kitchen was a small room with a wooden shutter in a window recess. In the middle of the floor stood a barrel on legs with a large handle attached. Here, the cream from the urn was poured into the barrel and my aunt, George or I would turn the handle, spinning the barrel round and round for arm-aching hour after hour, slowly churning the cream into butter. Then the butter had to be removed with wooden scrapers and the pale watery whey poured out into buckets. This process was repeated again and again until the urn had been emptied of all its cream. The cloudy, watery whey was fed to the pigs in the byre.

The week had a regularity that was soon recognisable. Saturday was the day when everything and everybody was washed. From early in the morning, fire raged under the copper in the washhouse to accompany a procession of water buckets from the pump. As soon as the first water was hot, it was used to fill the big iron bath. My aunt had first use, then all the family men followed, with several water changes as the next copper was heated. When I too had had the final turn in the warm soapy water the bath was finally drained, the water gurgling and splashing into a channel in the stone floor and out through a hole in the wall to a soak-pit in the orchard.

Then all the bedding was boiled up in the copper, rinsed in the large copper bowls on each side and hung on ropes to dry, outside if it was fine, inside the wash-house if not. This work took the whole day, with my cousins and I all helping.

Apart from having to feed or milk animals, Sunday was for God and family. Dressed in our best clothes and squeezing aboard both the gig and the dray, we crossed the valley and trotted up the long winding hill to the small village of Castledawson and a stone church built by the Dawson family on the edge of their estate. Church services for young boys seemed endless and tedious but we would vigorously stand to sing hymns that stilled our growing restlessness. Eventually, when the distraction of hard wooden pews on numbing bottoms was almost unbearable, the service would end. After another seemingly endless time of waiting while the adults met and talked with other local families outside the church, we would return home.

In the mid-afternoon we all gathered around the long table for a dinner, with my uncle reading us long passages from the bible both before and after. Then, toward evening, we were allowed into the parlour room to sit around in the high-backed comfortable chairs. My aunt and Charles could both play the piano that stood against the wall away from the fire and I, who had never heard such a musical instrument before, soon enjoyed joining my cousins in singing to its cascades of sound. These Sunday evenings being together as a part of such a large family became a special time for me. I began to feel that I belonged.

Weekdays were dominated by going to school. This too was a new experience for me and initially at least, not a very good one. A few days after my father had left me, my aunt told me I must be going each day with George to school. The first day Harry, George, my aunt and I went together in the dray (the gig was too small for my aunt), up the Leitrim Lane, down into the valley, over the bridge across the river, then along the valley to the village of Magherafelt, the largest village in the area. After that day and for the years that followed, the three of us would mostly walk.

Having not been to a school before, I did not know what to expect. My aunt had given me only one warning:

'John, you must try to speak slowly at school, or they will not understand you. The way that you are talking is different from the other children here and it will take some time for yours to change, to be like theirs. You are a big boy for your age and your cousins are also there to take care of you if the other children should try to make fun of you.'

The initial attention of sounding different and because of my size, looking different, soon passed. It took a lot longer for me to catch up with the schooling I had missed compared with other children of my age. But I was very much aware – and those feelings were with me for a long time – that my height, my Scottish speech, my lack of reading or writing, and not having a father or mother of my own, made me very different from the others. It also made me very determined to try harder, to catch up and to be accepted.

Those conscious inadequacies affected me in other ways. I strove to run faster, to throw stones farther and more accurately, to climb trees higher, to whistle louder or, in whatever competition we would be involved, I was equally determined to beat the others. I also discovered that I could punch harder and was much stronger than most of the boys in our 'young' part of the school, though having older cousins there who were both big for their age also helped to deter any serious fights.

After the long walk home each day we still had work to do around the house and yard; carrying wood and peat sods for the fires; pumping and carrying water; feeding potatoes, food scraps and buckets of whey to the pigs, hay or smelly grass silage to the cows, grain to the poultry, dusty chaff to the horses. Summer, this early time after my arrival in Ireland, was the best and most relaxed season of the yearly cycle. When the first yellowing leaves began to appear on the trees, it changed.

For a short time, we stopped going to school; these breaks in our schooling were coincidental with each of the farming community's peak working, when everybody including children had to be available to help with the season's tasks.

Our days now concentrated on the harvesting of the potato crop. A two-horse team dragging a plough-shaped implement steered from behind by one of my cousins, strained its way slowly along each heaped row now topped by the yellowing, withering remains of the plants. The crumbly, dry sandy soil slid away to the sides of the heaped row, exposing a jumbled carpet of pale-brown, almost yellow potatoes in every size and shape. The hard work which all of us were bent to, was to gather these fruit out of the soil into large wicker baskets.

When a ragged line of heaped full baskets dotted the ground behind us, the horses were harnessed to a wooden flat-topped sledge in place of the plough. Two of the men loaded the heaped baskets onto the sledge and when the deck was completely covered, slowly led the team away over the fields toward the house.

Back in the yard, the full baskets were heaved up and emptied into a steeply-sloping wooden chute which at its lower end narrowed to a small hand-shuttled wooden gate. A coarse woven sack was held beneath the chute, the wooden gate slid open and a tumbling stream of potatoes would fall, until just before the sack was completely filled, the gate would be shut again. Each bag was stitched closed by hand, using a large curved sack-needle along the full length of its top. Great crossed heaps of filled bags built up in the yard as day after day the work continued.

Although we were a large family of mostly-grown men, working by ourselves we could never have harvested the seemingly endless rows of potatoes that by the end of each long day seemed hardly to have diminished. Just as the potato tops were yellowing and drying in the fields, groups of people began arriving at the farm – men, mothers and children. They arrived walking down Leitrim Lane, carrying bags, rolls of belongings and cooking pots on their stooped backs or swinging from short poles over their shoulders. They were small people, much shorter than us, with dark hair and dirty-looking skin, dressed in poor-looking patched clothes. They were *'tinkers'*, homeless labourers from further south who wandered about the countryside looking for work on the estates and large farms such as ours.

As each group arrived they were taken to the two-level stone barn at the west end of the yard. Behind each of the small wooden doors set into the wall of this barn fronting the yard was a dark space too small to be a room, about high enough for a small person to kneel upright, as wide as a big bed and as deep as the full width of the building itself. With a scattering of hay on the floor, each of these alcove spaces was the brief home for a tinker family. The early arrivals soon filled the spaces at ground level, later arrivals had to climb wooden ladders leaning against the wall to reach the doors of the upper level.

All the tinkers worked – men, women and even young children. Women and children gathered potatoes from the earth into the wicker baskets; men loaded baskets onto the sledge, filled the chute in the yard, sewed the tops of the bulging sacks and staggered about under their weight to heap them up around the yard. My uncle moved about constantly from field to yard and back, keeping everyone organised and working. My cousins drove the horses pulling the plough and the sledge and operated the chute in the yard.

In the evenings during the long twilight, the tinkers lit fires in stone-lined pits in the field immediately behind their building, cooking and eating their food in the open. I was not allowed to go near, nor to play with their children.

Eventually, when it seemed almost never-ending, the potato harvest was finished. For a few more days, orange carrots and white turnips took their place. The tinkers were paid by my uncle, given as many vegetables as they could carry, and wandered off up the lane. In following days, a procession of drays arrived in the yard, each to be loaded up with as many sacks of produce as they could carry to the port at Belfast, where they were shipped to England for sale.

* * *

The last of the brown leaves fell from the trees, we three returned to school, the days quickly shortened, and winter followed. It seemed to last forever, wet, dark and cold, but not the cold of winter as I remembered it in Melvich, nor did snow lie deep upon the ground.

The byre was now filled with cows. Feeding them, the pigs and horses was the main farm work for my cousins, so we spent much time inside the big house. The fire in the kitchen and another in the parlour burned strongly day and night, keeping the whole house warm. My aunt began to teach me to play chords on the piano, we played games, recited poems, or read books.

Another pastime was to wrestle. The dray would be dragged into the yard, hay spread on the floor, and in the light of oil lamps, my cousins would wrestle with each other. Even George and I were taught how to grapple, to manoeuvre into position for a throw, how to place our legs to trip each other, or seizing an arm with our opponent off balance, to roll a shoulder down and throw them over backwards to the ground. Then there was a variety of arm and leg holds and headlocks and several combinations of these. To the amusement of my grown cousins I even wrestled with them, practising all they had taught me until contesting much larger men, at least on a friendly basis, held no fear.

When the days lengthened, new leaves had appeared on the trees and the warming sun encouraged the cuckoos to sing their distinctive song in the woods, we had another long break from school. Again, families of tinkers magically appeared down the lane, a smaller number this time. Day after day, two groups laboured steadily in different parts of the farm.

One group – most of my cousins – led two teams of horses ploughing the bare ground back into heaped rows. When the brown soil lay piled in long knee-high rows, the men tinkers carried wicker baskets filled with newly-sprouting seed potatoes, held over through the winter on wire trays in the loft over the byre. The women stabbed a hole every foot in the top of the row with a short trowel, quickly placed a seeder with its new shoots uppermost, covered the hole over and moved to the next. Even the children helped.

Meanwhile, in the green fields a line of stooped men stood, rocking from one leg to the other, turning from right to left in a swinging arc, cutting through the freshly-grown grass with scythes. Slowly they advanced, the long blades swishing over the ground, tumbling a swathe of grass flat with each swing of the strangely-twisted shafts. Behind them, others raked the cut grass into lengthening windrows. In turn, these were lifted with pitchforks onto a horsedrawn sledge until, piled with as much as it could carry, it returned to the yards. On the farm-side wall of the byre, the sweet-smelling grass was forked off onto a long stack, then jumped and rolled on to pack it down. For George and I much of this was fun, not work.

Eventually, all the potatoes were planted, many of the broad fields of grass were all cut, and the great stack of grass behind the byre was covered with a thick layer of soil. Finally, the last fields of grass were felled and left lying scattered to dry in the warm sun, then it too was gathered in on the dray, to be forked high up into the loft over the byre. The tinkers, carrying their distinctive bundles of possessions, trickled away up the lane and we went back to school again for the summer.

So the cycle of seasons was repeated, varied by being earlier or later, hotter or colder, wetter or drier. The seasons slipped into years and my fresh memories of the life I had left in Scotland seemed to fade. I felt comfortable and safe in my new family, looked after by my aunt like a new mother as if I were no different than one of her own.

She continued to teach me at times to learn the piano and had a strong interest in how we were learning at school. George and I were consciously growing, the gap between us and Harry visibly closing, our vigorous appetites filled by the huge daily meals of meats, potatoes and other vegetables, milk, butter and endless bread.

I was taught by my cousins to safely load and fire a musket. Using it became a new passion, as I avidly hunted around the 150 acres of our farmland and woods, shooting at crows and squirrels, stalking and bringing home rabbits and hares for the kitchen.

From hunting grew a new interest in the birds and wild animals that shared the farm with us. When time was spare I would happily spend hours in the summer twilight sitting in a copse among giant beech trees, their starkly bare trunks soaring sixty feet up to the first branches while bats flitted like hallucinations between them. There in still silence I could watch foxes, some so close they would bark and leap away with surprise to find me there, until in the near dark, shadowy badgers shuffled from their deep holes in the ground.

As I grew older, my aunt would also tell me about her earlier life with her brother, my father. The earlier Fraser family, she told me, were millers in Inverness and my grandfather had moved to the north coast to escape the terror after the war with the English ended at Culloden, building a small mill on a stream at Bighouse, near Port Skerra. It was there that my aunt had met her future husband, now my uncle.

According to my aunt, my father had little interest in milling and wanted to become a blacksmith, besides, the small mill would not provide enough work or money to support all the growing family, so he set up a small smithy. Later, when my aunt had married and moved to Ireland, their parents had both died and the mill was closed. My father had then moved to Melvich and set up the smithy that later became my home.

The Bruce family my aunt had married into had also originally come from Scotland. They had a history of support for the English and had fought on the English side at Culloden Moor against the Scots patriots, including our Fraser clan. In the late 16th century, Colonel Lord Dawson was awarded a large estate on the border of Antrim and Londonderry counties in Ireland by the English as grateful thanks for his service to the Crown during their invasion of Ireland. The Bruce's were his 'Factors', or overseers, of his lands in the Trossachs and moved to Ireland with him to take up a similar role for his newly-awarded estate. Colonel Dawson had a huge new stone mansion built on the estate which, because of its size and dominant position high on the hill, became known as Castle Dawson.

The Bruce's original home was built on that estate. Many similarly awarded estates were not properly supervised by their absentee owners and became occupied by squatters. Other squatters regularly attempted to settle on the Dawson estate only to be forcibly evicted by the Bruces. In one of these violent confrontations, the Bruce's home was attacked and destroyed by fire. As compensation for this loss and as a reward for their loyalty and devotion to protecting his interests, Lord Dawson gave the family 150 acres of land in Leitrim Lane on the edge of his estate. The great house in which we all now lived was built there in 1754, with its two-foot thick stone walls, deep recessed windows, stone outbuildings and protective walled yards designed for defence against any further attacks.

The Bruce family continued to supervise the Dawson estate as well as farm their own lands. They were a respected and well-known family in the area, with many contacts in the English administration, but envied for their comparative wealth. Many years later, through marriage, the Dawson estate passed by marriage to the Phillips family whose descendants still lived in the Dawson home, or 'castle'. Over the years, a small village had gradually developed at the entrance to the estate which now I knew as

Castledawson. The Phillips and Bruce families were still close friends and we were quite often invited to their home on the hill.

Learning about my family in Scotland and the new family I now felt part of in Ireland helped to rebuild a sense of stability and security in my young life. I was also taught that as a member of a prominent family in the district, we were expected to care for the less fortunate, to be well-behaved, responsible, to be educated and to learn a trade or profession.

* * *

In 1845, when I was 11 years old, a darkening shadow crept quietly over Ireland. It first appeared in the autumn at the big table in the kitchen when we were all tiredly eating dinner at the end of another long mid-harvest day. Amid all the talking which my uncle actively encouraged at the table when meals were ending, his words suddenly stopped all conversation.

'I was at the market in Magherafelt today. There was talk there about the potato crop in some places to the south. They say it has been cursed by God: the plants go black almost overnight and die, the crop rots in the ground before it can be harvested. They say it started in the south and has quickly moved north. Quite large areas have been affected and some of the harvest there is being lost.'

A silence followed. We all stopped eating. We were all staring at my uncle.

'What do you think it is? Has it been seen near here?' asked Charles.

'It sounds like a strange new disease that's being carried or spread somehow. Nobody I talked with has seen it yet, but we must get our crop harvested as quickly as we can, before it should appear here. If the stories are right and the crops in the ground itself are destroyed, it's as well that it's appeared so late in the season, or else what would there have been to feed the people through to next harvest.'

Another long silence as we all were lost in our own thoughts.

Alexander wondered, 'What if tis a new disease that comes back again next season? P'raps we should hold back more of our crop for extra seed?'

'If it is a disease that can survive the winter, having more seed won't help us. We don't know if it attacks all the crops or only the potatoes, but as God himself knows, Ireland lives on its potatoes.

We soon had some answers.

As we continued digging up the rows, gathering and bagging the crop with a new feeling of urgency, the Phillips came from Casteldawson with news of the black disease sweeping through the remainder of their own crop, reducing the stalks and yellowing leaves to a slimy mess within a day. Although we ourselves had but a few rows unharvested, within the week those, too, lay devastated on the ground. Uncle ordered that they be dug up, but not be taken into the yard. Filled baskets were left standing in the ploughed field. The tinkers were paid off and given crop from the bags in the yard.

Each day we watched closely, but the green-topped carrots and turnips still left in the ground were not affected. Meanwhile, the baskets of potatoes left standing in the field turned quickly to a stinking putrescence. We buried them in deep holes where they stood and then burned branches on top of them.

When the first dray arrived to collect a load of bags to be shipped from the port at Belfast, it was not alone. Lazily following behind were two slouching soldiers on horseback with muskets slung across their backs, cutlasses in scabbards at their sides. So it was with every dray that followed.

'It's just a precaution,' Uncle explained to us, 'we hear tell that some peasants down south stopped the transport and made off with part of the load. It won't happen here, the escorts are just a warning.'

My uncle was a careful and thoughtful man. In the early winter, leaving Hugh in charge of the farm, he and my two eldest cousins Charles and Alex went south, travelling the countryside, attending meetings of estate owners and talking with officials in the Stormont government. When they returned, they set about building a long wooden extension to the byre building, all along its side facing into the fields not covered by the silage stack, covering the sloping roof with sheets of iron.

Behind our washing-house at the edge of the enclosed yard by the gate into the orchard, the packed paving stones were lifted to expose a large area of bare earth. Then with spades and picks, we began digging a square hole for a new well, deeper and deeper into the ground, lining the sheer sides with heavy timbers as it went down. One of my cousins at a time would climb down a ladder fixed to one side, to dig in the dark earth below, filling buckets with soil to be hauled to the surface on ropes. Slowly the digging continued until finally, water was reached. Before winter was over, two large iron lever-pumps and sections of iron pipes were brought from Belfast and installed on either side of this well.

When the new leaves appeared on the trees and bluebells again carpeted the woods, my cousins returned from brief journeys into the country with cows uncle had bought, until our little herd had grown several times over. The byre was emptied of winters' deep layers of manure and straw, the floor of a large bay was scrubbed clean and a large new churn set up in the middle. Until the first of the tinkers arrived again down the lane, milking all the new cows, separating the cream from the milk and churning the cream to butter kept the whole family working.

With the tinkers there to help, ploughing and planting of the potato crop began once more. But this time, my uncle kept two large fields aside to be sown with turnips and parsnips. When the crops were all planted some of the tinkers wandered away, but several families were allowed to stay living in their dark alcoves in the building at the end of the yard, to help with the cow herd and dairy. From them, my cousins heard more stories of the strange potato disease at the end of last harvest and of many people in parts of the south that did not have enough to eat during the winter.

That summer of 1846 was wet and warm. The grass grew so fast it was cut twice and the silage stack by the byre doubled its usual size. The cows bore calves and bulged with milk. The stone byre was filled with young pigs swilling all the extra whey. Out in the crop fields the bare earth quickly disappeared beneath the flourishing green tops of potatoes, turnips and parsnips. At church on Sundays, all the people seemed brighter and happier in anticipation of the harvest that would surely follow such a good growing season.

Just as the summer reached its peak, the first news arrived of the black disease sweeping anew through the crops to the south. This time, so the word came, the curse of God was everywhere and almost nothing was being spared. Very soon, it appeared in the crops around Magherafelt and then in ours. Within a few days, most of the freshly flowering potato heads that had been vigorously topping the rows lay wilted and black upon the ground. Strangely, small tufts of green where some plants had been spared were dotted about the fields. But the turnips and parsnips nearby were unaffected.

Now at church, the gaiety was gone as men and women gathered in small groups, to talk in low voices. The usual talk around the long table in our kitchen was subdued. Some of the older children stopped coming to the school in Magherafelt.

The potato fields were left to lie. When some of the tinkers returned, each plant that still survived was dug up by hand and a pitiful few baskets returned to the yard for storing as seed. The green tops of the parsnips and turnips were cut off in the field; but unlike potatoes, they did not come clean from the ground and the roots caked with wet soil were brought to the end of the yard by the new well, to be tipped into long open troughs fed with water through a canvas pipe from each of the pumps. Then each root was washed clean by hand, the rush of silt-laden water spilling over the lower end of the trough, out through the gate into the orchard.

The tedious work of washing roots was interrupted one afternoon by the rhythmic clatter of horses' hooves on the cobbles and around into the yard rode two pairs of mounted soldiers. We all straightened up and took our hands from the troughs. They reined up together unsmiling, sitting stiffly, as their officer swung smoothly to the ground, a leather bag in one hand. He and my uncle talked briefly together, then he remounted, and the four rode away.

At the kitchen table even before dinner was served, we all waited expectantly for uncle to speak.

'This disease plight is now very serious. The Government has requisitioned all the food supplies in Ireland. Our crops, the butter and any meat we produce will be taken from us by the army. We're no longer permitted to sell anything except the milk. We will only be allowed to keep a small portion for our own use, and our few potatoes for seed. All the rest will be taken under escort to Belfast and transported to England by ships of the navy. It's not just us – this is happening to farms all over Ireland'

My cousins all spoke at once but it was my aunt's voice that prevailed. 'So what are the people of Ireland to do then? What're they going to eat? With the country's food being taken from them, they'll surely starve. The Governor must be leaving enough here to feed the country until next season! Surely the government wouldn't do such a thing – it can't be true that they'd deprive the people of Ireland of their food!?'

But it was – and they did.

Just as we had been told, soldiers came escorting the wagons to take our stacked harvest away, carefully making records of all that we had left stored in the loft, our cattle, pigs, even our poultry. Not that it seemed to affect us much at first. We still had plenty available to eat; though we all longed for potatoes, we even adjusted to parsnip or turnip every night, otherwise our life seemed unchanged.

In late summer, we heard and read frightening stories of hungry people in the cities of Dublin and the south country with yellow fever and dying of the black plague, but fortunately it didn't reach the north or out into our countryside. When winter came, so did pitiful bands of tinkers we had not seen before, shuffling into the yard in ragged clothes, huddling together in the dim light as the men begged for food and shelter from my uncle. We were afraid they could be carrying the horrible diseases and reluctantly they were sent away.

Being a cautious man, my uncle decided we should set a guard at night in the yard in case of any attempt to steal our livestock, poultry, or stores. A space was cleared among the hay in the loft over the byre, where a shutter was removed to give a sweeping view over the approach to the byre and the entrances to the yard. My grown cousins took turns to spend every night up there in the cold, each armed with a gun, but nobody came.

Later, toward spring, more families or groups of people would appear across the land, begging for food or offering work in return for anything to eat. They weren't tinkers, just peasants driven by hunger from their poor homes to scour the countryside for food. We found others, even the children, scrabbling in the earth where our crops had been, searching for anything that might have been left behind in the ground after the harvest. The sight of these people, obviously starving, with bony faces, sunken staring eyes and pitifully thin bodies, many barefoot, dressed in tattered rags, drove us all to an anger of helplessness.

Now, my aunt and uncle gave what they could – milk, cheese, a few eggs, pig-fat, or some vegetables – whatever could be spared that was not on the requisition list. They even allowed peasant families to stay in the barn alcoves for a night or two, but my cousins still kept their nightly guard in the loft.

By the summer of 1847, the situation in Ireland was desperate. It was now two years since the black blight had first appeared in the potato crops. The previous summer was the first season of almost total destruction of the potato harvest, followed by a long winter of hunger, famine and fever, made so much worse by the cruel policy of the government to take whatever food was left, by force, feeding England by callously starving the people of Ireland. We even heard of starving people crowded by the roads, watching in sullen resentfulness as wagons escorted by dragoons took away to England the food that could save them.

Now into our second season since the blight, all we farmers were at least better prepared for growing other crops that seemed to resist the disease, but famine, fevers and death had already swept the land. There had been scattered violent armed protests in the south. The English army was everywhere, arresting people for stealing food to survive, even imprisoning and deporting them to the penal colonies for speaking out against the government. We heard that many thousands of people were escaping their plight by fleeing from Ireland. Taking passage on ships for America to find a new life began as a trickle but quickly had become a human flood.

Our family was not, nor could not, be isolated from the turmoil which life throughout Ireland had become. Although our basic needs for food were well supplied from the farm, all that was produced was taken under requisition and, George told me, payments fixed by the government were very low.

Discussion and conversation at our kitchen table in the evenings, which had always been encouraged by my uncle, had changed from enthusiasm and laughter amongst my cousins, to long heavy silences. Their frustrated anger with the government's actions which had caused such misery for the people of Ireland, had created a tension in the family that we could all feel, though now never discussed.

My older cousins' criticism of the English, the English Governor and the consequences of their harsh rule imposed on the people by the army, was strongly answered by my uncle.

'We aren't Catholic Irish people – we're Protestant Scots. Our family came here with the English 200 years ago because we supported the English, the parliament and the Monarchy. The English and the Scots founded our port city of Belfast – gave us our land – built our churches, our schools, provided our government and justice. If not for them and our support of them, we would not be here now, would not have this land and our home, nor this way of life and all that we value.

'These troubles are a calamity of nature, that will pass. Any government or monarch can make mistakes. We must be tolerant of what we judge as mistakes they make in coping with such calamities and their right to take whatever actions they judge to be needed. But 'tis a time to be staunch in our support of those actions – difficult though that may be for each of us – standing together with our community and unwavering in our duty to the administration. I'll have no more such talk as I've been hearing in this house, none of it! It must stop!'

Less than a month had passed when, in the darkness of the room we shared together, George whispered to me of further turmoil about unfold in our family. 'Some of my brothers are leaving us. They're leaving Ireland too. They're going to the Argentine to work on building railways.

'They wouldn't be staying here anyway, even without the troubles. Charles is the eldest and one day he'll take over the farm from my father. Alexander's next, and until he has a wife he'll stay to help. But the rest of us have to find our own way – there isn't any place for us here, no money, no future.

'Hugh, David and Arthur are going together to the Argentine. New companies have set up there, calling for men to help build railroads all over the country. For working on the railroads, they're given land grants and money to start farms of their own.

'Harry wants to leave too, maybe to America or Australia – he hasn't decided yet. And I'm being sent to Belfast, to be articled as a clerk. My father knows Mr Stevenson, the owner of Stevenson's Iron & Steel Works and I'm going to learn the iron and steel trade.

Until you return to Melvich, I think they'll keep you on with school.'

And within another month, except for Harry, they were gone. Together, Hugh, David and Arthur rode off in the dray for Belfast on what they regarded as a great new adventure, my uncle driving, while my aunt stood crying farewell in the yard. They had always seemed like other adults to me, so I felt little emotion with their leaving us. George was next to go, but knowing he was only half a day's ride away and would often return for brief visits was neither as final nor as sad, though as we were like brothers, I sorely missed him.

Then finally Harry – tall thin Harry with the straw-coloured hair, freckles and smiling eyes who had given up his room to my father and I when we arrived Scotland; my guardian at school, shooting instructor and wrestling teacher, my mentor for farm work and animals, rode away up the lane. As he left, I was reminded of the day my father had made the same journey, only this time my aunt stood sharing tears with me in the lane as he disappeared from sight, bound for a farm in the Antipodes after changing his mind about going to America. It was like losing my eldest brother.

Now the big house seemed so empty; without Harry and George to fill the age gap, I more felt like the child of the family again. The room George and I had shared for so many years was lonely, the loneliness accentuated by my now doing all the usual farm routines and pastimes by myself.

However, like a young tree given more light when those sheltering it are cleared away, I soon began to feel more responsible, more conscious of my place, more aware of my capabilities. In the house or around the farm, we each seemed to occupy more space than before, neither the gap nor the feeling of emptiness left by my cousins' departures lasting for long.

At school I was alone without an older cousin for the first time since I had begun there six years before. I was also among the older group of children still attending after many had left when the harvests failed. I had always been taller than others my own age, but now I was changing with early maturity, I grew even faster. Being both the tallest and the largest in the small school began to cause me acute feelings of self-consciousness. My reaction was to avoid attracting any further attention.

Quite suddenly I began to be very aware of girls that had shared school with us almost unnoticed. First there was Margaret Alderton: tall, with long thick dark hair, a high forehead, squareish face and prominent cheekbones. I found that she was often looking at me but would avert her flashing eyes when I looked back, tossing her hair back as she did so. Whenever she came near me, to my embarrassment I could feel my face heat up with redness, which I could not control. Naturally this just increased my self-consciousness even more.

Then, as an almost exact opposite, came Jessica Franklin. This time it was I who was aware of her first: short and dainty, straight fair hair cut evenly short at the level of her chin, blue eyes slightly squinting from time to time because of some difficulty with her sight, and a soft sing-song voice that tinkled like pieces of ice on a pond. Sometimes we walked together down the road from Magherafelt when school classes had finished. I wanted to try to hold her hand but would be overcome by a wave of almost uncontrollable emotion when I made an attempt, then the flushing redness would well up on my face again and I'd break away. I spent much of the day thinking about her, every night picturing the perfect smooth pale skin of her face as I fell asleep.

Soon one, then the other of these girls left, along with many children in the area who were forced away by the effects of the famine on their families.

Throughout these years, my Aunt Colina would send an occasional letter to my father in Scotland, telling him of the difficulties of life in Ireland and of how I was growing and learning. Every year near Christmas a letter from him would arrive back, but there was never any suggestion that I should return to Melvich – a Fraser I might be, but the Bruces were my family and here in Ireland was my home.

Now nearing being the oldest boy at the school, my thoughts and those of my family turned to what I should do upon my leaving. There was no pressure to do so despite the difficulties of the times, but obviously my schooling was approaching its end. Just as I had as a young child in the forge in Melvich, I still enjoyed doing things with my hands and was drawn to any mechanical or moving devices, developing recognition from my uncle and cousins that I had some ability to build or repair such things. At school my best interest and ability was in arithmetic; it was a subject which seemed to come naturally to me and the only subject at which I excelled.

My uncle suggested to me that I should become an engineer, which would combine my mathematical skills, my interest in anything mechanical and my enjoyment of working with my hands. The more he described the work of an engineer and the more I thought about it, the more I convinced myself that it was what I wanted to do. Fortuitously, my uncle's friend Mr Stevenson, owner of the Iron & Steel Works where George was happily articled as a clerk, also owned Stevenson's Engineering Works in Belfast. After some enquiry by my uncle, he agreed to apprentice me to train as an engineer. In August of 1850, my uncle signed the papers to article me as I stood by watching, filled with a swirling mixture of excitement at the beginning of a new adventure and apprehension at leaving this home where I had been so secure for what had been the much larger portion of my life.

Just as my cousins before me, now it was my time to hug my crying aunt, look around the yard where every stone was so familiar to me, climb up into the gig alongside my uncle and together trot out through the back gate into the Leitrim Lane. As we moved quickly between the hedgerows up to the first corner I clearly saw again the day when my father had begun this same journey. But I sat turned right around, looking back, waving vigorously in case my aunt was watching from somewhere, holding my last glimpse of the great stone house with its yew tree-lined front path, until it was lost from sight.

THREE

Years later and during my lifetime, engineers were taught their craft at universities, but at the time I learned mine it was a long, painfully laborious and exacting process defined by a syllabus, each step of which had a prescribed number of hours to be completed.

During the five years it took to fulfil the time requirements, three-quarters of it or nearly four years were spent in practical manual labour on the floor of the engineering works. Having just finished my schooling I had finally been at the pinnacle of that period of learning, feeling accomplished and mature compared with most others in the school, aware that being senior contributed significantly to my self-confidence.

But now I was in no doubt that at the beginning of the process to learn engineering, I was as nothing again. New apprentice engineers at Stevenson's were a particularly low form of life, their utter lack of status being reinforced at every opportunity by those who had progressed further through the course in order to better establish their own seniority. Thus I had to endure the humiliations of spending many tedious weeks cleaning floors, gathering scraps, shovelling coal into boilers, filling grease-caps, sorting tools and being ordered about by each and every person until I had completed some undefined 'rite of passage'. Only then, when I was deemed to have properly learned my place in the order of things, was I placed under the tutelage of more senior men and given slightly more constructive tasks to undertake.

At least being in Belfast had one compensation – I was reunited with my cousin George again. Together we shared a room, boarding in a house owned by a Mrs Robertson, a kind and motherly grey-haired elderly widow, who cooked us delicious meals at the end of long days, washed our dirty clothes and fussed over us as if we were her own. In return, she received virtually all the small sums that we earned.

Every second month we were allowed to stop work at mid-day on a Saturday which, combined with Sunday, gave us both just sufficient time to make the journey home to the farm and back. Though these visits became less and less frequent as time passed.

Despite the effects of the famine and emigration from Ireland, it was a very active and busy period for Stevenson's in both their businesses. The Engineering Works was mostly divided into two sections; one built machines and pieces of equipment to order, the other produced many parts, shapes and fittings for shipbuilders.

During my first three years I mostly worked in the former of these, the 'job-shop', so named because each construction was an individual or unique 'job'. Central to this section was a large steam engine driving a huge spinning flywheel and heavy shaft. From this shaft, long leather belts snaked away overhead to drive other shafts fixed on the walls and roof, from which further belts extended down to power machinery such as lathes and drills.

From the boiler producing the steam that drove the stationary engine, a seeming tangle of pipes led off to other heavy machinery such as stamping mills, power hammers, forming mills, guillotines and several cranes.

Progressively, I learned the purpose and operation of all this thundering, hissing, crashing, thumping, cacophony of power equipment that determined the abilities and limitations of the Engineering Works at that time. It all seemed like a gigantic extension of childhood memories of the forge in Melvich. Although we worked twelve-hour days, six days each week, they passed so quickly I almost resented our Sunday off.

The men of the Engineering Works were mostly Scots. Belfast having been established by the English and Scots as their town and port after the invasion of Ireland, it was not surprising that most business was owned or controlled by one or other. But for some inexplicable reason, the Scots seemed to have an affinity for engineering. Thus the English Stevenson family owned the business but employed mostly Scots to work in it. Like most Scots supplanted to another country, I had retained some of my earlier accent, though being so young when I arrived in Ireland, it was but a vestige which neither my aunt nor my school had fully managed to eradicate. Now amongst Scottish-accented men each day, much of my earlier accent began to return.

At the end of three years, George and I both seemed to have done little but work. Such long days and long weeks allowed neither time nor energy for anything else. During much of the year we left for work in the dark, returned to Mrs Robertson's in the dark, ate a large hot dinner, read or talked for a while and went to our beds.

Just as I was beginning to feel I had some command of the machinery in the job-shop, I was moved to the design office. Once again I had to start with the lowliest of tasks, even sharpening pencils, mixing inks or cleaning drawing utensils. It was however, both cleaner and quieter.

I began to learn the knowledge of engineering. The rules, the formulae, of stresses, leverage and moments; the physics of force and motion, power and pressure, the effects of temperature, the structure and performances of materials. My mathematics was challenged and extended. I learned geometry and trigonometry that was applied to drawing and draughting. Now I began to understand some of the very core of this profession I had decided upon.

As 1853 unfolded, the demand for parts for shipbuilding increased. The discovery of gold in far-off Australia took many ships away on long voyages, leaving a shortage of ships for the normal trade and coastal routes. Shipbuilders directly across the Irish Sea on the Mersey around Liverpool were frequent visitors to Stevenson's. Not only was there an increasing use of steel or iron parts in wooden sailing ships, but many more smaller vessels, both paddle and even screw-driven were needed for the coast or to service ports. Even in the port of Belfast, tugs and tenders were small steam-driven, side-paddlers and the larger vessels tied alongside the docks were a mix of wooden sailing ships and ironclad paddle-steamers.

The shipbuilding shop at Stevenson's made an increasing variety and number of parts for both wooden and iron ships. Wooden vessels needed large curved plates which when bolted together, strengthened the base of masts; these plates, some eight feet long and nearly three in diameter, were cut sheets of steel, drilled, then formed and flanged in huge steam presses. In a similar procedure, long strips cut from plate, drilled and pressed on small-diameter cast iron dies, when rivetted together as two halves formed long tapered tubes which were used to replace timber for bowsprits, spars and yards.

For both types of vessel we designed and built knees and elbows for the keel, chine and gunwale junctions of the many ribs forming the outer shape of each ship. These were large shaped sections of plate cut and drilled which were to be bolted or riveted on both sides of the join in each section. For iron-clads, we cut and shaped sections of ribs themselves and parts of the stems and transoms, according to the detailed drawings supplied by the ship designers.

West across the Irish sea came visiting designers and Mersey shipbuilders; back east to Liverpool were transported all the various pieces and parts we had made for the builders or riggers.

My first and only sea voyage from North Sutherland to Ireland was still a vivid and fascinating memory. Now being involved in the design and construction of ships' parts, even being in the distant company of ships' designers and builders themselves, I decided that it was marine engineering which interested me most and resolved to make it my future.

After nearly a whole year in the design office, most of which was occupied by learning engineering theory and principles as well as the practical aspects of designing the types of work that Stevenson's were required to produce, there remained only one year to complete for my qualification. There seemed so much about engineering of which I knew nothing, yet with only one quarter of my articles to finish, it seemed an impossible task. The more I learned, the more I became aware of the narrowness of my knowledge.

Fortunately, the Master of the design office Mr McBride, an austere man with ginger bushy mutton-chop sideburns almost meeting at his chin and a large prominent nose down which he stared at us forbiddingly from a tilted-back head, had noticed my keen interest in both the shipbuilders who visited us and in the often complex parts we were commissioned to build for them. For most of my time in his domain, he had rarely spoken directly to me (for which I was thankful), but now as my period of service there was almost ended, I was called to his office.

After some questioning of my interest in marine engineering, he advised that it would be necessary for me to gain knowledge of steam engines and propulsion devices. 'It is all a'changing laddie' he commented, 'yesterday it was all oak, teak and sail; today the iron steamer with paddle and screw. 'Tis only the quality of iron that's stopping the steamers taking over from sail, but tomorrow that may change. The steam engine has more power than the sail, the screw more than the paddle; steel plate is stronger than oak. Mark my words young Fraser, before you're an old man you will see screw-driven iron steamers drive out the sail.'

On leaving the design office, I had yet to spend nearly a year in the marine shop, learning to operate the cutting, forming and riveting machinery. But Mr McBride said he would speak with Mr Stevenson himself and with his permission, I might be temporarily transferred to the shipbuilding works of the Laird brothers at Warrington on the Mersey. Mr McGregor Laird, a good friend of Mr McBride, was the Works Manager for his older brother Mr John Laird, a prominent designer of iron ships and steamers. As Stevenson's did not have experience of or involvement with steam engines, I could not be given tuition in their works; in such cases, transfers were permitted to other works that could give tuition.

But first, I had to spend many months on the machinery in the ship-parts fabricating shop.

From the plans drawn in the design office I had just left, each part was marked out on a sheet of steel plate. The plate, slung horizontally with ropes and pulleys and swung to the bed of the steam-guillotine to be cut to outline, was drilled by a belt-driven capstan borer and fitted with temporary eye-bolts. Now hooks could be attached from light chain running to a chain block hoist and up to a wheeled bogey sliding on rails in the roof. This simplified moving the sheet around on the bed of the borer or across to the steam-former where angled flanges or other shapes could be pressed.

Finally, parts could be assembled on the floor to ensure they properly fitted together, or sub-assemblies could be riveted in place, before being carefully identified with marks ready for transporting to the shipbuilders.

Although the men on the shop floor of Stevenson's were very experienced, there were many accidents during my time there; crushed hands and feet, broken bones, or even the complete loss of fingers happened quite frequently. Occasionally, one of the long leather drive belts overhead would break sending us all scattering for cover as a loose length of it flailed about wildly.

George and I had now been boarding with Mrs Robertson for nearly four years. It was like a second home and the old lady still fed us well and fussed over us like we were children. George had long-completed his articles, continuing to work seemingly happily for Stevenson's Iron & Steel. His work covered the purchasing of supplies from the mills or casting-shops in the northeast of England, pricing and shipping stock to businesses and farms in Ireland, and helping to maintain all the records. From listings in newspapers, Stevenson's were also receiving written enquiries from businesses in the many growing colonies of the British

Empire.

Since French farmers in Bordeaux had recently found that the mixture of oxide of copper with crushed limestone which they used to protect grapevines from mould diseases would also give potato crops some protection from the black blight, business activity in Ireland had slowly begun to improve. Too late for the thousands of Irish people who had died of hunger or the plagues that accompanied it; too late for the hundreds of thousands forced to emigrate to stay alive; too late to change the brutal policies of the English authorities which had so heartlessly exacerbated the destruction of Irish life.

Like many who had fled across the Irish Sea to Liverpool to escape the famine or find work, relatives of my uncle had been forced to leave their cropping farm. This cousin of my uncle, Mr Alfred Bruce, had found work with Joseph Steel & Sons, a long-established firm of shipbuilders close to Liverpool. Now in 1854, war with Russia had broken out in the Crimean peninsula, causing a further demand on the already-scarce shipping fleet. Yards such as Steel & Sons were very busy.

When my temporary transfer to the yard of Mr McGregor Laird drew near, it was arranged that I could stay with the Liverpool Bruces until I could find lodgings closer to the Laird's yard in Warrington.
Reluctant as I was to leave my familiar surroundings and friends at Stevenson's, the opportunity to learn more in the special area of marine engineering was exciting. Knowing I would soon return, the goodbyes from my family, George and Mrs Robertson were easily taken and I sailed out of Belfast light-heartedly. My second-only sea voyage, across the Irish Sea in a small single-masted coastal smack was seemingly over before it had even begun. I spent most of it holding tightly to the rail in the rounded bows, revelling in the lift as we crunched into steep waves coming from the north-east and watching the patterns of rainbow- light caught in sheets of spray flung off into the wind.

In the port of Liverpool I was surprised to see so many ships, more than I could have imagined, rafted together often four abreast, mostly sailing ships adding to a forest of masts and spars, but also a number of smaller steamers. Paddle-tugs, smacks and coastal paddlers moved about along the shore and out in the grey water of the Mersey. The docks were a mass of people, piles of goods, horse-drawn wagons and carts. Off the smack and carrying a wooden trunk filled with clothes and draughting equipment, I hailed one of the many hansom-cabs waiting on the nearby streets. We headed northwest out of Liverpool, following the instructions sent by my relatives.

Behind one of many wooden doors opening right onto the streetside of a reddish-stone building that seemed to stretch for the full length of the road, identical to rows and rows of similar chimney-potted buildings in street upon street in this area, I found my relatives whom I had not seen for some five years. What a contrast was this cramped home of a few dark rooms from the more spacious farmhouse they had left in Londonderry; how different these bare, narrow crowded streets of featureless stone facades from the rich greenness of tree-speckled soft rolling Irish countryside. However, Mr Alfred explained that this part of Liverpool was now filled with families who had left Ireland in the famine. Together they made a community of common voices who supported each other in a sea of often-hostile English for whom the memories of the ferocious war waged against them by the French and Irish in Ireland only some 50 years ago, still rankled. I was pleased that now I spoke more like a Scot.

Southeast of Liverpool in the flat coastal Cheshire plain exposed to the cold wind beating in the from the Irish Sea, I soon found Laird's shipyards. From some distance off, the skeletal frames of ships under construction rose up out of the earth, topped by the derricks of cranes. Closer, I could see smaller vessels under construction along the bank of the river Mersey, surrounded by a vast seemingly chaotic mess of timber, rusty steel and discarded materials scattered over the bare earth. Nearby, the name J & M Laird topped a large building of red brick with small-paned windows on each of its levels.

Mr McGregor Laird to whom I was soon ushered was not unlike his friend Mr McBride of Stevenson's whose notice of in my interest in marine engineering was instrumental in my now being here in Warrington. Mr Macerator, as he was known, was a large-girthed man with a round, red face topped and fringed with bushy ginger hair and full beard. He wore calf-length boots, his waistcoat strained at its buttons across an expansive chest laced with a chain and fob watch and the corners of his eyes were creased with deep wrinkles. He was the most friendly, happy, always-smiling and most helpful man I had encountered since I began my training.

With lodgings arranged in a boarding-house in the nearby town of Warrington, I was soon at work in the design and supervision office on the upper floor of the building. The lower floor and its rearward extension was divided into two sections: in one, all the various parts and pieces arriving from outside engineering works such as Stevenson's were checked, assembled and organised; in the other much larger area, the drive-shafts, gears, bearings and propulsion systems were manufactured, constructed and assembled, together with the steam engine that would provide the drive.

Away out in the yards, each vessel being built was in the charge of a Ships' Overseer, under him a number of Foremen, who supervised the work of the tradesmen, artificers and labourers doing the heavy manual work. Wheeled steam-trains moved materials about the site on flat-decked wagons.

Vessels of various sizes and at differing stages of construction were arranged in the yards parallel with the riverbank. When I arrived, several small paddle-steamers for coastal and port work were being built, but two huge vessels on which work had commenced dominated the yards. The smaller of these, an iron steamer of 179 feet overall, later to be called *The Queen* was the first large ship built by Lairds to the new iron-ship construction rules drawn up by the Lloyds Register, London. The other on which work had recently commenced was an immense vessel, the hull of an iron clipper with a design displacement of 1460 tons, to be called the *Sarah Palmer*.

My work in the office of Laird's was totally absorbing. Though still just a student, I was very conscious of being involved with engineers at the forefront of using the power of steam and the strength of iron and steel to change the very nature of marine transport. Steam pressure was a force greater than the power of men and most of nature; only the cleverness and skills of engineers could devise the means to control it, otherwise it had the ferocious capacity to destroy both the men and their machines that harnessed it. Applying such a force to drive a fragile vessel out on the ocean in the face of the power of nature itself, for me was the pinnacle of daring and skill. My year had passed before it had seemingly begun.

At Christmastime, 1854, I returned to Ireland and Stevenson's, to have my Articles verified as completed and be admitted to the Guild of Engineers. My uncle Malcolm Bruce came from Castledawson to be present at the ceremony of presentation of my Certificate by the Masters of the Guild. It was a moment of immense pride, a feeling that at last I was grown into the age of men. But I was also now unemployed.

Fortunately, it was a matter of choice. Back in the familiar comfort of my home on the farm, being fussed over by my aunt Colina again, I discussed my situation with my uncle and family. In one direction, I was offered a position back with Stevenson's in Belfast, in the ship-parts works. But before I had left Lairds, I had been called into the office of Mr McGregor Laird, to say goodbye and to thank him for his generosity in employing me.

Standing before this kindly, warm-hearted man, I had felt quite saddened. He had been the first gentleman I had met, the first supervisor (let alone an owner), who exercised no superiority, power or authority, who spoke with all those around him as if they were his equals. Yet he inspired respect, even devotion. In a glass frame on the wall of his office, visible immediately behind his desk, was a single calligraphically written sentence on a clean white page. It read: *'It is not the job that maketh the man; it is the man that maketh the job.'* So did he live this and such was his personality, that he brought to whatever task he undertook, even the simple or mundane, the most profound impression of importance and value. Wherever he led or whatever he undertook, all others clamoured to follow. The respect in which he was so highly held was not because he was The Owner but for himself.

'Well Fraser' he said, coming around his desk and holding out his hand, 'we have been pleased to have had you work with us. You have a talent for this new age of engineering ships. If you should want to return to us, Laird's will have a position for you and would be the better, if you chose to do so.' My old childhood emotion at feeling wanted and accepted surged inside me as I shook his hand.

'The honour that you should make such an offer Sir, is mine. It has been a privilege to have been here and to have worked with you. I shall not forget my time here, nor you Sir. I shall advise early in the New Year of my next intentions. Thank you, and goodbye.'

So now, sitting around the old wooden table before the open fire in the kitchen of the great stone house on the Leitrim Road, it was time to make a decision.

I could stay here in Ireland, close by this family and home which had become mine and was familiar, comfortable and secure. George had stayed with Stevenson's in Belfast, why not me?

But returning to live amongst the English across the Irish Sea, amidst the very country which with callous indifference had inflicted such suffering upon the Irish people only because they were regarded as a lower form of life, was not itself attractive. Yet the Lairds were Scots, who had proven themselves to me to be devoid of the haughty superiority and self-aggrandisement of the English owning-class. Their shipbuilding and engineering work was challenging and inspiring; I had, after all, just spent nearly a year there.

So it was not really such a difficult choice to make. I wrote a letter to Mr McGregor accepting his offer and a more difficult one to Mr Stevenson to decline. Once again I said goodbye to my family – this time with less certainty as to when we would meet again – and began the journey back to Warrington, stopping with George at Mrs Robertson's in Belfast briefly, to thank the Stevensons for all they had done for me.

Back at Laird's, the frame of *The Queen* was rising up from the earth as if to welcome me back. The gaunt steel ribs supported by a lower palisade of timber formed a double row, like the rib-bones of some great beast. Further down the yard, the keelson, stem and transom of the *Sarah Palmer* now taking form showed the outline of what a massive vessel she would become.

My new position, announced to me by a welcoming Mr McGregor, was as an assistant to the Overseer of *The Queen*, particularly to work on the construction and assembly of the power and propulsion system.

Through this new work, I soon met the other brother, Mr John Laird. Also as tall as Mr Macerator, he was of different build, a thin narrow-faced man, with a dark beard as sideburns meeting at the chin. He was as cold and austere as his brother was warm-hearted and expansive. Mr John lived in Liverpool where he was a partner with Mr John Grantham in Page & Grantham, the foremost ship designers in the north of England. Mr Grantham, among the best designers in the whole of Britain, was also a renowned naval architect.

Mr John had mostly designed *The Queen*, taking a close interest in her construction now that it was taking physical shape, with frequent visits to the Warrington yards. Several times, he brought with him a Mr Alfred Holt, a civil engineer, business and ship-owner of Liverpool, who was becoming quite famous as a developer of steam engines especially for ships. Because of my work on the propulsion system, over a period I came to know Mr Holt quite well.

The engine he was building and providing for *The Queen* was much larger than those installed in the smaller coastal vessels, but otherwise typical of engine development at the time. Slowly we assembled it at

Lairds. A large boiler, like a furnace, was filled with tubes made from the best commercial-grade steel available. The tubes when filled with water from a tank and then heated by burning coal, generated the steam. A steel manifold collected the steam which was then piped directly into the giant single cylinder of the engine. As the piston was driven down by the pressure of steam, it drove a cranking-shaft attached to a flywheel fixed to the long drive shaft. At the moment the piston reached the bottom of its stroke and released its steam through a port, the crankshaft was also at the maximum point of its reach. The momentum of the flywheel turning drove the crankshaft and piston back up to its apogee as the steam pressure built up again in the cylinder. Steam released from the cylinder on the piston down-stroke was piped to a condenser cooled by saltwater and recirculated to the water tank for reuse.

As Mr Holt explained to me, the future development of steamships was being frustrated by the design of engines. In turn, engines could only operate at the pressures that could be contained by the quality of the steel in the boilers and cylinders. Improvements in making iron and steel during the last 20 years had allowed steam pressure to be increased from 5lbs per square inch up to the 25lbs being used in the engine of *The Queen*. At these pressures, engines were still so inefficient that they burned large quantities of coal to generate the vast volume of steam required.

If pressure could be doubled, the amount of coal needing to be carried for burning would be halved. Every less ton of coal carried could be replaced by another ton of cargo shipped. Meantime, sailing ships were by far the most economic means of moving cargo across the oceans. Even the invention of the screw propeller which had proven its superior driving force compared with paddlewheels could not overcome the inefficiency of the steam-engine driving it. The outline of the enormous clipper *Sarah Palmer* taking form in our yards showed that although iron was replacing timber for shipbuilding, large sailing vessels far-surpassed steamers as cargo-carriers.

Mr Holt had devoted his energy, money and skill to inventing a better steam engine but without stronger iron from the smelters, *The Queen* had the best that could presently be built.

At least the recent changes in the near century-old Lloyd's tonnage measurement rules had allowed Page & Grantham to design the long graceful lines of the *Sarah Palmer* for us to build. In place of squat, fat, short, blunt-bowed and flat-sterned ships that had to be forced slowly and heavily against the ocean, the long, narrow, sharp-bowed *Sarah Palmer* would slice her way quickly through the seas. Speed and cargo capacity together, with non-burning non-rotting iron to outlast wood – it was a new generation in shipbuilding and here I now was at its very heart. What better place could I be, than here on the Mersey?

No wonder then, that so many years thus passed so quickly.

* * *

I lived in Warrington throughout the years of my twenties. *The Queen* was built, and launched with cheers, steam whistles and a crashing roar of water, sideways into the Mersey – the first ship I could take some pride in having been involved in her construction.

Eventually the *Sarah Palmer*, at least completed to the deck-line framing but without her teak decking in place, was slowly slid into the river; towed by a steam tugboat she disappeared down river to the rigging yards whilst all the army of workers at Laird's cheered her sadly from sight.

Other vessels took their places. In 1857 we started to build Laird's first large screw-vessel, the collier *James Kennedy* also designed by Page & Grantham, to be driven by Mr Holt's latest design in steam engines. Her speed and reliability of passage was calculated to bring the total tonnage of coal shipped by her in a year to almost double that of a collier driven by sail. I learned to deal with the engineering problems of a long shaft running through half the full length of the keel from the engine amidships, needing to be supported by large bearings supplied with animal grease.

Improvements continued to be made by the smelters in the quality of iron. During his many visits to Laird's, Mr Holt would discuss with me his ideas and plans for more efficient steam engines. By heating the ore to higher temperatures using forced drafts of air and by adding increased amounts of charcoal to raise the carbon levels, the smelters now could produce much stronger iron. But the higher carbon content and hotter temperatures made the iron more brittle which meant that the large castings such as those required for big engines were likely to crack as they cooled. This was not a problem for making the thinner-walled tubes required for the boilers, which could now sustain much higher pressures.

Mr Holt was quite excited by my suggestion that he should try to design a two-part or two-cylinder steam engine. The first cylinder could be a smaller casting made from the highest-quality high-carbon iron, operating at the highest possible pressures; the steam would exit from the first cylinder to a conventional large second cylinder operating at lower pressure. If it were possible to design such a two-stage engine, there would be a very significant increase in its efficiency, effectively doubling the thrust from the same quantity of coal burned. Mr Holt soon produced some designs; a succession of small experimental engines following during the next two years, each improving on the other.

Living in the social structure here in the northwest of England was very strange. It was as if there were three societies living beside each other but separately.

One society was of the English aristocracy, of inherited titles, wealth, land and property, most of whom did no useful work. It seemed a class of idle, mostly-educated gentlemen and their ladies, who occupied themselves with frivolous pastimes, staying aloof and separated from all that surrounded them.

Then there was a society of commerce, to which the Lairds belonged, consisting of mill owners, industrialists, traders and shippers. These were hardworking energetic people who had created or continued their own family businesses, building, manufacturing or moving goods. Similarly, they formed a separate society of their own amidst the structure that surrounded them.

Although I had virtually no involvement with them, there was a third, much larger society of the poor who owned nothing, lived in dirty soot-stained, crowded, ramshackle tenements, row upon row in coalsmoke-shrouded streets. They worked long hours in factories or mills to earn barely enough for survival. It seemed that consuming excessive amounts of cheap gin was very common, which helped the people to forget the horrible conditions in which they lived. Adults and children alike often lay drunken in the streets. It was the society of most of the northern city of Manchester.

The two societies of commerce and aristocracy did not mix together. For myself, I belonged nowhere. The MacGregor Lairds were kindness itself to me, often inviting me into their home or to accompany them to functions held among the commercial society. I met many young ladies at such functions or at dances held in private homes, but was quickly made aware that as an employee (not a principal), I was not to be socially accepted. I felt very isolated even amidst this large community in a way which I had never been aware of in Ireland. Much as I longed at times to court some of the attractive daughters of commercial society, it was not to be.

Yet at the same time, because I was educated and qualified I was also well aware that the great masses of working people would perceive me to be part of some higher class, completely unrelated to their way of life. I was conscious of not belonging anywhere.

I was also very aware of being different just in stature. The English here in the northwest were all short stocky people amongst whom I was frequently both head and shoulders taller. In a busy street in the town of Warrington, I could easily see over the whole crowd; to enter a shop or tavern I would have to stoop low to avoid hitting my head on the low door-lintels. Some taverns even had a pit in the floor in which taller people like myself could stand to avoid constantly stooping beneath the ceiling beams.

I had now been living in Warrington for a very long time, fully occupied and absorbed in the engineering work of shipbuilding. Although the continual cycle of new vessels to construct provided a challenging variety, after all those years there was a tedious sameness to my life, constantly touched with loneliness.

In the autumn of 1860, George married Lucy Gibson, one of five daughters of a Belfast carriage builder. I took leave to attend the wedding and travelled back to Ireland for the first time in many years.

At the farm in Castledawson, my dear aunt still sat in her special chair by the hearth in the kitchen, but she and my uncle had both aged considerably. Charles, married to Anne and now with two children of their own, lived together with them in the great stone house. Hugh, who had not married, still worked around the farm, living in a rebuilt part of the barn across the yard. The patterns of life seemed otherwise unchanged.

Slow, steady, reliable George had married short wiry Lucy, overflowing with uncontainable, enthusiastic energy. As opposites, they provided a matching balance to each other, but Lucy had a visible restlessness that did not sit easily with George's more complacent nature. It was bound to change him. It soon did.

'John, we have been thinking of leaving Ireland and going to the Argentine,' he burst out before I left them to return to England, as smiling Lucy looked up at him, hugging his arm. 'Mother has had many letters from Alex and David.

'Both of them have been very successful – they've made money on the railroad construction and have each bought land of their own to farm. They say it has wonderful earth, rich and fertile. The winters are not cold, the summer rains grow lush grass. They graze herds of cattle across big open spaces. It sounds like a paradise full of opportunities compared with a life here in Belfast. Lucy thinks we should go out there to join them. Why don't you come with us?'

Back once more in Warrington, my own life seemed very purposeless and empty compared with my cousins' in Ireland. I could easily see years of the sameness stretching forward before me. Thoughts of the Argentine kept returning to my mind.

Shortly before Christmas, a letter arrived from George. He and Lucy were still determined to start a new life for themselves by leaving Ireland, but there had been some change in their plan to join my cousins in Argentina. Instead, a new possibility had appeared.

At Stevenson's Iron & Steel Works, George was responsible for obtaining, preparing and shipping orders of iron and steel to customers in the colonies, some themselves having emigrated from Ireland during the bad times of the famine. One of these far-off customers, a Mr John Burns, had recently placed another but much larger order for iron goods with Stevenson's. At the same time, Mr Burns had written separately to Mr Stevenson, asking if any man with a good knowledge of the iron and steel trade was interested to accompany the shipment and on its arrival, join his business in New Zealand. With recent discoveries of gold in the area, Mr Burns was expecting his business there to grow substantially. For George (and Lucy), it seemed timely and opportune; besides, George reminded me, my cousin Harry was somewhere in New Zealand too.

They would go. Would I, George wrote, join him and Lucy on their venture?

I sought advice from Mr MacGregor Laird. To leave all that was familiar to me was a big decision in itself, but to leave my position at Laird's Shipyards was irrevocable, especially after all the consideration that the Lairds, Mr McGregor particularly, had extended to me.

His usually smiling, cheerful face became sombre and grave as I discussed George's letter in the library at his home in the country near Warrington He poured us each a short glass of whisky.

Finally, when I had nothing more to say, he looked at me intently. 'John, you are a man of some engineering talent for shipbuilding. If you were to stay with us, I can truly say that you would have a fine future. We will build some grand new ships. Mr Holt will succeed with new engines. Iron screw-steamers will replace sail.

'Both Mrs Laird and I have much regard for you – in many ways you have been like a son to us. But whatever, I believe that in life we must follow our fate, to fulfil whatever is God's plan for each of us. Just as that fate brought you here, perhaps now its hand is being held out to lead you on another path.

'Much as we would all not want to lose you, much as Mrs Laird and I would be very sad to see you go, you should follow your fate.'

Over several days, I weighed his words together with my own thoughts. Twice now in my life, I had left all that was familiar to venture anew, firstly being taken out of Scotland as a child, then secondly moving from Ireland to the shipyards here in England.

Did I feel I belonged here? – No. Not only did I feel no sense of belonging, it was also obvious that I would not easily be accepted into any of the defined classes of this English society. I did not like living with the English - my ancestry and the experiences of the famine in Ireland vividly etched in my memory reinforced that. My work was absorbing, though somewhat repetitive. Obviously from Mr MacGregor's comments, my future with Laird's was sound, but I would always be an employee, it would be very difficult to begin or own a business myself.

I decided to go.

Time was now vital: the iron order for Mr Burns was already being assembled in Plymouth and George and Lucy were expecting to embark with it from there aboard a vessel some time in February. I hastily replied to George, suggesting he should come to Liverpool, then meet with me in Warrington. Together, the three of us could take a train to London and travel west to Plymouth by coach.

Meantime, with Mr MacGregor's assistance, I sought and purchased a small steam engine still in very good condition, which had been used in a small Mersey paddle tugboat that had been damaged by fire. I also purchased a fine kit of engineering tools which we crated up in an iron footlocker. We arranged for their shipment to Plymouth.

Regrettably, I would not have time to revisit Castledawson to see my aunt and uncle again. Life already seemed to have had too many goodbyes. I wrote instead.

On a cold, dark day in January 1861, the three of us boarded a train in Warrington for the long journey south. Mr and Mrs Laird accompanied us to the station, standing in the rain to wave as our train moved away in shrouds of steam. I really wasn't sorry to leave northwest England behind.

FOUR

For much of our travelling to Plymouth, we discussed the long sea voyage we were soon to undertake.

For George and Lucy, the short journey across the Irish Sea to Liverpool had been their first experience of ships and the sea. For most of it, pitching through the northeast swells out of Belfast in an iron, sail-paddlesteamer, they had both been violently ill so that now the prospect of months aboard a ship filled them with apprehension.

On arriving by coach in Plymouth, we took rooms in the town away from the docks, expecting to wait some indeterminate time for the arrival of the *Black Swan*, but found on calling upon the shipping Agent next day, she was already alongside, taking cargo aboard. Leaving Lucy safely lodged, George and I went looking for her.

The docks were crowded with rows of ships end to end, rafted together as many as four abreast, their bare masts and yards forming a tangled forest against the grey sky. Sailors of the Royal Fleet, men with barrows, lines of horse-drawn drays and swirling crowds of people seethed noisily everywhere.

Eventually, by the expedient of checking the ensign at the stern of each ship, we found her. There before us, with the striped flag of the Union of States of America clearly hanging from a pole atop a towering flat transom, and the black and gold scripted words 'Black Swan' under the aft-cabin windows, she lay hard alongside.

As we pushed closer, I saw she was a large three-masted barque, square-rigged on the fore and mizzen, her lower yards so wide that they hung out over the dock where we stood. Even though the tide was quite low, her bulwarks were riding high above us. A long steeved sprit projecting forward from her bluff bows added some graceful line. A roped timber gangway swung from the gunwhale down onto the dock.

Stacks of cargo lay piled on the dock. I recognised many rectangular blocks of flat and corrugated sheet-iron locked in nailed frames of timber, with rows of iron beams waiting nearby on four-wheeled drays. Crates, boxes and barrels were stacked in heaps. Stevedores swarmed everywhere beneath the swinging arms of cranes.

Amidships on the *Black Swan*'s deck, stood a fellow calling down to the dock through the tapering tube of a hailer. I waited until he lowered it from his mouth, cupped my hands and shouted up 'Ahoy *Black Swan*. Can we come aboard?' The fellow with the hailer looked towards us, giving a vague wave of the hand toward the gangway which we took to be his permission. With George following closely, I led the way up the bouncing woodwork, hand over hand on the rope stays until we jumped on to the solid Malibar teak deck.

Confronting me, lowered hailer still in hand, stood a tall young man, not much older than myself. A cap, rakishly backward, perched atop a thatch of thick curly hair. As he spoke, I saw his open dark-blue jacket had strips of braid on the epaulettes – an Officer. 'State your business gentlemen!'

'We have passage aboard your ship – can we look around her?' and on seeing the frown, quickly added, 'I'm a shipbuilding engineer, so I know my way about – we'll keep out of your way.'

The frowning stopped. In an unexpected gesture, he thrust out his hand toward me, 'I'm Nathaniel Greene, the ship's Purser.' Both the accent and his manner were distinctly different, certainly not English.

'John Fraser, and my cousin George Bruce.' Continuing the unexpected, he shook each of us by the hand.

'Stay topside, don't go below, and keep well clear of the cargo. I can't accompany you – too busy here – but I come ashore at night for an ale and porter. If you want to talk, you can find me in *The Matelot's Arms* in Maidstone, behind the docks.' He returned quickly to his post at the bulwark.

We clambered around the main deck forward to the fo'c'sle: a shambles of loose timber, ropes, rigging and canvas surrounded the open hole of the large for'ard cargo hold set between the main and foremasts. From up on the fo'c'sle deck by the blunt bows looking back down aft to the poop, she looked huge. Accustomed as I was to large vessels, the *Black Swan* was at first sight a reassuringly impressive ship to take us to the Antipodes.

We made our way back down the main deck, noting the cannon between blocks with their long iron barrels set in the gun-ports of the bulwark. Just for'ard of the foremast, we passed the for'ard companionway leading down to quarters below deck. Between the main and mizzen masts, presently securely lashed, was the spoked steering wheel sheltered behind a low sloping wheelhouse. Immediately aft of the wheelhouse was the raised timber covering of the smaller aft hold.

Just on the aft side of the mizzen mast, companionways led down to the general passengers' quarters below deck. The long boom of the mizzen mast hung out over the poop deck, at the front of which were the doors to the Captain's quarters, dining-room and private passenger-cabins beneath the poop itself. On either side, railed gangway steps led up onto the poop deck. We climbed up.

A strong, decorative timber railing surrounded the sides of the poop deck, except for one empty cannon port on each side. Two large cannon secured by blocks were positioned facing directly aft and in the centre, hanging over the transom on hooked iron davits, was a securely-lashed longboat.

Looking up and for'ard from the poop deck against the darkening afternoon sky, I could see all three masts soaring upward, intersected by the horizontal spread of their yards, amidst a thick maze of rigging. I could make out double-stays near me on the mizzenmast, then four heavy backstays anchoring each of the main and foremasts. Lighter stays threaded the tops of the masts and the tips of the yards. A swathe of shrouds splayed down from each side of the two yarded masts to the top of the bulwark. Much of the upper rigging was bare of sail, rolls of canvas furled on the lower yards.

Having now traversed the entire ship from fo'c'sle to stern, we returned to the maindeck, saw Mr Greene with hailer still in hand leaning over the open hold and climbed back down the gangway again to the dock. We both stood looking at the ship for some time, knowing we were soon to trust our lives to her.

Later that night armed with directions from our lodgekeeper, George and I with Lucy firmly by arm between us, found *The Matelots' Arms*. Together we pushed through a rough-looking crowd of noisy men and women toward the back of the smokey tavern, trying to recognise our Mr Greene. He sat at a bench in a corner with two other men, tankards in hand, but rose up to greet us when we were close by.

We were introduced. 'Mr Fraser's a passenger, a marine engineer. Our First Officer Mr Holbourne, Second Officer Mr O'Reilly.' We completed the introductions, including Lucy.

Mr Greene explained he himself was both Third Officer and Purser. In port, all three officers took lodgings ashore, pleased to have the space, a variety of food, and normal beds. The Captain was presently away from Plymouth, visiting with friends, leaving Mr Holbourne in charge of the *Black Swan*. He, Mr Greene, was responsible for the organising and loading of the cargo; Mr O'Reilly for stowing the cargo securely down in the holds, both assisted by the Mates. When at sea, as Purser, he was responsible for all the passengers.

They were expecting to complete the loading of all the cargo next day. The cargo hatches would be covered and secured, the ship's longboats returned to their stowage atop the for'ard hold hatch-cover, the barge atop the aft hold. Then the ship would be watered and provisioned which, he explained, was a slow process because as it progressed, many live animals and poultry had to be taken aboard. Finally, the passengers' personal luggage would be carried down into the aft hold, where it would be accessible during the voyage. The passengers themselves could then board. The *Black Swan* was scheduled to set sail mid-February.

Next day, we visited the ship's Agents to pay the £25 each cost of our passage. We were required to sign a document agreeing to abide by the Voyage Rules, then being presented with a printed copy each. In the town, following the requirement of the Rules that we each must provide our own, we purchased bedding, linen and soap.

Several nights later, we returned to *The Matelots' Arms*, buying tankards of ale for Mr Greene and the two other Officers, both of whom were considerably older. He seemed pleased to see us again, asking many questions. George explained that much of the iron we had seen being loaded on the day we first visited the ship was destined for his new employer in New Zealand as well as being the reason for his leaving Belfast. They were all very interested in my experience with steamers, especially with Mr Holt's engine developments. We discussed the merits of screw power compared with paddles.

In turn, we learned more about our ship and her crew. The *Black Swan* had been completed in 1854, intended for the trans-Atlantic freight and passenger trade. When the surge of demand for ships followed the discovery of gold in Australia, her owners decided she was a very suitable vessel for the long journeys to the Antipodes, so that at launching she was named after the unusual black swan of Australia, itself a graceful, powerful and fast flyer.

At nearly 1000 tons, she was among the biggest ships to have come from the Maine shipyards, built of American oak sheathed with English copper to protect her timbers from sea-worm. Her masts and spars were of straight-grained white American pine, her sails Mississippi cotton canvas. She was registered in Maine but built according to the Lloyd's Register measurement rules prior to the changes of 1854, which explained her height, full bluff bows and racked flat stern.

The *Black Swan* was fitted out to carry more than 400 passengers, indeed had done so, from Dublin to New York several times and on one of her three voyages from London to Van Diemen's Land. However, our own impending voyage was mostly to transport freight, so she was only booked for 104 passengers (should they all duly take up their bookings). Besides, there were not many people wanting to endure the long voyage to New Zealand.

The Captain, officers and most of the crew were American, from the northeastern maritime States. Nathan – as he now insisted with an American lack of formality we should address him – was from Maine, but his commander, Captain King, was from Virginia; so too, First Officer Holbourne. The Second Officer Mr O'Reilly came from Massachusetts. After the voyage to the Antipodes, they expected they would return around Cape Horn, then north up the west Atlantic to their homes for the first time in two years. There were uneasy tensions reported between the southern and northern Atlantic States of the American Union and they were anxious to return to their families.

By the end of the week, we entertained ourselves by watching the loading of the provisions and livestock from the dockside. The hours of daylight were still quite short, so there was urgency to load as much as possible in the time available.

From Nathan we had learned that the *Black Swan* did not intend to stop for re-provisioning during the voyage, following a new, much faster route west and south that kept us well clear of Capetown, the traditional Cape of Good Hope port of supply for passage to the Indian Ocean. So whatever provisions were required to sustain us for the months to New Zealand had to be taken aboard now in Plymouth.

At first, row upon row of water barrels and many barrels of apple cider were rolled along the dock, hoisted aboard for storage deep in the lower decks. Then barrels of salted beef brisket in vinegar, cases of biscuit, chests of tea, cases of wine, port and brandy all arrived on a succession of drays, mostly carried aboard one by one by stevedores. Next followed goods packed in sacking; drays of flour, rice, salt, grain, potatoes, onions, turnips, beets, carrots – seemingly enough to provision a small army.

While we read our way through the pages of the Voyage Rules familiarising ourselves with all their detail, we watched tightly compressed bales of hay being carried below or stacked around the main deck between the masts and hatch covers, then barrels stamped 'Oats' and 'Corn'.

Next day, as we stood in the shelter of a dockside warehouse in a cold drizzly rain, came a parade of livestock and poultry, as if the *Black Swan* had become Noah's Ark itself. Three cows led the way, followed by some 50 sheep, then goats, calves and pigs. The cows disappeared below deck, the sheep, goats and calves packed close together into the boats stored before the mainmast and into the barge, the pigs in wooden pens up near the fo'c'sle.

Then came cage upon cage of poultry; fowl, geese, turkeys, in all several hundred, stacked in rows up around the poop deck. They were soon joined by cages of rabbits and more chickens. The topsides of the ship now looked more like a farmyard than a sailing vessel.

By this day, quite a large crowd was gathered on the dock to watch the loading. We assumed they were mostly our fellow passengers. Given that this was now the Agent's published departure date of February 15, we were several days late in boarding, but it was obvious the *Black Swan* would be made ready to sail soon thereafter.

The notice posted at the ship's gangway late that afternoon advised that passengers must board early on February 17, prior to sailing later that same day. Another notice on the board outside the Agent's offices read the same, but when we sought out Nathaniel Green at *The Matelots' Arms* that night, he told us to be ready for boarding tomorrow afternoon. If we arrived at the gangway immediately after darkness fell, he would sign us aboard, ahead of the general rush of passengers. We could then leave the ship for our last evening meal ashore, but return to spend our first night on board here in Plymouth Harbour.

At 4p.m. next day we duly arrived shipside accompanied by our trunks for stowage in the hold and drawstring-topped canvas sea-bags each, containing our bedding, linen, soap and clothing for the first period at sea. Ahead of us, in the light of lanterns, a line of men was carrying slatted crates of large round green cabbages up the gangway. When some of these returned to the dock, we had them help us with our trunks.

Nathan Greene met us on deck by the top of the gangway, signed us into the ship's passenger log, then called a steward forward to take George and Lucy to their berth in the deck below. Single men such as I were berthed in the bow quarters, where I was now led by a mate – one of several among the crew.

We descended the for'ard companionway into a semi-dark passage lit by a lantern, moving forward under the fo'c'sle deck. After following my guide for about 20 feet the passage opened to about six feet wide. Another lantern hanging from a hook overhead dimly lit two tiers of wooden bunks on either side, the lower at my knee height, the upper tier level with my shoulder.

On the proffered suggestion of the mate, I chose an upper berth on the starboard side. 'Through the tropical ocean the uppers will be very hot,' he commented, 'but in the southern latitudes where we spend much of the voyage, you'll be glad of it because they're warmer.'

My bunk was about six feet long, aligned from stem to stern, and about two feet six inches wide, with barely sufficient height above for a shorter man than I to sit upright. A high sideboard held my bedding and I from falling out. Foot and headboards separated the bunks from each other, but as the berth I had chosen was the aftermost, at my feet was a fixed timber bulkhead.

When the mate departed, I unrolled and laid out my bedding, using the seabag which now only contained some clothes as a headrest. So this dark, almost airless place was to be my home. At least I had had first choice.

I returned to the deck and went looking for George and Lucy, whilst I was able to visit their quarters; when the Voyage Rules applied when we sailed, single men such as I were not permitted to enter the married quarters. There were two aft companionways, port and starboard which below deck gave access to two rows of two-tiered bunk-berths similar to my own, except they were arranged sideways across the ship, not fore and aft like mine. The berths were only separated from each other at the sides by a higher dividing board, otherwise they were continuous on the same level in a long row, stretching away into the dark. When occupied, there would be no privacy whatsoever.

Lucy had wisely chosen port side berths for she and George, knowing that through the tropics sailing north-south, the port side was shaded from the hot afternoon sun as it travelled west; but in the cold southern latitudes during winter, then sailing west-east, port was the warmest side of the ship facing the northern arc of the sun. They had secured berths as far for'ard as they could, mostly to be clear of the busy passageway close to the bottom of the companionway, but also with the hope that with only 100 passengers for a ship fitted out for 400, they might have some empty berths around them.

Both of them looked rather discouraged; faced with the reality of their abode for the next several months, even Lucy had lost much of her normal bright, enthusiastic persona. However, after having a large portion of a bottle of whisky ashore, accompanied by a good meal, we returned to the *Black Swan* feeling more resigned to the voyage ahead.

Next morning, the 17th day of February, at first light, a long line of passengers stretched out along the dock, waiting to board, their trunks stacked up in a growing heap. Slowly they shuffled up the gangway, to be registered in the log by the Purser and directed to the berths in their respective section of the ship. I was surprised at the number of families with young children, though there were also many single men of all ages.

Beside a web of shrouds cascading down from the mainmast, we leaned idly over the bulwark railing close enough to the top of the gangway to view the passengers as they arrived on deck. Gradually as the morning passed, the line on the dock became shorter. Stevedores and porters carried most of the stack of cabin trunks aboard and down into the aft hold.

As the boarding passenger numbers dwindled in the early afternoon, I became more interested in watching the ships cooks and carpenter setting up the galleys immediately aft of the for'ard hold cover, where the ships' boats provided some protection from the wind.

At the clatter of horse hooves on the dock, I turned back to see a tall military officer in full dress of brass-buttoned scarlet coat, black breeches, dress sword and long black boots, climb down from a carriage. Porters unloaded a number of trunks and lockers. On deck, both the First and Second Officers appeared, to join Nathaniel by the gangway.

Almost immediately, the Captain himself emerged from the doorway under the poop deck. It was the first time we had seen him. He too was resplendent in a coat of blue with bright gold embroidery, black velvet lapels, cuffs and collar, waistcoat and breeches of a deep buff colour, a black stock loosely around his neck, a cocked hat firmly on top of his head, a pistol at the waist and a sheathed sword at his side.

The Guards Officer was greeted at the top of the gangway by Nathaniel Greene, welcomed aboard and introduced to the Captain, Mr Holbourne and Mr O'Reilly. We were not sufficiently close to hear these proceedings. A steward stood attentively nearby. A small line of porters had backed up on the gangway carrying the officer's trunks.

After some minutes, the Captain led the Officer aft and together they disappeared into the private quarters beneath the poop followed by porters with the baggage. We turned back to continue watching the building of the galleys. It seemed that most, if not all, the passengers were now boarded and the deck was quite crowded as the newly-arrived walked about inspecting all the livestock. All the people now suddenly around set off a huge noise from the animals which in turn provoked the geese and turkeys into a clamour. It sounded (and smelled) more like a farmyard than a ship about to set sail for the opposite side of the world.

Then again came the clipped sound of hooves on the dock. I turned idly back over the rail to see these latest arrivals. A gentleman in a tophat climbed down from a coach, followed by a woman. Shiny trunks were stacked on the back-rails. They walked over to the gangway. I leaned on the bulwark rail and looked aft. The ship's officers were again gathering on the deck. More private cabin passengers. The wealthy or important obviously wait to the last moment before they board.

I looked back to the galleys, the carpenter had almost finished his work, the cooks were stoking up a mound of charcoal for cooking the first meal aboard. When I glanced over the rail again, the gentleman was almost atop the gangway. For the second time, the Captain in his blue coat had arrived. Under the gentleman's tophat I could see he had grey hair and beard. Close behind him was his wife.

Just as I turned away, something made me stop. I looked at them again. Wife? No. Too young to be his wife? Very young wife? Travelling companion? Daughter? By now the gentleman was on the deck being greeted by Nathaniel Greene. The woman was close behind.

Suddenly she turned part-around and looked at me. I thought because I was now staring at her. Her eyes met mine. I felt some strange surge go through my chest. My left hand gripped the rail tightly. Our eyes were still locked together. Almost like burning. I could feel my heart jump. Her mouth opened slightly. A faint trace of a smile appeared. She turned back to meet the Captain and Officers. I was aware my hands were shaking, my knees feeling weak. It was like fright, but different. A reaction I had not known before. I turned to speak to George, but no sound came.

I stared at the woman again. Her back was now to me as she met the Officers. Then as the Captain began to lead them off in the direction of the private cabins, she suddenly turned her head. She looked directly at me. We locked eyes again. Even at that distance I could feel it. My heart raced. She gave a fuller smile. To me! I managed to smile back. Then she was gone. The doorway under the poop deck closed behind them and she was lost from my sight.

Oblivious to the noise and bustle around me, I stood holding the rail. Trying to make some sense from what had happened. My mouth was dry. I struggled to think. It was as if some tangible physical force had just passed between us. Some thing I had never experienced before.

I tried to recall. All that was in my mind was her eyes. Bright blue eyes. Looking at mine. Blue eyes – a blue bonnet, tied under her chin – curls the colour of wheat stalks spilling out from beneath the bonnet. A vision was returning. A wide mouth – even, white teeth – that trace of a smile opening her mouth. Eyes still fixed on mine. A shawl of some darker blue around her shoulders, crossed in front. A froth of white lacey collar upstanding around her neck.

How long did it last? Three minutes? Half a minute? A quarter? Why me – from amongst the crowd on the deck? A mistake of identity? But she had looked back a second time, no mistaking it. And smiled at me again. I did return it. How old was she? Less than 20? More? No, younger. Must be the daughter of the man in the tophat. Who are they?

Suddenly I realised George and Lucy were talking to me, Lucy tugging at my arm. The gangway was gone. The crew were already untying the lines holding us firm against the dock. A crowd on the dock were calling to passengers around us on the deck, lining the rail. Wherever I looked I kept seeing her face, eyes looking into mine. A paddlesteamer tug backed up near the bow was fixing a line to us; an excited Lucy had been trying to draw my attention to it. Whoever she is, I would find out – we were all on this ship together.

* * *

The line to the tug taughtened. A small cheer from those on the dock, cries from those on deck, and a gap of dark water appeared between us and the dockside as the *Black Swan* was pulled slowly away. The distinct shape of buildings in Plymouth in the late afternoon began to merge into greyness behind us. I looked back to the poop deck, but there was nobody there. I could still see her face.

As we neared Graves End we began to feel life in the deck beneath our feet. The first sense of lifting and falling. A midshipman stood at the wheel, flanked by the two officers, the Captain nearby with hands clasped behind his back. Seamen scrambled up the ratlines on the cluster of mainmast shrouds beside us, for'ard on the foremast too, spreading out to hang over the upper yards. Behind us to creaks and a chant in rhythm, the huge triangular sail of the spanker rose in bursts up the mizzen mast from the boom.

The line to the steam tug ahead was dropped. At the same moment the mainsail and foresails fell open from the yards. In fading light the sails flapped, then filled out. The wind leaned into the ship and we tilted slightly to port. The *Black Swan* was underway.

Quite quickly, the ship fell to an even, rolling pitching movement: a lift of the bows, a slow tilt over to port, a falling of the bow, a roll back to starboard, a lift of the bow again, the wind steady on our aft starboard quarter. Excited passengers and children still crowded the deck as lanterns were lit around the ship. George and Lucy plied me with question after question about the ship and the great confusing mass of rigging. But my mind was often elsewhere; thoughts of Melvich and my father whom I'd never seen again, the house at Castledawson with my dear aunt and uncle, Warrington and the MacGregor Lairds, now all left behind.

It was quite late that first night before we turned in to our berths. I lay there stretched out in the dark, listening to all the sounds about me. A clear vision of her in my mind as I fell asleep.

The next few days I fully expected the private-cabin passengers at any moment to appear on their private deck, the poop, but to my surprise, nobody appeared. I watched constantly during each day, staying down aft, hoping to catch sight again of the young lady who had so affected me and who continually returned to my mind.

The daily patterns of life aboard became established. The wind continued from the same northwest quarter at about 20 knots, hardly varying in strength. The seamen had set the topsails on the main and foremast, the small topgallants high up on the mizzen, and two small jibs for'ard down to the bowsprit. It looked to be close to a full rig of sail, driving us quite fast in a southwest direction.

The Captain, accompanied by all three officers, took a daily turn around the ship. When the sun briefly appeared, the Captain took sightings with a sextant to log our position. Ships' bells tolled the 12-hour change in the watch. Either Mr Holbourne or Mr O'Reilly stood near the steersman at the wheelhouse, checking the compass, watching the set of the sails, scanning the horizon through a glass, or calling instructions to the crew. Seamen on their watch were constantly about the ship, those off watch mostly below, asleep.

Long ocean swells came steadily down us from behind like even windrows in a ploughed field. They would surge under the *Black Swan*'s stern, lifting it higher as her bow dropped, then peeling down the length of the ship as the stern fell back into the trough, the bow rising as we rolled from side to side. Seabirds with seemingly fixed wings glided just above the surface through the valley of each trough.

Several times I had tried to speak with Nathan Greene alone, impatient for information about the grey-haired gentleman and the young lady with him, but in these first days he was constantly busy or below deck with other passengers.

Many passengers including children had been seasick from the unfamiliar motion of the ship. George and Lucy had found it particularly difficult in their berth below deck with the smell aggravating their already nauseous state. They spent as much time as possible, even well into the night, up on deck in the fresh cold air.

Sickness had almost silenced the constant chatter aboard. The cooks had little to do because few wanted to eat. Only one of the two galleys was fired up each morning and those of us who wished to do so could get access to make tea at any time; the Voyage Rules allowed passengers to make tea when the galleys were not being used by the cooks.

The main hot meal was prepared by the cooks during the morning and eaten about midday. Passengers lined up, families first, followed by the single men, to collect their food which was then eaten at tables set up around the deck. Meals were not permitted to be taken below.

In the evening, the food of the day was served cold. We each had a fixed ration of water, including that for making tea and all of us, even the children, were given a daily cup of cider with our meal to prevent the development of scurvy. The baker, who was also the butcher, baked fresh bread each day in heavy cast-iron boxes which, with cheese and thinly-sliced smoked bacon made an excellent breakfast.

On the morning of the third day, for the first time since leaving Plymouth at last I saw Nathaniel Greene standing briefly alone, drinking tea by the steersman at the wheelhouse. I hurried over to him. He looked up, recognising me with a quick smile. 'Ah Mr Fraser, – I trust you're well settled aboard ship?'

'Yes, thank you, I'm very comfortable. But I would like to ask something of you; I've been waiting for a less busy time to ask you.... Please – if it's permitted for you to tell me – who is the tall grey-haired gentleman with a private berth … and is the young lady accompanying him, his wife?'

He laughed and grinned. 'That would be Mr MacKay you ask of. No, the lady is not his wife, I understand he lost his wife just a few years ago. The young lady is his daughter.' I felt as if a weight had lifted from me. 'Mr MacKay is from Edinburgh … I heard him call her 'Elizabeth'.' He looked at me quizzically, 'Why do you ask?'

'I thought he looked familiar … somebody I have met before … but no, it cannot be.' Some passengers were now waiting to speak with the Purser; as I thanked him and turned to move away, he grinned slyly, touched my arm lightly with a hand, 'Don't forget the Voyage Rules.'

Her name ran through my mind … Miss MacKay …. Miss MacKay … it had a certain pleasing harmony to it. Miss MacKay … I wanted to meet this Miss MacKay, but how? 'The Voyage Rules' Nathan Greene had said, but which of the Rules?

Then the significance of some of the Rules I had read came back to me:

Main deck passengers were not permitted on the poop deck or even on the gangways to the deck.

Main deck passengers were not allowed to enter the private quarters without permission of the Captain.

We could not converse, or even attempt to converse with the private-berth passengers unless we were spoken to first.

There was even another section which threatened that *breaches of the Voyage Rules would result in arrest and detention in the brig in the fo'c'sle head at the Captain's pleasure, on a diet of bread and water.*

It had been impressed upon us that certain rules such as those for not smoking tobacco below deck, drunkenness, stealing, fighting, failure to obey directions of the officers, were certain to be punished severely. Then there were others such as single men not entering the married berths or vice versa. That was to be expected, but when I had read through their many pages, I had not thought that minor rules could so affect me.

How ever could it be possible for me to meet Miss MacKay? It would indeed be difficult. Conceivably, we could sail to the Antipodes on the *Black Swan* together for several months never more than a few hundred feet apart, but might as well be a world apart. An anger of frustration welled inside me; rules and strictures to enforce the kind of segregation of people by class such as I had seen so often among the English in Warrington. And aboard an American ship – did they not revolt against that themselves? Did not their famous Independence Declaration state that 'All men are created equal'?

Two more days passed. We had now been sailing steadily southwest for five days and nights. The daylight had already noticeably lengthened with the apogee of the sun increasing as we left the northern winter further behind. Passengers were recovering from seasickness, becoming accustomed to the rolling movement of the ship, turning out to eat again, talking in groups around the rails. Children gathered around the livestock.

In mid-afternoon, people suddenly emerging from a companionway onto the poop deck caught my attention. Since we had left Plymouth, only the Captain or the poulterer feeding grain to the caged birds had appeared on the empty deck above the aft cabins. Now I could see the Guards Officer, a shorter older man and woman and then the gentleman who must be Mr MacKay with his daughter at his side holding his arm. I moved quickly further aft. If only we were allowed up on the poop deck.

The cold wind had strengthened during the day and the crew had furled in the topsails. We were all more heavily clothed against the wind. The small group on the poop deck were wrapped with coats, scarves and hats. They moved to the fore-rail fronting the main deck, holding tightly to the rail while looking out over the deck or up at the masts. There, clearly, was Miss MacKay beside her father. My heart jumped. I hoped she would see me, even recognise me. If only…. But the group all turned back into the wind, moved aft, and disappeared again below the deck.

Soon after, the wind shifted to the northeast, directly behind us. The long ocean swells had been steadily growing steeper during the afternoon, now rolling white foam at their breaking tops, their troughs deeper. Back to the north, the grey sky was ominously darkening; we were obviously to encounter our first storm at sea. The Captain appeared in an oilskin coat and long seaboots, taking up station by the steersman, the First Officer at his side.

As the waves grew larger, well above the ship when we were in the troughs, the *Black Swan* which until now had seemed such a large ship, seemingly shrank. Irrepressible Lucy had grown more fearful, spurning our reassurances as, running before the wind, the ship buried her bow and spray burst in sheets over the fo'c'sle. The seamen had lowered the spanker, secured the boom and furled the mainsails. Even with two foresails and the jibs, we were moving quite fast.

Most of the passengers had already gone below. George took white-faced Lucy firmly with one arm and, holding tightly to the ship with the other, tried to call to me above the noise of the wind in the rigging, then disappeared down their companionway. I still stood aft, braced by rigging at the mizzenmast, exhilarated by the way the ship surged through the growing violence around us, water dishing up over the bluff bows, then falling off the fo'c'sle head into the scuppers under the bulwarks. Mr O'Reilly finally made his way along the deck shouting, 'All passengers clear the decks - go below!'

Down in our single berths we were away from the noise of the wind but being as we were, up close to the bows, the pitch of the ship was accentuated. After each swift rising up came a long fall, sharp enough to feel that some part of you had been left behind. In the light of the lanterns still swinging in the passageway, the men around me talked and joked together to hold their equanimity. We had no food, but even had we, few would have eaten.

With the lanterns turned down, we tried to sleep. The narrowness of our berths and their alignment fore and aft provided some stability, but sleep was fitful as we all woke continually to brace ourselves against the side rails. I knew that daylight must have returned, only by the time on my fobwatch. We relit a lantern.

One of the two stewards appeared, offering us biscuit and water. Without the galley fires there would be no other food. He told us that the storm showed no sign yet of abating, but was no worse. As the motion of the ship confirmed, we were still running before the wind, at least holding to our southerly course.

We passed the hours of day playing card games or trying to read in the dim lantern light. As we entered the second night, we could hear and feel the ship shudder as we hit the bottom of some larger troughs. Later, we again tried to sleep.

Some hours had passed fitfully when suddenly we were all startled by a violent bang and thumping noise somewhere on the starboard side. Then a shaking vibration through the timbers of the ship, followed by the same thump a second time. The *Black Swan* heeled well over to port, straightened up, then heeled back again. This same sequence – a deep thump, a vibrating shudder, heel to port, straighten up – kept repeating. Frightened men were standing in the dark in the passageway beside my bunk. Some called to me, 'Fraser…Mr Fraser…what is it? What is happening? Have we struck something?'

We heard shouting and the sounds of feet pounding on the deck above, but our companionway doors stayed firmly shut.

I tried to understand what it could be. Had we indeed struck something? Had we sprung a timber? Had something, a longboat or a spar, broken free and washed overboard but was still fastened to the ship? 'I don't know … I can't tell … something seems to be loose against the side.'

Again we swung over hard onto port, then straightened up. From the motion, I tried to work out what was happening to the direction of the ship. We had been running down wind. We must have turned sharply to starboard, begun to broach and rolled over to port. Then we straightened up, probably down wind again. Another turn to starboard, another broach, a long heavier roll to port, straighten up. I could picture the steersman frantically spinning the wheel as the ship began to broach, struggling to hold her course. Had we broken our steering? No, can't have … we wouldn't have straightened up.

Since last we straightened up, we had held there pitching up and down in a steady cycle, with a lean to starboard. I reasoned that on the last big roll we had come round into the wind and were now holding there virtually hove to, taking the wind and waves just onto the port quarter. The thumping vibrating sound had stopped. My companions in the berth regained some equanimity. I explained to them what I thought our motion had been. We lit a lantern. I checked my fob. It was only 3 a.m. – a lot more night yet to pass.

None of the crew had called us out, so whatever had happened, the ship must be secure. Apart from the regular pitching, she was stable. Perhaps when daylight returned, we would find out what had happened. Meantime, we could try again to sleep. The men returned to their bunks and we turned the lantern down.

Six hours later, the companionway door was opened from outside and faint light lit the passageway. Nathaniel Greene came for'ard through the berths, calling out: 'Passengers remain below please. Mr Fraser, where is Mr Fraser?' I swung down from my bunk, reaching for a shirt. 'I'm here!'

'Captain's compliments Mr Fraser, could you attend on deck please!' He turned away. I pulled on my boots, buttoning my shirt as I followed him up the companionway to the deck. Out there, the wind had died away to a steady breeze, just on the port quarter. We were almost hove to into it, two jibs and the spanker to its first reef the only sails. A group of men were standing by the wheelhouse amidships.

As Nathan led us toward them, I could see the officers, the Captain and several others. They faced toward us. 'Sir, this passenger is the engineer, Mr Fraser…' Nathan turned to me, 'Mr Fraser – our commander, Captain King.' The Captain dipped his head, 'Mr Fraser, morning to you. You're a marine engineer?'

'Yes Sir, but in iron steamers, not timbered sailing ships.'

'Well Fraser, we have something of a problem with this ship. Would like to hear your opinion … what you would recommend we do to fix it. Come with us.'

The Captain strode off for'ard with us all close behind. Mr Holbourne and Mr O'Rielly were beside me, the first and second mates, the bosun, the carpenter and three seamen followed. We lined up together at the starboard quarter bulwark and leaned over the rail. The Captain pointed down and forward, 'There Mr Fraser, you see that? Our sheathing on the chine's being ripped off … peeled back like the skin of an orange!'

It was obvious there, a huge sheet of copper pulled out from the hull, swaying about in the sea, the top of it dipping in and out as the ship rose and fell.

'We struck a big sea in the night. It must've ripped out for'ard, then peeled back abeam. The drag swung the ship to starboard. We lost way when she broached … that thing smashed back against the ship … then opened out as we straightened up, pulling us round again.' The noises in the night, the wild swinging of the ship – it was clearer to me now.

'Can't stay like this! In Maine we rivet the copper together in long sheets, beat it onto the timbers, then fasten it. English ships use small sheets. Long way to a port. Seems we must cut it free or the drag'll make it impossible to sail her. Not a simple matter to do that either….' He frowned severely, looking at me. 'Thought you might've a suggestion Fraser, something we've not thought of … what else could be done?'

I stared into the sea, thinking. The copper sheet surged in and out. Maybe if it kept flexing it would break off close in to the hull? But if it kept peeling back … not a good thought. Not many choices. They ran through my mind, the silence amongst us growing.

I took a deep breath. I spoke before the idea was consciously in my mind. 'Perhaps a solution Sir … I'm not sure it could be done.' They all looked at me, waiting, expectantly.

FIVE

The jibs luffed as the *Black Swan* was held close to the wind, still pitching in the swells.

'We could pass two long weighted lines under the stem, Sir', the idea taking more shape as I spoke. 'Walk them under her keel. Fix the lines on the port side to the bulwark just for'ard of where we stand now.' The Captain looked at me quizzically. 'We need two good lines under the ship but with the starboard ends aft behind that torn sheet. If we make the starboard lines fast to the bulwark just in front of the torn sheathing, then lightly weight their ends, we could sink the ends into the space between the copper and the timbers … with some way on, they would drift under the loose section, close in to the hull.

'If we fished for them with a line and hook aft of the sheathing and snagged them, we could bring them up again aft of the sheathing … then release their fore-fastening. Unless the bosun knows another way to get them round that thing down there….' I glanced at him.

'And then what?'

'Well, I'm thinking to get a heavy spar, like the one beside the longboats against the hatch. Secure two heavy lines to one end then fix the starboard lines to the other end. If we lower it vertically over the side and haul up the keel ropes taught on the port, then we would have the spar positioned vertically against the hull immediately aft the torn sheathing.' Some realisation now, but they waited whilst I continued.

'The purpose of two lines at the bottom of the spar coming up to port … keep one line exactly opposite the spar to hold it tight against the hull, the other line for'ard at least 30 degrees. Same with the two starboard-side lines.

'With all four lines separately on a windlass and some co-ordination, we should be able to roll the spar forward slowly against the copper sheet like a huge rolling-pin flattening pastry.' The Captain grinned, but I wanted to finish my thoughts before he spoke, so I rushed on.

'I don't know how much could be achieved Sir, but with all the jibs and staysails you can put on aloft, the full spanker sheeted tight and the ship on her beam to the wind, she might be laid over enough to get that torn piece clear of the water.' And then without a forethought, 'If the carpenter comes with me, I'm willing to go over the side. As your men haul the spar for'ard and work the sheath back in Captain, we could beat it flat and with some good nails, fix it to the timbers again as she goes....'

A silence lengthened. The Officers looked to their Captain. He stared at the deck, frowning, then looked up. 'Worth trying Mr Fraser. If it doesn't work, we can chop it adrift ... make for a port ... have her slipped ... lose two weeks! Let's get started Mr Holbourne!' Orders flowed.

'You take command of the ship. Get every piece of canvas you can find, up there. Mr Greene, it mightn't count for much, but I want every male passenger on deck and lined up along the leeward rail. All others stay below. Mr O'Reilly, you and the Bosun get some lines under the ship. When we're ready, you will take charge of the portside lines. I will stay here where I can see what's happening below ... call the instructions to you all when we need to move.

'Now Mr Fraser, you'll not go over the side of my ship unless I'm assured of your safety. Mr McGreevy the Mate here will go with you and Burton the Carpenter. McGreevy, if Mr Fraser does not return safely to this deck, it's you I will hold responsible! Mr Burton, prepare all that you and Fraser need to repair this thing.'

They moved away. The Carpenter and I discussed what we would need, deciding on large hammers fitted with wrist-straps and leather waist-pouches filled with the largest copper ships' nails he had, each fitted with a brass domed-rivet. I went below to change clothing as best I could, choosing a heavy shirt, tight-fitting breeches and laced short soft boots.

When I returned on deck, Mr McGreevy the bearded stocky Mate was waiting with a tangle of leather strapping, buckles and rope. 'These here harnesses Mr Fraser, are "bosun's chairs". We'll fit these straps under your buttocks Sir and around to the ring at the front.' He held it up to show me. 'Then these straps up your back, crossed over your shoulders and onto this upper ring. Then this heavy piece fastens between the two rings. Trussed up like a turkey at Thanksgiving you'll be. With a line to the top ring and a spare to the lower, you will be secured to the rail. Same for the Carpenter and I on either side of you.'

Passing weighted lines under the bow and under the ship proved easier than I expected. O'Reilly used very light lines. It was more difficult to sink the ends of the starboard lines under the swaying copper sheet and fish them up again aft of it, but three seamen with small grapnels soon had them hooked and back on deck. O'Reilly then attached heavy hemp ropes onto the ends of the light lines and hauled them through under the ship.

It took six seamen to carry the unlashed spar from the hatchcover to the bulwark. The ropes to control its two ends were securely fastened then clamped in place with iron collars. A breechblock was slung from the starboard end of the lower foremast yard and a rope through it attached to the spar lying in the scuppers. The Bosun explained that when we were ready, the men would haul what would be the top end of the spar up into the air with the rope through the block, swing the lower end with its port-side ropes passing under the ship attached, over the side, then lower the spar down into place.

I was surprised at how much canvas had now been rigged aloft; three large jibs for'ard, three staysails between the fore and mainmasts, three between the main and the mizzen, and the huge spanker aft. A rectangular mainsail, one of the larger sails in the ship's wardrobe, had been rigged fore and aft beneath the upper staysails between the main and foremasts, almost down onto the deck below.

The Carpenter reappeared with our equipment. I checked the nails for length, the brass rivets for diameter. Mr McGreevy fitted the bosuns-chair leather harness around me. The Carpenter and I belted on our pouches of nails and I made sure I could reach and open the flap easily. We slung the hammers from our wrists. McGreevy attached the lines to us. The seamen hauled on the rope through the breechblock and the top end of the spar lifted in jerks into the air. A long line of curious male passengers looked towards us from all along the portside rails.

The spar was lifted higher. The lower end was swung over the side. The breech rope was eased and the spar lowered. O'Reilly's men hauled in the portside ropes attached to the lower end of the spar, the Bosun's men the ropes beside us attached to the top end. The spar was in place, exactly behind the loose sheathing. I was aware of breathing faster, my apprehension rising. The Captain called an order to the First Officer by the wheelhouse and the *Black Swan* swung away to port off the wind.

As the still-moderate wind caught her as we turned, she began to lay over, more than I expected. Now almost fully on her beam-ends, each swell that surged down on us pushed her further over. Shouts from the men at the port rail as it dipped toward the sea. Then in the trough, we righted slightly.

The Captain waved. McGreevy called out, 'Let's go Fraser!' and the three of us swung over the rail.

Held by the tight line from above, my feet apart on the sloping side of the ship, back to the wind and the advancing swells, I felt more secure. I waved a signal to be lowered. Below to my right beyond the carpenter, I could see the loose sheathing mostly clear of the water, swaying wildly. Down lower we went. If the spar should move, we'd be crushed by it.

We reached the chine line where the ship's copper sheathing began. The carpenter had a foot against the spar. He waved his right arm for'ard. I looked up. The Captain's face above, watching. The spar moved slightly sideways, tilted more at the top. Shouting from above. It straightened up. I could see it pressuring the loose sheet from behind. My mind racing, but clear.

I realised the tear in the sheathing was not as bad as I had thought. The copper sheets fastened on the timbers were in fathom-wide strips, ends tapered fore and aft. A long parallelogram. The loose sheet wasn't torn – had freed from the timbers at the fore-end, then peeled back. In the troughs, the lower edge was lifting clear of the sea. I jumped out and sideways to the right, swinging off the rope above. McGreevy on my left. Shouted to the carpenter: 'More movement on the spar!'

He waved for'ard again. The spar crept some more, rolling more of the sheet in against the timbers. It works!

The carpenter was almost directly below me. We both reached for nails. I grabbed the hammer dangling from my right wrist, pounded the first nail in, flattening the dome rivet. Then another – and another. We stopped, close to the spar. I looked down, the carpenter waved for'ard, the spar moved slowly. Another jump out and to the right. We nailed some more.

Gradually, very slowly, concentrating, almost unaware, we were pulling it in, nailing it fast. I could sense the loose end was not swaying out so wildly. McGreevy close on my left, one hand holding tight to my harness strap called out encouragingly 'keep going! keep going!' The carpenter was still below me, often in water up to his chest as the swells swished up the sloping side of the ship, reaching to my knees, then draining back down.

We almost had the main section of the sheet fastened home. The carpenter had reached the end of the lower edge of the sheet and began work on the upward-sloping piece, the spar now well for'ard. He waived to be hoisted up higher. My supply of nails was getting low, my right arm ached from swinging the heavy hammer. The carpenter and I were now beside each other. I looked over his shoulder for'ard, the end of the sheet clearly in sight. Nearly finished.

I heard anxious shouts from above and we looked up. Men at the rail were pointing outward. I turned and looked back over my shoulder – sensed something rather than saw it. Coming toward us was a huge wave, dark and menacing. Only seconds away. It would be on us before we could be hoisted up. Its crest toppled forward in a rolling roar of white foam. McGreevy shouted 'hold on!'. I tensed my legs, pulled my head down to my shoulders. It hit us.

We were buried. Green water. Cold and hard. The carpenter crashed into me. I was knocked off my feet. My left shoulder smashed into the ship. Swirling spinning around, no control, under water, still holding breath. Lifted by the wave. A tangle of bodies and rope. Can't hold much longer. My chest near bursting … a ringing in my head. I felt the harness rope tighten hard … water sucking down past my body. I fought to turn, face the ship, pull my feet up, get them back on the side. My face clear … at last a breath!

Oh wonderful air!

The wave drained away with a violent surge below us. I dangled there, feet hanging free, gasping air in, pain through my left shoulder. The three of us were piled together, our lines twisted above us. In front of me I saw the spar, still vertically in place. The ship was righting herself again. McGreevy's voice right in my ear, 'are y'still with us Fraser?'

I lifted my head, answered, 'I'm alright!' The carpenter turned toward me, his face white with shock, 'damned close thing!' his voice shaking in fright, 'God saved me again!'

I was surprised to see the hammer still dangling from my wrist, the flapped nail-pouch at my waist. We began to untangle ourselves, rolling over each other until the twisted lines above were free. Faces stared down at us from above. I heard the Captain call out. McGreevy waved.

I saw that the carpenter beside me had blood streaming down the side of his face. 'You're hurt Mr Burton. Looks like a cut on your head. Get them to haul you up, I'll finish this. Give me the nails you've left.' I turned to the Mate, 'The carpenter's injured. Get him hauled up. We can finish this together, there's not much left to fix.'

McGreevy waved again. I was feeling more composed, the immediate pain in my shoulder easing. The carpenter was hauled up, his feet braced against the ship disappearing past me. The Mate and I bounced our way together over to the spar to my right. I turned to him with a grin, 'You watch the waves behind us, I'll nail the last of this. If another one like that appears, get us hauled up fast!' He grinned back.

Pain burned in my left arm and shoulder as I held each nail, but I managed to keep hammering them in. The spar was moved forward and was now just on the end of the sheet where it had first broken free. I made a pattern of nails in close rows, increasing the density as I reached the final end of the taper. Then it was finished. All finished!

I turned back to the Mate at my side. 'That's it. Let's go,' and together we waved to the men at the rail above to haul us up. I hung there limply as we rose up in jerks, walking my feet up the side of the ship as we went. At the rail, hands reached to clutch us and heave us over onto the deck. I winced with the pain in my shoulder. A small cheer rose from the men along the port rail.

Already the ship was turning back into the wind. Men crowded around us, unfastening the ropes and the bosun's chair harness. For the first time, I was aware that I was wet and beginning to shake with cold. The Captain was there with O'Reilly and Nathan Greene. 'Well done Mr Fraser! That was a close run thing. Now get below and get dry. Mr Greene, have a long shot of rum brought for these men.'

I turned to the stocky figure of the Mate. He looked relieved to have the deck under his feet. I put my right hand on his shoulder, 'My thanks for your help Mr McGreevy. Let's hope it stays secure – I'm not anxious to do that again.' He grinned through the beard, 'I'd have drowned too if we'd lost you – wouldn't want to have faced my Captain again if we had!'

George came below to my berth with me. When the wave had hit us, he was sure we'd be lost. The ship had been laid over, the top of the wave sweeping up over the windward rail and across the deck. Some fearful minutes had passed before he had known we were safe. The women and children were still all below, so he had yet to explain to Lucy what had happened. He went off to find her. I changed into dry clothes and lay on my berth until Nathan himself arrived with a mug of rum. Then despite the continual sound of feet on the deck overhead, I slept until evening.

The next day was Sunday, the first Sunday since we left Plymouth. According to the Voyage Rules, we were allowed access to our trunks and lockers on the first level of the aft hold, for changes of clothing. There would also be a short church service held on the aft deck by the Captain late morning, before our mid-day dinner.

Just before we single men began to leave our berths in the morning, the Purser arrived, making directly for my bunk. I looked up, surprised to see him here again. 'Good morning Mr Fraser. I trust you are well rested? With the Captain's compliments, he invites you to join him for dinner in his quarters this evening.' Nathan could not hold back a smile, 'Can I tell him you accept?'

The Captain's quarters. Dining at his table. With the private-cabin passengers. I felt my heart jump. So I would get to meet her at last! The impossible is possible. 'Yes, of course Nathan, please thank the Captain … I accept his invitation with pleasure.' I too could not stop grinning.

While the women and children remained below, we single men were allowed to wash ourselves thoroughly with soap at large tubs of seawater set up on the deck. I made a more complete effort than most, carefully shaving the bare skin of my cheeks and chin with a sharp razor before a mirror hanging from the mast.

Later, we were allowed below deck aft to find our trunks and lockers in the side wings of the upper level of the hold, for changes of clothing. I found my best evening jacket, deep maroon velvet with black cuffs and buttons, then a white shirt with high wing collar and gathered facings down the front. With black breeches and boots, I hoped I would be more fitted for dining at the Captain's table.

I soon found George and Lucy, to tell them of the Captain's invitation. Lucy was to help me trim my hair and sideburns and would check my dress when evening came.

I was impatient for the day to pass. At noon, we all gathered on deck in front of the poop for our first Sunday service of the voyage. The Captain and Officers stood together at the poop rail, overlooking the deck. I could see the private berth passengers were standing further aft behind them but screened from view. The Captain, then Mr Holbourne, each read passages from the bible. The Captain recited a sailors' prayer for the safety of those in peril on the sea. We all sang the Psalm 23, then the Hymn 'Abide With Me'.

I was restless with anticipation and a growing excitement all through the afternoon, not able to settle to any pastime. Repeatedly I ran through my mind how the evening's conversation might flow, recalling the many evenings I had spent with the McGregor Lairds and their guests in Warrington, the topics we discussed and those we didn't.

At last it was time to prepare. I dressed slowly, checking every item, my nervousness rising. George and Lucy met me at the head of the companionway on deck, where Lucy carefully examined me, playfully finding non-existent marks or tears on my clothing just to heighten my anxiety. Then feeling very conspicuous among my staring fellow passengers I made what seemed the longest walk aft down the main deck to the door which led into the private quarters under the poop. I could feel my heart thumping in my chest, more loudly with every step.

The Purser was already there, waiting for me. 'Evening John. If you're ready, follow me. And good luck!' I held my upturned hand toward the door and he opened it as I quickly took several deep breaths.

We stood briefly in a small outer room. The heavy door to the main deck closed behind us. To my right, an open door led into the Captain's own quarters; to my left as I turned, behind a single glass-panelled door I could see into another room with a large chart table, lighted by windows in the ship's side. Ahead of us were two double glass-panelled doors with the movement of people in the room aft visible through them. Nathan pushed opened the doors and we entered a large open saloon.

A long table crossed the centre of the room. We went to the left of it toward the people grouped further behind. A row of windows along the rear wall looked out over the sea trailing behind us. The Captain, resplendent in a white jacket with heavy gold braid on the shoulders and down the front lapels came forward toward me. Nathan stood aside. I was aware they were all looking at me.

'Ah, Mr Fraser, good evening. I trust you are well recovered from yesterday's ordeal?'

'Captain King, good evening Sir. Yes, thank you, a dip in the ocean was probably good for us at this stage of the voyage….'

'Allow me to introduce you to some of my passengers. Our ships' Doctor and Surgeon Dr Carrington and Mrs Carrington (a short dumpy middle-aged couple. I shook his outstretched hand and nodded to his wife), and Lieutenant Oliver Haile of the King's 4th Guards Regiment.' Haile, a crimson-jacketed man about my own age, standing very straight with heels together, slightly dipped his head toward me, saying nothing. I did the same. No other passengers. A momentary silence.

Suddenly I was aware of her. I could sense she was there before she appeared from behind to my right, coming through a door at the side of the saloon, the tall grey-haired man at her side. I stepped back, turned, feeling my heart racing. I heard the Captain again, 'And our other two passengers Mr MacKay and his daughter Elizabeth…' That smile again, her eyes looking directly into mine. I felt weak, almost faint, hands trembling at my sides, feet fixed to the floor, only just aware of the Captain speaking again… 'Mr John Cameron Fraser'

I tore my eyes away from her, looking at the others. 'A pleasure to meet you all, indeed.' A slight tremor betrayed the nervousness in my voice. I could feel her presence there, close beside me. As if the space between us, the air itself, had turned solid. My acuity heightened, every nerve-end tense.

'We are in some debt to Mr Fraser. But for his suggestion and then his valiant efforts yesterday, we would have been forced to interrupt our voyage for a port and repairs. Would have lost two weeks, perhaps longer.'

I tried to contain some self-consciousness, looked at Mr MacKay who was watching me. He was tall, nearly as tall as me. A high wide forehead fringed with short grey hair, wide-spaced dark eyes, prominent high cheek-bones, a grey moustache angling vigorously downwards over the sides of his mouth, very bushy at the ends, joining sideburns either side of a shaven chin. The appearance of a strong physique, a strong character, no smile, no expression.

The Captain broke the brief silence, 'Come ladies and gentlemen, Mr Fraser, let us be seated.' He moved toward the table behind us, taking his place at the head. 'Dr and Mrs Carrington,' he indicated to chairs immediately on his right, 'then Mr Fraser, seat yourself there,' also on the right. 'Lieutenant,' a wave to his left, 'Mr MacKay, Miss MacKay.' With a conscious effort of will, I looked away from her.

The ladies took their seats, the Captain next, then we men. She was directly opposite me. Close enough to reach across and touch. Our eyes met again, we both smiled. She was even more beautiful than I remembered, her eyes the intense blue of harebells, her blonde hair without a bonnet a jumble of rolling curls, flawless smooth skin. The smile lightened her whole face, crinkly lines in the corners of her eyes, a full top lip slightly raised in the centre, a wide mouth with white even teeth.

The silence was broken as the Doctor spoke with the Captain, Lieutenant Haile opposite making some comment I could not hear. A steward was waiting at the table, bringing some sweetmeats to us on a silver tray. The Captain spoke again in a louder voice, 'Well Mr Fraser, as guest at our table this evening, I'm sure we would all like to hear more about you…' The Carringtons turned toward me. I could feel all eyes were upon me. Another deep breath. 'You are a marine engineer are you not, from the north of England?'

'Yes Sir. I have been fortunate to have worked in the ship building industry in the English northwest for some years. But I am not English….'

Lieutenant Haile: 'You are from Ireland then?…I believe I detect some Irish tones to your voice?'

I looked to him. 'Well not exactly, Lieutenant, but yes, I have spent many years in Ireland. In fact I am Scottish. I was born on the north coast. My mother died when I was but a young child … my father took me to Ireland. His sister, my aunt, has a large family on an estate in the north. My aunt and uncle took me in as one of their own. I was educated there, then trained as an engineer with a business in Belfast. It was owned by friends of the family. Later I was invited to join a prominent shipbuilding company near Liverpool.'

Mr MacKay, a deep voice, face expressionless: 'From the highlands … then to Ireland … so are you Catholic, Fraser?' An intrusive question. I could feel a hard edge to his tone.

'No Sir, we Frasers are Protestant, of Presbyterian faith. My family came originally from Inverness … they were millers. They fought on the side of Prince Charles at Culloden, not because they were Catholic, but for Scottish freedom. After the war they fled north to escape the persecutions of the English. They set up mills again in Halladale, at Millburn. Eventually, my father was not interested to continue as a miller … he moved to Melvich near Port Skerra in North Sutherland and established a smithy.

'His sister, my aunt, married a Scot from Tullamore in Ireland. He took up the family estate in the north on the premature death of his elder brother.' I smiled, but Mr MacKay remained stone-faced. 'And you Sir, you are from Edinburgh?'

'Just south of Edinburgh. And our family supported the English at Culloden, Fraser, loyal to our King and the British Crown. Not to the Catholic French foreigners who sheltered your Pretender, then fought in Ireland supporting their rebels against us not very long ago.' There was force and antagonism in his voice again. No, I must avoid this… change the subject. I turned toward the head of the table.

'Captain King, I observe since leaving Plymouth we have sailed quite westward, south and west. Can you explain our course for me Sir?' He looked relieved to do so.

'You are familiar with Mercator's projection?' and not waiting for an answer, 'on that flat map of the world, the shortest distance between two points is a straight line. So it was believed the quickest route from England to India and the Pacific was directly south to Capetown, a stop to reprovision, then onward to the east or the north. At least that is the route that was taken, until a decade ago.

'But the world is not flat. On a globe, tracing a line more westward through the Atlantic in fact is a shorter route. To prove the point, pioneering voyages were undertaken in 1852. Then it was found, sailing to the southwest, that the winds there are more favourable, more northerly and avoiding the doldrums off the African coast. Deeper south in the Atlantic, the winds turn due west, speeding a voyage to the east. It seems the winds around the Atlantic are a vast anti-clockwise rotation. The new route proved much faster, less than 100 days to New South Wales.

'Deep to the south in the Atlantic, the westerly winds become stronger, called the 'roaring forties'. Catching these winds means we are well south of Capetown, so it's not just shorter, it's also a much quicker voyage not stopping to reprovision. Not so liked by passengers Mr Fraser, as you will experience, but much more profitable for shipowners.'

I could feel the atmosphere was more relaxed, the tension from MacKay's comments now drained away.

'And pray what takes you to the Antipodes, Fraser?' Lieutenant Haile asked, then a touch sarcastically, 'they don't build ships there to my knowledge.'

'I accompany my cousin and his newly-wed wife, who are here with us on the *Black Swan*. My cousin George Bruce is responsible for much of the cargo aboard this ship. A company in New Zealand, who was his client of long-standing, has sought his knowledge of iron and steel. He

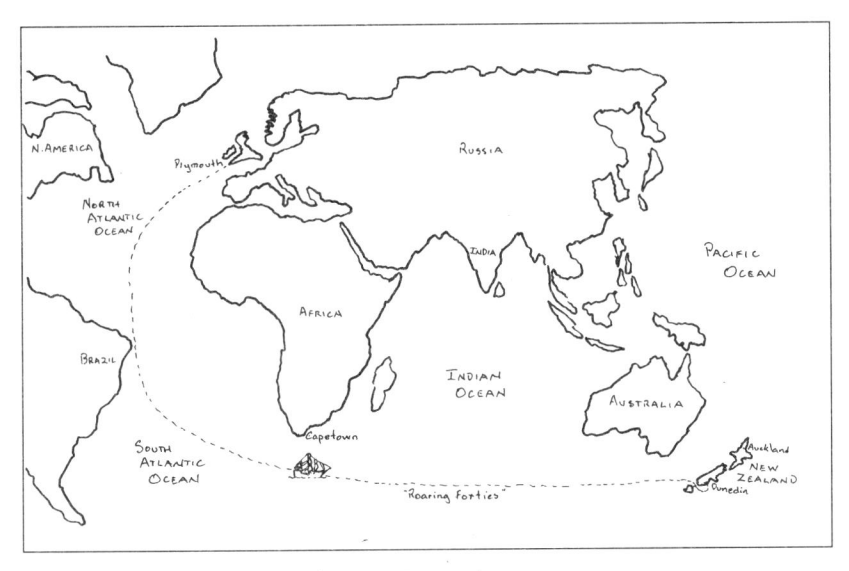

The voyage of the Black Swan, *February – June 1861*

and his wife decided to begin a new life there and they invited me to travel with them.

'My cousin has a brother somewhere in New Zealand; two other brothers who are now successful landowners emigrated to the Argentine some years ago.' I could feel her eyes upon me.

'To your other question Lieutenant, I have in the hold, a small steam engine. In New Zealand if there is a suitable opportunity, I propose to purchase or build a vessel in which to install it. Then seek contracts to transport goods around the coasts or in the rivers. If the prospects are limited, then I will sail on westward to join my cousins in the Argentine.

'And you Sir, if I may ask, what takes you to New Zealand?

The steward had arrived with a large piece of roast kept hot in the galley since the midday dinner. The fresh meat from Plymouth was now exhausted – now the calves and goats filling the longboats were the first to meet the butcher's knife. I hoped the roast before us was calf. It was.

The Lieutenant replied as the steward carved and served. 'No wish to bore my fellow passengers who know the story already, Fraser. Seems there's some restlessness amongst the aborigines in New Zealand. An aggressive lot of natives, as natives go. The Governor's family and mine are somewhat related. So I'm seconded to the colonial army. Train and arm the troops. A demonstration of trained soldiers with modern munitions will soon quieten them down, no doubt.'

Miss MacKay had still not spoken. Whenever I stole a glance toward her, she was looking at me, that same faint smile lightly apparent. How could I shift the conversation toward her. I breathed deeply once and tried again….

'Mr MacKay Sir, you also have friends in the Antipodes?'

'My father, Mr Fraser, has been appointed to the colonial Government.' She had spoken! My heart leapt at the first sound of her voice. She had spoken directly to me! A lovely soft melodious voice. I looked straight into her eyes. 'Papa is to be the Gold Commissioner for the southern island,' she said to me with obvious pride. Did I imagine, or was her speaking for him, a reason to speak to me? At least, a reason for me to address her in return….

'Miss MacKay, please pardon my lack of knowledge,' I tried not to stumble with the excitement of speaking directly with her, 'such an important position, what duties does it carry?'

But MacKay himself answered in that same unreadable voice. 'Gold was discovered in the north of New Zealand some years ago now. That gold is in veins embedded in rock, it must be crushed with heavy machinery, not with labour. A Gold Commissioner, a geologist, was appointed to set up and administer mining rights.

'I too have a knowledge of geology. There have been some small gold discoveries in the southern island. They are finer powders loose in sands, easily won by men hand-washing the gravels that carry them. In Australia, there has been anarchy and violence in similar goldfields. A wild rabble of criminals, violent revolutionaries and exiles. New Zealand has not been a penal Colony; its pioneering people are landowners, pastoral companies, gentry from England and Scotland. There is order, peace, respect for the law. An English society is being established.

'If more gold should be discovered, the Governor is rightly determined to administer it properly. We shall not tolerate the violence and disorder of that wild rabble in Australia. The Gold Commissioner is the authority to ensure order, uphold the law.'

So there lay the explanation for his rather forbidding demeanour. An authoritarian. How does such a severe man have such a sweet daughter?

Whilst MacKay was speaking, I had looked beyond. Between the doors into the private cabins, the saloon walls were lined with a library of books securely behind glass frames. Lanterns with high glass stacks were hung all around. The steward offered and poured us wine, the deep red glowing with light captured from the lanterns.

The Doctor who had been occupied quaffing several glasses of wine, now spoke for the first time, leaning forward to see me: 'Pray tell me Fraser, you have knowledge of steam power, what's the future hold for steam and sail?'

'Perhaps I have some bias Dr Carrington. I was privileged to work beside some of the prominent marine engineers of this age, pioneers of iron ship design and steam propulsion. I have to say, from that knowledge, steam propulsion driving screws will eventually take the day.'

Mr MacKay interposed, contestably, 'Not for ship-owners Fraser. There are far more sailing vessels still being built than there are steamers in total upon the seas. Sail is far more profitable – the wind costs nothing – the wind does not have to be carried in the holds like coal. Paying cargo is all that is carried!'

A brief silence. I could feel tension again. Why does this man keep pushing at me…?

Fortunately, the Captain replied: 'The navies have already taken a lead. Your English navy is building many iron steamers, screw and paddle-driven. A steamer is fast, always certain to travel in any desired direction, even directly against the wind. The wooden sailing navy is finished. Even the fighting ships being built by our Union are all steam-driven monitors.'

'Mr MacKay is presently correct,' I offered uncontentiously, 'the economics today certainly favour sail. But I had the honour of working with Mr Alfred Holt, the foremost inventor and designer of steam engines for ships in Britain, perhaps the world. Mr Holt has already invented the steam engine for the new age, a two-stage machine so efficient that it will drive sail into history. I have seen Mr Holt's own construction of such an engine in a moving but non-working form. All that it waits for now, is sufficient improvement in the quality of the iron to build it, to sustain its pressures. The iron makers have been gaining quality at a pound of pressure, each and every year for the past fifteen. I believe that further improvement Mr Holt requires will soon come.'

The discussion was taken up amongst the men at the top of the table.

For a moment, I was not participating. I turned immediately to Miss MacKay, still looking at me expectantly, 'I do apologise Miss MacKay, this must be a very tedious conversation for you. Are you enjoying the voyage so far … how have you occupied your time aboard?' The others at the table seemed not to notice us.

'Oh no, Mr Fraser, please, no apology from you is necessary, it has been a most interesting matter to hear you discuss and one of great importance for the future.

'I am now more accustomed to the voyage thank you. The first days were difficult, the motion of the ship made us both unwell. Then the storm … it was quite frightening. You were very brave to risk yourself with repairing the ship.

'Now my father and I seem both more settled. We occupy ourselves with games of draughts, or chess. I have begun some small tapestries and I spend much time reading. But we are only one week on this long voyage … I fear I shall soon miss my music and the company of people my own age.'

Still the others appeared to be holding their own conversation. Our meal was almost finished. 'And you Mr Fraser, when you are not repairing our ship (she smiled, eyes shining in the lantern-light), how do you pass the time?'

'Mostly, Miss MacKay, I have been reading. Or in conversation with my cousin and his amusing new wife – Lucy has such a bright and happy disposition…' Surely she must see the captivation I felt I could not hide from my face. If only we can continue talking together like this.

'Perhaps I shall meet her….' she commented.

The Captain raised his voice. 'Are we all finished ladies, gentlemen? Shall we adjourn to more comfortable seating aft?'

We all rose. I helped Mrs Carrington from her chair beside me. As the Captain led us away, our two groups from either side of the table merged together. Miss MacKay, following her father, now stood close beside me. I felt the same overwhelming almost uncontrollable urge to take her by the arm, to touch her, as I had with Jessica Franklin all those years ago near my final days at school. With an acute sensitivity I felt our arms brush lightly together as we walked, an exhilarating sensation that almost made me stumble.

The Doctor's wife and Miss MacKay took seats near each other. We five men remained standing in a half circle. Trying to be inconspicuous,

I moved as closely as I could to the side of Miss MacKay's chair. The steward asked us each in turn if we wished for a glass of port wine or brandy. I chose a brandy, feeling the need for something strong to balance my excitement.

I tried again to initiate some distracting general discussion. 'Captain King, Sir, your opinion if I may.' They all looked to me, even Mr Mackay. 'There is much comment in our newspapers, of tension amongst the States within your Union. What do you make of that Sir, and how do you believe it will eventuate?'

'That is a very difficult matter of which you speak Mr Fraser. I fear to think upon its consequences. Myself, I see it as a matter of the rights of the States within the Union … the right to determine policies within a State or whether a policy agreed by the President and the Congress of the Union can be imposed on a State against its will. Then if such a State shall not agree, does it have a right to secede from the Union, just as it had a right to elect to join?

'Or will the Union impose a policy on the State by force of arms? Prevent secession by force of arms? Such difficult issues. The southern States and northern States seem set upon different paths. The north is more populated, becoming more industrialised and the south more agricultural with great estates and land-ownership, a large population of black slaves, a different culture from the north. And around the edges, north, west and south, the French stirring trouble.'

'The consequences are almost unthinkable. Take this ship. Built in northern shipyards, owned by southerners … myself, officers, crew, all from many different States. What if we should be forced to choose sides? How does one divide the Union army, the navy?

'What is your opinion Mr MacKay, Lieutenant, if the southern States secede from the Union and form a Confederacy, what position would you expect England to take?'

MacKay answered first, predictably: 'I would expect the King and Parliament to support the south. The south I understand, is a land-owning aristocracy much like ourselves; we share much shipping and commerce, it is the source of cotton for our industries, tobacco, sugar. Our history with the north's rebellious colonies was bad and bloody. The French sided with the north, even today they give succour to the Irish émigrés, fellow revolutionaries. People who have little respect for our culture, our institutions, our empire.'

The discussion continued amongst the four men. I carefully withdrew slightly, turned to Miss MacKay seated beside me. Before I could speak first she looked up to me, her head tilted coquettishly to one side. 'And where on this ship is your cabin Mr Fraser?' she asked.

'We single men are awarded the most difficult berths on the entire vessel, Miss MacKay. The motion of the ship is most pronounced toward the bows, and the most stable is here aft where we are now, so with chivalry, single men occupy the most forward berths up near the fo'c'sle.

'You mentioned that you spend much time reading Miss MacKay, what is it that presently interests you?'

'I have been reading the illustrated journals of Mr Banks, the botanist who travelled with Captain Cook on his voyages of discovery to New Zealand. I have been learning of the natural life we will find there, to prepare myself. Did you know that New Zealand has no native animals, only birds and insects and some birds are so tame that they have no wings, and that all the trees keep their leaves throughout the seasons?'

I felt light-headed, the two of us talking personally together like this, every sense heightened. 'I too have been reading in preparation … to understand. But no, I've not read Mr Banks, only the journals of Captain Cook himself. It was a long time ago now of which he writes, a whole century. I hope that today the natives are more peaceful, have given up their cannibalism and have been converted to Christianity by the missionaries.

'I've also read some of the Wakefield papers, the founding of settlements in the south where our voyage arrives. The towns of Christ Church and Dunedin. It sounds quite civilised. Have you read any of Mr Dickens, Miss MacKay, his books were very popular where I lived in England?'

Was I really thinking of my questions, my replies, hearing her respond? Or was I so overcome by her beauty, her presence, our closeness, our actually being here together, that my conversation was not making any sense?

'Oh yes, Mr Fraser, I have read *Oliver Twist*, and recently *David Copperfield*. What horrible pictures Mr Dickens draws, so horrible it's difficult to believe that people live in such circumstances. I found it compelling reading, but not enjoyable.'

'Then I would not recommend Mr Charles Kingsley's new novel to you, Miss Mackay. His book *The Water Babies* is a story to rend the heart.'

'Oh why do they write stories so injurious to the spirit, Mr Fraser. I do prefer literature that is more enlightened, uplifting, like the novels of Jane Austen, I would not suppose that you have read Miss Bronte's *Wuthering Heights*?'

'I regret no, I have not yet done so. But if you recommend it, I shall. I believe Mr Dickens and Mr Kingsley are writing to awaken us to the hardship and injustice in our societies. I myself have seen people in the industrial north, near Manchester, living in conditions much as Mr Dickens describes. Even worse perhaps. Such misery has weighed upon me Miss MacKay – perhaps otherwise I may not have been aboard this ship today.

'I expect that we will find life in the colonies to be very different Mr Fraser, but I hope not too different. Papa tells me that the town where we are to live, Dunedin, is being called 'the Edinburgh of the south'.

'For you Miss MacKay, I hope that you will find it so. For myself, I hope the Colony is a new society somewhat like America, without the rigid social divisions of England, but where men can be respected for their enterprise, their skill and hard work. Not for the accidental fortune of their birth or self-assumptions of superiority.'

She leaned forward, smiling, and lowered her voice, rather conspiratorially, 'Why Mr Fraser! I do declare! Such opinions are what my father might say are revolutionary!'

I noticed the Doctor's wife seated nearby straining to hear us. A change of subject was needed. 'Mrs Carrington, please tell me, you and the Doctor are from America? And for where are you bound?'

She was obviously pleased to be included in our conversation. 'Yes Mr Fraser, the Doctor and I are from Charleston in the State of Carolina. The *Black Swan* was sailing south from New York to catch favourable winds for crossing the Atlantic. Dr Carrington and I, we thought to travel with her to England and thence to the Antipodes. From New Zealand, the Captain intends to call at a port in Peru, then around Cape Horn to return us again to America. A truly wonderful experience.

'I believe you and Miss MacKay were speaking of books Mr Fraser. Have you read our American author, Mr Mark Twain?'

'I regret not, Mrs Carrington. But I hear they are very popular stories of frontier life in America?'

'That is so. The Captain has two of Mr Twain's books here in this extensive library of his. I'm sure Miss MacKay can get them for you. Would you like to read them?'

'Thank you Mrs Carrington, yes, very much so if that were possible for Miss MacKay....'

The Captain looked across to us and raised his voice, 'Well now gentlemen, we must allow the ladies to retire if they wish. Come Mr Fraser, on your way out, I will show you in the chart room, our present position and our course....' He began to lead toward the saloon doors, turned, waiting for me.

So my evening was ending. Will we talk together like this again? Would she want to? How can I? The thoughts tumbled in my mind...then I reasserted some control of myself. 'A pleasure to have the opportunity of meeting you, gentlemen (dipping my head toward MacKay, the Lieutenant), and ladies, your company' (a last lingering look into those blue eyes holding mine and then with a conscious act of will, I turned away).

I followed the Captain out through the double doors, thinking I could sense her eyes still on my back, that same awareness of a tangible something between us. Or was I just imagining it, wishing that it were so?

I struggled to concentrate as the Captain showed me the chart laid out on the table in the room opposite his quarters, my thoughts elsewhere. Then we were at the door to the main deck. 'Thank you Captain. So generous of you to invite me Sir ... a most enjoyable evening, and with such company.'

'A scant reward for risking yourself to help the *Black Swan*, Fraser. My pleasure indeed ... good evening to you'.

I stepped out into the cold air, the deck visible in the light of a half moon overhead, the night sounds of the sea swishing past. I felt light-headed, exhilarated, thoughts and visions of my evening still whirling. Almost unaware, I made my way forward and by the companionway to the single berths, stopped, leaned against the bulwark rail and stared out to the darkened sea. I stayed there for some time, trying to arrange all the competing pictures of her in my mind. The thoughts and impressions of the evening ... what to make of her father's coldness toward me, Haile's aloofness, motherly Mrs Carrington, my role in the conversation. Was I only imagining there was a rapport between us, a pleasant tension, just because I wished there to be so? Had I been too forthright ... not exercised good manners? What did she think and how could I ever get to see her again?

Eventually, still unable to answer myself or slow the torrent of thoughts, I made my way below. In the darkness, staring upwards at black nothingness, I concentrated on visions of her opposite me at the table, seated beside me looking upward, eyes radiant, then knowing she was there down the other end of this same ship, here on this same ocean, bound for the same destination, until I drifted asleep.

SIX

I was out on deck early the next day awaiting George and Lucy, eager to relate to them my experiences of the night before and wanting to ensure I was visible there all day should Miss MacKay emerge on the poop deck.

We had now been sailing to the south-west for a week and except for the half day lost with the sheathing repair, the winds on the aft quarter had been driving us fast, day and night, bringing us into a more temperate climate as we travelled closer to the equator.

Grey skies had given way to blue, dotted with even-sized fluffy puffs of white cloud as if carefully placed to be equidistant from each other. Whereas the sky and grey seas had earlier merged into one without a discernible horizon, now we could look out to a clear distant line sharply dividing the deep blue of the ocean from the lighter blue of the sky.

The ship was dressed with all the sail she could carry: the foresails, mains and topsails on the fore and main masts, all bellied out full; the jibs and staysails between the masts raked and taught, topgallants billowing from the mizzen mast, and the great spanker swung wide to catch the wind. The *Black Swan* danced over the well-spaced swells to a steady even rhythm. Leaning against the starboard bulwark rail, looking both up and outward, I was consciously absorbing the pleasure of every moment.

With longer daylight and warmer, fine weather, most of the passengers were enjoying being on deck. It had become quite crowded, more difficult to find some space to oneself or to think without the intrusion of others' conversation. It was mid morning before, waiting with growing impatience, I eventually saw George and Lucy appear from below deck.

They were almost as anxious and keen to hear my account of the evening, as I was to give it. Recounting it was like reliving it; I tried to remember every part of the conversation, every detail. Lucy wanted a description of the clothes being worn at the Captain's table, but I was surprised to discover that I had no clear picture at all. I had been so concentrated upon the discussion, so affected by my nearness to Miss MacKay and so captivated by her, that I had no memory of what she was wearing, nor even the colours. Only the Captain's jacket and the Lieutenant's uniform dress were still in my mind.

I described to George the seeming cold remoteness of Mr MacKay – his challenging, almost combative comments and questions – and the aloofness of Lieutenant Haile. How different they were from the more relaxed and friendly Carringtons, even the Captain himself. Lucy, listening, suggested magnanimously that if Mr MacKay had only recently lost his wife and now had left his family home for the uncertainty of living in a small remote Colony, it could explain his sharpness of manner. English military officers, she also explained, were mostly reserved and aloof, coming as they did from the aristocracy and often with purchased commissions.

During our dinner in the early afternoon, the Purser joined us. 'I trust your evening with the Captain was enjoyable Mr Fraser,' he commented, adding with a smile 'and successful too?'

'Thank you, and yes to both. I did enjoy it very much, I'm very grateful to the Captain for the chance to meet the private-berth passengers … I only wish that all of the passengers on this ship could mix together more freely.…'

'Some of them would not always welcome that,' he replied with some conviction, 'but there might be further opportunities, no doubt.…'

Throughout the day, I kept aft, watching the poop deck frequently, hoping and expecting at any moment for the private-cabin passengers to appear. But nobody did. The poulterer with his buckets of grain, feeding all the caged birds was the only person to interrupt the otherwise emptiness of their deck.

In the evening, we three stood together at the rail as usual, watching the redness of the sun deepening as it sank slowly toward the horizon, growing in size before it seemingly plunged into the sea and disappeared. The almost three-quarter moon was already quite high in the sky, brightening as the night darkened behind it. The breeze crossing the deck now had definite warmth.

We parted company, Lucy and George returning to their berth. I was left there alone feeling subdued, my expectation of seeing Miss MacKay again, unrealised, knowing that she was just back there behind those doors. So close, but so far away. Frustratingly. At least, when eventually I too went to my berth, I drifted to sleep thinking about her.

The next day was again as perfect for sailing as the one before. George, Lucy and I met up mid morning, making our way aft through the milling passengers to a place beside the rail with the poop deck near us. We had not been there long when I heard the cackling of the geese in their cages out of sight on the deck above. Their noise was a certain signal that they had company.

All the private-berth passengers appeared on the deck. Miss MacKay holding a small parasol as shade against the sun was holding her father's arm. As they moved forward, leaving the other three behind, I could see she was not looking out to the ocean like her father, but was scanning the main deck crowded with passengers.

I waved, feeling my excitement surging. I was sure she had seen me. She said something to her father, then released his arm and came forward alone to the railing of the poop overlooking the main deck. As she did so, I moved quickly until I was directly beneath. I called up to her, 'Miss MacKay, good morning!'

'And good morning to you Mr Fraser. Such a beautiful day to be outside. I have the book by Mark Twain for you from the Captain's library.' Her voice was like a song I had been waiting to hear again. Her curls fell forward around her face as she leaned over the railing. 'I shall ask Papa … perhaps he will allow me onto your deck to bring it to you. And to meet your cousins.'

She turned and walked back to him. They stood facing each other. I waited, hope and anxiety mixing as they talked together for some time. Then she touched him lightly on the arm and was off quickly toward the companionway. I grabbed Lucy and George by the arms. 'Come with me!' I urged, and we walked to the door under the poop. It opened, and there she was, coming toward us.

'Miss MacKay, what a pleasure! Allow me to introduce my cousin George Bruce … and his wife Lucy.' She smiled happily to them both. For the first time, I noticed that she was about just over five feet tall, the top of her head in line with George's chest – and mine too. 'Lucy, please meet Miss MacKay, my companion at the Captain's table….'

'Oh Mrs Bruce, such formality. I would be pleased if you would call me Miss Elizabeth – and you Mr Fraser, if my father is not hearing us, are welcome to do the same.'

'Thank you Miss Elizabeth, 'I hastened to say, relishing the opportunity to use her name. From behind her back she produced a book, holding it out to me, those eyes looking directly into mine, shining.

'Here is the book by Mr Twain, the Captain has loaned to you. There is another when you have read this.' I took it from her, acutely aware that our hands had touched. I stood in a struck silence; certain she had deliberately held the book in such a way that I could not have taken it from her without our touching. Fortunately, Lucy quickly broke in, 'Come Miss Elizabeth, I will walk you around our deck to see all the animals,' and as they moved away together, she glanced briefly to me with a smile.

George and I stayed by the rail watching them go, Lucy animatedly chattering to her. Thank God for Lucy!

They were gone for some time, slowly walking for'ard along the port side, then back down the starboard side toward us. They were talking animatedly whenever I caught sight of them. I glanced up to the poop deck several times, once seeing MacKay come to the rail and look out over the deck, a hand cupped over his eyes to shield the sun, obviously checking to see his daughter. Eventually they returned to us. I was waiting impatiently.

'With Mrs Bruce as my guide, I've now seen around your part of the ship Mr Fraser, and even the stairway down to both your quarters' she said directly to me. 'But I must confess it isn't very nice to see all the poor animals that must yet sustain us for the rest of our voyage.'

I noticed from my peripheral vision that George and Lucy had moved away slightly. I turned toward the ocean. 'Have you noticed how the colour of the sea has changed Miss Elizabeth, now so blue?' she too turned so that we stood side by side looking outwards.

'Yes, it is so beautiful, and Mr Holbourne tells me it will change again as we reach the tropics. I do enjoy just watching the patterns of light on the sea, the colours are all so very bright.'

We talked together, Lucy standing close to her but not so close as to need being included in our conversation, George silent on my left. After exhausting an explanation of the sails and the purpose of all the various sheets, shrouds and stays that made up the rigging I was near to struggling for another topic to hold her attention when she herself provided it.

'Mr Fraser, you mentioned at dinner the other evening that you lost your mother when you were very young … it must have been very hard for you.'

'It's difficult now to try and remember just what I felt at the time, Miss Elizabeth. I was very young, and so much has happened since. Only a few memories, the stronger ones, still remain. When I do think of it, it is more the effect that it had on the course of my life afterward, that I reflect upon.'

I was leaning with one arm on the rail, partly turned toward her. To my surprise, she lightly touched my arm, the shock of her touch almost making me pull it away. 'Losing a mother at any age is a terrible thing, as I have so recently experienced myself … how sad that you remember so little of her. It is only two years since my own dear Mama passed away. In some ways perhaps, the longer they are with you then the harder it becomes. It is so, for me'

The smile lines had gone from her eyes and mouth. 'And my poor Papa, Mr Fraser, I fear he too still has much difficulty … I think it is the reason why he decided we should go to New Zealand … to have a new life away from everything that gives us such painful memories.'

She looked at me quite intently, 'I ask you Mr Fraser, as I know that you would … please be understanding of him if he should seem restrictive, over-protective of me, and very guarded in his manner toward you, or other young men. I have no brothers or sisters … I am all that poor Papa has left now. He means you no ill will, I'm sure. My dear Mama and I did look so alike, I'm sure that I just keep reminding him every day of her….'

I fought an urge to put a comforting arm around her shoulders. I put my hand over hers instead. 'Of course Miss Elizabeth. I can understand … it can't be easy for you.' A silence, then I spoke again.

'My own mother died when I was very young. My father left me in Ireland. He promised to come back for me, but he never did. My brother, Robert, he must be 35 now; I've never seen him again.

'Life seems filled with partings from those we love, who have been so much to us. I hope you will find that new doors can open for you, that new comfort comes to replace that which you have lost. And your father, much as he may be burdened by his loss, I hope that he will also see the wisdom of not loading that upon you.'

I took my hand away, she hers. Lucy stepped between us, her bright smiling face lifting us immediately. She took Elizabeth by the arm. 'Whatever it is that John says to you Miss Elizabeth, I advise you to take as lightly as possible … he can be too serious for his own good, sometimes! Now, did you see all the fine dresses the ladies produced last Sunday …' and they walked away again together, leaving George and I alone.

In following days Miss Elizabeth would appear on our deck on most afternoons. Usually accompanied by Mr Holbourne or another officer, occasionally even Captain King himself, she would appear through the poop-deck doors, often with her father watching from the poop railing above. Together they would walk around the main deck until she found Lucy, then the officer would disengage and leave her in Lucy's company. Ostensibly Miss Elizabeth was seeking out Lucy for company but I felt (or hoped or imagined) that she was also using the opportunity to spend time with me.

The *Black Swan* was now approaching the equator in mid-Atlantic. The blue sea of the Temperate Zone that had long replaced the green-grey of the north changed to deeper tones, then to the deep indigo of the tropics. We sailed slowly in light winds with a full wardrobe of sail aloft, the heavier sails like the lower main and the spanker barely filling or hanging listlessly as the breeze waned toward evening.

Often we were surrounded by towering Grecian-like columns of fluffy cloud suspended evenly-spaced in otherwise blue skies. Sometimes as the day progressed, many of these columns would reach higher, billowing out at their apex and darkening below until dazzling flashes of lightning would dance between them. The crack and roll of thunder would shake the air, followed by heavy cascades of warm rain.

In the tropical heat, the decks needed to be continually wet to prevent their caulking from drying out. In the mornings, the male passengers would draw buckets of warm seawater over the gunwhales with which to wash, sluicing ourselves down in the hot sun. In the afternoons, the seamen would take over the buckets, methodically working from stem to stern to wet the decks.

Miss Elizabeth enjoyed joining many of us at the gunwhale railing on the foredeck to watch for flying fish. As the ship dipped into each swell, white foam curling away from off the bow-stem, the concussion would frighten the flying fish to burst out of the face of the wave. With their vivid wing-like pectoral fins flapping frantically and their long thin tails held tautly behind, they could glide along the trough of the wave for more than 100 yards before suddenly vanishing back into the sea.

Miss Elizabeth would stand there close beside me, even touching against me if the ship dipped more sharply or other passengers pressed around us. Should this happen I would instantly be aware and the contact with her would send a surge through me that would send my heart leaping.

In the tropical heat, most of the passengers were on the deck during the day, lying around under shade from the sails or, when the galley fires were not in use, making tea from our daily ration of fresh water. Some passengers would sit for hours teaching reading and arithmetic to groups of children.

Others, under the guidance of sailors, would trail fishing lines from light spars out over the sides to catch Dorado, a powerful blunt-nosed dolphin-like fish that chased flying fish. The sailors would collect flying fish which would frequently land on the deck during the night and use these as bait on the lines. Excited shouting would signal that a Dorado had taken a bait and several men would seize the line whilst the huge fish thrashed wildly about on the surface. Finally the exhausted creature would lie gasping on its side, brilliant silver and blue uppermost, then be hauled up and heaved over the gunwhale onto the deck. The Dorado were excellent eating and provided a welcome change in our meat or poultry diet.

Even the private-berth passengers would sit out on the poop deck in sling-back chairs beneath an awning of sailcloth, reading, sleeping or watching all the activity on the main deck below. I would also see Lieutenant Haile, still dressed in a full uniform despite the heat, walking steadily round and round the poop deck, first clockwise then reverse, keeping exercised. Often MacKay would be seated there too, but would never acknowledge anyone except the Captain or the Doctor and his wife.

We were told by the officers that our crossing of the equator would be marked by a ceremony-of-passage and a special dinner prepared by the cook for the whole ship's company. This event soon became the main topic of conversation as the anticipation rose daily.

In the tropics there was virtually no twilight; one moment it was light, then the sun would deeply redden and plunge below the horizon and seemingly it would immediately be night. The evening air was so warm that many passengers would stay on deck until quite late before going to their berths below. So we were not surprised to learn that on the day of the ceremony-of-passage, our special dinner would be in the evening instead of the usual mid-day meal. All the passengers including the private-berth passengers would dine before dark at the long tables set up on the main deck. The bright moon, now approaching its apogee, together with lanterns hanging from the rigging would provide light for dancing on the poop deck.

Excitement rose as the day neared. We all took a new interest in the Captain's or Mr Holbourne's daily sightings with the sextant as they plotted our position which, in the prevailing calm, changed so little until eventually, Captain King declared that next day, our thirtieth since leaving England, the equator would be crossed.

The cook and his assistants laboured throughout the afternoon heat, shrouded in swirling smoke from the galley as they turned pork and mutton on spits and heated huge pots of soup. That morning, all passengers were given access to the cabin trunks stored in the aft hold to find their best clothes or make a change.

In the late afternoon when the intensity of the sun had waned and a light breeze promised some refreshing coolness for the evening we all crowded the main deck, the ship's crew gathered on the foredeck and in front of the doors to the private quarters under the poop, chairs were placed for the Captain, Officers and the private-berth passengers.

I ensured that Lucy, George and I were close by when Miss Elizabeth emerged with her father and the others, led by Lieutenant Haile in his full dress uniform of scarlet and black, complete with dress sword. When we were all assembled, Captain King stepped up to the poop deck rail and addressed us, reminding us firstly that the easiest and more pleasant part of our long voyage would soon be over.

Crossing the equator was an event for us to be proud of achieving but it meant that we were leaving the Northern Hemisphere for the Southern where, at this time of year, winter was approaching. The longest and stormiest part of our voyage now lay closely ahead, a time of danger and discomfort which would be difficult for all to endure. So, he urged us, we should enjoy this brief moment of tropical respite.

As the Captain spoke, gasps, squeals and laughter greeted an apparition that appeared from outside the aft-deck rail, a sailhand daubed with black soot, a huge wig of frayed rope atop his head and grasping a large iron three-pronged trident in one hand. Captain King interrupted his speech to welcome aboard 'King Neptune, Guardian of The Depths, from his home beneath the equator'.

When the Captain returned down to the maindeck, 'King Neptune' presented each passenger with a small printed scroll which recorded that we had made a crossing of the equator on this 19th day of March, 1861. From another large bag, he gave each of the children a large sweet-biscuit. Barrels of wine and cider and kegs of warm beer were tapped for the passengers as we gorged ourselves on the rich soups and smoky roasted meats.

As the sun dived below the horizon in the west, a large glittering orange moon began to emerge from under the ocean to the east. Lanterns around the deck were lit as the debris from our feast was cleared away. Several passengers produced violins and were joined by sailors from the foredeck with fiddles, flutes, and a round string-instrument from the Americas – the first time I had seen or heard this instrument called a banjo. Their music, first one group then another, soon held us enthralled and prompted some of the crew and passengers to jig and dance.

The officers moved most of the musicians up the gangways onto the empty poop-deck ringed with lanterns. As a special occasion, the Captain suspended the Voyage Rules and permitted passengers who wished to dance to take to this reserved deck, the only large clear-deck area of the whole ship and apart from cages of geese, devoid of other animals.

Before I could anticipate even that it might happen, Lieutenant Haile took Miss Elizabeth by the arm, led her onto the deck, bowed formally and watched by a crowd, they began to dance. Very quickly, other couples joined in until the deck was a milling swirl of people, George and Lucy among them. Sailors on the maindeck were dancing hornpipes to the tune of flutes, watched by crowds of passengers.

I stood by the port rail, consciously alone, feeling envious as I caught glimpses of Miss Elizabeth together with the Lieutenant. Eventually, after a seemingly endless sequence of music, the fiddlers and banjo players stopped for a rest and further refreshment. I caught a glimpse of George and Lucy driving a path through the milling throng of people and as they reached me, I suddenly saw Miss Elizabeth almost hidden behind.

I could feel my heartbeat quicken. 'Oh Mr Fraser…' she greeted me, those pale blue eyes even in the half-light, shining with excitement, looking up to mine, '…do you not dance?'

'I do with great pleasure Miss Elizabeth, when the opportunity is available, and I will again this evening if you would do me the honour of accompanying me when our musicians return. But I would not wish to deprive you of the company of the Lieutenant – or others – if that is what you would prefer?'

'Why no, not at all. I was afraid that either you did not dance, or that you would not invite me. I would indeed be delighted to accompany you…'

We didn't have long to wait, the musicians taking up their instruments again as we made our way through the crowded deck, Miss Elizabeth holding tightly to my arm and I, exhilarated by the pressure of her hand upon it. As we began to dance, her gloved hand lightly in the clasp of mine, I struggled to be aware of our surroundings and the music, so distracted was I by the light touch of her fingers burning against my hand and our being so close together. A confused mixture of excitement, a shy self-consciousness, thumping heart in my ears, and a strange feeling of lightness almost overwhelming me. We said nothing, just looked and smiled at each other. I wanted to shout. My chest felt as if it would burst. And then it was over. I reluctantly released her hand, stepped back and bowed.

In the next two hours we danced together again several times. Each time, the same feelings returned to me. In between, I danced with Lucy and Miss Elizabeth with the Captain, Dr Carrington and the Lieutenant until, eventually, the musicians tired and returned to the maindeck.

George, Lucy, Miss Elizabeth and I moved slowly for'ard, leaning against the starboard rail at the base of the foredeck. The near-full moon had risen high into the night sky, sufficiently bright to cast a white light over the ship and twinkle scattered reflections on the calm ocean. We leaned over the railing, watching brilliant phosphorescence curling away from the ship's bow as it dipped now and then into the light swells. I could feel the pressure of Elizabeth's shoulder against my side, fighting an urge to put my arm about her and hold her close.

We were slightly separated from George and Lucy, sufficient that they did not participate in our conversation. We talked about the events of this night and the splendour of the full moon in a sky filled with stars. For the first time, I felt we were together sharing our own small space, apart from the 150 others all around us on the *Black Swan*.

I felt emboldened: 'Miss Elizabeth', I ventured, 'I have so enjoyed your company this evening – in fact, each time I have been fortunate to be together with you!' I stumbled on, the words coming before any conscious forethought. 'I want to say, that I have felt a special warmth toward you ever since I saw you join the ship in Plymouth, before we had even met … I don't know … it was as if we had known each other before.'

She looked up at me, a smile lighting her eyes, the corners of her mouth turning upward. 'And I too have had much pleasure from your attention Mr Fraser, you are not alone in that regard, nor in the strange feeling that we have met previously.'

'I would hope, no, I would ask of you Miss Elizabeth, that when we have reached our destination in New Zealand, I may call upon you and continue my friendship with you?'

'Yes, of course you may Mr Fraser, I would be very pleased if you should do so and would be disappointed if you did not. However – and please understand that I am not wishing in the least way to dissuade you – I have a strong responsibility for my dear Papa and for his happiness. My first duty, until I am assured that he is well settled must be to him, for his wellbeing and to accord with his wishes.

'I must not think of myself, nor put myself and my own interests before his. Equally, as I have already commented to you, I do not think that at present he welcomes the attentions of any gentleman toward me – it is not a prejudice against you personally. He means no malice and I would entreat you not to be dissuaded by his indifference toward you, should that continue either now or when you refresh our acquaintance in New Zealand, as indeed I hope that you will.

'And now Mr Fraser, I must reluctantly take my leave of you and return to our quarters, lest Papa confines me there for the remainder of our voyage! I do thank you for your company this evening, it has been both enjoyable and memorable.' And turning toward George and Lucy, she bid them goodnight.

I escorted her back down the ship, the decks still crowded, until we stood before the doors to the private quarters. Then with a smile, a squeeze of her hand upon my arm, a slight toss of her head and a quick 'Goodnight Mr Fraser!' she was gone.

I joined with a large group of other passengers sitting on the aft hatch covers in the moonlight still drinking cider and singing until quite late. When the moon began to sink toward the west, we tired and drifted off to our respective quarters. I lay on my bunk in the dark, so dark that I could not see the timbers of the bunk above, visions of Miss Elizabeth and of our evening together parading before my eyes, reflecting on the strange path that life had taken me; from Scotland to Ireland, from England to this small ship floating in the vastness of the Atlantic Ocean. And after all that had passed, now here, a new experience – a consciousness that I must be in love with Elizabeth MacKay. The realisation I probably had been, since the very moment I first saw her.

* * *

We sailed languidly on. The inescapable heat continued, relieved only by the frequent flushing of the decks with seawater and the opportunity to douse ourselves in the process. The private-berth passengers sat beneath their awning of sailcloth providing some shade, waited upon by a steward. All other passengers spent the whole of daylight on deck, making tea with the daily water-ration, in small 'learning-classes', fishing or sleeping. Even the Purser Nathan Greene was not constantly in demand from the passengers, spending time with George and I to discuss America, the causes of tension between the States and potential consequences should it turn to violence.

Below decks in our quarters the odour of accumulating sweat and stale air was becoming unbearable. George and Lucy said that on entering their own quarters where most of the passengers were berthed, the stench of humanity and hot air was so strong as to make them gag. Sleep itself in the stifling heat was increasingly difficult for all of us, many passengers instead choosing to sleep out on the hard deck.

In response to complaints from the passengers to Nathan Greene, Dr Carrington accompanied Mr Holbourne and Mr O'Reilly on an inspection of all the quarters. Captain King declared that all the berths were to be cleaned out and swabbed down with carbolic, then the floors spread with chloride of lime, lest there should be a risk of illness. That activity occupied several days, providing a break in the normal dreary routines.

Much as I wished it, I did not again meet Miss Elizabeth until stirring breezes from the northwest returned to inject a new vigour into the *Black Swan*. Our listless sails filled once more and the deck moved beneath our feet with renewed life. The *Black Swan's* bow lifted and dipped into the growing swell, peeling off hissing sheets of spray, casting small rainbows in the bright sunlight.

As if suddenly shaken from the tropical torpor, Miss Elizabeth appeared again at the poop deck rail, waiting until she caught sight of Lucy, then after a wave of her hand, came down to join her on the main deck. Together they made a turn of the deck, inspecting our visibly shrinking menagerie of livestock and poultry. When they returned to George and I waiting by the aft rail, a hot flush of self-consciousness began sweeping over my face as I struggled to keep my excitement contained.

'What a pleasure to have you visit with us again Miss Elizabeth,' I greeted her, reaching forward and taking both of her hands in mine. 'And mine to be here,' she replied spontaneously, smiling coquettishly up at me, a light pressure on my hands before releasing hers, 'I was hoping that I would find you during this brief time when Papa allowed me to come again.'

George and Lucy moved slightly away, leaving us somewhat alone together. We continued a light discussion of events on ship since our last evening together but as we talked, I noticed an increasing agitation as she glanced repeatedly up toward the poop deck. Shortly, she apologised that she must return to the private quarters, quite quickly thanked Lucy for accompanying her, wished us all farewell and disappeared again through the aft doorway.

As she left us, I stood staring wistfully until she was lost from sight. When she had gone, Lucy playfully pushed her hand against my chest: 'Well John Fraser, unless I should be mistaken – which I think not – you are quite captivated by that young lady. And I believe Miss Elizabeth portrays more than just a casual friendship toward you also.'

'The former I must admit and cannot disguise; if your intuitions are correct Lucy, the latter would be more than I could hope for. I wish that this voyage would speedily end, so that I could continue to pursue my feelings without the barriers that our present circumstances impose upon us. But an ocean still exists between us and our destination in more ways than one!'

As if in answer to my wish, the wind from the west slowly strengthened during the next several days driving the ship farther southward with encouraging speed. The noticeably cooler air made the nights below deck again endurable for all the passengers.

During the days, I passed much of the time with George and Lucy, both now seasoned sailors at ease with the renewed motion of the ship, at the lee rail facing aft, exhilarated by the wind against face, watching the great sweep of the larger swells rolling away beneath us. Above us the sails billowed tautly, still an almost complete suite of canvas straining against the yards, continually being trimmed by the crew under the direction of the Officer of the Watch. All around, the hemp and coir sheets creaked noisily against the belaying pins along the gunwhales. Breechblocks squeaked as the strain on the sheets rose and fell with the slow roll of the ship.

I was fortunate to see Miss Elizabeth again a number of times as we drove deeper into the south Atlantic. On each occasion, ostensibly to visit Lucy for a walk around the main deck, she would bring me some new book, which she had read already from the Captain's extensive library. I would return the one I had finished and we would stand in the lee of the poop deck for a brief exchange of our opinions of the book and the abilities of its author.

Gradually these excursions became less frequent as the daily temperatures continued to fall, the winds to freshen, the long swells to rise and the days to shorten. Each time, I would try to hold the last vision of her uppermost in my mind, never knowing when she might again return, or whether it might be a portrait I would have to cling to for some much longer time.

Fewer passengers ventured on deck to brave the more vigorous elements and rolling banks of darker clouds reappeared, as our course increasing became south-easterly instead of due south. At least the new more-easterly bearing marked a turning-point in the voyage, carrying an expectation we were at last entering the next significant phase of the journey, but also an awareness we were closer to the wildness of the southern oceans.

Frequent rainstorms began bearing down upon us, beating the ocean white with the size and density of the drops, lashing over the decks and pouring in rivulets from the sails above. Still the Captain maintained an almost complete sail set, with the ship heeling and surging as each squall fell upon us.

The first albatrosses appeared, huge birds whose angled wings stretched some six feet from wingtip to wingtip, gracefully soaring through the troughs between the swells with not a beat of their wings, riding the wind pressure close to the surface of the waves. They would sweep downwind toward us, then catching the disturbed air thrown off by our ship, suddenly soar gracefully into the air almost to the height of our masts, peel over to a sharp angle displaying the pure white of their under-wings and dive back down into the wind, skimming mere inches from the surface. Yet not once would they touch the water, nor beat their wings. We amused ourselves by tossing small food scraps over the side, watching the birds display an agility belying their size by lifting these off the sea in their hooked beaks while in full flight.

The next Sunday, given access to the hold and our cabin trunks, we all drew our warmest clothes and coats, warned by the officers that it might be our last opportunity to ensure we were properly clothed for the cold weeks ahead. Just in time.

As we plunged deep into the Southern Ocean, we emerged on deck one morning to find a fine coating of ice crystals clinging to the lower rigging. Showers of hail replaced the rain. Below deck in our quarters, the air became a damp chill. Still we forged onward with a south-easterly bearing, the intensity of the cold noticeably increasing, the strength of the wind on the aft port quarter daily growing stronger, the long rolling swells visibly higher and with a great jumble of smaller waves scattering their surface. Now when we sank into the troughs we could see nothing but the grey walls of water around us, then lifting up over the crests would reveal a quick glimpse of a turbulent ocean out to a broken horizon far away.

Cold pervaded the ship, a cloying penetrating cold with no respite, no escape, even striking through the wrap of bedding in our berths. Above deck, the constant wind never abated, pushing and tugging at us, rattling the shrouds, whistling through the rigging, throwing shafts of spray up over the gunwhales and over the decks. The greyness of the sky was unbroken, just lower and darker patches of cloud appearing, bursting forth with sweeping columns of rain.

The cooks struggled to supply hot food, fighting against the wind and rain to light the galleys. When they succeeded, partly shielded by protective screens of heavy canvas, stewards carried tin panniers below to the passengers who now rarely appeared on deck, except some of the men in the mornings to empty their chamber-pots over the side.

The Captain sent word around the ship that we were now almost as far south as our route would take us, any further south might take us into the path of icebergs which could have drifted north from the Antarctic. From this point our course would lie due east for more than another month and until we approached the southern end of New Zealand.

Another month! At least.

Gradually, passengers became more accustomed to the rigours of our new environment and daily, more of them appeared on deck, assured of the ability of our ship to ride the great swells that bore down on us from astern. Heavy grey skies stretched from horizon to horizon but there was no rain. The cooks worked assiduously behind their heavy canvas shields and regularly managed to cook our midday hot dinners despite the heave and roll of the ship.

Aloft, we still carried a fair measure of canvas and the *Black Swan* surged eastward at an impressive pace. George, Lucy and I would meet on deck every day, shrouded in our heavy coats against the wind, to walk back and forth between the poop and the fo'c'sle, or watch the albatrosses from behind some shelter. But of the private-berth passengers there was no sign. Only the relentless march of long grey waves from the west bearing down on us from astern, evenly-spaced and with a long low easily-sailed slope from trough to crest.

Lying in the dark each night listening to the creaking of the ship, I would recall clear images of Elizabeth, longing that I could see her again, missing the light lilting sound of her voice, her smile, her blue eyes, the intense touch of her hand on my arm. I decided if I could not get to meet her, then I would write her a letter which I was confident that the Purser could deliver for me. Nathaniel obtained paper, ink and pen and under the curious gaze of other single men in our quarters, I sat in the dim lantern-light writing in the best hand I could exercise.

My Dear Miss Elizabeth

My cousins and I trust that you are enduring the privations which our passage now inflicts upon us, in comfort and good heart.

We ourselves yet endeavour to take the deck most days, finding the exercise, the fresh airs and the elements quite invigorating. Although cold and colourless, we find much in the pattern and life of the ocean that is of interest which helps to breach the monotony of the voyage.

We have all missed your company and presence, this writer particularly, and our days would be greatly brightened if again we were honoured by having you visit with us. Your safety and comfort would be assured should you so venture, accompanied if your father wishes by the Purser or an Officer.

We will continue to hope that your circumstances will permit you to be with us again, however briefly that may be. In the meantime,

I remain

Sincerely Yours
John Cameron Fraser

After the Purser took the sealed letter from me, confirming that he had indeed delivered it into Miss Elizabeth's own hand, I waited expectantly for a reply or for her to appear out on the deck. But as the days passed with neither response, my hope slowly faded into despondency. Why, I wondered, had my letter not spurred some reply? Perhaps, I reasoned, MacKay had objected, or else Elizabeth herself was awaiting a suitable opportunity.

Talking in the shelter of the steering dodger amidships with Mr Holbourne, I learned that we were now estimated to have passed well south of Capetown having made fast progress with the strong ceaseless wind from the west. Our position below the south-western edge of the Indian ocean was reputably among the most dangerous of our voyage – warm air off the east coast of Africa was drawn south by the rotation of the globe, colliding with cold air in the great southern ocean to cause storms of great turbulence. So it proved to be.

The wind strengthened during the night. We were awakened in our for'ard berth by the thud of seamen's boots on the deck above and the thump of the ship falling off larger waves. Lying in the darkness I thought of the courage of the sailors who would be aloft in the windy night clinging to the yards as the ship rolled about, struggling urgently to furl the heavy canvas. Braced in my bunk, unable to sleep, I listened to the louder sounds of a rising storm, then felt a deep shudder shake the ship as a crest rolled beneath her and the blunt bows buried deep into the trough.

In the grey light of morning, followed by several other venturesome fellows, I stumbled along the companionway, rolled the hatchway aside and stepped out onto the deck. The wind itself was not as strong as I had imagined but we were surrounded by towering masses of enormous waves in a great confusion. Clinging to the shrouds of the foremast, as the ship rose up I could see beyond the immediate crest; instead of the even regular lines of waves out of the west directly on our stern, now there was another succession of huge swells coming simultaneously from the quarter.

The convergence of these lines of waves was creating such a confusion of sea. As they meshed across each other the *Black Swan* was shaken violently to starboard then at the same moment lifted and thrown forward in a corkscrew roll. Holding tight to the shrouds, I looked up and saw that the fore and mainmasts carried only a foresail apiece, with a staysail between each of the masts. Yet amid the violence of the ocean the thousand tons of our ship was being tossed about like a small cork in rapids and even with so little canvas, was surging forward apace.

When mountainous crossing waves collided they reared up violently into frightening vertical peaks over 50 feet high, then crashed down in a roaring mass of tumbling froth and foam. The wind hurled off clouds of foam from the summits as the walls of water collapsed, creating a dense haze that limited visibility to a few hundred yards. We were all alarmed at the prospect that one of these giant rearing waves would collapse upon the ship itself but just as that seemed fearsomely imminent, the *Black Swan* would race forward, leaving the huge crashing maelstrom of roiling water behind.

Despite our apprehension and fear, there was some exhilaration amongst us from the danger and the continual escapes of the ship just when catastrophe seemed imminent. But our venture onto the deck was short-lived – Mr O'Reilly the Second Officer appeared from aft toward us, holding hand-over-hand to safety-lines or the rigging as he came, then shouted to us to return to the safety of our berths.

For four days and three nights the storm raged. It was impossible for the cooks to fire the galleys so we were without proper food or hot drinks, sustaining ourselves with hard ship's biscuit and our water ration. I could only imagine what the conditions were like in the main berths for most of the passengers, with whole families crowded into their dimly-lit narrow bunks, trying to calm their fears and those of their children whilst the ship tossed violently about.

Days and nights in our lantern-lit berth merged and we slept whenever it came upon us. Only the time on our fobs told us when day changed to night. On the fourth night, I was awakened by increasing cold that had penetrated even into our berth. Lying in the dark, I noticed that the violent corkscrew motion of the ship had changed; the roll from side to side was more regular and even but the pitch and rise from bow to stern was much steeper.

When day returned, Nathaniel Greene came to tell us we could again go out on deck, where the cooks would later try to fire the galley. Outside, the sea and the wind had changed. It was bitterly cold, a gale of a wind that cut through our thickest coats. Bearing down behind the ship came huge steep waves with rolling foaming tops, 'greybeards' O'Reilly called them, that pitched the ship up onto her ends so the poop deck was angled high above us. Then as the wave crest surged beneath amidships with dark sea swirling up to the gunwhales, the *Black Swan* would hurtle forward and the fo'c'sle rear up as the greybeard cleared the ship, dropping us back into the deep trough behind.

Long ragged lines of foam scattered down the back of the passing wave. Lumps of spume torn from the foaming crests by the wind flew through the air, splattering the deck. A clutch of officers stood by the wheelhouse as the steersman swung the wheel back and forth, fighting to hold the ship on line and avoid her yawing. But at least now the seas, although enormous, only came directly from astern and the motion of the ship, although extreme, held to a regular cycle.

I managed a short shouted conversation with Mr Holbourne, anxious not to distract him from controlling the ship. The storm he said, had driven us further south from our intended course and we were now in a gale-battered cold region called the 'roaring 40s' from its southern latitude. We could only hold to this course and hope that the fierce wind would abate or shift to a more southerly quarter that would push us northeastward again.

With some shelter from a small dodger, the cooks managed to set up and light a galley, sufficient to braise chunks of brine-salted beef and boil up churns of soup – our first hot food or drink in four days. Even some breaks in the dull grey cloud appeared to the north exposing glimpses of pale sky. But to the south, low toward the horizon, were ominous banks of deepening blackness.

Passengers, mostly men, appeared from the main berths. I saw George among them and we exchanged experiences as we chewed ravenously into pieces of quickly-cooling meat in our hands. As the afternoon drew on, the wind rose even further, shrieking and rattling through the rigging until again we were all ordered below. The dark sky to the south was riven with flashing stabs of lightning as we struggled back to the fo'c'sle.

In the night, lying wedged in my berth I could hear the ship protesting the rising violence of the storm again upon us. Above the noise of rain lashing the deck overhead came rolls of thunder. Sleep was impossible as the ship continued to be driven eastward before the wind.

Hours passed. I prayed that our repair to the copper sheathing would hold fast. The lanterns in our berth had been turned out. Lulled a little by the regularity of the ship's motion, severe though it was, I drifted in and out of sleep. Suddenly, I sensed or felt a pause in the regular lifting of the stern. I tensed, instantly awake. The ship must be lying level in a deep trough.

Then a violent shudder and a roar from aft and above. Shouts from the deck. A shaking crashing roar. Thuds and thumps. The hatch door to the fo'c'sle burst open. A blast of cold air and a torrent of sloshing water burst into our berth. Panicked shouts from fellow passengers in the darkness. A touch of fear ignited all my senses. I leapt from my berth into knee-deep freezing water in the companionway. I shouted out 'Keep calm men! We've taken a wave aboard – there's water over the floor!'

Against my bare legs I could feel the water surging back toward the fo'c'sle door. I groped my way toward it in the blackness. The urgent clanging of bells sounding 'all hands on deck'. The sound of boots on the deck above us. A shout from the direction of the door: 'Ahoy in there! Are you men safe?'

I recognised O'Reilly, and called back: 'O'Reilly, it's Fraser … we're unharmed but there's water in the fo'c'sle … I think it's draining back toward you. What of the ship? What's happened?'

Anxiety for my cousins and for Elizabeth suddenly swept through me. O'Reilly and I were now close in the darkness. I could hear other men in our berth coming aft toward us, calling to each other. 'The ship's all sound, Fraser! A giant wave came over the poop, some water through the ship. We're assessing the damage. Captain will try to hold our course till daylight, it's too risky to go about in the dark and these seas.'

Then in a louder voice shouted down the companionway: 'This is the Second Officer! You men stay below! You'll be safe here! We'll shore up the hatch … the water'll drain quickly. Get your lanterns lit and go back to your berths till the deck's dry. I'll return.'

Shortly he did so, accompanying Burton the carpenter who worked quickly to shore-up the stoved portion of the fo'c'sle door in the dim light of our lanterns. The water that had been deep over the floor had somewhere drained away. I anxiously pressed O'Reilly for news:

'Tell us O'Reilly, what's happened to the rest of the ship? What of the passengers? '

'All the passengers are safe and unharmed, though some are bruised or wet and most are badly frightened. A huge rogue wave caught us when we were in a trough, swept up over the port quarter of the poop. It's stoutly built as you would know ... we lost most of the poultry off its deck but the pinnace in its davits was secure ... water filled the companionway from the poop-deck but the doors held ... only a small amount entered the cabins. The passengers there are shaken but unharmed.

'The wave came down off the poop and over the wheelhouse. Holbourne and the men went under but their safety-lines held them. Holbourne has an injured shoulder ... they are all battered and bruised. The water drove down the main-berth companionway ... smashed the doors open like this one ... flooded into the berths. Several passengers were swept from their bunks ... got tumbled about and bruised. Greene and some others are trying to dry it all out ... there are many spare bunks deeper in the berth for them to use.

'The wave tore along the port side. A longboat came loose, smashed against the foremast stem. I think we've lost all the livestock on the port side. The last of the wave hit against your doors here but didn't go over the fo'c'sle deck. We've all seen worse than this before Fraser. The *Black Swan's* a strong ship and Cap'n King well-knows these southern oceans.'

They left us, the carpenter barring the door from outside. The berth reeked dankly with seawater. In the dim light of swaying lanterns we returned to our bunks but fright had driven sleep far away. I wished that I could go to Elizabeth, comfort and reassure her, imagining how frightened she must have been, frustrated that she was so near to me but so inaccessible. And George and Lucy – how had they fared? Poor Lucy with her fear of the sea. And the livestock gone ... would we have sufficient food now to last the voyage? Jumbled questions and concerns filled my mind.

It seemed to become colder. Probably a consequence of the flooding I thought. I pulled up more bedroll, burrowed well beneath it, trapping the warmth of my own breathing in the space around my body, tried again to sleep.

I awoke again. Body warm, but my feet and lower legs very cold. I pushed my head out above the bedroll into now-freezing air. There was banging at our outer door, then a gust of frigid air. I heard O'Reilly call: 'You men can come on deck if you wish – but take care and be warmly clad.'

I was first to do so. Through the door, I was surprised to find the ship coated in white. Deep snow lay on the deck. A trough of footprints led aft. Above and around, wind-driven snow or ice clung jaggedly to masts and spars, coating all the fixed rigging. Drifts piled up against the gunwhales and the fo'c'sle head. Further aft, the main hold hatch-cover lay buried beneath a rounded mound of white.

The whitened ship was bright in the dull morning light, contrasting against the grey sea. The wind had dropped to a light westerly breeze; the long swells bearing down from behind us, though still huge, less tumbled about, less menacing. The sky, so pale as to be seemingly grey as the sea itself, mostly devoid of cloud. The violence of the storm had passed.

The Bosun appeared, carrying shovels. 'Lend a hand Mr Fraser, we must free the ship! We need all the men to shovel this snow away. Knock the ice off the rigging with the handles. If we start down aft, the cooks can set up the galley as soon as the deck is cleared.'

We set to vigorously, quickly warming with the activity. More men appeared from the main berth. We worked together in small groups, gradually clearing toward each other, showering long tinkling shards of ice off the rigging as we went.

I met up with George. We shovelled steadily, shoulder to shoulder. I learned that in the night, water nearly three feet deep roared through their berth, sweeping up everything in its path, washing some passengers from their bunks, tumbling them along the companionway screaming and shouting in the dark.

Lucy had been terrified; like many others, imagining the ship was foundering, clinging to George, aghast that they might imminently be drowned. As the water surged for'ard its depth and velocity diminished, dissipating before it reached the berths of families with children. The passengers in a panic had leapt from their bunks into knee-deep water. Apart from being wet and scared, only those who had been scoured from their bunks were injured. They were now all busy cleaning up the mess, trying to keep warm in the freezing dampness.

As we cleared the snow from around the main hatchcovers, the cooks set up the galley. We worked our way further aft, then up the gangways to the poop deck. Shovelling our way along the deck, I felt a nearness to Elizabeth, knowing that she was there somewhere, just below the deck under my feet, willing her to know that I was here, just above.

Feeling uplifted and warmed by the strenuous activity, we all heaved the last of the snow over the side just as the cooks produced hot tea. By midday they had cooked a comparative feast of onion soup, hot corned beef with potatoes together with flat squares of hot bread-like dampers. The wind and seas had abated sufficiently for tables to be set up and quickly the deck was crowded with passengers and crew, ravenously gorging the first hot food of substance for days, all relieved to have survived the terrors of the night.

The *Black Swan* sailed on eastward relentlessly, driven by moderate winds and the regular march of well-spaced long even swells from the west. The journey seemed endless, the ocean depressingly vast, empty, cold and forever grey. Days lapsed into a monotony of days. A monotony of weeks.

Having lost much of our remaining livestock when the wave swept over us, even the food was repetitively dull. The cooks tried hard but each day we awoke knowing we would face again the daily fare of boiled or roasted beef salted in brine vinegar.

How much further was this voyage to the Antipodes? How many more days of sameness must we endure to reach the bottom of the world? We began to long for journey's end, to see land again, feel earth beneath our feet, to look at green grass with trees, walk among houses, eat different food, taste fresh water. But every day was as the day before, another day closer but seemingly no further.

In an effort to lift our spirits, we talked of the happy times behind us sailing through the tropics, of warm nights singing and dancing on the deck under star-strewn skies, hot languid days. Of the day when surely this voyage must end, the food we most looked forward to eating again; peoples' plans, hopes and dreams. But each day that followed was the same again.

I wrote another letter to Elizabeth, hoping that she might again visit us, suggesting her radiant presence would brighten otherwise dreary days for us all. I waited. Days of expectancy turned to days of anguish, but this letter too spurred no response. I spent hours staring at the empty ocean, trying to reason why, mostly ending in a building resentment that probably her father had intervened in some harsh way, his cold unsmiling image still strongly in my mind, Elizabeth's sweet words of duty to him still in my ears.

The officers advised that the great mass of Van Diemens Land far to the north had now been passed. The Captain predicted that in only a few weeks we could be sighting land. Oh yet still more weeks of enduring our condition! We all ached for the day of liberty at journey's end; longed for it, dreamt of it, prayed for it.

As the expectation of an end to our incarceration steadily increased, the days themselves took longer to pass; with their hours of darkness increasing, even longer. As if to add to our exasperations, we entered a calmer period, the wind which had so inexorably driven us from the west, faded to a light breeze, then almost to nothing. We wallowed in the shelter of the troughs with the staysails all luffing, heavy dark clouds looming low overhead as if to burst suddenly upon us.

The last passengers cleared from the decks for the night. I lay in the stillness of our darkened berth, trying to picture Elizabeth in my mind before drifting to sleep. Suddenly a violent shudder went through the ship. From below came a deep rumble, then a harsh grating sound and a sharp jolt seemed to thrust up beneath us. The anxious clanging of the 'All Hands on Deck!' bells and the thud of seaboots. I jumped from my berth, all senses racing. Shouts from everywhere. We spilled out of the fo'c'sle onto the darkened deck.

In a burst of moonlight I could see passengers streaming from the main berth below out onto the deck, a milling mass of confusion and anxiety. There was a mix of orders, calling and shouting, 'What have we struck? Are we fast aground? Gather the women and children! Where's the Captain? What do we do? Prepare to launch boats! Stand to! Are we foundering?' all heard above the noise of fear. But the *Black Swan* sailed serenely onward as if nothing untoward had happened.

Gradually the tumult died away and near-quiet returned. I recognised the tall figure of MacKay, together with Haile and Dr Carrington emerge from the poop and gather beside the officers. We all stood there together in the dark, waiting tensely for some imminent change in our circumstance that would indicate the ship was damaged. But minutes passed, and nothing occurred.

Officers and seamen who had been moving quickly about the ship were returning aft to report to the Captain standing by the wheelhouse with Holbourne, O'Reilly and Greene. They remained close in conversation. The ship sailed inexorably eastward, apparently quite untroubled by whatever had taken place, even I noting that she was riding quite normally with no sign of listing or sluggishness that would indicate she was taking water. We waited, shivering, poorly clad for the cold of the night.

Captain King climbed the companionway to the poop deck, stood to the rail facing down to us, his features clearly visible in the lantern-light.

'You may all return to your berths! The ship is safe and sound. We are in deep ocean, with no recorded islets, reefs or rocks. We believe we have been struck by a quaking, or tremor, of the earth on the ocean floor below - such events are known but not experienced by my officers or me. Our passenger Mr MacKay, a geologist, advises that such a tremor in the ocean floor would be conducted through the sea above with violent effect. In the absence of any signs of our ship having struck an object, nor suffering any damage, I concur. So you may return below now – all is well!'

Back in the fo'c'sle, sleep did not come easily after such a frightening experience. I sat at the table in the varying light of the swaying lantern recording the extraordinary event of an earthquake at sea in a letter to my Uncle and Aunt back in Ireland, and noting the date as May 23, 1861.

Within a few days, the Captain reported that from his latest sightings, we must at last be closing toward land. As if in confirmation, thousands of seabirds appeared, swirling like a black fog across the ocean in every direction. We lined the rails watching as the birds – black shearwaters - surged frantically about in a flight like flying fish, a frenetic beating of wings then a long glide barely skimming the sea. Their wingtips seemingly scraping the water, they hugged every riffle and wave. So many and so dense, it was impossible to follow the path of a single bird; flying, diving, bursting back to the surface, then a beating of wings whilst running with webbed feet on top of the water until again airborne, then lost into the wheeling mass of millions.

On occasion, for no apparent reason, all the birds would be flying without stopping in the same direction, passing by us in their millions all on the same heading for hour upon hour. Or else all resting on the surface, like a thick black scum out to the horizon, only moving aside sufficiently to allow for the passage of our ship. We stood staring in amazement at this natural phenomenon.

We were urged to watch for signs of land, expected to appear on the port side toward the northeast, or possibly directly ahead due east. Excitement at the prospect could be felt throughout the ship. Wagers were made amongst the passengers as to the date and time that land would be sighted. Given the long nights, I believed it probable that land would appear in the hours of darkness, only being clearly visible as the pale light of dawn returned.

Our patience and tolerance of our long incarceration aboard the *Black Swan* which was already stretched became tautly so at the prospect of an imminent end to our journey. We became more restless, more conscious of being confined within the small perimeter of the deck, surrounded by the mass of rigging, our view of the sky above obscured by canvas. All this which for so long had been our security, our home together, now an increasing frustration. But still the ship rolled along eastward under grey skies, even the shearwaters forsaking us, leaving the ocean again empty and us alone. The last days of May passed tediously into June. Our mood of excitement waned and we all seemingly retreated deeper within ourselves. Conversation among us virtually ceased.

'Laaaand hooooe!' The unmistakable cry, repeated again and again hauntingly from aloft, woke me from sleep. I was caught up in a rush of men. We crushed together around the hatchway, tumbling out into the half-light of dawn onto the deck. Passengers from the main berth aft burst out of their companionway, leaping and laughing, slapping each other on the back, men hugging wives and children. Tears of joy on many faces. I found George and Lucy and with arms about each other's shoulders we danced around, cheering in an excited jig, as others joined in.

Crewmen surged aloft up the ratlines for a better view of land. We crowded along the port rails, anxious for our first glimpse. Then as the light strengthened we could see beyond the broken sea-horizon to the northeast, a long low roll of cloud like a bank of sea-fog. But slowly, solid and unmoving above, the form of land took shape, rising darker, high over the cloud, up to patches of stark white mountaintop snow contrasting clearly against the grey sky. Our destination and our destiny. The Antipodes at journey's end. New Zealand.

Excitement was overcome by the magnitude of the moment. The crowd stood still, hushed, staring, not wanting to glance away lest the vision vanished, nor wanting to break the silence of emotions.

So we remained, immovable for hours at the rail, each wrapped in our own solitude, emotion borne of 103 days since Graves End had slipped into darkness behind us; 103 long days of restless, featureless, empty ocean, devoid of the sight of land.

Mountains to the north-east rose up higher as we closed toward the land, their heights drifting in and out of cloud, then gradually fading as darkness returned. Despite the cold evening, many of us remained on deck until late, now willing to discuss our plans and priorities when the voyage ended. Mostly we talked of food; of juicy beef, eggs, fresh vegetables especially green ones, fresh untainted water, tankards of beer, any food not tasting of salt. George and Lucy first wanted such a feast in a tavern – I first wanted to bathe in a deep hot tub, all the better to enjoy the feast to follow.

When day returned, the mountains were to the north directly abeam the port side. A long stretch of lower land extended from them along the north horizon off toward the east. Off the starboard quarter to the southeast, another low bank of dark green land had appeared. Our heading was directly between these two pieces of land some 30 miles apart, an area of empty sea that must be a channel or a strait separating them. O'Reilly circulating about the ship advised we were indeed navigating a strait between Stewart's Island to the south and the south end of New Zealand's South Island to our north.

By dusk, Stewart's Island to the south had passed us by. To the north, the land was falling lower to the horizon, barely visible. The ship's bells rang and with a cheer from the crew, the *Black Swan* heeled to starboard and our course changed fully 50 degrees, to head nor-nor'east. Our relentless journey westward was at an end. We were sailing up the eastern coast of the southern island to make our landfall at Port Chalmers.

All day I had watched the poop deck closely, expecting, hoping, to see Elizabeth and her fellow-passengers appear, to view the passing coast. But the deck remained bare.

Whilst standing for hours at the rail reflecting ahead beyond the end of our voyage, I resolved that I could retain my feelings for her unspoken no longer. Freed from the strictures of the Voyage Rules, I would be free to call upon her and Mr MacKay at their residence whenever I so chose. I would declare my love for Elizabeth and if reciprocated – as I fervently hoped – continue my courtship. Then after whatever passage of time required, seek the approval of her father for our life together in marriage. I struggled to keep such thoughts from dominating my mind, by thinking of building a vessel in which to install my steam engine and creating a rewarding enterprise.

We passed nearby the mouth of a large river, the Molyneaux, and then a large area of low land backed by higher rolling hills. In the afternoon came a long stretch of steep bush-clad hills plunging directly into the sea, broken by small bays with sandy beaches. Rounding the end of these hills, we saw they had been masking a long narrow inlet also flanked on its landward western side by even-higher forested mountains.

As we crossed the entrance to this inlet or sound, the *Black Swan* rounded into the wind and we watched as the sailors swarming aloft furled the sails down onto the great spreading yards. The ship luffed, held by the jibs, staysails and spanker, then tacked back and forth across the entrance of the sound. Shortly, we saw coming up the sound toward us, a small boat with a stack trailing black smoke, the first other vessel we had seen for months. As it closed with us we could read the sign 'PILOT' across the front of the wheelhouse.

After an exchange with Captain King by voice-trumpet, a line was thrown to the *Black Swan* by several dark-skinned men aboard the pilot-boat and as we were taken in tow, the last of our sails were dropped. Crewmen lining the yards above and all the passengers crowding the deck cheered and clapped. Lucy, George and I, almost overcome with mixed feelings of relief, exhilaration and excited anticipation stood together, pressed by the crowd, watching the mountainous shores on either side slide by on a long tow down the sound. We pressed on, until eventually we could see ahead to starboard, the outline of buildings, then the clustered masts of several ships at the small port of Port Chalmers.

The pilot-boat drew us achingly slowly inward, then a paddlewheeler tugboat came toward us, made fast to our starboard side and drove us more quickly toward the quayside. The forested hilltops rose up quite steeply, their tops and full height shrouded by swirling cloud as a fine drizzle rained down upon us. The town of Dunedin was somewhere out of sight, further up the sound.

A small crowd had gathered on the quayside, flanked by horses, carts, gigs and drays. Looking aft, I saw the private-berth passengers had at last appeared on the poop-deck to watch, clustered together in a small group, but I could not separately see Elizabeth herself, nor did she detach from the group to look for us.

The tug pushed the *Black Swan* against the wooden side of the quay and to cheers from the crowd on shore, a signal-gun was fired from the poop deck. To three-cheers from all of us on board the ship, we were made fast alongside.

The date was the 5th of June, 1861, the end of our non-stop voyage of 107 days since we had left England and without loss of life. Relief that it was finally at an end overwhelmed me as I stared at the mist-coated hills around us, knowing not nor caring whether it was rain or tears streaming down my bearded face.

SEVEN

We stayed on board the ship that night. Our arrival was too late in the day for us to retrieve any of our cabin trunks from the main hold, without which we could not disembark.

Not all of us remained on board however. Once a gangway was fixed to the jetty, men swarmed aboard carrying fresh provisions. The ship's agents and officials from the Provincial Office clustered about the Captain and officers. Visitors permitted aboard to greet passengers crowded the deck and a clerk from the office of Burns & Co soon sought out George and Lucy. Amongst this activity, the cooks had fresh food now and were firing the galley to give us our last meal on the *Black Swan*.

Distracted by all the noise and crush, I almost missed noticing the private-berth passengers had left the ship. A carriage had crept through the crowd on the quay, close to the gangway and suddenly, in a space cleared near the carriage doors, I could see the well-dressed figures of the Doctor, the Lieutenant, Mr MacKay and, at his side, Elizabeth with hat and heavy coat. I pushed frantically through people toward the rail. Just as they were about to climb into the carriage, Elizabeth looked back to the ship. I hadn't yet reached the rail, but raised my arm and called out over the crowd, 'Miss Elizabeth … Goodbye!' I thought that she could see me, and with a half-raised gloved hand she gave a small wave and climbed inside the carriage.

At first light next morning, amid the chaos of unloading from the uncovered hold, we took our leave from the ship. Captain King, Mr Holbourne, O'Reilly, Nathaniel Greene, Burton the carpenter, the Bosun (whose name was never used) farewelled those of us who had befriended them.

'Your repair to my ship has served us well Fraser,' the Captain said. 'We'll slip her on the beach before we leave Port Chalmers again and have the shipwrights replace the torn sheathing.'

I thanked him for bringing us so far across the world unharmed and in some comfort, then talked with each of the officers in turn. Nathaniel Greene wished us well for our future in the Colony and arranged to meet us ashore.

Stepping onto solid earth again was an unnerving experience. We could not understand why the ground – even the buildings themselves – seemed to move and sway. We staggered about, as did other passengers, struggling to maintain our balance. Instantly we let hold of a fixture, the dizziness would return. After more than 100 days surrounded by constantly-moving ocean, on land and surrounded by stable solid structures we were suddenly unsteady. Having taken many days at sea after leaving England to accustom ourselves to the motion of the ship, now we had to restore our 'land-legs'.

George and Lucy were provided temporary lodgings by Burns & Co which I was able to share. A luxurious bathe in a deep tub of hot water, a change of clean clothes, then to a tavern for a huge meal of freshly-roasted beef with green cabbage, potatoes and gravy washed down with a large tankard of beer celebrated our arrival in New Zealand.

Back at the ship, my steam engine and tools were unloaded by a hand-winched boom-crane onto a dray, to be taken to Burns' yard until I had found a use for them. George was already in charge to supervise and check each swinging load of steel as it too was carted away.

The town was crowded and busy. Everywhere, groups of men gathered or milled about in the streets and hotels. Horses, carts, wagons and gigs surged back and forth.

Dunedin was abuzz with stories and rumours of gold. We soon learned that small pockets of gold had recently been reported at a number of sites in all directions near to the town and quite close to the coast. One discovery further inland to the northeast on the Taieri River had prompted a rush of miners to the area but had quickly been worked out. The two ships we had seen alongside the quay had both arrived from Victoria only a week before us carrying hundreds of Australian miners, 'diggers' they called themselves, enticed by the news of the gold finds. There was a tense expectancy that at any moment, a 'mother lode' would be found and a rush begin. The Provincial Government of Otago had posted a reward of £2000 for any discovery that would yield more than a certain quantity of gold within a year of its finding and had engaged experienced prospectors from Australia and California to search inland for a productive field. The appointment and arrival of Mr MacKay from the *Black Swan* as Gold Commissioner seemed very opportune.

Also adding to the air of enthusiasm was word that further inland in this Province of Otago, huge areas of land suitable for grazing was just waiting to be found and claimed by any man willing to venture. Already many had done so, droving their flocks of sheep purchased from farms near the coast, off into the hills.

The town of Dunedin further inland up the harbour from the old whaling port of Port Chalmers had been long-settled by paying immigrants from Scotland, farmers from the Trossachs and businessmen from Edinburgh and Glasgow. Several large stone buildings including a church, a bank and a school dominated the town which was set on a strip of undulating land gently sloping up from the seashore to the base of high bush-clad hills that loomed above the town to the west. From there, small burns tumbled vigorously out of more rugged hills to provide the town with fresh water.

The town had several main streets laid out parallel to the shore, with others running inland at angles along small side valleys. There were many wooden buildings, some of two levels in the centre of the town, with facades directly onto the dominant street, Princes Street. Further along and up the side streets, were rows of wooden houses, some quite substantial, with surrounding grounds. The streets were very rough, even quite muddy in places when wet.

Surrounded as it was by mountains – even on the seaward side the peninsula of land enclosing the sound leading to the port was also very rugged – the sun barely reached the town even on fine days. Often low cloud, mist and fog shrouded us or persisted with a fine cold drizzle. White frost often clung to the streets throughout the day without thawing.

It was rumoured that the first settlers had traversed up and down the coast seeking a suitable place to establish their town. Each time they passed by Port Chalmers, it was wrapped in mist, gloomily shaded by the mountains all around, reminding them of Scotland and rekindling memories of home. And so, it was said, for that reason they chose it as a suitable site for their new settlement.

I visited the offices of the harbourmaster and several shipping agents seeking any boat or vessel in which to install my steam engine. Nothing was listed for sale and it was mostly suggested that I would have to build such a boat myself, which if necessary I was prepared to do. However, dining with George and Lucy one evening in a Jetty Street tavern frequented by shippers and sailors, I learned of an old whaleboat lying beached in the shallows south of the town.

Riding a hired horse along the shore, I found a cove of muddy flats where a number of wrecks and derelicts lay abandoned, washed by the tides. Among them, I saw the whaleboat lying partly on her side, held down with sand washed in and out by the tides. She was a typical whaler about 22 feet long, pointed and high at both bow and stern, very broad-beamed with heavy wide sweeping gunwhales, of lapped timber construction and full rounded chines. All her ribs and strakes that were uncovered appeared to be still in good condition.

Cleared the next day of yards of sand, emptied of water, and hitched abeam to my horse, I pulled her upright out of the mud, only to find the apparent reason for her abandonment. Her back was broken – a large break was clearly visible right through the keelson (the main lengthways beam along the bottom to which the ribs were secured), now sagging open as the bow and stern settled back onto the mud. All her other timbers and structures were surprisingly otherwise very sound.

But immediately the remedy for this was obvious to me: to mount my steam engine and boiler would require several long beams of timber or iron to be fitted securely lengthways through the bottom of the boat which, when cross-braced together between the chines and the keelson would provide a strong and secure structure all around the break. When previously the whaleboat was rowed by about eight oarsmen, such a repair would not be so obvious, nor practical to allow free movement about the boat when chasing whales in the open sea. But installing an engine on its bearers would provide its own solution. After securing permission from the harbourmaster for her possession, I set to work.

With large props under the gunwhales, the boat stayed upright at low tide, further props at bow and stern held the broken keelson together and bags of sand as ballast kept her sitting securely on the mud. The crew of the *Black Swan* were now all staying ashore and I sought the help of the carpenter Mr Burton to install the hardwood engine-bearer beams carried out from town on a dray.

Next, we shaped and fitted timbers between the gunwhales which would provide framing for a foredeck, working back from the bow almost to amidships. Mr Burton, keen to earn some extra money whilst in port, repaired the rudder, fitting horizontal strips of brass to strengthen it and shaping a new long curved tiller. We worked hard from daylight to dark.

Although absorbed in rebuilding the boat, my thoughts would continually drift to Miss Elizabeth and the passage of sufficient time to the day when I could acceptably call upon her in their new home. Already, by enquiring in shops in the town, Lucy had located the MacKays' residence at the north end of Maclaggan Street, the knowledge of which only served to raise my anticipation and impatience for the time to pass.

With the boat rebuilding nearing completion, I decided to name her the *Lady Colina* in memory of my dear aunt in Ireland who was equally of broad a beam and stout of heart.

While working alone one day standing in the bow installing the decking timber, I was surprised to see a man approaching slowly across the mud. When nearby, I noticed his head and beard of thick black hair, dark brown skin, wide flattened nose in a large round face, broad drooping shoulders and heavy arms. An aborigine, a native.

I stopped working. Alongside, he looked toward me but not at me. I could see his dark brown eyes downcast. He spoke in a deep slow voice, to my surprise in quite clear English: 'Kia Ora, you are the man called Fraser?' – more in statement than as a question.

'I am. Who are you and what is your business with me?' In slight trepidation that he may be about to claim prior ownership of the whaleboat now that it was being rebuilt, unsure of speaking with the first dark-skinned person I had ever encountered.

'White men call me Daniel, Daniel Ellison. My *Maori* name is Erihana. I have work on the pilot boat.' Again the deep slow sonorous voice. He had an unidentifiable presence about him, some strange but perceptible stature. I recalled having seen two natives aboard the pilot boat when the *Black Swan* arrived at Port Chalmers. I put down my tools and climbed from the boat onto the mud. Now his eyes briefly glanced directly to mine. I was unsure what to expect.

'My name is John Fraser…. When you have two different names Mr Ellison, by which name should I call you?'

He looked down at the mud, then at the boat, now slowly back to me at waist-height, the silence growing longer. Perhaps he did not understand me? 'You, Mr Fraser…' a seemingly thoughtful pause, 'you may call me Erihana.' Another silence.

'And what then Erihana, is your business with me?'

'My people are of the sea Mr Fraser. I myself have been with whalers. I know boats and ocean from small child to man. Work with the pilot is not long – many days, no work for me. I need work, food for my family. We hear you want this boat … you repair it …you bring an engine on *Black Swan* to drive it. When you need help on your boat, I will work with you.'

So that was it! 'I thank you for your offer Erihana, but I have no work to offer to you. First I must complete my construction, then I too must find work that will reward me for my effort.'

'You will find work for this boat Mr Fraser. When you do, we will work together. Many *Pakeha* in town know me … you will ask for me please … I will come.'

I was aware that he was asking me, but his speech was like soft commands. I did not want to disappoint or discourage him, but was at a loss to know how to reply. Before I could, he just turned about and walked slowly away back to the shore. As he went, I noticed that he wore no boots, his broad bare feet leaving a trail of footprints rapidly filling with water, across the firm mud.

We built a for'ard hatch, completed timbering over the foredeck, then built two bunkers for wood or coal exactly abeam of the engine-bearers. A solid floor aft beneath the tiller, narrow seats also doubling as steps along both sides and the topsides of *Lady Colina* were almost complete.

Burns & Co had amongst their stock, a large brass screw propeller. Although the casting was quite rough and pitted with air-holes, they balanced and trued it on a lathe, cut a new keyway and fitted it to a long shaft. It would suffice.

By removing the timber props along the port side, at low water *Lady Colina* rolled down until the chine rested on the mud. With Mr Burton's help, I lit a driftwood fire back on the shore and with a combination of heated rods and a large drilling brace, we burned and drilled an angled hole through the keelson for the screw-shaft, plugging it firmly with a caulked peg.

On successive low tides whilst Burton carefully checked and repaired the caulking between all the clinkers, I bolted a heavy false-keel of tapered timber from in front of the shaft-hole up to the base of the stem. Finally, we brought the shaft and screw out from Burns & Co and with several of their engineers assisting, fitted the whole drive-assembly in place. On the next high tide we were ready to float *Lady Colina* and tow her with the steam-tug back to the quay to install the waiting steam engine.

In the water, I was very pleased to see that she rode well, balanced fore and aft, beam to beam. Although under tow and therefore not a reliable guide, she responded quickly to small movements of the tiller which required little pressure. All too quickly, this first short journey was over, ending with being securely moored to a small jetty at the end of the quay.

I worked with a sense of urgency from daylight till dark installing the steam engine, driven not only by my need to have the boat in operation commercially but even more so by a commitment to myself that as soon as she was completed, I would pay my first social visit to see again the lady with whom I was in love. The weeks, indeed months that had passed since last we had been together on the ship had only increased my longing to see her. The sound of her voice, the toss of her hair, the steady gaze of her blue eyes, the touch of her hand on my arm, returned to haunt my thoughts daily.

Such images rarely left me as first the engine was lowered by the 3-ton crane from the jetty into place and mounted securely over the shaft on its bearers, then the boiler. Two copper water-tanks were fitted to the deck for supply to the boiler. Burns' engineers helped to connect the engine piston to the crankshaft driving the screw-shaft and we were soon ready for our first low-pressure firing.

Dunedin was fortunate to have a supply of coal brought by dray from a new mine on the coast not far south. Only a small amount was needed to fire the boiler, building just the minimum pressure to drive the piston and turn the shaft. Heavily secured to the dock, the *Lady Colina* strained at the mooring-lines as the screw gently turned its first revolutions. A small crowd of Australian diggers, easily drawn from their listless wandering around the town by some new activity, watched from the dock above, noisily vying with each other to shout ribald comments down to us.

With a successful test of the driving system completed, we were ready for a maiden voyage under power at first light next day, before onlookers would gather on the quay. Mr Burton arrived with the bosun's mate from the *Black Swan* together with two engineers from Burns'. We fired up the boiler to a higher pressure, closed the steam-valve, cast off from the quay and were underway. I stood holding the tiller, feeling some excitement from the swish of the water passing, the rhythm of the engine, the trail of dark smoke coming from the stack. A steam-boat of my own!

Although the screw turned only slowly, its large size drove *Lady Colina* strongly through the calm water as we travelled around the port, effortlessly tossing aside the wash from our own wake when I deliberately turned her to cross it. We continually checked the glands for water-tightness, the bearings – which were only warm to the touch – in case of over-heating. All was well.

Low on coal and water after several hours cruising around the harbour, we returned to the south end of the quay, making the boat fast. *Lady Colina* was ready for whatever work could be found: my time to visit the MacKay's had come. Finally.

Freshly bathed, hair and beard neatly trimmed, polished boots over my best moleskin trousers and an unworn jacket purchased before I had left Warrington around my shoulders, I made my way to Maclaggan Street with growing anticipation. Now I was on the street where she lived, where she herself probably walked. My tread felt light, as if gravity itself had almost gone. Visions of Elizabeth filled my mind as I sought out the house Lucy had described. I felt tense and excited. I stood on the street outside, breathed deeply and tried to calm myself, conscious of my loud and rapidly thumping heart.

A large two-level wooden house, set back from the street, a side path to the rear for tradespeople, a wider main path secured by a double gate through which I went, led directly to steps before a large front door. Steps low enough to take two at a time but too deep to do so. I gently lowered the iron knocker on the door several times and heard the sound reverberate inside. Footsteps on a wooden floor were coming closer.

The door opened. In front of me stood a maid, smartly dressed in dark blue, white collar, ruffs and a while bonnet tied under her chin. I took a quick deep breath, trying to calm myself.

'John Cameron Fraser presents his compliments to Miss Elizabeth MacKay. If Miss MacKay is in residence, is it convenient for me to visit and pay my respects?'

'Please come in Sir and I shall acquaint the Mistress of your presence. This way Sir, if you please.' She led me deeper down a wide hallway, opened a door to the right, ushered me into an anteroom, my boots seemingly pounding on the wooden floors.

'If you would mind waiting here a few moments Sir, the Mistress will join you shortly, or I shall return with further advice.' I nodded in acknowledgement. She left through another door. I could not see what lay behind.

Hands clasped firmly at my back, aware that they were shaking, I walked softly to bay-windows overlooking a small garden, not wanting to be seated, striving for some distraction. I waited. Heart thumping – so loud. Anxiously. Impatiently. What would she say? What would I say? How would I greet her? If only my heart would not pound so loudly.

An interminable wait. Then I heard footsteps returning. Louder, coming closer, approaching the door. I turned, quickly moved back in centre-room. Elizabeth, at last! The door opened.

Into the room strode Mr MacKay himself. The same unsmiling man from our meetings aboard the *Black Swan*, stiff and coldly staring at me as before.

'Fraser! I was not expecting that we would meet again. Nor that you would come calling upon me in my home. Is there some matter requiring my official attention that has brought you here?'

Surprise tumbled my thoughts. 'Why no Sir. I trust that you and your daughter are well rested and recovered from your long and arduous voyage. (I rushed the explanation.) Your daughter Sir, the last time we met, kindly extended an invitation to call upon her when we were settled in Dunedin. It is to that invitation I am responding. I was hoping Sir – with your permission of course – to renew my acquaintance again with Miss Elizabeth.'

He looked at me, showing no visible emotion. 'That will not be possible, Fraser. You will not see my daughter.'

I stared directly back at him, waiting, the silence growing. I broke it: 'I'm sorry Sir, but I do not understand … is it that I will not see your daughter, or that Miss Elizabeth herself perhaps does not wish to see me…?'

'I assure you Fraser, as her father I am well able to speak for her. My daughter would definitely not want to meet with you again. You must have quite mistaken her Fraser! Obviously you have presumed too much from some casual conversation – in the confines and boredom of shipboard life you have allowed your wild imagination to overcome your reason'

'But definitely I…'

He cut in: 'You grossly over-reach your station Fraser, if you believed that my daughter would wish for your attention, let alone that I myself would sanction it.'

'I had reason to believe that Miss Elizabeth would welcome my visit today Sir … indeed she encouraged me to do so, or I should not otherwise have come. Perhaps Sir, you would be good enough to advise her that I am here in response to her kind invitation and wish to see her.'

His voice hardened further, 'You do not understand, Fraser! You are obviously unaware that my daughter is betrothed to marry Lieutenant Haile … and with my blessing!'

I stared. Stunned. His words ringing. Unsure if I had heard them or just imagined them. The impact still striking me, my mind resisting. Not wanting to have heard. Not believing that I had.

'Lieutenant Haile is of an excellent English family. He holds my daughter in the highest regard. I am in no doubt she will be well cared for, and I myself am pleased to grant him my permission to marry her.'

He took a step back, turned slightly away, visible signs our brief conversation was almost ended. Wild thoughts raced through my reeling mind. 'But what of Miss Elizabeth herself … what are her true feelings in the matter?'

He swung abruptly back to face me. 'You have no right to ask such questions! I've warned you Fraser, you over-reach yourself! It is only my sanction that is of any consequence! If you reasoned to believe – to grossly presume – that I would allow you, the abandoned son of a Highland blacksmith, to have paid court to my daughter, you are indeed very mistaken!'

I struggled to contain myself, wanting to attack him. Consumed by anger, I almost shouted at him. 'You MacKay…' I fought for breath, 'you should have stayed in England where you belonged! Not brought your prejudice to this Colony! We seek new beginnings here … a life free from the constraints – your old society, we chose to leave behind! Your notions of class, your archaic views, will not I hope be welcome here. And I for one will work to make that so!'

He drew himself up, tipping back his head, vainly trying to reach my height, his eyes level only with my chest. Shouted: 'This conversation is ended! Leave my house immediately!' He threw open the door from where he had entered, called out: 'Robertson, this man is leaving! Show him the door and see him from my premises!' He marched briskly away, stiff-backed, his boots pounding angrily on the floor.

I didn't wait. Stepped into the hallway. Through the front door. Stumbled down the steps, through the gate, into the street, just wanting to get away, heedless of the rain now falling from a leaden sky.

Elizabeth, my love, gone. My dreams, my plans destroyed. A life together never to be. I plunged down the street. How could it have happened? Somebody, somebody tell me that it isn't so. MacKay … he didn't like me from the outset … perhaps he's just driving me away!

I struggled to breathe. Bands like iron clamped themselves around my chest, suffocating me. A powerful pain grew deeply inside, crushing in on my heart itself. A great unseen weight pressed down on my shoulders. I staggered, struggling to walk straight, my sightless eyes seeing but images not registering. Aware that people were on the street about me, but not avoiding them. Rain soaking through my coat to unfeeling skin. Time stopped. Sounds unheard. I was in a void, a sightless silent void. The world about me receded to a nothingness.

Had darkness come? I was still stumbling, wandering aimlessly, caring not where my feet led me, untroubled by wet and cold. My soul, my life itself, seeming to drain from me. Pain replaced the anger – the tension. Waves of pain swept over me, leaving behind a tired remoteness, an exhaustion. A hopelessness. Effort failed me.

Somehow, unthinkingly, without conscious intent, I had reached the quay. The *Lady Colina* there before me. I climbed wearily down to her, almost fell, devoid of strength collapsed onto a seat, leaning against a water tank. My whole being imploded. Staring vacantly into the night, feeling nothing, hearing nothing, seeing nothing, thinking nothing.

I was aware that daylight slowly returned, but I had sat there unmoving and sleepless, the night through. It was as if I had withdrawn, retreated inside a glass sphere, knowing that life was there around me, but I was no longer part of it. As if from far off, I heard men hollowly calling down to me from the dock above, calling my name, asking of me, but they were outside the sphere, in another world beyond my reach. I could not respond, as if my life was ended, my soul itself had gone, only my body remained slumped here in the boat, separated from me.

I know not how long I was there. Time itself had no meaning. I stared vacantly out at the sea. Vacantly at anything. People came and went. Some spoke. Hearing vaguely as if from far away, not listening. I wanted them to go away, leave me alone.

The light began to fade. I was aware that George and Lucy were suddenly there, standing before me, anxious faces recognisable. Urgently they spoke, but I could not answer.

I could hear their words as if from down a long tunnel, understood they were appealing to me, Lucy in front holding tightly to my arm, George's hand on my shoulder. 'John, what is wrong? Please tell us, what is it … what has happened to you?'

I heard, but I could not reply. They were beyond my sphere, on the other side. I stared back, wanting to speak, to answer, but nothing came. Instead, tears suddenly poured uncontrolled from my eyes, spasms crushed my chest, and I leaned forward into Lucy's arms.

They helped me from the boat in the darkness, holding me by the arm on each side, led me blindly away from the quay. We sat together swaying in a gig through lantern-lit streets. To my room in the house that we shared. Lucy talking softly, but I was still locked away inside the sphere. George removed my wet clothes, my boots, laid me down on my bed, went away. I heard hushed whispers from far off.

Blissful silence returned. I lay staring upward into a blank black void. Perhaps I slept, perhaps not. In either state, the same blank void. No thoughts, no words, no images, nothing.

Daylight again. Lucy appeared. I smelled hot tea. For the moment, the sphere had gone, replaced with a deep crushing weariness. I was back in the world again, but not wanting to be. I felt thirst, some hunger even, startled that sensations had again returned.

'Are you feeling better John?' dear Lucy, 'I've brought you some tea'.

I just looked blankly at her, not sure that the power of speech was restored, not wanting to converse, to engage. She waited, clearly anxious, uncertain of me. Instead I reached to the bureau for some paper, shakily took a pen. Lucy watched. With a conscious effort of exhausted will, I wrote, not wanting to use her name: *SHE IS BETROTHED TO HAILE.*

Lucy stared at the paper, suddenly comprehending, turned and left the room.

For days I wanted to be alone. I rode my horse to the south of the town – a long stretch of low land between the hills of Dunedin and the hills of the peninsula enclosing the port. A flat desolate place of scrubland, marsh, swamp and sand exposed to the battering wind.

On the ocean side, I wandered the long deserted beach swept by tiers of great rolling waves driven from the open sea by southerly gales. Occasional seabirds were my only companions, sharing my loneliness.

Pain still swept my chest, weight still crushed upon my shoulders. On successive days, when I tired of the empty beach, I roamed the trackless dunes, plunged deeply in thought, trying to comprehend how I had lost her, what had happened….

It had been nearly two months since we had sailed south in the Atlantic, before turning eastward. As we entered the southern ocean, the colder, often-violent weather had kept the private-berth passengers confined to their quarters. In fact, on reflection, I had barely sighted them again until we had reached New Zealand.

In all that time, Elizabeth had shared the saloon, the library, the dining-table, with Haile: was probably in his company every day, in conversation, being entertained. MacKay himself would have shared the Captain's table with the Lieutenant, drank the Captain's port-wine together, smoked cigars convivially.

Haile would have impressed MacKay: his family well-placed in English society, a family of means; Haile himself, wealthy, well-educated, a purchased commission, a career-officer in the Guards. Obviously an excellent suitor and match for his daughter; a husband who would provide for her in comfort, confer immediate status in the colonial society.

By comparison, even if MacKay thought about it, what did he know of me? As he himself had flung at me, 'son of a Highland blacksmith', raised in Ireland by farmers, an articled tradesman without private means who would soil his hands in work; a man perhaps tainted by the French Revolution with thoughts of equality, fraternity with others quite outside his social level. Quite unsuitable for his daughter. A threat, to be dealt with….

But I also recalled Elizabeth's own words to me about her father, could hear again the sound of her voice saying them: 'My first duty is to him … to accord with his wishes.' At least twice she had appealed to me to be understanding of him, that he meant no malice, that I should not be dissuaded by his indifference toward me. Yet such malice he had shown.

Had I imagined her encouragement of me, her positive responses to my attention? How could I have mistaken that powerful indefinable 'something' that passed between us the first time we saw each other? And subsequently. I surely had not. So the only reasonable conclusion I could reach – though it brought no satisfaction nor eased my pain – was that Elizabeth had acquiesced to her father's wishes, was following his bidding, was doing what most well-bred young ladies would do – being ruled by her sensible head, rather than her unpredictable wild heart.

And thus I had lost. But the realisation as to why, only served to revive my old feelings of rejection, of not belonging, of being looked down-upon by the aristocracy of Warrington from above whilst being not accepted when I reached into the society below me. Perhaps then, this Colony was the best place to be, a new land of courageous independent people who had deliberately left England behind, wanting a new beginning where men were more likely to be judged on their human qualities, what they would achieve through their skill, daring and hard work, what they did for their fellows.

Another day, I rode the horse to the top of the hills southwest of town. Under a weak winter sun, I lay among the tall tussock grass. From there I could look out over the coastal plain along the south coast, over the swampy valley of the Taieri River, then westward inland to the convoluted rising moors of the Lammerlaw Range. In the far distance there was snow. Gazing out onto the great empty spaces, watching the light change on the hills beyond, seemed to restore some stolidity to my mind. Oh if only I could spread my anguish and sadness out even thinly over the vastness of the land before me, it could all be gone.

Lucy had sought out the MacKay's housemaid, had waylaid her in the street on pretext of enquiring after her shipboard friend Elizabeth. Miss Robertson had confirmed the betrothal, added that Lieutenant Haile was awaiting a sailing-ship to the northern island to fulfil his military duties to the Colonial Government: upon his return, however long that may require, he and Miss Elizabeth would duly be wed. To be told what I didn't want to hear, only pained me further.

I revisited the long lonely beach of St Clair. Wandering the sands with only the pounding surf accompanying me, I fought to lift myself out of this depression into which I had fallen, reasoning that the strength of purpose which had carried me thus far through my life, if applied to a constructive plan, would serve me again to rise above this tragedy. Only with such determination could I reclaim my life, find a new future.

I decided I could not remain here in this Colony. To do so meant a certainty that at some future time, if not many times, I would be confronted by the Lieutenant and his Mrs Haile, probably even with their children. To do so would be unbearable, would only reopen the wound. Even should a chance meeting be avoided, the knowledge of their presence together in the same town, the same province, the same country, would constantly remind me of what might have been. For years, some cold hand would come from somewhere – a word, their names, whatever – stroking the scar, reminding me it was still there. Surely, it was better to leave. Put it behind me … begin again.

It was now late June, the *Black Swan* was still in port, due to sail for Callao in Peru on the 7th of July and thence to California. Captain King had decided that in the event of armed insurrection by the southern States, his mixed-state crew would be safer on the west coast of America than the east. I decided to take passage upon her – then travel overland from Callao down through South America to the Argentine – find my other cousins who had been so successful there. Opportunity for an engineer must still abound.

Meantime, I would immediately seek a buyer for the *Lady Colina*. If a new owner had not been found by the time of my departure, surely George would continue the search for me through the shipping agents and the Harbourmaster. Parting with my new boat would be unfortunate, but should turn a good profit.

Such decisions made, strengthened me. I could feel some of the heavy weight lift from my shoulders. I felt able to discuss my plans with George and Lucy, who though understanding, were saddened by the thought that I would leave them, hopeful that one day I might return. It was our friendship that had brought me here, perhaps one day it would bring me back.

Still I had difficulty drawing myself away from my own sorrow, limiting conversation, avoiding contact with people. To pass my time, I took long rides on the roads north and south of the town.

The north road was steep and winding, barely more than a track, climbing up the rugged high hills that surrounded Dunedin to the north, picking its way around rocky spurs, through wet bush-filled gullies, before descending again down near the sea. Further north after lesser hills, the road divided, one to carry on northward, the other to branch directly inland. This inland road was quite well-travelled; apparently crossing more steep hills then opening out into a long high valley of the upper Taieri River. Some small finds of gold had been discovered there, and a number of diggers bored from waiting in the town or warned from excessive drinking in the many hotels, walked this road to prospect some more.

The south road was better-formed, even travelled by a Cobb & Co coach. Once over the hills to the south of the town, the road descended to a plain shielded from the salt-wind coast by a long range of hills. On one hill in the range, Saddle Hill, a seam of coal had recently been unearthed. Farms had been established on the fertile but wet flatlands along the lower Taieri River. Here the road divided: one branch turned inland, crossing the Taieri River westward at Wylies Crossing, then climbing up to the windswept moorland of the Lammerlaw Ranges and off into the vastness of central Otago Province; the other branch, continued southward. Passing several small swampy lakes, the south road reached the north bank of the Taieri River, crossed by a ferryman. Further south, was a larger lake, Lake Waihola. A small ferry also crossed this lake to the western shore, from which a horse-trail wandered from farm to isolated farm inland.

Otherwise, the south road skirted around the eastern shore of the lake, then climbed gradually through a long valley between coastal and inland ranges. Although I did not pursue it, I was told the road entered the valley of the Tokomairiro River, then eventually reached the north bank of the mighty Molyneaux – the mouth of which we had passed on the *Black Swan*. The river, probably the largest in the Colony, could be crossed with difficulty by a ferryman and was a formidable barrier to pass. There was a small hostelry on the north bank for travellers waiting to cross; on the south bank, the small settlement of Port Molyneaux also including a hostelry, was clustered near to a timbered wharf which formed a little port inside the estuary. Travellers could rejoin the coach or obtain horses on either side.

Beyond, the road turned inland to the southwest, thence to the valley of the Mataura River in the new province of Southland.

George advised that Mr Burns was discussing with several business colleagues in Dunedin the possible purchase of the *Lady Colina*. Apparently, the valley of the Molyneaux River had already been settled by a number of graziers and farmers, into some of its many lower tributaries, even far inland. But access was difficult, if not impossible. Most farms could only be reached on foot or by horse or bullock, along tortuous trails winding from farm to farm. Such was the size and velocity of the Molyneaux itself, there were as yet no boats that could navigate it beyond the estuarine stretches near the sea. Although supplies could be shipped by sea from Dunedin to the ferry-landings at the crossing, further distribution up the river was not yet possible.

Mr Burns and his associates believed the steam-powered screw-driven

Lady Colina, although not fast, might be sufficiently powerful to forge her way slowly up-river carrying supplies to the farms and out-stations along the way. If so, the prospects for business for he and his colleagues in Dunedin would improve. There was, for example, quite a demand for sheets of the corrugated iron imported from Belfast, but such sheets could only be carried to farms deeper west in Otago Province, strapped a few sheets at a time to a bullock or packhorse. Ploughs or other heavy farm machinery were almost impossible to transport.

Purchasing my boat and sailing her down to the Molyneaux for a trial was the only way to find out. They were debating the risk; she could always be brought back to Port Chalmers or modified as a coach-ferry across the Molyneaux, if the trial did not succeed.

I had revisited the *Black Swan* to discuss my passage to Peru with Nathaniel Greene. Back on board her, I was struck by the stale human-stench still coming from the quarters amid-ships and the fo'c'sle; living with it during our passage, we had ceased to notice. Captain King had had the ship slipped on the sand over several tides and a full repair had been made to her damaged sheathing. Fortunately, Nathaniel said that as there were no other passengers leaving for Callao (or America beyond), it was likely I would have the use of a private berth in the poop. The thought that I would be using the same quarters that Elizabeth herself had occupied would not rest with me easily. The *Black Swan* would carry only bags of sand as ballast with no cargo apart from some bales of wool.

June turned to July and I only had to wait another week. Dunedin was cold, dark, wet and gloomy, or else heavily frosted. I would not be sorry to leave the town or the painful memories of my brief visit here, far behind. Listless groups of diggers from New South Wales – deported Irishmen, released or escaped convicts, ex-whalers, even miners from the exhausted goldfields of California, wild men all – still wandered about the streets, frequently causing trouble with fights or drunkenness. Some had drifted off prospecting, others had left to join the militia being formed by the Governor in the far north. A regiment of Mounted Police was being formed to keep order in Dunedin – and beyond.

As I rode slowly through the town one morning, heading south again for a few hours' ride, I saw several men running in the street, stopping briefly when they came to others, gesticulating wildly, then running on. Others started up, rushing off to do the same. Some news or mischief was afoot.

I nudged my horse forward across into their path. Several men ran past, avoiding me, not looking or stopping, but one slowed, twisting round though still half-running. I leaned down toward him. He looked up, open-mouthed, eyes staring wildly. 'Stop!' I called. 'What is it man? Tell me what's happened?'

'Gold! Haven't you heard? They've found gold! The rush, it's started! Don't stop me!' and he ran on down the street.

I swung the horse back into the road the way I had come, back toward the centre of the town. Groups of men were still rushing in every direction. Making my way to the building where the Mining Commission was located, I saw a large mass of agitated men had gathered, some looking up at the closed front door, others talking excitedly, groups breaking hurriedly away. Horses and gigs at all angles blocked the street.

I dismounted outside the crowd, tethered my horse to a post, shouldering my way through the men pressing toward the door of the Commission. The door was firmly closed. A notice nailed to the door was being read by the man closest, who turned and shouted excerpts to the crowd that briefly quieted to hear him, then broke out again into a noisy babble.

'Gold at Tuapeka! A major discovery! It's genuine this time, he's brought back the gold! More than 100 ounces in just a few days! A Government prospector, Mr Read, he's claiming the reward! The field's open to any man who stakes a claim! The first diggers there will get the best paydirt!' He jumped from the step, the crowd opened and those around him surged away while others who had just arrived pressed forward.

As I returned to my horse, remounted and rode away southward again, I pondered what the discovery of gold would mean. Around me, the town seemed to be swept by some madness. Everywhere, determined-looking men were rushing about, some visibly excited, some waving, gesticulating frantically to others.

Almost every shop in the street seemed besieged as laden men struggled to get out against others trying to get in. I saw one group of men working on a small building, put down their tools and rush off up town. Others poured out from Jetty Street, emptying the taverns. Riders hurried past, their horses stacked haphazardly with gear. It seemed every man was in a race to be first out of the town.

Further south, the same urgency, but more determined order. Men, singly or in groups, most on foot but some mounted, all headed in the same direction. Most carried loads, some with bedrolls across their shoulders, tents or swags on their backs, pots or billies dangling, many carrying short-handled shovels in their hands or a panning-dish under an arm. Even at a distance, I could see long ragged lines of these men already strung out up the hilly south road. Those on horses were overtaking them. Closer, nobody was speaking as with heads down and backs leaning forward under their loads they strode away as if men possessed. I had heard tales of gold-fever before – now I was seeing men possessed by it with my own eyes.

EIGHT

At George's house that night, both he and Lucy – like most of Dunedin no doubt – were brimming with stories and rumours of the gold discovery and the events of the day which it had ignited.

Lucy's stories mostly related incidents in the town as men suddenly became miners, miners bought, seized, stole or fought for whatever stores they believed they needed before rushing off south. Some men had abandoned families; others had just walked off from their employment, all seized by the same madness. Regardless that it was now mid-winter, that there had already been some snowfalls with many more yet to come, the miners either intended to shelter in flimsy canvas tents or had no protection at all. To Lucy's amazement, a large number of men had set off southward with no apparent food supplies, trusting they could find or buy whatever they needed when they reached Tuapeka.

George, having been at Burns' offices all day, had been somewhat isolated whilst the town went mad. Some stories had trickled in with customers but he was now anxious about the new day lest Burns' had lost employees to the rush. He was however, enthusiastic about the effects that the discovery – if proven to be large – would have upon the town, the province, and his personal prospects in Mr Burns' business.

Late in the afternoon, Mr Burns had called George to his office, to ask if I might call upon him personally early the next morning to discuss a proposal for the *Lady Colina*.

George and I arrived together the next morning at Burns & Co, George taking me directly to the owners' office where we were both invited in. Mr Burns was a short stocky man, nearly bald but with a large bushy moustache meeting his beard on either side. His eyes were warm and his smile friendly. George introduced me.

'A pleasure to meet you Sir,' I said as we were offered chairs in front of his large desk.

'And you also Mr Fraser … indeed a pleasure to meet a cousin of Mr Bruce and of whose activities I have already heard so much.' I thanked him for generously allowing me to have stored my steam engine at his yard when we had first arrived, hoping that my employment of his engineers to install it had in some measure repaid him.

He quickly turned to the events of the previous day, providing us both with much more information than I had learned from my visit with the crowd to the office of the Gold Commission.

Mr Burns related that Thomas Gabriel Read, a prospector and explorer had arrived in Dunedin from Victoria, Australia in May. Read – with others – had been encouraged by the Provincial Council to investigate the many scattered small claims that had recently been reported and to prospect the southern country for gold or silver. Read had first travelled southwest into the Mataura Valley in the Province of Southland to investigate a reported discovery there, but only found isolated traces of gold along the banks of the Mataura River.

Intending to return later to prospect tributaries of the Mataura, Read had then returned back up the south road, recrossed the Molyneaux to the north bank, then made his way on foot north-west through the trackless land to the Tuapeka River where a find had been reported by an unreliable scoundrel named 'Black Peter'. Given that a number of so-called gold discoveries had proven to be false claims as a means of cheating desperate miners, Read had expected to find that Black Peter's report, like others, was also false.

He began by prospecting the lower reaches of the Tuapeka River, a tributary of the Molyneaux, starting at its confluence and working steadily upstream. Just as he had expected, mile after mile of the gravels yielded nothing. Read kept to the main flow, leaving side branches of the river until later.

A long way back from the Molyneaux, where the forested valleys of the Tuapeka closed in and the hills to the north dominated the skyline, the river flow had dwindled so much that the main course was no longer obvious. Forced to choose at a junction, Read chose the right branch because he happened to be already on the right bank. Not far up this gully, he stooped to wash sandy sediment from the tail end of a large pool surrounded by boulders. As the sand swilled from his gold-pan, he was amazed to see small pieces of dull gold appear around the edge of the sediment remaining.

Read quickly returned downstream, collected the two other men of his party who had set up an encampment and together the three of them worked at intervals up the small stream from his first sign. All along this gully they found gold. Although continuing to prospect along both banks rather than to work the most promising site, the three men recovered 112 ounces worth £431.

Gabriel Read was more concerned to have his name recorded for history as the discoverer of the first significant gold field in Otago than he was to make his fortune digging it. Staking out their claims – at 60 feet stream frontage by 24 feet deep per man – Read remained with one of his companions to dig whilst sending the third man, John Hardy – a Provincial Councillor, to Dunedin to report his discovery and lay claim to the Government reward.

Beginning on his long journey to Dunedin on foot, Hardy had stopped overnight at a small stone hut in a nearby gully, being recently settled for farming by a Mr and Mrs Wetherston. On being told of Read's gold discovery, Mrs Wetherston had taken a pan, gone down to the stream just below their cottage and excitedly returned as darkness fell with small pieces of gold in the palm of her hand. Obviously, Read's gully was not the only one in the region that contained gold.

Turning directly to me, Mr Burns said 'This goldfield could bring great wealth to our Province and our town Mr Fraser, if it proves its promise. There are fortunes to be made here, not just by the men who dig for it!' His eyes widened. He stared at me directly, intently.

'When Mr Bruce told me that you intended to resume your voyage to South America aboard the *Black Swan* – that your intriguing steamboat was for sale – some business associates and I discussed purchasing it. For some time, we have been interested in the prospects for developing commerce in the valley of the Molyneaux with its becoming settled by farmers, but there is not a vessel capable of forcing the river, let alone carrying a cargo. As you may know, the Superintendent of the Otago Assembly owns the coastal screw-steamer *Queen* which can enter Port Molyneaux but not the river itself. We speculated that your boat may be such a vessel for the river and were willing to risk an investment in purchasing it, to find out.

'It is said that more than a thousand men left the town yesterday for the goldfield. I myself may have lost men from my employ, lured away by the chance strike it rich. A thousand men Mr Fraser, need a vast amount of provisions – stores, liquor, equipment, materials for shelters. If Read's gully is indeed a rich find, those men will have a lot of gold to pay for all their needs!

'There is no way to get all that cargo to Tuapeka, Mr Fraser. Although in a straight line it is probably only 40 miles from here, it is a difficult journey. As you may have already learned, there are no roads. First you must cross the long lake Waihola by boat. Then there are only walking tracks, leading inland, fording the Tokomairiro River, thence over steep ranges, winding their way from remote farm to farm. By horseback, the bridle trail must pass south of the lake, then thread through a formidable maze of swamps before reaching the hills and the walking tracks. Gabriel Read's man Hardy, himself took many days to get back here to report his discovery.

'Without food supplies, most of the diggers will have to abandon the goldfield, or starve. If it snows, without proper shelters they will die of cold.

'But there might be a way to get goods to them, Mr Fraser. The Tuapeka River is a northern tributary of the Molyneaux. The Molyneaux itself is known to be navigable upriver well beyond the Tuapeka. If your vessel can force the passage of the Molyneaux, there is money to be made here Mr Fraser!

'If it can, my business associates and I can ship all the provisions and equipment for the goldfield by the small steamer *Queen* from Port Chalmers to Port Molyneaux. Your boat can transport it up the river to a landing at the confluence of the Tuapeka or further upriver at Beaumont's landing. We will build a store there. It is only a short distance by bullock or packhorse either up the valley of the Tuapeka or over the hills from Beaumont to the goldfield in Gabriels' Gully.

'I can see opportunity Mr Fraser – for you and for us! If all that I surmise comes to pass, there will be much to be done here! My colleagues and I will need to organise almost immediately. We will have no time to spend owning your boat, crewing it, operating it. We need you yourself to do that Fraser. And you can share in the wealth such an opportunity will derive.'

Mr Burns paused for breath. I waited, his comments swirling in my mind, implications of such a venture spilling over each other. When next he spoke, he addressed us both, continually turning from me to George and back.

'There is no time to lose. We need a decision from you now Fraser! Delay your departure from this Colony! If the goldfield is proven, there will be other ships, many ships, coming to Port Chalmers and then on to England around the Horn, stopping at Buenos Airies in Argentina en route: you will be able to resume your voyage at any time, should you wish to do so.

'Meantime, we can all make some money. To help you decide, my colleagues and I are willing to charter you and your vessel to sail from here to the Molyneaux, then to try forcing the river. If you succeed, pay a rider to bring us the word. We will ship stores to Port Molyneaux by the steamer *Queen* immediately, as soon as the weather allows, and together we will be in the business.

'If your cousin listens to your advice Mr Bruce, I appeal to you to impress upon him for me that he has not much to risk – only a delay to his departure for Argentina – but an untold opportunity if he can succeed! I shall leave you both alone in my office for a short period to confer. When I return Mr Fraser, I need your answer to my proposal!'

He left. I sat in silence, thinking. George pleaded with me to accept, hoping that I would stay with he and Lucy in the Province. Even Harry, dear cousin Harry who was up in the northern island, might come south to join us. He emphasised the financial opportunity the venture might prove to be for me. That there would be other ships on which I could travel to Argentina, if later I chose so to do. That in reality I had little to lose. All were true.

But I deeply grieved over my loss of Elizabeth; was only just beginning to lift myself from my depression by resolving to leave, my departure imminent. Only by leaving (I had thought), could I better put her from my mind and avoid being reminded of what might have been, find a new life to replace that of which I had dreamed, now lost. But then if I stayed, this venture would at least take me away from Dunedin. I would have no need to return to this town. What new directions might open to me with the goldfield? The venture itself would provide some immediate distractions. And if I could not shed the pain, forget lost love, or the venture fail, I need only wait for another ship which could take me directly to Argentina, perhaps even arriving there sooner than if I had travelled overland from Peru. Indeed, Mr Burns was correct, there was little to lose.

I heard heavy footsteps returning. George stood, looked at me expectantly. The door opened and Mr Burns looked to me smiling hopefully, the corners of his eyes crinkling. He stood still holding the door.

'Well Fraser, what is your decision, will you join us or must we buy your boat?'

I breathed deeply … sighed … somewhat resignedly. 'Very well Mr Burns, let us try! But before I do, can we agree on a sum for my boat should she not overcome the Molyneaux and I return her to Port Chalmers?'

He laughed. He reached for and shook my hand vigorously. 'A good decision – my colleagues will be pleased you will join us! I am confident you will succeed and not regret this day.' George grinned elatedly.

He paused, serious again. 'With regard to your boat – I should have known a true Scot would drive for such a bargain. I will back my confidence Fraser – I'll wager £250 for your vessel should she fail, unless you can better that sum.'

I agreed, hiding my elation that my cost was more than covered. There was now no time to lose – Mr Burns hopeful that I could depart from the port this same day. I took leave of them both, returned into the town, mindful as I went that I could not manage the *Lady Colina* alone. To enter the Molyneaux, then navigate the river, I needed an experienced boatman. But with so many men having left town in the rush for the goldfield, it was unlikely I would find such a man.

That was confirmed at each place I hurriedly visited: the Harbourmaster, nobody; the shipping agents shook their heads, smiling; the taverns in Jetty Street, empty. Nobody. Then spurred by desperation I remembered – Daniel Ellison! Probably he too left in the rush? If not, where would I find him? Would he suffice? He had claimed experience at sea, was still actually employed on the pilot boat. I retraced my steps, asking in each place was he known, leaving word that I was seeking him or any other experienced boatman willing to join me.

Until I could find a deckhand to go with me, I could not depart, but at least meantime I could prepare. First, I loaded the *Lady Colina* with extra cans of fresh water for the boiler, filling the two coal bunkers and stacking further sacks of coal against them. Provisions of porridge, salt, dry cheese, a side of bacon, potted meat, flour and some cooking utensils were stowed for'ard in boxes under the foredeck. Several sheets of corrugated iron from Burns & Co that had come with us on the *Black*

Swan were secured across the deck in front of the engine.

Then in the town I unsuccessfully tried to buy some canvas for a tent-fly, but every piece of shelter had already left with the miners. At least I did have some iron. I also managed to find a hand-drawn map of the country from Dunedin to the Molyneaux (with many areas blank) and a copy of an early chart of the southeastern coast.

Very mindful of the cut-throats and ex-convicts who until yesterday had been aimlessly roaming the town but were now on their way into a wilderness without adequate food or shelter, I decided to buy some arms for protection. One general merchant in Princes Street was also a gunsmith, from whom I purchased at great expense a new Westley-Richards breech-loading carbine and a Beaumont Adams six-shot .44 calibre revolver, with ammunition in steel boxes for both weapons. The carbine came in a leather scabbard suitable for horseback, the revolver with a leather flap-holster that could be fitted to a belt.

A cold drizzle began to fall from the clouds low over the town, so I returned to secure the boat. As I approached, the figure of a man who was already aboard her rose up from the seating aft. A prospective deckhand perhaps? A heavily-bearded man with long hair…a dark-skinned man. The native, Ellison … Erihana!

He greeted me, his face impassive. ' You are seeking me Mr Fraser. I have come. You have some work for me?'

I explained, using simple words – not knowing if he understood much English – that I could offer him payment for one week if he would accompany me to Port Molyneaux, then attempt to travel up-river. If we succeeded, then more work would follow but if we failed, I would return him to Dunedin with me. As I spoke, he looked at the ground near my feet, then slowly nodded his head. I felt uneasy, unsure how to converse with an aborigine, especially when he would not look directly at me as I spoke nor indicate that he understood.

'We will go. This river you call Molyneaux Mr Fraser, is a river of my people we call Matau, our way to the land of *pounamu*. We know this river from Murikauhaka at the sea to its birthplace where the land reaches to the sky.'

I did not understand some of what he said, but it sounded helpful. I continued to explain that the *Lady Colina* was prepared, that I was ready to leave, intending to steam out through the sound to the entrance into the open sea, then shelter at anchor for suitable weather and daylight for the voyage to Port Molyneaux.

He nodded seriously. 'You are ready now? – Then we go!' I noted that he carried nothing, had only a coat, shirt, and worn moleskin trousers frayed at the cuffs. His feet were still bare.

I asked him to wait for me while I returned to the Bruce's for my clothes and bedroll, said goodbye to Lucy, then after leaving my horse at the stables took a gig back to the quay. The rain had stopped, the sky breaking to the south. I estimated there was still just sufficient daylight to allow for firing up the boiler and steaming up the sound toward the entrance. If we did not reach there when evening fell, at least we would be well-positioned for the next day.

Getting steam pressure up in the little boiler seemed to take most of the afternoon. Erihana seemed to know about firing the boiler to its operating pressure from his work on the pilot-boat. Visibly he had more patience than did I during the long wait. Finally, I closed the valve, the piston began driving and we untied the *Lady Colina* from the quay. Although still lined with other small ships, the quay was empty; there was nobody to see us leave as I turned her away, pointing the bow down the harbour.

It took us longer than I expected to reach the two islands that nearly blocked the channel at Port Chalmers, but with Erihana at the bow directing me, we successfully navigated between them into the wider half of the harbour leading toward the open sea. With such short days in midwinter, darkness soon began to fall before we had reached the harbour entrance, which even in the fading light I could see was not far-distant. Erihana who seemed to know the coast of the sound well, directed me to a small tree-lined cove on the southern shore with deep water in close where we would be sheltered for the night. With at least most of the journey down the sound behind us, I was satisfied that we were well-positioned to cover the distance to Port Molyneaux next day.

Very conscious of the stories I had heard about the perfidy and savagery of the aborigines of New Zealand, who until recently – perhaps even still – were vicious cannibals who ate the flesh and body parts of slain enemies including white men, keeping their smoked heads as trophies, I was quite apprehensive of a night aboard *Lady Colina* with a native whom I did not know. Although Erihana dressed in some European clothes, spoke some English, had taken or been given the European name Daniel Ellison, claimed to have been to sea with whalers, he was still a brown-skinned native who might attack me to steal my boat during the night.

However, wrapping himself in a blanket, he was soon curled up on the floor in the stern apparently asleep. For several hours, I sat up by the warmth of the boiler, loaded revolver in my hand, listening to the sounds of the night, watchful in case he should stir, trying to push painful visions of Elizabeth from returning to my mind again. But all remained quiet except for the lapping of ripples against the side of the boat as I too drifted to sleep, waking frequently through the night at the slightest sense of movement to check on my companion huddled aft. I kept hold of the revolver in my lap, hidden beneath a blanket.

Daylight returned with a wind from the south. Although we were well-sheltered by the peninsula, I could clearly see lines of large waves marching past the entrance to the harbour eastward. The speed of clouds appearing from the south over the hills of the peninsula quickly convinced me we would not be continuing our journey this day.

Erihana unrolled from his blanket, looked at the sea and the sky, looked toward me. I shook my head, said that we must wait until the wind had passed before we could enter the open sea. I needed food and water, but as I took bacon from the front hold, Erihana stopped me.

'We go to the land Mr Fraser. Water is deep here, your boat can go very close. You make a fire, I get food from the sea!'

With the anchor at the stern, we paddled the boat closer to shore with oars until Erihana dropped off the bow onto the steep beach, taking a rope to a nearby tree. When we were fast, I was able to lower off the bow into knee-deep icy water, then onto the beach of tiny smooth stones. While I gathered driftwood from above the tide line for a fire, Erihana stripped off all his clothes, producing a concealed knife from inside his belt in the process. Then seemingly oblivious to the cold, he walked into the sea where rocks ended our short beach.

Though even at knee-depth the intense cold of the sea had made me gasp, to my surprise Erihana now began to swim along the shoreline close to the rocks, stopping every few yards, then swimming on, sometimes disappearing momentarily completely submerged. He appeared completely immune to the near-freezing cold water. Each time he stopped, I saw that he threw objects up onto the rocks. After some 15 minutes I saw him returning, swimming powerfully through the water back to the beach. I watched in admiration – the first time I had seen anything other than a fish swimming in water, let alone a man.

While I struggled to get damp wood to burn, Erihana dressed again, then climbed barefoot around the rocky shoreline where earlier he had swum. He came back carrying in both arms, a pile of what appeared to be large plate-sized round stones. When he dumped these onto the shingle by the fire, I saw they were not stones but some type of giant shell-covered limpet with a rough grey stone-like coating over the rounded outer surface. The flat inner surface was fleshy, alive, slowly moving but shapeless, black and slimy-looking.

Once the fire was burning well, I followed Erihana's lead, arranging the limpets flesh-side uppermost in the embers against the smouldering wood. We sat in silence, watching them stop squirming, then steaming around the edge of the shell as they slowly cooked in their own liquid, while we poked the fire with sticks to keep the grey ash from smothering the flame.

I climbed back aboard the *Lady Colina*, collecting a billy of fresh water to boil on the fire for tea and some porridge in case the limpets proved to be as inedible as they appeared unpleasant. By the time I was back ashore, Erihana was already scooping around the edge of a limpet – '*paua*' he called them – with his knife, freeing the steaming cooked flesh from its shell. Holding the ugly black mass speared through the centre with his knife, he bit into the black part of it, tearing off pieces with his teeth. I picked up the large empty shell to examine, amazed at the beauty of the smooth interior, a magnificent glistening pattern of swirling blue-green-black iridescence, the colours changing as I tilted it in different directions to the light.

The beauty of the shell encouraged me to try eating one of the shellfish myself, despite its unappetising appearance. I copied Erihana (who was now eating his third), cutting around the perimeter of the hot shell, stabbing the lump of black flesh through the centre with my knife, then taking a tentative bite into the black meat. It had strong but not unpleasant fishy taste with quite tough chewy meat.

Erihana, pushing another from the fire with a stick was watching me without looking at me directly, waiting for my reaction. 'It is good, eh, Mr Fraser?' I nodded, mouth full with a chewy piece, and for the first time since we had met on the Dunedin shore, I saw him smile. As I had seen Erihana doing, I ate only the black meat of the shellfish, throwing the remainder containing the gut back into the fire. When we had eaten all the paua, I chose two of the most colourful shells to keep. I lay back on the pebbly beach drinking brewed tea to wash away the strong aftertaste, thinking that such a feast in such an attractive cove was some compensation for losing a day of our voyage.

Erihana disappeared into the low bush on the hillside behind the cove. I waited with growing apprehension until he returned some hours later. He said nothing of where he had been or why. The wind kept blowing without change. I lay on the beach in patches of weak winter sun watching the pattern of passing clouds against the sky.

A sudden shout from Erihana startled me upright, to see a him waving to a long thin boat being paddled by several natives, now making quickly toward us. I chose the moment to return to the *Lady Colina*, ostensibly to adjust our moorings now that the tide was rising but really for the security of my guns, not knowing if these Maori with such a fearsome reputation, who now out-numbered me five-to-one, could be trusted. I laid the carbine on the seat out of sight below the gunwhale then slung the revolver in its holster behind my back.

I moved about in the boat to give the appearance of being busy while I watched the natives beach their hollowed-out log canoe and all leap ashore. Three were dressed in European clothes of shirt and breeches, the fourth wrapped in a large blanket fastened at the neck in front. All were barefoot.

They appeared to know Erihana, approaching him with smiles and talk in their language, putting their faces against each other in some form of greeting. For several hours while I stayed watchfully on the *Lady Colina*, they squatted or sat by the fire on the beach. Apart from some glances toward me when they had first arrived, I was otherwise ignored; from their hand-movements and position it seemed they were deeply involved in discussion. Then abruptly they rose, the visitors pushed their canoe into the water, resumed their places with paddles in hand, quickly vanishing around the corner of the cove in the direction of the entrance.

In response to my questions, Erihana said that the men had come from a native settlement just inside the harbour entrance beneath a mountain called Taiaroa which dominated the end of the peninsula. The people, who survived mostly by fishing, were the remnants of a previously much larger community which had suffered from disease and hunger. Many people including children had died. The people of the church in Dunedin were helping the natives by giving them clothes and building materials to better protect them from the wet and cold, but the natives were concerned that the white settlers really wanted to take their land on the peninsula for new farms. For that reason, the natives had remained in their settlement despite the hardship, sure that if they abandoned it, their right to the land would be lost. Although Erihana knew the natives in this settlement, he himself did not belong with them.

It was the longest conversation I had had with Erihana who until now had kept himself quite withdrawn, speaking rarely. Throughout his explanation his face had shown no emotion; just his eyes, looking down, not at me, almost sadly downcast.

Brief as my contact with the natives was to this point, I began to feel a little less threatened by them. Erihana himself seemed to have some presence or stature about him which I had noticed the first time we had met. The men in the canoe appeared to have come to consult with him. It struck me that these men had come purposefully into our cove as if they knew we were there; that when Erihana himself had arrived across the mudflat to my boat the first time we met – and again when I found him waiting for me at the quay only yesterday, he knew I would be there. Perhaps, I mused, these people had some strange perceptive sense, a forewarning or awareness, otherwise how had they known?

The afternoon passed. The wind kept blowing clouds over the peninsula. We spent another night huddled under our blankets in the moored boat, thankful it was not raining.

At dawn next morning, the silence told me that the wind had stopped. I set the fire in the boiler immediately – while Erihana still lay curled in his blanket – anxious that we make an early venture to the open sea, hopeful that we could head south to the Molyneaux. When steam pressure was eventually reached after an impatient wait, we paddled the bow around and headed down harbour, soon passing to starboard the small native village at Taiaroa Head with several canoes drawn up on the shore from where our visitors had come the previous day.

Against the lightening sky I could see long evenly-spaced swells moving steadily from the south but though quite high, the crests were not steep, nor the ocean rough. In their regularity in the silver-grey light of early morning they looked like giant even furrows in the sea. As we rounded the head to the steady beat-hiss of the steam engine, I was confident that the *Lady Colina* could sail safely in the conditions provided the wind did not rise again.

We rose up the long sloping face of the first large swell effortlessly, over its rounded crest, then surged down the slope toward the almost-level trough. I stood aft on the port side, steering the tiller with my right hand. Erihana waited by the boiler ready to shovel in more coal if the steam pressure should lower. Brown smoke from the stack trailed back over me but I cared not, exhilarated by the breeze on my face, the lively motion of the boat beneath my feet, the even beat of the engine and anticipation of the voyage ahead.

After passing the most-eastward projection of Cape Saunders on the peninsula we sailed our way steadily south quite some distance out to sea. The coast to our starboard swung in a long sweeping curve westward away from our direct line south, then gradually came toward us again as our line slowly closed with the shore around midday. While Erihana took the tiller, I prepared a meal for us of potted meat with slabs of bread washed down with tea from water heated on the stack.

At mid afternoon we passed by the clearly visible mouth of a large river which I identified on the chart as the Tokomairiro (confirmed by Erihana), the river carving a wide cleft in the high beach and surrounded by wheeling white flocks of gulls. I knew that the Molyneaux was now not far to the south ahead of us.

As we progressed, I could see steadily rising on the southern horizon the long eastward shape of a projection of land which Erihana pointed toward, calling 'Kaimataitai'. On my chart, this was probably Nugget Point on the south side of Molyneaux Bay. Although it did not appear far off, I was anxious that we make Molyneaux mouth in daylight lest we have to stand off in the open sea through a precarious long night.

Fortunately, by late afternoon we arrived off the first mouth of the Molyneaux. Without the chart I would not have known there were two mouths of the river, but Erihana explained this was the Matau, the lagooned smaller northern mouth; the larger mouth of the Koau was still several miles to the south. The two rivers were separate branches of the Molyneaux, merging together again into one some miles inland from the sea. Port Molyneaux was on the deeper Koau branch.

Lines of whiter breaking waves inshore marked a wide sandbar on the southern side of the Koau mouth as we approached in light which was now beginning to fade. The entrance itself was clearly visible, facing northeastward toward us as we steered closer.

'The channel, Mr Fraser – the flat water over there!' Erihana shouted, pointing to an area of less-disturbed water at 45 degrees to the shoreline.

I aimed the *Lady Colina* directly at the long stretch of calmer water on the northern side, the breaking waves of the bar piling up on the southern side. As we ran in, the breakers towered above to port, threatening to collapse over on top of us, then dissipating as they were caught by the force of the water in the channel running out from the river. What had looked apparently like calmer water from seaward was in fact a long stretch of fast-flowing water coming out through the mouth, pressed up into rows of short steep pressure-waves by the force of the current.

We surged up and down struggling to make any headway with the steam-valve fully closed, the piston hissing bursts of steam and the screw thumping loudly beneath my feet. There was no time to think of fear, only concentration to keep us on line. Locked in the grip of the current with the crash of rollers on the bar close by us and unable to make any forward progress against the rip, I swung the boat diagonally from side to side across the channel, trying to gain forward speed by angling in both directions instead of taking the current directly onto the bow. Tossed about by the pressure waves and fighting to hold the tiller against the rip, I sensed rather than saw that at last we seemed to be moving upstream.

Suddenly we were surrounded by a patch of calmer water and I could see that we had made inside the bar, through the mouth into a wider smooth estuary. Erihana moved quickly to the bow, prominently indicating with either arm where he thought the best channel appeared to lie. Two days since we had left Dunedin – and at last we were on the Molyneaux!

We forged on upriver, anxious to reach Port Molyneaux itself before darkness forced us to find an anchorage. Then just as I was deciding we must find a suitable place to moor against the bank for the night, I was relieved to see some lights ahead on the left shore. Erihana directed us in toward a long pier of logs lining the bank, I eased back on the valve and we had soon made fast.

The port seemed empty, silent, only the pale light I had seen from the river as we approached showing that some habitation was occupied. Erihana had been here before, telling me that there were several wooden houses set back from the pier at the beginning of a road leading inland, one of which provided lodgings. Just upstream on the same bank was the native village Murikauhaka whose people he did not know.

I climbed ashore, leaving Erihana aboard *Lady Colina* curled up in blankets near the still-hot boiler with instructions to tend it during the night so that we could make an early start when daylight returned next morning. Warmth from the boiler on this freezing night was an incentive to ensure the fire remained stoked.

The surprised owner of the lodging-house, a Mr Bissett, who had not heard our arrival in the near-dark, welcomed me to his fire, only too pleased to provide me with a bed for the night for a small fee. He was now alone in the port, the other few European inhabitants having departed immediately on hearing news of the gold find. Only the handicap of an injured leg had prevented him from joining them.

Concerned about our enterprise, I asked how any visiting ship would cope with unloading or loading cargo, should that need arise in the absence of the departed men, but he assured me that natives from the village nearby could generally be persuaded to provide their labour. I then explained the purpose of my visit to the port and our intention to attempt navigation of the river, learning from him that the water flow in the river was now at its lowest period of the year. In mid-winter, the massive inland mountains – the source of the whole river system – were heavily covered in snow and the intense cold froze solid any water which might otherwise have fed into the river itself. No rain fell in the mountains, only snow. Until the thaw came in the spring, the Molyneaux would remain at low levels.

This, Bissett explained, was both advantageous and disadvantageous. On one hand, the river flowed slowly, the currents more gentle; on the other, the shallows were more frequent, the navigation more difficult for my boat with its screw at risk of striking rocks which bestrewed the riverbed. Also, he pointed out thoughtfully, unless *Lady Colina* easily forced the river at its present low flows, it would not be sufficiently powerful to force it when fast currents returned again in the spring.

In the morning, well-rested and fed I returned to the pier as the sky lightened in the east, carrying a hot pannikin of food for Erihana who showed no apparent gratitude, taking it from my proffered hands as if it were expected of me. With the boiler already still burning dully, some fresh wood and coal soon had the steam-pressure rising. I sat watching the sky becoming brighter, impatient that although we had reached sufficient power to leave, we needed better light in which to navigate the shallows that were surely ahead.

When I felt more confident that we could see effectively, we cast off, leaving a watchful Bissett standing on the pier. At least I knew from his description that the first winding section of the river was easily navigable beyond its junction with the northern Matau branch, nearly up to the ferry-landing of the north-south road.

The darkened water reflected the first grey clouds as we surged along on the smooth wide river, low tree-lined banks on both sides. The river swung slowly back and forth in wide sweeping curves, with rolling hills off to both north and south. As we rounded each slow bend I expected to see some new scene revealed but mile after mile passed by without change until we reached the obvious junction of the northern Matau branch, marked by a strip of rising ground on the right bank. As we passed by, well to the left side, I judged that the Matau carried only a quarter – at most a third – of the total volume of the river.

Now that the river was as a whole, currents were clearly visible. The balanced V-shape of our wake no longer stretched aft to reach from bank to bank as it merged into the current. Erihana took up a position at the bow, beginning to indicate with either arm the best directions to steer the boat which still forged ahead quite effortlessly, even with boiler pressure at its lower operating levels. The regular thump of the piston and the hiss of steam escaping at the end of the stroke were the only sounds.

Erihana held his hand high, signalling a course in mid-channel as we rounded another long left-curving sweep of the faster-flowing river. Suddenly on the short straight ahead I saw a movement on the left bank, men on a small jetty crowding in a solid mass back on the land behind. At the moment I saw them, I could also see a boat across the river at another jetty on the right bank from which men were climbing ashore. The north-south ferry landings. A loud shout went up, a roar, a mass of waving hands from the south side. Was something wrong?

As we approached, I swung *Lady Colina* closer to the noisy throng at the southern jetty. More than a hundred men thronged the shore, calling, pushing, jostling, waving to us, threatening to tip the men already on the small jetty into the river. Other men appeared, running from among low trees behind, drawn by the noise to join the crowd. Those on the north bank had all stopped still, turning back at the noise to watch us.

I eased the valve back, slowing us almost to the speed of the current until we held level with the end of the jetty, gradually creeping us closer. The noise of shouting reduced. The huge crowd was mostly stilled. Voices called out 'Take us across! Take us across! There's money to take us across!

Come and get us!'

Isolated on our voyage from Dunedin for three days, it had been easy to forget that men all over the province, seized by the prospect of finding easy riches, were still rushing in a wave of madness to the new goldfield. This huge crowd of men on the land beside us must have been drawn up from the south, overwhelming the capacity of the ferry to transport them across to the northern bank.

As I swung us carefully closer, a group of men at the end of the small jetty turned around, lashing out with fists at the men pressing them from behind. Several fell into the river on both sides as the men at the jetty's end, shouting and cursing, drove into the mob behind with a hail of punches. An uproar in every direction. Stones and pieces of wood being thrown through the air. Erihana and I watched the struggle in amazement, keeping well clear out on the river.

Gradually, the small group on the jetty prevailed, forcing the others back off the short jetty onto the land. One particular man, his back to us, fists pumping, stood out clearly, his head and shoulders towering above the others. A giant driving the mob before him.

The jetty was narrow – the width of three or four men standing shoulder to shoulder. Now that the crowd had retreated onto the land, these men still with their backs to us, looked to be holding the jetty, preventing any others from boarding it. The shouting receded – the sticks and stones stopped flying. The giant turned around toward us, called out: 'Take us across Mister! I'll pay you well!'

I cupped a hand, shouted back: 'We're not going *across* the river! We're going *up* it!'

'All the better! Take us with you. I'll make it well worth your while – whatever you ask! Help us please – you won't regret it.'

I held us there out in the river, hesitating, thinking. No need for us to complicate our attempt on the river with passengers, nor their weight. Besides, this giant and his men could overpower us, seize our boat. But some extra hands could be useful as would the money. They couldn't sail the boat without me. However far upriver we could get, I could put them onto the north bank, be paid for carrying them.

'How many of you?'

'Four, with our swags.'

'Five pounds a man in advance? '

I could see him grin. 'Done! I'll pay. Just get us off here!'

I moved the tiller slightly. We drifted closer. 'Five pounds for however far I can take you. I'll put you on the north bank!'

'Agreed! Get us off or this mob will rush us!'

I held the tiller with my left hand. Felt for the comfort of my revolver in its holster. Pulled it round just by my right hand, clearly in view. Called Erihana quickly back aft beside me. Shouted to the giant on the jetty: 'I'll come alongside. Jump on the foredeck when you can. Then stay there! Don't move 'till I tell you!'

The giant waved a hand in acknowledgement as he turned quickly back to join his three men holding the end of the jetty. I saw him seize a length of wood like a shovel handle, waving it wildly in the air, menacingly.

The crowd stood back, watching, silent. I swung the tiller gently then straightened up as the boat moved within a yard of the end of the jetty, holding against the current. Two of the four men quickly pulled back, came down the jetty towards us, jumped with a thump onto the foredeck and crouched down with their swags.

Nobody in the crowd of men on the land moved. Not even as the giant, still facing them dangerously swinging his stave, backed along the jetty toward us. The third man turned, jumped onto the deck. The giant took the last few steps backward toward us, glanced over his shoulder and in one quick movement dropped his stave, leapt onto the deck with a crash, nearly falling over the side and was grabbed by his companions as I pushed the tiller hard over. We swung away out into the river as Erihana closed the valve for more power and we surged forward.

NINE

Across the river, I saw the ferryboat returning empty toward the jetty as the crowd again surged onto it, then we were leaving them behind. The men stayed huddled together with their gear, but the giant kneeling, called aft to me: 'Good work boatman. That was getting nasty – I thought it was either a fight, or into the river.'

He grinned, teeth showing through a mass of black beard which spread up the sides of his face to become one with a thatch of black hair. I called back to him over the noise of the engine, 'You can come aft here now if you like, but the others stay there.' I grinned too, 'And bring your money!'

He unravelled himself from the deck and I could see fully just how big he was, at least six feet five or six, with broad sloping shoulders to match, long arms hanging down to the top of his knee-boots. I turned slightly to be sure he could see my revolver as Erihana moved aside to let him pass when he stepped down off the deck into the boat. He swung past the engine toward me, smiling through large dark eyes, holding an enormous hand out, it's back thick with dark hair. I was instantly aware that he was the first man I had encountered in a long time who was taller than me, as consciously I looked up at him.

'M'name's Fox, Irishman.'

'I'm John Cameron Fraser,' I said as I gripped his hand tightly, 'and I'm neither Irish – nor the boatman. I own this ship you're on.' We stared directly at each other for a moment, measuringly.

'Jesus Christ.'

I started at his sudden blasphemy, 'What's wrong?'

He grinned again. 'Oh, nothing – it's your initials, 'JC'. And your appearing from nowhere was an answer to a prayer itself. So where are you bound upriver? – we're off to Gabriel's goldfield, though I thought for a moment those bastards were going to have us, back there.'

'We'll go as far up the river as we can navigate, Mr Fox. We'll be pleased if it's close to the goldfield, for that's our intention. And this is my boatman, Daniel Ellison,' I said, indicating with my hand toward Erihana, 'and my bosun and navigator.'

Fox just ignored him. Erihana turned stiffly away. 'Those men in my party up there, we've come from the south at Mataura. There's no worthwhile gold there. We came north when we heard of Gabriel's find but there was a rush. We all ended up at the river, hundreds of us. We've been there two days, waiting to be ferried across. It was getting violent, – all those men held up on the south bank of this damned river knowing that whoever gets to the field first, gets the best ground. We were nearly next on the ferry, then you came along. A bloody miracle, I call it, JC.

'So here's your money, and I'm pleased to give it to you,' as he fumbled with both hands at a leather pouch, placing the sovereigns into my hand.

I hurriedly directed Erihana to take up his station on the bow, suddenly aware that we were forging upriver without clear directions, the screw beneath our feet pounding away and needing at least half a fathom of water below to avoid striking the bottom. I concentrated on watching Erihana's indicating arm, talking again to Fox.

'While on this boat Mr Fox there are some instructions you must follow. You and your men will do exactly what I tell you. Stow your swags under the deck. Two of you will stay for'ard, no more than two can be aft at any time. You'll keep out of my way – I must have a clear view of my navigator at all times.

'Provisions and feeding yourselves is your own concern. I judge that it's forty to fifty miles up this river to the vicinity of the goldfield. If we can navigate the river all the way it will take us at least two days, perhaps more. If we're still making our way upriver tonight, I will stop in daylight when I can find deep water close in to the bank. You and your party will sleep ashore; Daniel and I will stay on the boat.

'If we run aground or we're in shallows, I'll need all of you instantly over the side in the river to push us clear – otherwise Mr Fox, your journey might have to continue on foot. But if we find an impassable barrier in the river, I will put you all ashore on the north bank at whatever point we have reached. Meantime, I will also get your help to keep the boiler stoked with coal – Daniel will show you how when he comes down off the bow.

'Now Mr Fox, relay what I have said to your men, then any two of you can come aft here with me.'

He looked down at me, his dark eyes steady under the black eyebrows. 'Very well, JC, if you get us to the goldfield, or even close to it, we'll be indebted to you. And the name's 'Fox', not "Mr" Fox.' I was watching Erihana, responding to his directions as he indicated the channel following a long curve to the left close by a steeper sandy bank. Fox pointed for'ard: 'My mates up there, that's "Gray" on the left, James McLeod and Dusty Brown.'

The river was winding through a wide valley of rolling brown hills with higher ground visible in the distance toward the northwest. A cold breeze came towards us downriver, ruffling the surface so that I could no longer see clearly into the depth immediately beside us. I had to trust that Erihana was guiding us from his knowledge of the shape of the river, reading the swirls, the movement of the currents, the dark and light patches indicating deeper or shallower water ahead.

Fox went for'ard to speak with his men. They stowed their swags under the deck. He came back aft, the man he named Gray coming with him. This man was older, his face heavily lined, framed in bushy grey hair above a long grey beard flecked with white, saggy shoulders as if weighed down by gravity itself. 'Gray', or 'Grey'?

My eyes stayed fixed on Erihana, watching his every arm movement but simultaneously I tried to keep Fox and Grey in my peripheral vision, mindful that I did not know these men who were quite capable, if it was their intention, to take my boat from me by force. I still carried the heavy Beaumont-Adams revolver clearly visible on my belt.

The river seemed to run strongly within its channel, the bends long and slow so that no shallows formed on the lee or off-side bank. Mostly the on-side banks were high above the river, often quite sheer with exposed stony ground or thickly covered with brown kanuka scrub. Off-side banks were also frequently steep, so that a fast current spread evenly across the river, offering us nothing to break its force or provide slower water toward either one bank or the other. Occasionally, the off-side bank would be low, stretching away from the river in a swampy thicket of trees or clumping billows of dark green flax. Then Erihana would direct me to that side of the river, escaping the full force of the current and allowing us to make much faster progress.

Away from the river channel itself, we were slowly progressing up a wide valley surrounded with hills to both north and south, rising in the distance to the west where we were headed. Off to the north the land was in a series of rolling ridges clothed in brown scrub as if vast waves had swept down the valley in ages past, piling the land up in giant ripples at right angles to its course. Further beyond, the apparently treeless hills rose up to the north, convoluted and creased like a crumpled blanket on a bed, folds and creases randomly in every direction. In the far west distance on the south side lay the dark shadow of high mountains.

Shaded for most of the day by high ground on both sides, the valley lay chillingly cold now in the winter when the sun – briefly such as there was – crept low across the sky. When the light was lost in the later afternoon on days clear as this, heavy frost would bite the land.

As we slowly struggled in mid-river up a long straight, Erihana came off the bow to restoke the boiler, Fox and Gray watching closely as he swung a bucket on a rope over the side to top up the header-tank with water. I could feel puffs of warm air from the open boiler door when Erihana threw in shovels-full of black coal onto the glowing embers.

When Erihana returned to his navigating station on the bow, Fox and Gray lounged in silence on the seats on either side near me, staring out at the valley drifting slowly behind us. We traversed mile after mile of uninhabited river almost monotonously similar, to the steady throb of the screw and the regular hiss of steam from each stroke of the piston. Erihana stood resolutely on the bow like a figurehead, constantly indicating to me with his arms the best part of the channel to follow. Fox tended the boiler and topped up the header-tank whenever I asked. Thus far, forcing the Molyneaux had been quite uneventful, given that the boat appeared suited to the purpose and we had an experienced native guide.

Before the light had begun to fade, I looked for a suitable mooring for night, eventually picking a place where the river ran evenly on a short straight, the north bank rising steeply up from the water for about six feet then shelving to a level terrace covered with scattered kanuka trees. Deep water ran close in as we edged the boat toward the bank, eased off on the valve with a hissing burst of hot steam into the cold afternoon air and Erihana leapt ashore with a rope, scrambled over the low bank and tied us fast to a tree. Gray swung over the side aft, pulling the stern in hard against the ground.

Fox and his men unloaded their bedrolls, then busied themselves gathering wood from among the kanuka trees for a fire and cutting piles of the soft springy foliage to lie upon. As the early chill of frost swirled about, they grilled lumps of sheepmeat skewered on sticks, the mouth-watering smell of burning fat wafting about, while I boiled salted beef and potatoes for Erihana and me.

Afterward, we sat around the fire, our faces tinted red from the glow, our day-long hunger at last satisfied. The night temperature dropped further below freezing, the cold creeping deep into my clothes on whichever side was away from the flames. Erihana didn't join us, kept away from the circle, barely visible, only the whites of his eyes shining in the firelight.

To be sociable, I ventured a question. 'So tell me Fox, where have you and your men come from?'

All four suddenly looked directly at me, even James McLeod whose sly eyes constantly danced shiftily about.

'From your question JC, you must be new to the colonies yourself, or you would know better than to ask it!'

I raised my eyebrows in surprise at his answer as a silence lengthened, then he continued.

'You should know that many men in Australia would take exception to a question such as yours, sometimes with violence, nor would they think to ask it of others. Most men in that Colony are there for a reason they would like to forget: either they've been transported in chains against their will, or they've fled there to escape incarceration. Some have committed a felony – transportation locked in irons and crammed into foul prison ships is the first punishment, whether stealing bread for starving children, or for an act of violence. The second punishment is supposed to relate to the seriousness of their crime; the years they've been sentenced to be incarcerated in the Colony's prisons if they've survived the voyage to get there.

'Others have been transported to exile, for political agitation against the Crown or fomenting resistance to British rule. Many have been banished there from Ireland for such reasons, even Scotland, forbidden never to return to their homes and families.

'Some are there of their own free will, choosing to flee there voluntarily to escape the penalty of incarceration should they be arrested and hauled before the Judges. Better to go voluntarily as a freeman than be transported in chains – at least they mostly avoid death in the ships and the lash in the prisons.

'So men keep their own counsel, JC, knowing that most have a past to hide. Many have taken new identities and names, or like Gray over there, answering only to one given them by their mates. Only the police or the penal authorities ask a man questions about his past....'

The others said nothing as Fox spoke, sometimes nodding or dipping their heads in agreement.

'But some virtue comes from shared adversity, JC. Whether felons or patriots, we mostly stand by each other. We respect authority only in those who inspire it and resist any that try to impose it. We judge each other by what we do now, not what we did before. We make our own rules based on fairness, not on privilege or position; and every man succeeds or fails by his own endeavours, not according to some social class he inherited.

'But despite all those bonds formed from shared adversity, Australia's a place where the toughest and strongest survive the country, the climate, the authorities and each other – a man soon learns to fight for himself first and then to look after his mates second.' The others murmured or gave short laughs in agreement.

'We all four came separately from Victoria where we were diggers on the goldfields. The easy gold there that a man can win by his labour alone has gone, so when we heard all the stories of gold finds here, we came to New Zealand. A large group of us joined an expedition in Dunedin, paying good money to a thieving lying bastard calling himself O'Neill, who claimed he had discovered rich gold on the Mataura. For a price, he would lead us there to his secret place.

'So we paid up and went with him, only as soon as we got to the river, he vanished into the night, making off with all the good money we'd paid him. There was no payable gold. We spent weeks washing gravels all along the river, finding nothing worth the labour, only small traces. If ever we find him again, I'll kill the bastard myself if I'm not beaten to it.

'As soon as we heard the authentic report of Read's discovery, we four left and came north the same day, but the rush had already started. If you can get us there tomorrow, we might still find some good ground to work, before it's all taken and the easy gold all gone. If the good ground's gone, I'll go off prospecting myself – I'll be bound there's other gold than Read's, waiting somewhere to be found.'

He paused.'You're not a temperance-man are you Fraser? – All this talking's made me thirst for my whisky! I'll share my bottle with you if you're a drinking man.'

'There's n'eer a true Scot that wouldn't help you drink it when it's offered,' I replied as Fox rummaged in his swag, flourishing a bottle that had already lost some of its contents. He sloshed a generous portion into the mug I held out, then drank straight from the bottle himself. Dusty and Gray on the other side of the firelight both produced bottles of their own, pouring from them into a mug for McLeod.

'Better this golden brew than that cheap stinking gin these mates of mine drink,' Fox said. He took another long pull on the bottle, then turned back to me. 'And you JC, why are you and your aborigine not off to find your fortune on the goldfields too?'

'I'm an engineer Fox, with some knowledge of building ships; I know nothing about mining or digging for gold, though there are probably many others who don't, that have already joined the rush. I saw hundreds of men leaving good jobs in Dunedin, the day of Read's report, joining the rush as if possessed by some madness. This is mid-winter, but they gave no thought to their shelter, nor where food for so many would come from. Their gold fever will cool quickly when cold and hunger set in.

'If men like you want to stay digging in Gabriel's valley, food and shelter will have to come first, the gold second, otherwise you'll starve or freeze to death. The Molyneaux will become the road for your supplies to travel along, if we can succeed to navigate it. Some of your gold will find its way to my pocket without my having to dig for it, when you pay for the essentials to live. That is why I have come here.'

While we slowly drained Fox's whisky bottle, I told him of accompanying George and Lucy to New Zealand on my way to South America. I explained that but for Read's gold, I would now be on my way to the Argentine to join my cousins. Only the prospect of this venture had diverted me temporarily from that course.

The warmth of the fire held us by it until quite late as the cold of the frost intensified. The others emptied their gin bottles, then huddled down in their bedrolls. Fox and I talked quietly on, long after the whisky had gone. Erihana waited silently on the edge of the firelight, then rose to join me as we walked in starlight back to the Lady Colina. We stoked more coal into the boiler to hold it for the remainder of the night, then rolled in our blankets under the foredeck.

The return of daylight gradually revealed a thick coat of white frost covering most of the boat, patches of mist swirling softly on the river. Erihana tended the boiler while I prepared our porridge ashore, sharing the fire relit by Fox's men.

We cast off from the bank when the mist had lifted, the river turning from grey to pale blue as the light strengthened. The intensely cold air attacked my eyes as we headed upriver, Erihana resolutely guiding us from the bow.

We passed by the mouth of a large river, joining the Molyneaux on the north side, but from the rough chart I carried, it was much too soon for us to have reached the Tuapeka. Not far beyond, the valley began to widen out, the banks of the river spreading as it did so. We slowed as the water became shallower, forcing us to choose a channel from among several as the river divided itself.

Erihana must have had forewarning of these shallows for now he held a long pole cut from the kanuka trees the previous night, plunging it into the water to check the depth as we crept forward. One channel we chose swung toward the south bank, then back to mid-river where its blueness suddenly turned to grey. As Erihana shouted a warning, we bumped and shuddered to a stop, the bow running against a steep bank of round stones on the riverbed. I threw the valve open. A cloud of white steam burst up into the cold air as the boiler lost pressure. Fox leapt from the bow into the river pulling Dusty with him, waist deep in the freezing water. I called McLeod and Gray aft to avoid weighing the bow down.

As Dusty pushed, Fox thrust hard up under the gunwale, his huge shoulders bunched together as if his head and neck had sunk between them. The bow lifted with his effort and as Dusty pushed harder, we began to swing away clear. Fox hauled himself back onto the bow, dragging Dusty with him by one arm. They huddled alongside the boiler to get dry while we drifted quickly back down the channel, swept by the current. Erihana used his pole to fend us from the shallows on either side.

With pressure rebuilding, we returned to the deeper pool where the channels had divided, chose another and tried again. Although this channel appeared to carry less volume, it meandered back and forth between banks of grey gravel, but remained navigable. After several more anxious miles the valley gradually closed again, bringing the riverbanks closer with it, driving the divided water back into one deep course.

To the steady thump of the screw and the hiss of steam from the piston, we forged steadily onward, zigzagging diagonally across the river from bank to bank, using the force of the current obliquely to increase our speed. Mountains to the south and higher broken hills to the north gradually closed toward us as mile after mile of river passed behind us. Occasionally, the dull brown of the hillsides, particularly on the north side, was broken by greener valleys splitting away from the river with twisting drifting smoke indicating some pioneering farmer had already settled there.

Later in the day Erihana pointed to some cloudiness appearing in a thin stream along the north bank of the river, contrasting clearly with the otherwise grey or blue of the water. Quickly this cloudiness became thicker and darker until suddenly on rounding a long slow bend, we saw the mouth of a larger river joining into the Molyneaux from the north. This tributary looked sufficiently wide and deep to be navigable, but its water was murky with a pale brown silt. Erihana called out, pointing to me from the bow, 'Tuapeka Mr Fraser, it is Tuapeka!'.

We slowed as we approached. I looked quickly at the hand-drawn map of the Molyneaux which Mr Burns had given me, to confirm Erihana's conviction, then turned to Fox.

'Indeed this looks to be the Tuapeka, Fox. You can be put ashore here if you wish and make your way some distance up the river valley until you find the goldfield. Or you can stay aboard while we try to reach Beaumont's landing further up the Molyneaux, then find your way overland from there. My map indicates that Beaumont is closer to the goldfield than this confluence with the Tuapeka, but the choice and its consequence must be yours.'

I waited while he talked with the others, holding the boat steady against the current.

'Y'see that colour in the river JC? I'll bet a sovereign it's from all the diggers washing their paydirt up in Gabriel's gully already! We've not a moment to lose. Put us ashore now and we'll make a run for it from here!'

I eased back on the valve and swung the tiller over. The boat turned into the mouth of the Tuapeka, Erihana checking the depth in the discoloured water with his pole. As we nudged against a steep bank, he made us fast to a tree. McLeod and Gray leapt ashore. Fox hurled all their bedrolls and swags effortlessly up to Dusty on the bank. He came back aft, held out a hand.

'Good luck to you JC. If you ever catch the gold fever yourself, come and join me – you and I could do well together. And if an engineer'll ever help me get more of the gold, I'll come and find you!'

We shook hands firmly. He swung up on the tree onto the bank, heaved his swag onto his shoulders, the four of them strode off into the trees and quickly disappeared from sight.

I studied the map before steering the *Lady Colina* back out into the river. The place marked as 'Beaumont' was an area rather than some physical feature, a wide sweep of flatter fertile land on both sides of the river which was long-settled by men farming flocks of sheep walked inland from the coast. Prior to the recent gold find, it was the principal destination that Mr Burns and his Dunedin business colleagues had in mind for transporting farm equipment and supplies along the Molyneaux. Now, by coincidence, it appeared also to be the closest point on the river to the gully where Read had found his gold.

As we forged further upstream, high forested mountains clothed in deep-green bush rose closely along the southern bank of the river, their bare tops in places brushed with the whiteness of new snow. The valley now was sunless, tightly enclosed by high ground casting cold shadows. Ferns carpeted the banks beneath kanuka on the north bank, mosses shrouded the black trunks of beech trees along the south side. The river was dark, flowing swiftly between steep banks which plunged almost sheer into the rushing water.

We angled abruptly back and forth, striving to make way against the strong current, only making ground by using the deflection. Erihana crouched on the bow watching the hillsides slip slowly by. Gradually we could see ahead to brighter light, as if passing through a long roofless tunnel, until at last the close hillsides began to fall back from the river, the high mountains on the south side sloping away to the southwest. The river widened, the current slowed. Kanuka-covered flats appeared again above the lower banks.

Clear ground appeared on the north side, blackened trunks and stumps of kanuka still showing signs of having been burned. We saw dirty grey sheep foraging among the brown clumps of tussock, lifting their heads in alarm at the strange sounds of our engine, their nostrils spurting steam on the crisp cold air, then a stone and log hut came into view near the river, smoke drifting upward from its dominant chimney.

A man materialised on the bank further ahead, waving. Then several more huts scattered on the plateau. Flat, cleared ground stretched away for some distance on both banks. Another hut on the south side, a large log canoe pulled up on a sloping shore on the north. This must be Beaumont – our destination. We had succeeded.

Although it was still winter when rain was locked on the land as frost and snow, thus reducing the volume of water in the river, the *Lady Colina* had forced the Molyneaux with ease. As the spring thaw came, the shallows would disappear but the current would be stronger. But I was confident that by using the current to deflect us when angling back and forth across the river, the boat's big slow screw could drive a good load from Port Molyneaux at least up to here.

Several men were now watching us from the shore near the canoe, so I eased back on the valve and headed toward them, calling to Erihana that we would make our landing. Moments later I ran the bow up onto a small sandy beach and Erihana jumped ashore holding a paynter.

The men arrived beside us, their questions tumbling over each other, surprise apparent on their faces. We exchanged our names. They ignored Erihana, turning their backs to him as they faced toward me. They confirmed that this was indeed the area called Beaumont, the mouth of the Beaumont River joining the Molyneaux just around the next bend. I explained from where we had come, why we were there. One man, a Mr Denniston, invited me to along his hut and when the engine was shut down, I left Erihana minding the boat and went ashore.

Denniston's hut was made from stacked stone rammed between with earth, the stones a mixture of smooth rounded grey river-stones and flat dark slate. Denniston had been in the valley for two years so had had time to add a small second room onto the larger first which was dominated by a large open hearth and chimney. The floor was bare ground, the sloping roof of Kanuka poles covered with a layer of cut tussock overlaid with pieces of canvas greased with mutton fat. The only light inside came from either candles or the fire. The room smelled strongly of smoke. A carbine leaned against a wall by the open doorway.

Arthur Denniston himself was a short burly man with long dark unkempt hair and a similarly long beard. He wore the usual thick woollen shirt, very worn moleskin trousers and calf-length boots. Despite his lined face and worn hands, he was probably not yet 40, visible signs of a man who had spent his years working outdoors. He had obviously not bathed for a long period, but the hut was quite clean.

When Read's gold was discovered, Denniston and several other farmers in the Beaumont area had elected to stay on their land rather than join the miners nearby, not willing to lose their squatters' rights to the land after two years of hard labour clearing it of kanuka, for the risk that they might – or might not – win any gold.

He and the others had sold as many of their sheep as they were willing to spare to hungry miners who were scouring the nearby countryside for food. Now they were all having to guard their flocks, especially at night, against hungry marauding bands of miners determined that if they could not buy sheep, they would steal them. The settlers were taking turns to patrol the Beaumont flats every night, frequently firing warning shots at stealthy figures in the dark. (I was reminded of our being on guard nightly at Castledawson in Ireland during the potato famine). Even by day – as I had seen – they all kept carbines close at hand, treating any strangers with suspicion.

Denniston was eager to assist me, not only to make money but hopefully to secure his property and livestock against the depredations of the miners by helping to supply them with the food and materials they so badly needed. Not only was he willing to transport goods I shipped upriver from Beaumont to the goldfield, using the oxen from all the farms in the area to draw a rough sled, but he also offered to build a secure storeroom for them if I provided iron for the roof. Some of the sheets of corrugated iron we had brought with us on the *Lady Colina* would be put to good use.

My immediate priority however, was to get word carried back to Mr Burns in Dunedin that by successfully reaching Beaumont, our shipping venture could indeed proceed. Denniston believed that many of the first miners were already being driven from the goldfield by hunger and cold, being forced to return to Dunedin for food and better supplies; if I were to ride to the goldfield on Denniston's horse next day I would surely find many willing hands to carry a letter, especially when paid to do so.

I returned to the boat before dark. I wrote a short note addressed to Mr Burns:

The Molyneaux is successfully forced. I have reached Beaumont. Ship supplies as soon as possible: food, canvas, tools, grog, iron sheets, to the care of Mr Bissett at Port Molyneaux with all haste, especially food. Include full account of your costs. I will return downriver to the port to await your shipment.

Faithfully yours, John Cameron Fraser.

Then I wrote another:

My Dear George and Dearest Lucy;
Passage of the Molyneaux is achieved with ease. The venture with Mr Burns can proceed. If the gold continues to be won at Gabriel Reads', prospects for our further enterprise are very good.
There is much to be done. Should you know how to find your brother Harry in the north, I suggest you send word to him immediately that there is opportunity if he comes south to join me.
I expect to remain working the Molyneaux for as long as the gold is won and the rewards can be made.
Affectionately, your cousin,
J.C.F.

I rode Denniston's horse along the valley next morning following a vague track and the directions given to me of the most direct route to the goldfield. After sidling over some tussock-covered ridges, I came to a larger stony stream, the Low Burn, which I had been advised to follow north to the first branch. The going was very easy, almost open grassy tussock with patches of a spiny thorn-bush down in the valley floor to be avoided, the horse ambling along breathing slowly, lifting its head occasionally as if knowing the way forward. Half a mile after turning east up the first branch, its valley sides closed in sharply until soon it abruptly ended in a rounded hillside. The track angled directly up this to a low point, a saddle, on the ridge, the horse now breathing shafts of steaming air from its nostrils, snorting and blowing with the steep climb.

At the ridge, directly in front of me, the ground fell less steeply away into a wider U-shaped valley, which Denniston had told me was the headwaters of Wetherstons' Gully. Beyond lay a much higher ridge lying north-south which increased in height and steepness to the south. Over this ridge directly beyond Wetherstons' Gully, was Gabriel Read's Gully.

Within a half-hour I had reached the top of that ridge, resting the panting horse while I looked down into the valley below. Even from where I stood, I could see the moving figures of men scattered along both sides of the stream which wound along the valley floor. A soft pattern of smoke-haze hung in the still air. I mounted the horse and rode down.

The first men I came to stopped their activity suddenly when they saw me, looking toward me in silence. Several held the shafts of shovels, two were standing knee-deep in the stream, a large metal dish in both hands. They all stared sullenly at me. Closer, one of the men in the water called out sharply: 'Get away mister! We've claimed all this ground!'

I hastily explained I was not looking for ground to claim, merely directions to the largest part of the goldfield. They waved me off downstream, then returned to their labour.

As I rode further down the valley, the number of diggers increased so that both banks of the stream were being worked by men in an almost unbroken line of claims, until I rounded a shoulder in the valley side, to be confronted by activity virtually across the entire valley floor. The wide grassy valley was scattered with men individually or in groups, digging into the earth, heaping up mounds of stones, standing up to their knees or even thighs in the small stream washing gravel from their pans. Crude shelters dotted the tussock landscape – small walls of stacked stones, pieces of canvas and calico, sloping bivouacs of poles covered with a thatch of tussock. A few tethered horses grazed on small patches of grass. Further down the field was a line of canvas tents or calico screens held up with ropes outside of which, as I drew closer, I could see various wooden signs. One clearly said 'BANK'. Another which was just a screen not high enough to reach the conical hats of men inside was well sign-written 'Cobb & Co.' A third, with its sign roughly drawn, 'Miners Committee' had a cluster of men crowded outside.

At the Bank tent – the largest of the three – I was told that a bank officer escorted by armed men from Cobb & Co was travelling almost daily to Dunedin carrying miners' gold and mail, bringing back money, mail and food supplies on the return journey. For a small fee, they would carry my letters which I handed over, the next day.

Then I pushed my way through the crowd gathered outside the Miners' Committee tent. Inside, several men sat on gin boxes at a rough table made from planks nailed to saplings driven into the ground, talking with others standing in a line. I waited until eventually I shuffled to the front, to face a thickset man frowning through his beard. Without looking up from a large open ledger-book he said, 'I'm Gillies, the Committee Chairman. Register here (pointing at the book) and be given your claim!'

'I'm not here to claim. I want to find a miner just arrived named Fox, with three of his mates.'

Still without even a glance at me, he ran his finger over the names back up the ledger, then stopped at one. 'Here – Fox, Dusty, Gray, O'Neill. You'll find them in Wetherstons', not here in Gabriel's. Claim at post 48 on the west bank. Next!'

I rode out of Gabriel's Gully and around into nearby Wetherstons', picking my way carefully past the diggings of labouring groups of men all bent to their work. Dust hung in the still-chill air. A strange cry of 'Joe!' preceded me everywhere.

The lower end of Wetherstons', a similar symmetrical valley to Gabriel's, was more sparsely occupied by the diggers but even here I could estimate there were several hundred all along both banks of the small creek. By stopping and asking at the diggings from men visibly hostile at being interrupted, I progressed along the line of claims until I recognised the dominant figure of Fox ahead, standing knee-deep in the creek, a gold-pan in hand. Gray beside him held a heap of gravel in a short-handled shovel, O'Neill and Dusty were digging the ground a short distance away. They all stopped and looked to me as a rode up.

'Well if it isn't JC himself already,' Fox straightened up, took a stride out of the creek, 'come to join the diggers after all?'

'I came from Beaumont to send a messenger back to Dunedin. There's some time to spare before we head back down-river, so I came to see what goldmining is about.'

Fox came over as I dismounted from the horse, handed Gray the pan on the bank of the creek. He and O'Neill resumed their work.

Fox explained the four of them had adjoining claims side by side along the right side of the creek, each only 24 feet by 24 feet, but worked all of it as a single piece of ground. Initially the gold – as fine grains or as small irregularly-shaped pieces – was mixed in with sandy sediment in the bed of the creek, especially below heavy stones, but they had quickly worked this out in the short distance of creek beside their claims. Now, by digging aside the grassy topsoil cover on the nearby ground, they had exposed sediments previously deposited by the creek over the valley floor. They carried this gravel by the shovel-full over to the water where it was laboriously washed by a swirling rotating motion in the large round gold pan. As the lighter sand sediment spilled over the edge of the pan, the gold grains being very heavy for their size, sank steadily down into the lower bottom of the pan. Eventually, by careful washing and spilling of the coarser gravel over the edge of the pan, mostly just the gold itself remained.

Fox pulled a leather drawstring pouch from around his waist, opening the top sufficiently wide for me to see the dull gold inside. I had expected to see gold as a gleaming bright metal, but it had a disappointingly tarnished, almost dirty look. Fox, his eyes shining above the black beard, said there was 'pay-dirt' all over the valley. Already in the brief time they had been working, the three of them had gathered by his estimate, more than 32 ounces of gold which at the standard gold-price was worth over £120 – a promising reward for just over one day's work.

Fox was clearly anxious to get back to his work. 'Maybe there's better ground than this somewhere else, but we've got 162 square yards here to dig over – the sooner we find how much of it's pay-dirt and dig it out, the quicker we can we can claim some new ground that might be even better. There's a bigger fortune to make here in the diggings JC than you'll ever find on the river if you want to join us!' And with that, he turned back to the creek and in a few strides his giant frame was again stooped over in the water, pan in hand.

For a while I sat in the saddle watching. The grassy valley stretched away to the north, narrowing further upstream but there was nothing to provide shelter, nor to give any protection against the weather or even provide fuel for a fire. I wondered how long men could survive in such a bleak place, where what brief winter sun there was, barely crept over the steep hills on either side and the air hung heavy and cold over the valley floor. When next the wind came, carrying rain or snow, the hot lure of gold would quickly chill. Men could die here.

I rode back to Denniston's at Beaumont, returning his horse with undertakings to return up river as soon as the first shipment of supplies arrived at Port Molyneaux. In return, he undertook to begin work immediately to build a stone shelter to store the goods we would deliver and to secure the oxen from his neighbours to transport them to the diggings.

We fired up the boiler on the *Lady Colina* once more, using the last of the coal remaining and pulled away out into the river. Running downstream with the current was an exhilarating experience compared to the slow journey upriver. Our speed combined with that of the current itself swept us furiously along as I struggled to maintain steerage with the tiller. Erihana crouched on the bow trying to indicate the best course but there was no time for me to follow his directions as we plunged along almost out of control.

Quickly I learned that movements of the tiller had to be extreme in order to make even slight gradual changes to our direction. Unless I anticipated the surge of the current toward one bank or the other, we would be swept into it before the boat would respond, yawing wildly as the kanuka on the banks clawed at us racing past. After several frightening such experiences and one violent crash when we struck the bank, spinning sideways into the current again unable to steer, I began to read the shape of the river in the valley itself so that I could begin correcting our course before we arrived.

Only then could I exercise some control, but when we reached the braided shallows it was more prudent to let the steam go than risk damaging the screw on the gravel. So we drifted without power, frequently being run aground and both of us having to struggle in the bitingly cold water to push the boat free.

The wild journey back down to Port Molyneaux took us only one day. Erihana went off to the nearby native settlement he called Murikauhaka. I waited many impatient days with Bissett for the arrival of the Otago Assembly Superintendent's coastal steamer *Queen* with the first shipment of supplies from Mr Burns. On a bleak grey day in mid-August the hollow hoot of her steam-horn brought us hurriedly to the quay as she swung in toward the shore to make a landing.

The cargo when unloaded I estimated would take us at least five trips upriver. Allowing two days up to Beaumont, one to unload and one day back down, the *Queen* would return to Port Molyneaux with the next shipment before the 20 days of our five trips had elapsed. Images of men labouring in the open back at the goldfield without either adequate food or shelter impressed a feeling of urgency upon me. We needed to start immediately.

As if alerted again by his strange extra sense, Erihana arrived from Murikauhaka with several other native men willing to help us load our boat. Aboard went as many sacks of flour as we could safely carry, plus potted fish and meat, small tubs of butter, boxes of Letchfords vesta matches, bags of tobacco, wooden boxes each packed with four bottles of brandy and finally some rolls of light canvas. Fortunately, a seam of black coal had recently been discovered on the north side of the Molyneaux close to the mouth, so Bissett was able to supply us with enough to fill our two bunkers; the black coal would burn far hotter than the soft brown coal we had carried from Dunedin. The *Lady Colina* steadily sank lower in the water as the cargo was stowed aboard until I stopped the men, fearing we might be too heavy to make headway in the narrower sections of the river.

But when with the boiler fired up we eventually headed upriver, the large slow-turning screw drove the boat reassuringly forward against the current, though she responded only sluggishly to the helm.

And so we plied the river, Erihana and I, through the last weeks of winter, then into the spring. Arthur Denniston built the stone store at Beaumont as he had promised, hauling the supplies over to the goldfield on a pole sled drawn by four oxen. When the first load was dragged into Gabriel's, Denniston was besieged by a crowd of hungry miners who would have seized all the flour, but for being held back at gunpoint by two Sergeants of the new Otago Mounted Police. Together they doled out one pannikin-full per man as the miners' gold piled up in a piece of hide laid on the ground.

Gabriel's goldfields were proving to be rich ground. Miners seemed willing to pay almost any of it for the necessities of life which enabled them to remain on the diggings. I calculated that I was earning at least £140 per ton of supplies ferried upriver, sometimes more: others were also taking their share – Mr Burns and his colleagues in Dunedin who provided the bought goods initially, the Assembly Superintendent for shipping them to the Molyneaux on his steamer, then Denniston's reward for dragging them over the hill from Beaumont. I was winning more gold by supplying the miners than by digging the metal myself, without the vagaries of uncertain ground too.

I saw the Molyneaux in its many moods. Late August brought frequent snow showers sweeping over the hills from the south, coating the deck of the boat white, decorating the landscape with its scattered mantel. Rain with hail or sleet hurled itself downriver at us from the west, with Erihana huddling behind the boiler for warmth whilst I peered into the biting wind through the parted fingers of a hand across my face, struggling to see where our course lay.

Then came freezing temperatures with fog, turning to hoar frost. We groped our way slowly forward in the swirling murk, marvelling at the delicate coatings of ice that accumulated over every branch, every twig, each blade of tussock-grass, with spiders' webs like sparkling symmetrical patterns of lace dangling among the kanuka. The cold air bit into our throats as we breathed, crept stealthily through our damp clothes until we were forced ashore.

As August turned to September, so the blue skies of spring returned, lifting the brooding gloom off the river. Then in the monotony of long stretches of the river my thoughts would drift again to Elizabeth: I would see her eyes in the bright blueness above, her hair in the gold of windblown tussock on the hillsides, be reminded of the lightness that surrounded her by the sparkle of sunlight dancing off the ripples on the river. And feel the pain again, a melancholy sadness from which I struggled for days to release myself.

Also in September, we were suddenly pressured to carry men up the river in place of precious supplies. Diggers arriving at the ferry crossing at Port Molyneaux clamouring for transport upriver told us that the overland trail from Lake Waihola to Tuapeka was no longer safe; during one week a number of miners had been held up at gunpoint by a bushranger at Round Hill and robbed of all their possessions. Fortunately, the Otago Mounted Police troop which had recently been formed, chased after the robber, a well-known convict escaped from Australia, Henry Beresford Garrett. He was last seen heading across the island to the West Coast.

I learned more of Erihana. We shared the same food, drank tea from the same billy, slept huddled in our bedrolls in the same space under the same foredeck, endured the same cold, the wind; worked side by side at the same labour unloading supplies from the boat at Beaumont.

He seldom spoke, as if words were unnecessary, but it was always with importance or a deep wisdom when he did. He maintained a quiet dignity, his movements always at the same deliberate measured pace regardless of the circumstance. He taught me some words of his language, his people's names for the plants, the birds, the trees, surprised that I would want to know.

He showed me how to trap eels from the river; making up bundles of kanuka bound with flax, weighted with large stones, then lowered on flax ropes into deep pools close to quiet banks. We marked each place with pieces of calico tied on the scrub. When next we passed by, we swiftly hauled the large bundle of sticks up into the boat, any eels that had taken refuge among the thicket slithering out to writhe on the floor. Split and cooked over a low fire, they were a delicious change from the ever-present mutton.

Erihana knew the value of money, appreciated that his labour was worth what I paid him. But he had difficulty understanding why white men wanted the gold sand: were willing to risk their lives by starving or freezing just to separate it from all the other equally worthless sand or gravel in which it lay. To him it was after all quite useless stuff, no different from any other sand, the dull irregular grains being neither ornamental nor able to be made into weapons or tools. How could gold compare with the pounamu, the jade stone prized by the natives above all else; its deep green translucence, its glass-like smoothness to the touch, its hardness better than iron for shaping into weapons, cutting instruments, or delicate ornaments. For that, the natives would risk their lives. Talking softly by a fire ashore one night, he told me of his surprise that if gold was so sought after, why had it taken the white men so long to find it – his people knew of very many other places where the same sand lay.

Returning down river one late afternoon when the heat of the lowering sun told of the onset of early summer, we approached Port Molyneaux in a wide curve across the current to line us up exactly with the landing. A lone figure stood on the quay with hands on hips as if waiting our arrival. It was not until we were hard alongside that I looked up more closely at the stranger standing there. Beneath his tall conical hat and behind his light-brown beard, I recognised from 13 years before, my cousin Harry Bruce.

TEN

As one would expect, the years since I last saw Harry at Castledawson had changed him.

The freckles were still there on the high parts of his cheeks not covered with the fair hair of his beard and the smiling eyes had permanent wrinkles in their corners. I was only 12 when we parted; I fondly remembered him as being tall and thin – much thinner than all his brothers, but now the years had built more shape onto his frame.

After three of his brothers had emigrated to the Argentine, Harry had come alone to New Zealand. He had always been different from the other Bruce sons, even from George, with an almost-transparent empathy for others that I had recognised when my father and I first met him the day we arrived at Larne in Ireland, long ago. It was Harry who had taught me about the farm animals, to ride a horse, to load and fire guns, to hunt rabbits, make hay, milk cows, churn butter, want to help the poor starving tinkers who arrived at our door during the famine.

His voyage from Liverpool was along the old route down the coast of Africa to stop at Capetown, then east to Adelaide in South Australia before eventually onward to New Zealand. Avoiding the deep southern ocean, his journey was longer but less turbulent than ours; the worst event being an outbreak of measles which spread rapidly amongst the children crowded in the main berth, taking many young lives with the pneumonia which followed.

Harry had disembarked in the north at the main port of Auckland, now the seat of the Colonial Government. Initially he had found some work in a flourmill but the economy of the Colony was struggling and there were few jobs. Although near penniless, he tried to secure some land suitable to farm from the Government, but most of the land available near Auckland was already long-taken and the few parcels that did occasionally appear were awarded to friends of the Governor. Other potentially good land further to the south was held determinedly by the natives who were refusing to sell any more.

Regretting not having joined his older brothers in Argentina and without even the fare now to do so, Harry joined a coastal steamer, working for his passage down the east coast of the northern island to a wide fertile coastal plain ringed by an arc of mountains on its western edge. This area, named Hawke Bay by the early explorer Captain James Cook was already well-settled in productive farms but Harry was hopeful that more blocks on the lesser-attractive land rising off the plain to the west might become available for settlement. That did not happen: the natives resolved not to sell, the Government had no funds to induce them otherwise, nor would trade them the modern rifles they wanted instead of money; the temporary work he secured on established farms became permanent.

Like many other émigrés, Harry found himself trapped in a life of hard labour in poor living conditions, without any apparent future, nor the means to break free. His dreams of having his own land faded. With no money and no prospects he had no eligibility, so had not married. Not that there were many young ladies in the region even had his circumstances been different – most of the settlers were men, only a few with wives.

When the letter from George eventually found him, suggesting he came south to join me on the Molyneaux, it was as if God himself had heard his prayers. Scraping together every penny he owned or could borrow, he found passage from the port of Napier on a steamer returning south.

None of this I knew when we stood face to face in the dusk on the quay at Port Molyneaux, though I caught the glisten of tears in his eyes as we shook hands in the silence of emotion, words failing us both.

I called Erihana to us. 'This man is Mr Bruce – he is the son of my father's sister. We lived in the same family together when we were young. And Harry, this is Daniel Ellison, Navigator and First Officer of the *Lady Colina* – and a good companion.'

Harry lowered his head slightly, looked toward Erihana's feet. 'Kia Ora Mr Ellison'

Erihana stood straight, his eyes unusually directly at Harry. 'Kia Ora Mr Bruce. For the family of Mr Fraser, I am 'Erihana'.

'I asked my cousin to come from the north to work with us. I need his help Erihana, there is so much to be done here.' He made no comment and after gathering his bundle from the boat, walked off into the fading light to the native village.

Harry and I sat up very late that night before the fire at Bissett's lodging-house, trying vainly in one evening to trace all that had happened to each of us since he had left me at Castledawson. He brought news of George and Lucy, both very happy in Dunedin, especially Lucy who was expecting their first child early the next year. They had told him all the story of our voyage on the *Black Swan* including the unexpected end to my courtship of Elizabeth. It seemed ironic that Harry and I who could both have chosen to join his brothers in the Argentine had instead travelled to the Antipodes, yet both of us now for differing reasons regretted having done so. Perhaps, we mused, when Gabriel's gold had all been won, our fortune here made, we could voyage onward together to South America.

Harry knew nothing of boats – other than his experience of the sailing voyage to the Colony – nor anything of steam engines, so there was much for him to learn before he could take a fully useful role in our venture. On our first trip upriver together with three of us aboard, he was more just a passenger, but quickly adapted to our routines. At least he was well-accustomed to living in uncomfortable hard conditions in all weathers, often wet, cold or hungry. Having spent some years living in the north as part of a small white community among a much larger population of natives, he was quite at ease with the Maori, treating Erihana with no distinction; Erihana responded similarly.

So urgent was the need to keep supplies flowing to the growing population of the goldfield, there was no time to spare in Beaumont to visit Gabriel's with Harry. However, the land trail from Dunedin had by now been so well-worn by the travels of hundreds of diggers followed by packhorse trains, that bullock-drawn carts were forging the journey, taking several weeks for the return trip. This additional transport route seemed to have no discernible effect on the demand for supplies via the river.

Much warmer temperatures in late November had thawed the snow on the mountains in the watershed of the Molyneaux far to the west beyond Beaumont, such that the river levels had risen some four feet from winter. Whilst that made navigation easier, especially through what had been the braided section of the river – now completely disappeared – fighting upriver against the stronger current had added a further day to each voyage. However, the return journey downriver racing with the faster flow was an apprehension-filled test of nerve as we were swept along, often not in control of our direction, surging toward banks then at the last moment being swung off by the rebounding current, drifting beam-on downstream, struggling to regain our heading. At least we were back in Port Molyneaux by early afternoon and could be loaded again by nightfall.

For a man with no boating experience, Harry learned quickly. By the third trip he could stow cargo so as to maintain our trim, fire the boiler, and maintain its pressure and header tanks. He spent hours with Erihana watching the channels all along the river, then began short periods steering the tiller under my close direction.

When we arrived back at Port Molyneaux after Harry's third journey, we three stood in the dusk on the quay when the *Lady Colina* had been made fast. I held out a small pouch to Erihana containing sovereigns in payment of his recent earnings. To my surprise, he quite unexpectedly drew himself upright, and faced directly at me, a more serious look than usual upon his brown face.

'Mr Fraser, it is time for Erihana to leave you. Mr Harry is come here to work with you … you are not alone, or I would not leave you. But if the Pakeha will give so much money in return for gold lying upon the ground, then Erihana will go where my people know this gold lies, before the Pakeha finds it and with our land, it is all taken from us.'

He paused for a moment as if searching for words but not finding them. 'You are a good man Mr Fraser. You are my friend always. You Mr Harry also.' He held up a hand, palm facing toward us. 'Haere ra!'

I knew not what to say, just stood there staring at this dignified native with whom I had shared so much. He picked up his rolled blanket, turned away and strode purposefully off toward Murikauhaka. I stood watching him go, so stunned by the abruptness of his parting that I was almost uncomprehending it had actually happened; sorry that he should be gone after all that we had shared together, silently wishing him good fortune, idly wondering if we would ever meet again. He left me as he had come: appearing as if from nowhere at the very moment I needed him; now disappearing to nowhere when he judged he was needed no longer.

Now Harry and I worked the river together, renewing the strands of friendship formed when we lived together in Ireland. Within a few more trips, he was able to take an equal role with me in handling the boat, loading or discharging the cargo at each end of the journey.

I had strongly resisted having to return to Dunedin to meet Mr Burns and his associates, not wishing to risk any accidental contact with the MacKays or be reminded of the pain that still lay dull upon me. Instead, I wrote out long lists of goods that were required to be shipped to Port Molyneaux and a regular flow of correspondence between us was carried on each voyage of the *Queen*.

The overland route between the goldfield and Dunedin continued to be rapidly improved, allowing regular frequent wagon-trains to carry supplies in to the diggers. Although this transport was a welcome reduction in the miners' dependence on our constant river journeys, the number of men whom I was told were daily arriving at Gabriels' caused continuing demand for whatever we could carry.

With such surety of our business being maintained, I was encouraged to build permanent accommodation for us at Port Molyneaux on a piece of land purchased from Mr Bissett. In the days either side of Christmas, as 1861 drew to a close, Harry and I with labour from the natives who normally worked our cargoes, built a small house using bricks and iron shipped in from Dunedin, with flat river stones stacked for the fireplace and chimney. The large rectangular main room fronted toward the river with two adjoining rooms for sleeping or storage to the rear. The roof was thatched with dried rushes, then covered with corrugated iron. Finally we laid thick sawn timber boards over the smoothed earth floor.

The finished dwelling was the first permanent housing I had ever owned, a tangible benefit of the river venture's success. Proud though I was of that, its very presence implied permanence – a continuity even - to my remaining in this Colony, which in my heart I did not feel.

Having completed the building, we set out with a loaded boat once more upriver, in time to reach Beaumont before years' end. On Christmas Day I had made a promise to Harry that we would spend some extra time inland on our next voyage to visit the goldfields – the last day of the year seemed especially appropriate to spend among the men whose laboured privations resulted in such rich rewards for our enterprise.

On the last day of the year, leaving the *Lady Colina* in the care of Arthur Denniston, we set out on borrowed horses for the goldfield. The route I had taken previously over the several ranges had now been superseded by a trail well-worn by the wheels of wagons, that skirted around the valleys between those ranges until reaching the Tuapeka

River, then striking directly north to Gabriels' Gully itself. Even the fords over the streams in each valley had been carefully built up with large flat stones for easy negotiation by the wagons that carried our goods from Beaumont.

We smelled the goldfield before we sighted it; a sickly-sweet but pungent odour of earth, human waste, sweat and horses made worse by the heat of the day which wafted toward us.

I was quite unprepared for the sight that greeted us as we rounded the end of the ridge with Gabriels' Gully spread before us. The soft valley of rich grasses rising up on either side to brown slopes of tussock being tousled by the wind was gone. Instead, the earth had been rudely stripped bare, piled up into random heaps of stones and dirt. Among this chaos were many hundreds of tents, canvas or calico shelters in shades of white to grimy grey, scattered as thickly as mushrooms, even spreading up the sides of the valley, stretching along its floor as far as we could see.

The whole landscape was alive, flickering in constant movement as several thousand or more diggers laboured, shovelled, carried, rose, sat or just moved about. On reaching the periphery of the first diggers, I stopped the horse, staring in near-stupefied amazement at the transition that had taken place since my previous visit to this place. Not even in my extreme imagination on listening to Denniston's tales of the goldfield did I ever envisage such a scene as now lay before us.

Eventually we moved on, turning our horses back toward the entrance to this valley, then around the shoulder of its western ridge, leading on into Wetherston's. I was even more astonished at the sight of this gully, which on my last visit had been occupied by only a few parties of diggers, Fox's among them.

Now it was a town, or some semblance of a town. A bare strip of earth serving as a road was lined along both sides by rows of shanties and shacks of every size and description. Slabs of rough-sawn wood, canvas, calico, stacked brush, layered stones – anything which could be found or carried – had been used to construct these makeshift shanties, a number of them roofless, just flimsy walls to shield their interior from the gaze of miners outside. Hand-drawn signs on wood or canvas advertised hotels, general stores, stables, boarding-houses, drinking saloons, eating places; then further down the street toward the diggings came the more disreputable tawdry shacks – dancing halls, fighting and wrestling rooms, billiard saloons, gambling halls and (judging by the 'ladies' standing around their entrances) several bordellos.

Clustered in the centre of this shambling array of shanties a group of more solid edifices; the flimsy shelter which had served as a bank on my previous visit was now replaced by a solid building of stacked layered stone topped by a well-painted sign 'Bank of New South Wales'. Immediately adjacent, a smaller such building housing the Postal Office on one side and another 'Cobb & Co', then directly across the street, two more – another imposing stone structure signed 'Bank of Victoria' and a stark squat windowless building with a single sign, 'Police'. These more-permanently constructed buildings appeared to serve as an anchor for all the other shanties clustered around.

We rode slowly through the bustle of men milling about in the street, most of them with wide-brimmed conical felt hats, dressed the same in woven woollen shirts – many with sleeves rolled up in the heat of the day – woollen or moleskin trousers ending in at the knee in long leather boots. Many smoked large clay pipes.

We dismounted and left our horses at a 'stables' – just a row of small corrals made from kanuka poles – then headed on foot toward the diggings. Wetherton's valley was a repeat of Gabriel's with its appearance so totally transformed that I reasoned the only way to find Fox and his mates again was to skirt our way through all the claims being worked until we came across them. As we began to do so, struggling to avoid the tents, deep holes, mounds of earth and labouring diggers, a strange shout of 'Joe' passed from mouth to mouth ahead of us at the sound of which every digger nearby suddenly looked sharply at us, stared for a few moments, then resumed their work.

Just ahead on our right I recognised a side-ridge, now with its lower slopes stripped bare of vegetation, known previously as Blue Spur at the base of which Fox had staked his claim. As we picked our way carefully through the diggings, the shout of 'Joe' still spreading before us, I saw a figure start at the cry, standing fully upright to see us. By his obvious height and size, it could only be Fox. He threw down a shovel and came quickly toward us.

'Well if it isn't JC himself – come to join us in some real work!' He seemed pleased to see us, reaching out with huge grimy hand to take and crush mine, shaking it repeatedly. I introduced him to Harry ('So you're JC's aborigine now are you!' then turned to look for Gray, McLeod and Dusty Brown. Two other men whom I did not know stood nearby, leaning on their shovel staves, watching us.

'So you're still digging your fortune Fox. But where are the three mates I left you with here?'

'Pleased to be quit of them, JC. Gray was a lazy bastard, McLeod a devious one. Sold their claims to two better men and went over to Gabriel's before I could chase them off with a hiding. Dusty went with them.' He led us a few paces over to the two men watching us. 'These are two good men from Dunedin come to make their fortune… Peter Reid and his brother John.

And this (turning to me) is JC Fraser, a rogue of my acquaintance whose hands unseen are round our throats, fleecing us of our gold for all the supplies that he brings by boat up-river! And his cousin Harry Bruce who's come to help him do it.' He grinned. I swung a feint punch toward him in reply.

'I've brought Harry to the diggings, to see how men like you make their riches picking up lumps of gold free from the ground. It's the last day of the year, so I thought we should stay to celebrate your good fortune with a dram or two.' I swung the bag hanging from my shoulders onto the ground to be sure he heard the clink of the bottles I had brought with me.

The Reids resumed their work as Fox walked us to their tent at the rear of the claim away from the stream. 'We've worked out much of these claims since you were here last JC,' he explained as we went. 'The float stone – the loose quartz gravel in the stream itself – we cleaned out quickly right to the bedrock. It was the richest paydirt, the easiest too. Then we had to start on the bench, this flat area beside the stream. First strip off the cover – it doesn't have any sign – then work our way down from the grassroots into the alluvial deposits underneath. Way back in time, those deposits were the gold-rich bed of the stream when it followed different courses swinging throughout this valley.

'Often there's nothing, no colour at all, then if you're lucky you'll hit a lead of paydirt, follow it along as far as it goes. When we first staked our claim, we used pans on the float stone working in the stream, but now when we need to wash more dirt to get a yield, we use cradles. So many diggers here now all needing to take the water, there's not much of it left. Without water, we can't wash for the gold. Cradles don't need much water and we can use the same water many times.'

He took us both over to where the Reids were working. 'We built cradles, just like I used in Victoria. Now all the diggers are using them. It's the only way to wash the dirt when the water's so scarce.'

The Reids were crouched on the ground, each vigorously rocking what looked roughly like a small baby's cradle. A shallow rectangular box, clearly made from the wood of a liquor box, was mounted on two elliptical-shaped rounded bearers – one higher than the other – that sat on the ground. A vertical handle was attached to the end and side of the boxes with which each of the brothers rocked the cradle from side to side.

With the other hand, they poured small amounts of water into the cradle from a tin with a wooden handle fixed to it. At the lower end of the cradle, dirty water sloshed over a wooden weir into a small chute that drained to a panning-dish on the ground. To one side was a pile of sandy gravel – pay dirt dug and carried from the lead – on the other side, the heap of washdirt emptied from the cradle.

While they worked on, Fox explained that in the bottom of each cradle was a thick layer of coir or plush. As the cradle was rocked back and forth, swilling the load of paydirt around in the water, the heavy pieces of gold worked their way down through the gravel to be caught in the coir matting. Whenever they chose, the men would stop rocking the cradle, drain out the bath of water, scoop out the washdirt onto its heap and lift the coir into a panning dish. Then with a little clean water, the gold could be carefully flushed and picked out of the matting. All the water could continue to be recycled throughout the day, then left to settle-out the sediment overnight.

Between the three of them – two operating cradles, one bringing paydirt and working the lead – Fox and his mates could wash a large amount of gravel each day, using a minimum of precious water. From day to day they exchanged roles to relieve the monotony.

How frequently the cradle was emptied and reloaded with fresh paydirt was a matter of judgement. If the paydirt was rich, emptying the cradle too soon risked leaving some valuable gold in the dumped washdirt, but the more paydirt washed in a day, the more gold that was recovered. If the paydirt was poor, then it needed a thorough washing to be sure that even its smallest grains of gold were recovered, but long washing of low-yielding dirt still meant that little gold was recovered for that day.

As Fox explained, when a lead of rich paydirt was found, they all worked frenziedly in the excitement of seeing such riches accumulating by the hour. In their haste to wash as much of the rich dirt as quickly as possible, they probably threw out more gold left in the washdirt than would often be recovered on their leaner days.

We moved over to the side of the claim away from the stream to where their two tents were pitched. In front was a fireplace of stones, a piece of iron suspended between the stones stacked high on each side from which two tin billies were slung. Like everything else brought to the goldfield, even wood for the fire had to be paid for in gold or in cash.

After some hours in the valley, the stench we had smelled on our approach seemed less pungent, probably because we were becoming accustomed to it. Fox told us that sickness was rife among the diggers, the lack of clean water together with a dearth of vegetables exacerbating the ever-present dysentery. Every claim had an open hole – a cesspit – with no cover or even screening. For privacy, most diggers defecated in the darkness at night but when wracked with dysentery, men would have to rush for their cesspit throughout the day.

There were neither bath-houses nor facilities for diggers to wash themselves, their clothes or their bedding. Few of the men had more than the one set of clothes they were wearing. Lice in their hair and clothes were becoming an irritating problem.

Fox said that every gully here in the headwaters of the Tuapeka – not only Gabriel's and Wetherston's but the Woolshed, Munroe's, Waipori, Waitahuna – were all filled with miners. Every day, more men arrived to join the diggers, coming directly off the ships arriving in Dunedin from Australia several times each week. Most new arrivals were Irish peasant immigrants who had fled the famine for a supposedly better life in Australia, Irish or Scots deportees or ex-convicts now freemen, escaped 'ticket-o-leave' parolees, all of whom had worked the goldfields of Victoria. Highly suspicious of strangers, their shout of 'Joe' when we were wending our way through the diggings was their warning cry in case we might be police or bounty hunters come amongst them.

They squeezed into every small piece of land the Miner's Committee had left to allocate, even up onto the hillsides. It was not surprising then that the stench coming from the goldfields could be smelled from afar, nor that the Tuapeka River at its confluence with the Molyneaux – which we passed by so frequently – was filthy brown and laden with sediment.

Harry and I stood watching when Fox returned to his work with the Reids. Although it was repetitive labour in which they were engaged, anticipation built as shovel after shovel of paydirt was washed through the cradles. We crowded close later in the day as the water was drained out of the cradles, the final load of washdirt gravel removed and the coir mat lifted out into a large panning dish.

Like fish caught in a net, the tangle of coir was alive with the unmistakable dull colour of alluvial gold from irregular-shaped pieces the size of a fingernail down to grains as fine as sand. Carefully, they teased and picked the gold free from the coir, jiggling it gently. With Fox leaning over closely, the Reids added a little clean water to each of their pans, swilling the gold around in a final wash to float off strands of loose coir. The water was tilted off carefully and the gold poured into a soft leather drawstring bag. Fox estimated the yield from the two cradles to be about 18 ounces, which at the fixed price of £3 17 shillings per fine ounce would earn the three of them nearly £70. It seemed an easy way to make such a large sum but Fox emphasised that the present lead they were digging, now almost exhausted, was the richest they had found for many weeks.

With the sun lower in the sky but still well-above the ridge line (at this time of year darkness did not fall until nearly 11 p.m.) we sat around the lit fire roasting the chops of wild pork I had purchased from the Bissets in Port Molyneaux, brought upriver and carried in to Fox's as a gift. As the appetising smell of smoking pork-fat wafted from the fire, Harry and I both talked again of the apparent ease with which so much wealth could be won from the ground, just by the taking.

'If that's what you think JC, then come and try for yourself!' Fox rejoined. 'What you saw today is an exception, probably the last of it. For more than a month, we've just been working tucker-ground, poor diggings just earning enough to pay for our food. The best of it's long gone I'm thinking. We've spot-dug over most of these three claims that we've not yet worked, right down to the bedrock without finding much with strong colour.

'It's the same over most of the fields. The best time was early, the first month or so after I'd arrived. Why, in the middle of November, a gold wagon left here escorted by a detachment of mounted troopers armed with guns and sabres. After it reached Dunedin they reported it carried 35,000 ounces – nearly a ton of gold! A King's ransom! I'll wager there hasn't been that much won from the fields in all the weeks since.' Peter and John Reid nodded vigorously in agreement.

Fox reached into the smoke and retrieved his blackening chops. I poured more whisky into our mugs. Holding the chops by the ends of their long bones, we began to tear into the strong succulent meat at the eye. Between mouthfuls washed down with long swigs of raw whisky, Fox continued where he'd left off.

'I'm thinking there's only two ways to make our fortune out of gold, JC. Either we strike it rich by finding and mining it first – before any others. Or else clever engineers like you have to build us some machines that can wash large amounts of the gravel through in a day without needing much labour.

'We don't have any machines other than cradles JC, so for me, the only choice is to find a new field someplace else. Just think about it – all this gold has been lying here in Gabriel's for years, so close to the coast, just waiting for somebody to find it. The land's been walked over, it's been farmed by Wetherston and others, I'm told there was even talk in Dunedin for years that there were traces of gold here in the Tuapeka area, yet it still wasn't discovered until Read came here to prospect for it. Now it's been dug by the ton – found in every gully in this district. But it was here all the time!

'I'll wager that this is not the only gold in Otago that's lying there just waiting to be found. But I'm not just going to wager and wait. Soon I'll go looking for it.

'There were traces on the Mataura when I went south. Now here it is in the east. The country to the west they tell me is vast, filled with river valleys, mountains and gorges. There must be more gold lying there somewhere, just for the finding. I've been lucky to have won enough here JC to grubstake me for a long time searching for it. If we don't find another rich lead on this claim very soon, I won't wait around, I'll go off prospecting for it myself.'

He gave the fire a push with his boot, reached out for another fill of whisky. Small puffs of warm wind heated by the day's sun on the bare stony ground wafted around as dusk began to fall. Miners throughout the valley sat quietly around their fires. The first lantern lights began to appear.

'So what will you do JC, when the next gold's found? For certain there'll be another rush if that happens – the diggers will leave here in their thousands for wherever it is. The need for your cargoes up the river will leave here with them. Why wait for that to happen? When I go off prospecting, sell your boat whilst the business is still good JC, you and your cousin come with me!'

The Reid brothers looked at us, waiting to hear my answer. When the silence lengthened, Peter Reid spoke first. 'We've decided we won't leave here yet to go with him, Fraser. John and I are only recently here from Dunedin. We both have business back there – I'm a stonemason and John's a wheelwright. We want to be sure this claim is fully exhausted before we'll willingly abandon it. Better we keep digging in this place that we know has gold than to scour the country looking for other places that might. Or might not too. If or when Fox finds a new field, we'll be pleased to help him work it, but meantime, we're staying here.'

Around the valley, lamps, candles and flares flickered. The horrible scene of daytime desolation disappeared in darkness. This years' end night, more than most others, seemed to draw the diggers together into a community of shared hardships, shared isolation, as scattered voices began to join together in song. Around the valley came the sound of fiddles and concertinas as hundreds of voices sang music-hall ballads, or the mournful lilts of Irish and Scottish folk-songs. The soft night air felt heavy with sentiment and nostalgia, for every man of us here had some far off place we'd once called home left long behind.

While others took up their refrain, I sat looking into the fire, comforted by having Harry here at my side as thoughts of all that had passed this year now gone swept over me. The growing line of empty whisky bottles around the stone hearth reflected the flames. At the close of the year around midnight, the strains of the Scottish farewell, 'Auld Lang Syne' took hold until the whole valley resounded emotively to the strength of more than a thousand voices singing in unison. A moment of silence, then ragged cheers as the old year passed. We five all shook hands, wondering what the New Year might hold for us.

* * *

Under a warm summer sky, Harry and I steamed lazily down the bright blue river next day, heading back to the Port, Harry stretched out on the foredeck whilst I sprawled aft at the tiller, drawn off into thought. Fox's words of the previous night kept drifting into my mind. I had not replied to his suggestions, just left them hanging unanswered in the air.

Of course he was correct; it was obvious to us that our lucrative river trade would be lost the moment gold might be discovered elsewhere. There would surely be another rush of miners that would empty Gabriel's within days, all eager for the rich pickings that could await the first to claim ground on a new field.

Fox's was not an original thought: I had warned Harry when he first arrived south that we had to take all the trade that offered while gold was still being won from the Tuapeka, for who knew when it might run out. Already, growing competition from wagons on the overland trail since it had been improved had caused us to ease back on our freight charges, though we still earned a large margin. Even Arthur Denniston had discussed with me the prospect of the Beaumont settlers buying the *Lady Colina* should I decide to sell, so dependent had they all become on the river transport and the prospect that its continuation held for all the farmers along the Molyneaux valley.

But I kept reminding myself that I had no commitment to this Colony; to the contrary, I had strong reason not to stay, such reason which I had continually to repress from my mind. Only successive circumstances had led me to this venture on the river, holding me here, with its opportunity to build myself some wealth before I moved on. Now Harry was with me with the same intent – we had already resolved that whatever direction we should next pursue, we would do so together.

However, as we both discussed Fox's proposal we concluded there was still such good money to be made here on the river that we should not abandon it for a tenuous life prospecting. Should Fox or others in fact discover gold elsewhere, the allure of a quick fortune that might be made could not then be ignored – if such an event occurred, we would have nothing to lose by joining the diggers for a short period whilst we tried our own luck. If not, we would maintain our present venture as long as it remained lucrative, then probably join Harry's brothers in the Argentine.

We worked on diligently throughout the heat of summer, interrupted only by the need to haul the boat from the water at Port Molyneaux to replace the worn bronze bearings and aft seal on her shaft. Using a team of bullocks, at high tide we dragged her steadily over logs as rollers, up a sloping bank. At low water there was ample ground on which to remove the rudder, withdraw the shaft, repair the bearings with new bronze sleeves from Burns & Co, then reposition the shaft. I carefully checked the points where her back had once been broken but the beams I had installed on which to mount the engine had kept her securely joined. Only some additional caulking was needed to maintain her watertight.

Back on the river, the water levels dropped steadily under the hot summer sun, making navigation quite difficult. Our frequent labours in the water pushing *Lady Colina* off gravel banks or through shallow channels were a welcome relief from the heat of the sun. The deep valley of the Molyneaux seemed to trap the hot air, not cooling much at night, then building to an even higher temperature each day. When a northwest wind came, it was like a blast from a desert, drying and cracking our browned skin, sucking the moisture from our eyes and mouths. The only respite was the chill river water itself of which we drank copiously, poured over ourselves with buckets or wallowed in when evening came.

I did not manage to return to the goldfield until late April. Arthur Denniston went on the round trip to the Port, with Harry managing the boat alone for the first time, whilst I rode back to Wetherstons. The lines of shanties were unchanged, just more of them. Crowds of diggers filled the street even in mid-morning while shouts from the wrestling tent indicated that a bout was in progress. I passed close by a tent with its front flap rolled open diagonally; inside I could see men sitting on gin boxes playing a card game at a rough table, an unmistakable lustre of gold piled in the centre.

I left the horse in a corral, walked through the shanties to the first of the diggings. The same desolate scene of bare ground, bigger heaps of stones, the movement of diggers everywhere. Again the cry of 'Joe' spread before me as miners turned to look, then resumed their labours. Picking my way through the diggings past Blue Spur, I expected at any moment to see the towering figure of Fox working on his claim. But only the Reid brothers greeted me. Fox himself was gone.

Whilst I waited for Harry to return, I stayed with the Reids, helping them to work the claim. They told me that Fox had left some two months previously, deciding that as the lead they had been following appeared to be almost worked out, he would try his luck at prospecting further westward up the valley of the Molyneaux.

The first frosts had come early to the goldfields, presaging a long cold winter ahead. Already now at the end of April, the air had a distinct chill even in the middle of the day. Although Peter Reid had used his stonemason's skills since my last visit at New Year to build up a small hut of layered rocks, it only provided shelter from the winds which swept through the valley. The cold – as well I remembered from my childhood in Scotland – would seep into the stone, then radiate from the inside walls to freeze the hut to the same temperature as the frost outside.

Digging and carrying gravel early in the morning was an excellent antidote for the white frost that lay crisp upon the ground, not yet so cold that the ground itself was frozen, as it would do so further into the winter. The Reids were following a small new lead at the rear of the claim which was providing just sufficient gold to maintain their interest. While they rocked their cradles, I dug the gravel for them from this lead, standing down waist deep in a hole which exposed the layers of gravel as a bank beside me. This cross-section of bank clearly showed itself as having been laid down in time long past, with layers of sand, small pebbles, coarser gravels and larger rounded stones as wide horizontal bands. No gold was visible, but because gold was so heavy, it was most likely to be buried amongst the sediments deeper in the hole, closer to the bedrock which underlay the valley floor, but one could never be sure exactly where it might lie.

Whenever either of the Reids stopped to empty a cradle, I hurried over to see what gold, if any, was revealed in the coir mat, the expectation having built up during the tedious hours of washing. After the fines were shaken from the mat into a pan, then swilled off, only small grains of gold remained for all our effort. But just as easily, had the ground been rich, the result could have been hugely different. I began to understand more lucidly how the lure of undiscovered fields had led Fox away prospecting; the anticipation that the next creek, the next sandy bank, the next beach of the next river, would reveal the gold lying there thick and rich for the taking.

The first cold breaths of approaching winter combined with the disappointing yield from the claim had prompted the Reids to consider returning to Dunedin. As John said, they both had trades they could resume there, in warmth and shelter away from the privations of bleak Wetherstons. In their six months as diggers, they had won sufficient gold to reward their effort quite handsomely – if a new field was discovered where this experience could be advantageous, they would probably join in any new rush.

Already quite a number of diggers, tired of the arduous conditions, the harshness of their surroundings, the prospect of a bitter winter soon ahead and the lower yields being won, had abandoned their claims to return to Dunedin and settlements along the east coast. Some claims had been abandoned, fully worked out, but were now being reworked by small groups of Chinese people who had come from Victoria, patiently sifting through the discarded piles of previously-washed gravels for even the smallest particles of gold that might have been missed in the early weeks of the rush in the diggers' haste to wash as much of the richest gravel as quickly as possible.

When I took leave of the Reids to return to Beaumont, I deliberately passed close by such a group, the first Chinese people I had ever seen. Four or five small dark men, each almost hidden in a shapeless dark-blue garment like a gown that fell from a high collar under the chin completely to the dirty ground, huddled together in a crouch, swilling gravel in pans. On their heads were strange tight-fitting caps from beneath which a long rope of plaited black hair hung down each of their backs at least to waist level. They did not look up as I passed by, nor even so much as glance toward me, but continued their panning, staring into the pans intensely.

When Harry and I returned back down river under a cold dull grey sky, I felt quite despondent. I could foresee that if many other diggers like the Reids left the goldfields for the coast with the onset of winter, we too would be spending much more time in the cottage I had built at Port Molyneaux as the need for our cargoes reduced. I had now spent nearly eight months plying back and forth along the river in return for which I had accumulated more wealth in my account at the Bank of New South Wales than I ever imagined possible. Although having Harry with me was enjoyable companionship, I was not enamoured at the prospect of spending the next few months sitting idle in Port Molyneaux.

* * *

The first snows of the 1862 winter came early. In late May we headed down river into a fierce southeasterly wind driving up the valley with sleet, then snow, being flung into our faces. Harry crouched in the shelter of the boiler, but I had to stand at the tiller, a hat pulled low, the collar of my coat masking much of my face, trying to see through snow-stung eyes where best to steer. Eventually we were forced to stop, pulling in to a bank overhung by kanuka bush for some protection as the storm swept over us, turning afternoon into an early night.

Frost followed the snow. Days of frost, then fog in the valley with white hoar frost coating the land, each day more cold than the day before, the fog so thick as to hide what sun there might have been. Ice built up in layers on the banks of the river and all the streams that flowed into it. The river level began to drop quite quickly as snow replaced the rain in the mountains and ice froze the watershed that fed the Molyneaux.

June brought more storms, some wet with gales from the north, mostly bitter cold with snow from the south. We tried to avoid the worst of them, but the diggers needed food, barrels of oil for their lamps and kegs of brandy to alleviate their misery. Sitting by a fire in the warmth of my cottage at the port listening to the wind howling over the roof, my earlier feelings of despondency returned. Why was I just waiting for some inevitable change in our circumstances to arrive unannounced? Why not choose now, ourselves, to pursue something new, rather than wait to be forced at a time not of our choice?

Perhaps the time had come to sell the *Lady Colina* to Arthur Denniston whilst there were still diggers left on the goldfield. Perhaps it was time to leave this Colony.

Having encouraged Harry to come and join me, it was not a decision I would enter into without his agreement. Fortunately in the short time he had been with me, even after repaying the people up north their loans for his voyage south, he still had saved more money than he had had in his life. Though it was far from sufficient to buy land for a farm, it would easily cover the cost of a passage to South America, should we choose to go. Whatever my decision, he would be party to it; wherever I decided to go, he would come.

When the weather abated, we made our way back up river. We were agreed that I would test Arthur Denniston's and the Beaumont settlers' willingness to purchase my boat and the business, a percentage of any payment for the latter to be shared with Harry.

We picked our way carefully through the shallows of the braided section of the river, the water level the lowest I had yet seen. Further inland, the Blue Mountains to the south and even the lower hills to the north were crusted with deep snow.

As the beech-log and river-stone quay at the mouth of the Beaumont River hove into view, I could see the familiar figure of Arthur Denniston already waiting there for us, drawn by the steady thump of our engine echoing between the hills of the valley.

Closer, I looked again. The man on the quay could not be Arthur Denniston. Such an unmistakable physique fitted only one man I knew. It was Fox.

ELEVEN

Fox looked gaunt. His clothes hung loosely around his huge shoulders, the long hair tumbling down to join his even-longer bushy beard could not cover sunken cheeks, the bones under his eyes quite prominent. But eyes glowing, he seemed pleased to see us.

'I've been waiting for you JC. Came back to the Reid brothers only to find they've left for Dunedin. Knew if I waited here for a while, you two would show up.' He took a paynter, tied us to the quay, then helped us unload.

'I've come here to ask for your help,' Fox said, when the three of us were sitting in the shelter of Denniston's stone store, 'but in turn, you I think you'll be interested to hear why.'

He told us he had left Wetherston's not long after we had visited at New Year. The lead they had been following on their claim began to run out without any prospect from all their spot-digging of finding a new seam of gravel that would offer any better than tucker dirt. Fox decided that having some months of summer ahead was an opporute time to set off prospecting on his own account, so he departed.

Initially he wanted to follow the Molyneaux further westward, checking some of its tributaries as he progressed. Most of those close to the Tuapeka had already been thoroughly prospected with – as in the nearby Beaumont River – none showing any sign of gold.

Upriver from the Beaumont settlement, the unnavigable Molyneaux headed in a long northwest curve for over 30 miles, much of which was through very steep rocky gorges between the Old Man Range pressing against the left bank and the Knobby Range on the right. The river then turned progressively toward the north for another 15 miles in a more open valley before again disappearing into high mountains.

Rather than struggle along the ranges or through the deep gorges immediately above Beaumont, Fox elected to take a different – apparently easier – route that first led north, then west, to join the Molyneaux again on its right bank in the more open valley beyond the Knobby Range. On foot, carrying a swag on his back, he followed a track from the head of Gabriel's Gully, up into the convoluted wilderness of barren windswept hills and meandering gullies that formed the Lammerlaw Ranges.

Eventually, this vague northern track Fox pursued interdicted the Dunstan Trail, a more visible track leading from the coast south of Dunedin to the far west, originally used by natives travelling inland and more worn latterly by pioneer graziers settling farms in the interior. Fox briefly described his journey along the trail to the west across a series of barren low ranges separating wide shallow valleys filled with seeping swamps that could sink a man to his armpits in mossy bogs. There was no forest or trees, just endless miles of open tussock-land occasionally rising to random higher ridges or peaks topped with rock. Across this deserted land, the wind blew unceasingly from every direction.

After many days of struggle, particularly with the swamps and the hundreds of soggy small streams that ran aimlessly in every direction, Fox descended a steeper ridge into a vast valley lying north-south. This much drier stony valley was coursed by the Manuherikia River which, to the south, eventually fed into the Molyneaux. Along the full length of the western side of the Manuherikia Valley rising up against the afternoon sun rose the rugged Dunstan Mountains.

Being much drier, the wide valley of the Manuherikia had extensive grassy plains that had been earlier settled by graziers along its forty mile northward reach. Most of these early farmers had each claimed grazing rights over huge areas of the suitable country, with the result that the land was very sparsely settled, each habitation far from its neighbours.

Fox explained that the trails here in the interior wandered from one habitation to the next, the farmers being sufficiently long-established as to have erected substantial houses and buildings made with the slate-like stone of the district mortared with a mixture of mud, sand and tussock. These clusters of buildings had the appearance of being stations along the line of a track, thus each becoming known as a 'station'. The farmers were generally very hospitable toward travellers, generously providing shelter, food and lodging to the footweary who came their way.

Fox stopped first at Moutere Station. During his stay the runholders, the Galloways, told him of rumours of gold traces having being found at scattered points far in the headwaters of the Manuherikia and the St Bathans mountain range which enclosed its valley to the north, but none had yet been substantiated. They also told of natives who had said that this useless gold stone the white men sought could be found in valleys to the west.

From Galloways', Fox followed the Manuherikia down to its confluence with the Molyneaux, a place known locally as 'The Junction'. Broad swathes of flat land lay on both sides of the Molyneaux at this point, on the west side rising to very high mountains farther to the south-west.

A clansman of yours JC, another Fraser – a very hospitable man too – has long-established a homestead on grazing land all along the west side of the Molyneaux, a place he calls 'Earnscleugh Station' which he reaches by a small boat across the river at The Junction.

'While I was staying there, intending to prospect some of the streams up into the mountains further to the west, two elderly men appeared. They obviously knew Fraser-of-Earnscleugh well, having called at the station several times previously. Although they kept closely to themselves, I learned that these hardened men were experienced prospectors from California, named Hartley and Rielly. They had spent months in the area, prospecting most of the streams along the west side of the Molyneaux and for some miles up-river, returning occasionally to Earnscleugh Station for supplies.

'They had already covered all the ground that I was thinking to prospect myself,' said Fox. But, they told him, their search having been utterly fruitless, they had decided to abandon further prospecting and return out to the coast before the onset of winter. They departed.

Fraser-of-Earnscleugh told Fox that Hartley had prospected up the Molyneaux as far west as the point where the Molyneaux divided into two separate rivers which formed it, the Kawerau River from the west and the Clutha River from the north. Fraser suggested that as the Californians had found nothing, Fox would have to prospect even further westward, or search in the headwaters of the Manuherikia where signs were rumoured to have been found. Fox chose initially to go westward.

Fraser-of- Earnscleugh drew Fox a map of the mountainous region to the west as best as he knew it. From Earnscleugh Station, a trail wound through and over the mountains to the west and south of the Molyneaux and Kawerau Rivers. The trail had been used for perhaps centuries by the natives who travelled over to the western coast to gather the green stone jade which they prized for their tools and weapons. Even now, they still used this route.

From Earnscleugh Station the trail went inland along the Hawk Burn which lay behind the rugged Cairnmuir Mountains that bordered the Molyneaux, avoiding the Molyneaux gorge region of precipitous ravines and bluffs already prospected by the Californians. Across a low saddle at the head of the Hawk Burn, the trail descended down the Bannock Burn to the Kawerau River, upstream from its junction with the Clutha and the Molyneaux. From there, Fraser's map was less certain. With as heavy a load of supplies as he could carry, Fox set out again.

I must have displayed some impatience at the length of the story Fox was relating to us, for he interrupted himself to comment: 'There is an end to this tale JC – as you will find – but if you and your cousin are to help me, you must hear me out.' We sat patiently while he continued.

The Bannock Burn meandered steadily down toward the deep valley of the Kawerau River. This was reportedly as far to the west as the Californians had prospected without success. At a place before the Burn dropped sharply from a terrace into a steep gully toward the river, the trail crossed over to its west bank. At the crossing near the edge of the terrace, Fox noticed white quartz stones mixed in the grey gravels, so panned a scoop of sediment from the edge of the Burn. To his surprise, the washdirt showed traces of gold.

Although he then panned upstream and downstream for some distance on both sides of the crossing point over the Burn, the sign was no heavier, though the same traces were present wherever he tried.

Thus encouraged, Fox decided to move further westward, attempting to follow the Kawerau River. The map which Fraser-of-Earnscleugh had drawn was less definite from this point; the country so barren and rocky that the trail frequently vanished. He tramped up a westward branch of the Bannock Burn leading up into the more-rounded mountains of the Old Woman Range.

'I cannot describe to you how wild and desolate that country along the Kawerau is, JC – only by seeing it for yourself, could you understand,' said Fox. 'It's a fearsome wilderness of the highest mountains I have ever seen; sheer walls of rock, cliffs and bluffs that plunge thousands of feet into ravines and gorges so deep that the sun doesn't penetrate. There are no trees or forests. Even the vegetation – what little there is – is as savage as the land itself; small leafless bushes made only of vicious thorns, thickets of sword-grass with stiff leaf-blades as long and sharp as a rapier that can pierce your boot or your leg just as easily.'

The Kawerau River itself could not be followed. It disappeared deep within an impassable canyon cut through near-sheer rock. Climbing high above its gorge as shown on the map, Fox had struggled painfully along the side of ranges bordering it, often finding his direction blocked by bluffs or deep ravines slashed into the hillsides. Any traces of the trail were long-lost on the bare broken rock. Slowly he picked his way around the aptly-named Mt Difficulty, the highest mountain in the range along the west side of the Kawerau Gorge, at times slipping on loose fractured rock or being caught in slides of soft shingle that filled many of the gullies.

Fortunately, Fox said, he had made that journey in summertime, in winter it would be impossible. The summer sun baked the black rock during the day, reflecting a fierce heat that was replaced at night by a bitter cold from the high mountains. There was no trace of quartz in any of the gullies but at least many contained trickles or seeps of water to sustain him.

Determined to keep going, Fox eventually rounded Mt Difficulty, from where he saw the precipitous walls of rock guarding the impassable side canyon of the Nevis River that itself barred the way any further westward. By following the map, he found again the trail that descended down a steep tussock hillside broken with grotesque outcrops of rock, deep into the gorge of the Kawerau River far below. When the vegetation ran out, the trail was marked with cairns of stones obviously placed by human hand. Scrambling on down nearer the river, Fox saw below as described by Fraser-of-Earsncleugh, the natural-arch bridge of rock spanning the tumult of the Kawerau, the only known crossing-point, found and used by the natives since back into time.

'I only crossed that bridge once,' he said, looking serious. 'I would hope never to do it again, nor recommend it to the faint of heart. The river at that place is squeezed between two great walls of jagged rock, hurling itself in a roaring white mass through the narrow gap. Gouts of wash tumble into the air, spray drifts over to wet the slippery rock. Spans of the bridge arch out from the walls on each side, becoming quite thin in the middle, some forty feet above the violent rush of the river.

'But the arch bridge doesn't quite meet in the middle – a section in the centre has fallen away. Although the top is quite wide, it's jagged all over, with unstable broken rock on both sides. One slip and a man is lost into the seething torrent below. I'm afraid of nothing, JC, but crossing that bridge....' He shook his head slowly.

'Yet many do it, the natives frequently and with nonchalance. Getting out along the bridge myself was difficult, then I had to leap across the gap in the middle. Christ Himself was watching me – despite all that I've said about him – or I wouldn't be here with you now. After that, all my journey since has seemed easy.'

Directly across the Kawerau, the rocky narrow valley of the Kittle Burn* angled steeply upward through thickets of thornbush and speargrass. Higher up into the Criffel Range, the Kittle Burn divided, the track following the Annie Burn* angling to the west slowly up into the tussock-covered tops of the Criffel. Over a saddle at a crossing-point in the Criffel, a winding gully led down a short easy gradient to the headwaters of the Cardrona stream, little more than a small creek. From the top of the narrow Cardrona valley, Fox descended down a terraced mountainside of the Crown Range from where he could see closely-sandwiched between more ranges of high mountains, the distant blue of a long lake, on the shore of which lay the homestead of a Mr Rees and Fox's destination.

The trail led down into the valley of the upper Kawerau River, upriver from the point at which it plunged into its fearsome gorges. The swampy valley, riven by streams, small lakes and several rivers that fed into the Kawerau, progressively widened out up to the rivers' source at the lake, where eventually Fox arrived at the stone homestead of Rees on the shores of Lake Wakatipu.

Being known to Fraser-of-Earnscleugh, Rees welcomed Fox warmly. Exhausted by his arduous journey that had taken far longer than he expected, Fox rested at Lake Wakatipu Station that Rees had settled years earlier. Rees had recently transported a boat, a ships' pinnace, by ox-wagon up the gentle valley of the Mataura River at the southern end of the lake, a benign route to the Wakatipu when compared with the horrors of the alternative journey from the east. Rees used this boat to convey supplies from the southern lake-head up the long arm of the Wakatipu to his station, taking two men two days in calm weather to row each load, less if a southerly wind would fill a sail.

Fox had intended using Wakatipu Station as his base from which to

---

*later named Roaring Meg and Gentle Annie

prospect the lake shore and rivers in the vicinity but, his journey having taken far longer than he expected, winter was now not far ahead. Rees warned him clearly of the savagery of winter here in the south-western mountains. From the homestead Fox could see the deep-blue ice-covered Alps forming the horizon up the western arm of the lake which Rees told him were deeply covered with permanent snow even throughout the summer, such was their height. When winter came, prospecting would be impossible as snow frequently buried the land in deep drifts, while frosts were so severe as to freeze small lakes and streams. Without good shelter, warmth and supplies, a man would easily die.

Rees employed a half-caste native to help row his boat transporting supplies and to watch over his sheep as they roamed the trackless tussock-covered hills. Rees disclosed to Fox that this man, 'Maori Jack' as he was known, had in his possession some pieces of gold he claimed to have found in the near-region to the homestead. Whenever Rees had closely questioned Maori Jack for the origin of these pieces, he had become secretive. Rees then displayed disinterest, in the hope that Maori Jack would reveal where he had found such apparently worthless objects.

'I befriended him during my stay at Rees's', Fox related. 'I pretended I had come to the Wakatipu searching to find the greenstone but he was equally secretive about its location too. When I then asked to see his strange 'gold stones', he produced one, a rough twisted piece of metal about an inch across. When I asked where he had found it, he looked quite sly, and would not answer me.

'I even shared some precious whisky with him in the hope that a little drunkenness would loosen his tongue, but the more he drank, the more secretive he became. All I learned was that he thought the gold 'stone' was useless, only keeping a piece he had picked up because it was so heavy he might use it as a weight on a line.

'Rees told me that for two years, Maori Jack had mostly stayed close to the station, only making trips to the south end of the lake with the boat or shepherding the sheep around the grazing land in the area. From that, I concluded he had found the gold somewhere nearby.'

Fox prospected for weeks along the shores of the lake and up the streams running into it. Although the ground looked promising, with a large quantity of white quartz stone everywhere, it was not auriferous.

He was discouraged by the total absence of any sign and by Rees's repeated tales of the severity of the winters. To the immediate south lay the valley of the Mataura where first Fox had gone a year previously on the fraudulent promise that gold would be found there. Now he had come almost a full circle. It seemed pointless to return down the Mataura again.

Rees described to Fox a much easier route back east that traversed the north side of the Kawerau instead of the fearsome journey Fox had followed on the south side, warning that it was a trail he should follow before winter came. So Fox decided he would return by this route into the headwaters of the Manuherikia, prospecting some of the area mentioned by the Galloways as rumoured to have signs of gold. Fox had found the interior of Otago was such a rugged mountainous wilderness over such a vast area, a man could spend his whole lifetime prospecting without covering even the tiniest portion of it. Far better to concentrate his efforts where hearsay suggested gold was more likely. If the upper Manuherikia Valley was unsuccessful, he would use the middle two months of winter out at the coast to outfit himself thoroughly, then return again to the Wakatipu when spring came, to renew searching for the location of Maori Jack's gold.

With all the supplies he could carry purchased from Rees, Fox retraced the trail east, over the saddle on the Crown Range into the head of the Cardrona Valley, up the side-gully leading onto the Criffel Ranges, down the Annie Burn to the Kittle Burn. But instead of turning south down the Burn to the natural-arch bridge over the Kawerau, he followed Rees's directions, turning left to climb up the Kittle's cascades northward, then turning east from its headwaters to cross the adjacent Pisa Range. Along the ridgeline at the top of the Pisa Range, he found – as Rees had drawn – signs of an old track that led down a gully of the Low Burn that eventually crossed several large barren terraces to reach the Clutha River. Just upriver from that confluence, the Clutha divided itself into narrow channels around several islands and by wading chest-deep in the numbingly-cold water, he managed to ford it.

Only one major barrier now lay between the Clutha Valley and the Manuherikia - the forbidding rock-strewn Dunstan Mountains. However, not far north from where he had crossed the Clutha River, Rees had drawn on the map a route that traversed a pass through the mountains rather than over them that would take him directly into the upper Manuherikia Valley. This trail followed a dry watercourse cut like a cleft into the centre of the Dunstan Mountain chain, at the top of which, on a low pass, Fox could see spread off before him the wide expanse of the Manuherikia Valley.

He knew that from where he was intending to prospect at the upper (northern) end of this huge valley, a well-defined trail ran due east out to the coast, north of the Dunedin settlement. For the Galloways and other settlers in the Manuherikia, it was that same trail by which they had first come west. Even Fraser-of-Earnscleugh frequently travelled to and from Dunedin via the Manuherikia in preference to the windswept desolate wastes and frequent swamps of the Dunstan Trail. If prospecting in the upper-Manuherikia was unsuccessful, Fox could then follow that same route out to the coast.

'Bear with me Gentlemen, for there is an end to my story,' Fox interrupted himself, 'and I am closing to it.'

Down off the Dunstan Mountains, Fox crossed the tussock plain to the Manuherikia River flowing sedately along its gravelly bed. On reaching the river, he turned leftward to the north, making his way slowly among large luxuriant clumps of wiry brown tussock growing waist-high from the moisture of the river.

As he did, he caught sight of horses being led by two men on the far side of the river. They were the first men he had seen since leaving the Wakatipu over a week earlier. They had not seen him, had just passed parallel with him, were now heading in the opposite direction away from him downriver with their backs to him. Hungry for human contact in this sparsely habited region, Fox turned and hurried after them.

Closing with them, though still on opposite sides of the river, Fox was sufficiently close to call out, when suddenly he thought that their manner of dress was familiar. To his amazement, he realised these two men leading heavily laden packhorses were the Californian prospectors, Hartley and Reilly.

'I kept low in the tussock,' Fox said, 'watching them, puzzled as to why they were again here in the interior, now heading back west with winter approaching, obviously well-outfitted. When they had departed from Earnscleugh Station they declared they were heading out east to the coast for the winter. Perhaps they had changed their minds about that, I thought. Or else they were a pair of cunning, deceitful, lying bastards!'

'I decided to follow them, careful to stay out of sight, at least until I knew where they were headed. I expected they would stop at Galloways, chagrined that to remain hidden, I would have to sleep rough in the tussock while they enjoyed the comforts of Moutere Station. But to my surprise, they crossed over the Manuherikia just upstream from Moutere, giving the Galloways' a wide berth. Rather than follow the Manuherikia down to The Junction and Earnscleugh, they angled away west across the flat land toward the gorge of the Molyneaux.

'At night they camped in a small ravine. I slept hungry nearby, close enough to see the light of their fire. Next day, they headed directly to the entrance of the Dunstan gorge, the same region of precipitous ravines and bluffs they had claimed to have prospected unsuccessfully previously, only they were now on its east side instead of the west.

'To remain hidden, I had to climb high up the steep hillside flanking the gorge, well above the Californians but able to keep their packhorses in sight down below me. Along this side of the gorge, the Dunstan Mountains which stretched for thirty miles northeast behind me, ended at the gorge, falling thousands of feet down to the rushing Molyneaux; opposite, the gorge was flanked parallel along its western side by the equally-precipitous Cairnmuir Mountains.

'Immediately inside the gorge, the Californians made camp again, but next day they did not move on, their horses remained tethered. I crept slowly through the wet tussock keeping screened as best I could by patches of thornbush until I was just able to see them. The place they had camped was above a small beach on the bank of the Molyneaux. Those two old bastards were down there in the water. They were panning for gold! Cunning lying bastards!

'Over the next few days, they kept moving up the gorge. I had to climb very high at times to avoid risking being seen. The gorge is incredibly rough and steep – in most places too sheer lower down toward the river to be traversed, especially with horses. The Californians would climb slowly up to where the mountainside was less-precipitous, then sidle around until they came to another ravine plunging down toward the river. The mountainside for miles along the gorge is reft by many of these ravines, cut like huge slashes into the hillside.

'They would leave their horses tethered high up in each of these ravines, then climb down. Some ravines just run out into deep guts of sheer rock that are impassable before they even reach the river; if so, they would return back up to where their horses were tethered and move on to the next, until they found one that would lead all the way deep into the gorge to the water.

'From behind and up higher, I could follow their every move. If they returned to their horses, took swags and descended down into the gorge, I would sneak down after them. Sometimes I had insufficient cover to be able to get close without being seen, but unmistakably they were panning along the gorge at every place they could reach the riverbank.

'By this time I was close to abandoning the pursuit. To avoid being seen, I had only lit a fire in the dead of night in the few places hidden from view. I was constantly wet from crawling through the tussock. The sun – such as there was – rarely penetrated the steep mountainside on this, the shaded side of the gorge. I had been very hungry for many days. It was always cold.

'Many miles up the gorge, the Californians eventually followed a large watercourse, more of an open gully filled with thornbushes and lush grasses than a rocky ravine, that led down to a beach several hundred yards long on a backwater of the river. They returned only after two days, removing in repeated journeys down to the beach all the loads that the horses had carried. The horses were left behind high up in the gully on long tethers.

'I crept down, using the spine of the gully as a screen. They were camped on a small terrace above the beach, with tents, a large fireplace of stones, piles of driftwood gathered from the riverbank – all signs they intended to stay for some time. Whilst I watched, they were already busy panning on the beach beside the river, but I was too distant to see with what success, if any.

'Sure that the Californians intended to stay in their encampment, I climbed further along into the gorge, upriver from them. Not very far, I too found a narrow gully plunging from one of the highest points of the Dunstan Mountains, that led down to the river. There was a thin strip of gravelly beach below a steep bank. The river surged darkly past.

'Confident the Californians were unlikely to move from their encampment immediately, I climbed down to the beach and scooped up gravel from the river into my pan.'

As he spoke, Fox took a familiar leather pouch from his breeches. He looked at us, his face impassive but his eyes shining. He loosened the drawstring on the pouch … held out his hand … palm uppermost.

'And look what I found!' Into his open palm he shook misshapen nuggets of gold. Harry stared openmouthed. Drew breath in a gasp.

'My God!' I exclaimed. Fox had a huge palm, as large as a small plate.

Four nuggets were almost large enough to cover it. He poured others on top from the pouch.

'Here, JC, hold it yourself.' He tipped the pile of gold into my hand. It must have weighed thirty ounces. 'I didn't stay for long by the river,' Fox said. 'Long enough to pan five or six pounds of gold just from the beach where I stood. It's lying there, thick in the gravel, waiting for us.

'I left, but not before marking my claim with sticks and piles of stones. Hartley and Reilly were still encamped at the bottom of their same gully, working the beach. I tell you, those old bastards are not only liars, they're clever, too. They knew there was gold in the gorge. But they've kept it secret.

'Look what happened here on this Gabriel's' goldfield ... the moment he found paydirt, Gabriel Read ran straight to Dunedin to tell the Gold Commissioner. All he wanted was the glory! Before he'd dug any gold for himself, the rush started. He was overwhelmed by the diggers. He didn't even wait to find out where the richest ground lay, it was claimed by Jenkins, Gillies, Lindsay and others. My own claim was rich enough and it wasn't even in Read's gully.

'Hartley and Reilly are smart; they're mining gold furiously in secret. The west bank they prospected earlier must have gold too, or they wouldn't have returned to the gorge in the middle of winter, well-equipped to stay. Where they're working on the east bank, I'm betting is richer ground than the west, or else they wouldn't be staying there. It was by chance that I saw them in the Manuherikia; by chance that I had met them before at Earnscleugh where by chance they had told me they were leaving for the coast because there was no gold in the area.

'Now chance has favoured us, JC... Harry. I couldn't stay there in the Dunstan Gorge myself, I was starving. I stopped at Galloway's only long enough to swage my hunger on mutton and oatmeal porridge. I decided I couldn't return to the gorge to mine alone. I needed friends I could trust; to make claims next to mine, to secure as much ground as possible. I need help to work the claim quickly, before the secret's out and another rush begins. Then we might have to defend it.

'I paid the Galloway's a fortune for a horse – they'll give me back 15 sovereigns if I return it. I rode back along the Dunstan track as fast as it would carry me, coming back to find you and the Reids. The Reids have gone, but there are still three of us.

We can make a fortune together! Are you with me ... or not?'

Fox looked at us. Harry was still staring at the gold piled in my hand. A hundred jumbled thoughts raced through my mind together. I struggled silently to get them in order, to think clearly, to see the priorities. We had, after all, come up the river this time intending to try selling my boat and the river-freight business to Denniston and the Beaumont settlers especially whilst the business still existed. Fox's proposition meant a further commitment for me to stay longer here in this Colony, to endure unknown hardships and perhaps risk our lives, in return for which was a near-certain chance of a small fortune.

'Wait here Fox. Harry and I will talk this over together, outside. Then we'll be back to give you an answer.' I placed his gold back into his pouch. We went outside, walked away from the store, out of hearing.

I could sense Harry's excitement. For one who had struggled for so long, who yet had little wealth but who still harboured a dream to have a farm of his own somewhere, I was sure of his decision even before he voiced it. 'We must go, John! This is our chance of a lifetime. We've nothing to lose and a fortune to gain!' He held my arm, squeezed it fervently. His eyes bright with excitement.

'Equal shares Harry, in whatever we find, as long as we are diggers together?'

'Of course.'

We turned and walked back to Fox who was now standing in the doorway, waiting anxiously. 'We're with you Fox,' I said, 'but we must outfit ourselves for it thoroughly before we leave here. There's no time to lose.' Fox grinned, nodding his head in agreement.

I went to find Arthur Denniston, urging Fox and Harry meantime to go quickly to Gabriel's' to try to buy themselves guns. All the other supplies we would need were already here in my stock of supplies in Beaumont. Harry was reluctant to buy guns: 'After the famine back home John, when we guarded our farm against marauders those years ago and English soldiers shot starving Irishmen, I swore I would never fire a gun at my fellow-man. So I have no need for one.'

It was time to be forthright: 'Harry, if you want to share in winning a fortune with us, then you must be prepared to defend it with us. Faced with any threat, Fox and I would fight. So must you!' He went.

By the time they returned, I had concluded an agreement with Arthur Denniston. He would purchase the *Lady Colina* and the freight business. I was not so concerned at leaving the boat – she had served me well, considering that she was only kept sound by the large beams I had installed on which the engine was mounted. But the engine itself, I was reluctant to lose, especially such a potentially useful machine, here in the far interior. So in selling the boat, I retained a bill-of-sale over the engine;

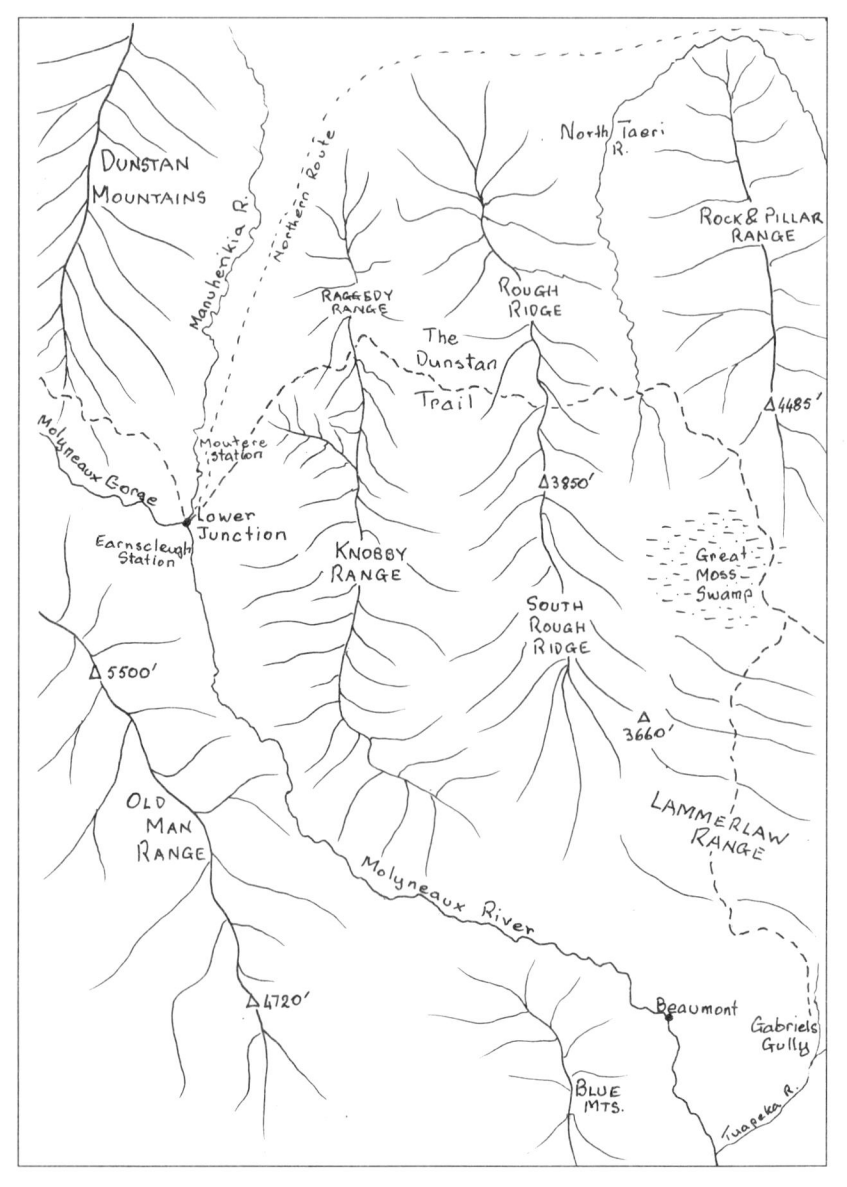

Gabriel's Gully to Molyneaux Gorge

perhaps a day might come when I needed it for another purpose.

As part of the payment from Denniston, I included two packhorses. From the inventory of supplies held in the stores at Port Molyneaux and here in Beaumont, I deducted all the flour, salt, oatmeal, canvas, dry cheeses, vesta matches, shovels and other essentials to sustain us, before transferring the balance to Denniston. Adding some sides of bacon, two small kegs of whisky and my chest of tools, would be all that the horses could carry. Each of us would pack our own swags.

I wrote letters of explanation to Mr Burns and to George to post when we passed through Wetherston's, while Fox and Harry prepared the loads for the horses.

Harry and I returned to the *Lady Colina*, unloading the supplies we had brought upriver before clearing her of all our personal gear. She looked quite forlorn – this boat that had served me and the miners of the goldfields so well for a whole year – lying against the quay with no trace of smoke coming from the stack, the boiler cold. Even if we were never to sight her again, she would continue to bear the name of my loved aunt and Harry's mother for the rest of her days.

We left at first light next day, making our way beyond the goldfield, up the track in to the Lammerlaw wilderness. The valley of the Molyneaux which I had come to know so well, receded from sight.

Previously I had only glimpsed the convoluted landscape of the Lammerlaws from the hills above Dunedin. Now I understood why it was described as a desolate wilderness. Short low broken ridges arose from nowhere, disappearing nowhere, interspersed by soft swampy shallow gullies winding aimlessly. Dotted with clumps of snowgrass, the tussock-covered semi-moorland sloped gradually upward to the northwest. With no dominant ridges or forest cover to provide protection, every wind raced unobstructed across the open land.

Having travelled this way before, Fox led us steadily upward over the featureless expanse leading the horse he was returning to Galloway's, Harry and I following behind with the heavily-laden packhorses, trying to stay on the short ridges but sinking to the tops of our boots in the many soggy little gullies that had to be crossed. Slowly we progressed to higher ground where white frost lay thick upon the ground, crunching loudly at our every step.

The faint track began to follow a more formed ridgeline as we continued to climb gradually. To our west lay steeper ground, rising more sharply up to Davidson's Top over 3000 feet against the sky, capped with snow. I pondered what quirk of nature had formed this land: the gullies just below us to our left (the west) were the headwaters of the Taieri River which then wandered some sixty miles north from here; yet the gullies just down to our right fed into the Taieri again on its returning journey back south. Barely a narrow low ridge separated the two, though the river flowed over a hundred miles to get from one side of that little ridge to the other.

With every mile that passed, the sharp ridges of a mountain chain rose higher into the northern sky ahead of us as we headed toward it. Near its southern end, Fox assured us, our track would meet the Dunstan Trail.

Just before dusk we duly reached the intersection marked with a cairn of stones, pleased to have achieved some thirty miles on our first day. In the treeless landscape, we used shovels as poles for a tent and cut tussock to burn for a fire. Another bitter frost froze the night, sending shards of ice scattering when we dismantled the tent in the morning.

Turning westward that day for the first time since leaving the Molyneaux, I felt that our true journey had just begun as the trail headed down to the first of many dangerous marshes, the Great Moss Swamp. This bog filled a wide depression between the 3000-foot Spiders' Hill to the west and the Rock and Pillar Range to the northeast.

We picked our way carefully, skirting the swamp which in places was thick with ice, obscuring the trail. In the lead, Fox stopped frequently to test the ground; the ice might only be resting on firm ground or could collapse suddenly beneath us and our horses, plunging us chest-deep or more into freezing bog beneath. At times the very ground itself appeared to be afloat on the swamp, as clumps of dead dry rushes and snowgrass would shake and sway up to forty feet either side of us as we passed. Large open areas of spongy moss up to a foot thick clothed the soft wet ground underneath.

Once beyond the Great Moss Swamp, the Rock and Pillar Range began to rise up ahead on our right as we climbed slowly. Its grotesque formations of rock scattered all over and sprouted up from otherwise barren brown tussock covered ridges as if some giants' playground. Strange twisted black rocks sat balanced at near-impossible angles on top of each other, interspersed with tall columns of layered rocks like irregular stacks of enormous dinner-plates.

Far across the shallow dished valley to the west were the lower ridges of the Knobby Range capped with broken heaps of rocks and against the distant western sky we could just see the line of snow along the Dunstan Mountains.

This vast empty basin of land stretching to the west and north seemed more like the interior of some continent rather than a mountainous island. With no wind blowing, the sun shining brightly in a clear blue winter sky, I felt no hostility from the land. For the first time, I could see beauty in the diversity of strange landscapes all about us. If only Elizabeth had been with me to see this country – how she would have enjoyed the magnificence of these hills and plains, the grandeur of distance and height, the emptiness and silence; the contrasts of colour, vegetation and rock, earth and sky.

The Rock and Pillar receded behind us to the east as we picked our way through the trackless labyrinth of rocks on the Knobby Range. Ahead, on the far western side of the Manuherikia valley, the stark Dunstan Mountains now towered up imposingly against the setting sun. We made camp that night up on the Range where the frost was not as severe as down in the lowland of the valley.

The trail next day turned southwest down the valley alongside the Manuherikia River which tumbled through deep pools between bubbling shallows of river-stones, near the place where Fox had first spied Hartley and Reilly passing by. Harry and I took our packhorses across to the opposite side, leaving Fox to return alone to Galloway's. While he returned their horse, we waited out of sight in the snowgrass well off to the west, eventually making a camp for the night on the slowly-rising plain that led to the entrance to the Molyneaux Gorge.

Fox enjoyed the hospitality, warmth and comfort of Moutere Station overnight; Harry and I struggled with the crushing cold of yet another frost, huddled together in our bedrolls trying to find sleep.

Keeping watch as the sun brushed the snow-topped Dunstan Mountains with pink light next morning, we soon saw Fox's tall figure striding through the tussock in the direction we were hiding. He had managed to return the horse to Galloway's without seeming to raise undue suspicion, claiming that he had managed to ride quickly east to the coast up the Manuherikia northern route, re-equip himself with fresh supplies including a large quantity of bagged flour in tins which he had cached in the foothills of the Dunstan Mountains to the north and was now resuming prospecting in the lonely valleys there. They returned his twenty sovereigns.

Fox led us plodding up the triangular plain that trisected the Manuherikia Junction, the south-western end of the Dunstan Mountains falling sharply into the Molyneaux to form the gorge, and a long placid stretch of the river between. Nearer the entrance to the gorge, we angled off toward the mountains, climbing steeply upwards, the laden horses choosing their footing, sidling back and forth. Whereas the vast basin of the Manuherikia was ideal country for horses, they needed coaxing to pick their way up these steep rocky hillsides.

Fox followed a route into the gorge similar to that taken by the Californians who had also led packhorses, climbing high up away from the river. Lower down, closer to the river, the hillsides plunged steeply into the gorge, cut by sheer bluffs, precipices and impassable rock ravines. Here, much higher on the Dunstan Mountains, the hillsides sloped less steeply, forming wider open basins above the ravines, filled with tall snowgrass and fearsome clumps of dangerous swordgrass growing in the better light. Just above us was the lower line of winter's snow. Directly opposite us, about a mile to the southwest, lay the stark jagged Cairnmuir Mountains, the Molyneaux Gorge a deep hidden slash in the land between.

By traversing across these high alpine basins, we progressed deeper along the gorge, the horses snorting long bursts of steam from their flared nostrils into the cold air. In several basins we saw signs where the Californians – as Fox had described – had previously left their horses tethered while they climbed down into the gorge seeking ravines below them that were passable all the way down to the river, the piles of dung on the frozen ground still looking as if they had been freshly-cast. Ahead far above us, the mountainsides soared upwards to the giant column topping the highest point, Leaning Rock.

As we sidled nearly across yet another of these basins, our horses suddenly became agitated, their upright ears pricked forward, pulling back against their bridles, champing jaws against the bits, violent quivers running across their flanks. They could smell or sense other horses nearby. Harry and I stopped, trying to soothe them as they rolled their eyes showing the whites, vigorously shaking their lowered heads, snorting noisily. Fox said quietly that the next hanging basin ahead was most likely that above the ravine where the Californians had made their final camp by the river below. Their horses might well still be there in the high basin, where Hartley and Reilly had left them on long tethers to graze on the alpine grasses.

We waited while Fox crept to the sloping ridge separating us from the next basin. We lost sight of him in the snowgrass, then saw his bare head rise up slowly on the ridgeline, before standing to his full height to wave us forward. The Californians' animals were no longer there, but the many piles of fresh dung littering the ground showed they had been there for some considerable time. Had they been moved further along the gorge, been taken lower down the mountainside, or had they gone?

Again Harry and I stayed waiting while Fox scouted, our horses gradually calming again. Eventually he returned. There was no sign that any animals had been in the next basin ahead, nor were they out of our line of sight immediately below. Fox saw no traces of smoke rising from down in the gorge, but he did not climb deeper into the ravine leading to the Californians' last camp. Given the apparent permanence of the camp they had established when Fox last spied upon them, he thought it unlikely they would have moved again such a brief time later. We resolved to press on to Fox's claim; if the Californians should encounter us now, there was nothing to be lost.

Another mile along the mountainside, we crossed over a ridge into the basin Fox declared was above his claim on the river far below. We carefully sidled the horses downhill. The basin narrowed in its lower centre, falling sharply into a steep ravine. Below, Fox assured us, the ravine opened into the head of another basin, narrower but longer than the one we were leaving, which would take us down much closer to the river.

We stopped to unpack the heavy loads from the horses; freed from their weight, Fox was confident we could safely lead the animals over the ledge below us down into the next basin where they could be tethered to graze. The load of supplies and gear we would then progressively pack down to the river on our backs.

Once over the ledge, we saw that the ravine from the basin above tumbled through a rocky bluff but on either side, although steep, the hill was well covered with vegetation. For the first time, still well below, we could see with anticipation, the dark ribbon of the river. With the horses securely tethered to outcrops of rock, we each climbed back up for a load of supplies.

Climbing down was almost more difficult than climbing upward, the footings less secure, the heavy loads we carried straining thighs and knees. We picked our way down facing sideways to the steep slope of the hillside, Fox leading, first the left leg taking the downhill steps, then turning about to use the right leg to take the weight, holding onto the tough snowgrass for support.

Small bluffs, broken outcrops of rock and short precipices frequently blocked our way down, Fox casting about for a way past while Harry and I waited above. As we progressed downward, the valley on both sides of the gorge was closing in, the light fading. Opposite, the Cairnmuir Mountains plunged almost sheer and barren into the gorge, riven with long guts of broken rock, studded with black precipices.

As we descended, the river now closer and growing ever-larger, our mountainside was becoming almost impassable until suddenly the near-vertical wall of fractured rock levelled out onto a narrow grassy bench some eighty feet or less in width, just above the swirling water racing past. I saw that we were on the outward side of a long sweeping curve in the gorge, the bench running for several hundred yards up and down the river with its narrowing ends blocked by huge bluffs falling directly into the water.

Fox's claim! He led us close by his previous campsite, a fireplace of stacked stones. With relief, we swung the loads from our backs.

Harry didn't stop, grabbed a pan, almost ran across the bench. Fox and I followed. A steep bank of stones some ten feet down. A sharply-sloping gravelly beach falling into deep water, fast-flowing.

Harry slid, jumped, almost into the water in haste. We watched just above. A swift scoop deep into the gravel. Stones and water swishing wildly. He stared for a moment. A shout. He turned, held up the pan toward us.

'John! We're rich! Look at this! Just look at this!' His hands visibly shaking, eyes wild, a grin stretching his mouth wide. Fox and I now down the bank. I clutched the pan from Harry, still heavy with gravel. There, unmistakably, several large misshapen lumps of dull gold among the stones.

I turned to Fox. He looked satisfied, nodded. 'I promised you a fortune here JC! Just lying in wait for us.' I reached out a hand toward him, clasped his in a firm grip. 'I've never doubted you for a moment, Fox. Nor could I want for a better man to be sharing it.'

Harry didn't stop to lift the lumps of gold from the pan; spilled it out onto the ground, waded into the river to his knees, awestruck at the riches around him. He scooped up another pan of gravel as dusk began to fall.

TWELVE

At the time, the emotion of this moment, of the wealth that lay there within our grasp, being the first to work the riches mingled in the gravel at our feet, was lost upon us. Only later did the uniqueness of this opportunity, that we amongst the thousands of men who struggled to find fortune in the silent empty spaces of this land, should be chosen by fate to succeed here in the gloom of the Molyneaux Gorge.

We three worked assiduously each day from early light to darkness, waiting until night to light a fire and avoid smoke drifting up into the gorge disclosing our presence, knowing without giving voice to it that our time alone to work this virgin ground was precious.

Along the back of the bench, just as the ground sloped steeply upward, we found piles of tangled driftwood worn smooth by its passage down river in some past flood. Several long pieces we selected to use for tent poles, shorter lengths were stacked high beside our fireplace.

By panning the shoad stone at places all along the water's edge, it appeared that the ground was richer toward the downstream end of the bench, poorer toward the upstream end. As a precaution, we carefully staked out three adjoining claims over the richest ground each with a frontage to the river of 80 feet, which we marked with sticks, and cairns of stones.

The gravel was so coarse that we could best work it by panning, not needing to assemble the cradles we had packed with us. After washing the pan clear of fine sand and silt, we could pick out the pieces of gold – which were quite large – clearly visible amongst the grey gravel. As we accumulated the gold we stowed it in saddlebags, not having brought anything better or large enough in which to keep it. With all three of us working long hours, the bags soon began to fill with many pounds weight.

Each day, one of us in turn would climb up to the basin high above to shift our horses because there was little feed among the snowgrass on the hillside. Within a few hours of being moved they would eat out their new ground. It was often difficult to find a suitable place to tether them securely and their leads had to be well separated to avoid entanglement.

The gorge was an oppressively hostile place. The mountains towered up so steeply and so high on both sides that the winter sun – still arcing low in the northern sky – could not penetrate. Each fine day of clear skies was followed by a freezing night, the heavy frosted air spilling down from the mountains to lie in the very bottom of the gorge. The cold was intense, our hands, feet, ears and noses even in daytime chilled numb despite the vigour with which we worked. At night we heated large rounded river stones beside the fire, then took them into our bedrolls with us for warmth.

In the middle hours of the night when the stone had cooled, the frost was fierce and the human spirit was at its lowest ebb, we would be wakened by the cold stealing into our bedrolls. Sleep was impossible. One or other of us would stumble out into the night to stir the embers of the fire and make a billy of tea. Warmed by the fire and the hot liquid – and with reheated bed-stones – we would retire again, to gain a few more hours sleep before daylight.

When the fine days passed and heavy clouds reduced the low light in the gorge to a gloom, the wind roared along the gorge as if being forced through a funnel. The tops of the Cairnmuir Mountains opposite vanished into swirling clouds, reappearing later clothed with snow. Only rain reached us down in the bottom of the gorge.

While we dug and panned gravel endlessly, I pondered where this gold had come from, why it was here. The stone on the hillsides was not quartz in which gold was usually found, it was a grey or black basaltic schist. But there was quartz in the gravels in the river. There was more gold present in the gravel at the tail end of the narrow bench than at its head where the current was swiftest. It suggested that the quartz gravel containing the gold had been washed down the river from upstream.

Fox, always restless, had soon tired of the daily tedious labour of panning gravel from the beach and as deeply as we could rake it with our shovels from in the river itself. He seemed driven much more by the quest for gold than by the actual accumulation of it, appearing far more excited by the new finding of gold than by the sheer amount that was accumulating in our saddlebags.

While we continued to work, Fox systematically dug holes all along and across the bench itself, down as deep as the bedrock, expectantly bringing shovels-full of gravel over to the river for us to pan. He found that the richest ground was deepest, down by the bedrock. It was also richer closest to the river – farther back on the bench toward the slope of the hillside there was but a trace – and that appeared as fine as sand, not the large pieces we were winning from in or by the water.

Discussing these findings by the fire at night, we agreed some conclusions. We considered that the source of the gold was not in the gorge: it had been carried here in the quartz gravel by the force of the river. The river surging through the gorge acted as if it were a giant pan itself; as the river tumbled and washed the gravels along the gorge, the heavy gold sank down through it to the lowest level. Thus the gravel closest to the bed of the river was likely the richest – just as we were finding it to be – and at the back of our bench, farthest from the river, there was barely any sign of gold at all. As the river during many years had deposited gravel to form the bench on which we were camped, the heavy gold had sunk down through that gravel until it laid on the bedrock itself, just as Fox had been finding in the holes he had dug. Although the ground we were working was almost unbelievably rich, we speculated that the very bed of the river itself could well be the richest ground of all, but the violence and depth of the river would long keep its riches beyond our reach if that were so.

I also pointed out to Fox that the line of driftwood along our bench was at the foot of the hillside or even up on the slope itself. It was obvious that it had been carried to that level by past floods surging through the gorge. It was now still late-winter: from my experience on the river, I knew that the water, which fed the Molyneaux, was presently locked upon the land in ice and snow. When spring came, it would thaw. Rain would fall in place of snow. The river, now at its lowest level would quickly rise, just as I had seen it rise in the previous year. The gravels below the bench, which we were working so richly now, would become covered by the rising water, perhaps even the very bench itself. We would then be driven off our claim; there was probably not much time.

It was mostly quiet down here in the gorge, except for when the wind blew. The river made a constant rushing sound but it was there as a low-level background noise; we soon lost our awareness of it. Sometimes a violent swirl would develop near to where we were working, the deep sucking sound of the whirlpool fading as, still wildly spinning, it was swept along downriver by the fast current. Occasionally, ducks would fly along the gorge low to the water but we refrained from shooting at any lest the silence be disturbed.

At night – especially on still frosty nights – we would hear the rush of stones broken off from the rock by the intense cold on the precipitous hillsides of the Cairnmuir Mountains directly across river from us, gathering into a rattling roar, then slowly fading as they trickled to a stop in some steep rocky gully.

* * *

On another quiet morning while all three of us were steadily panning by the water's edge, we were suddenly startled by the sound of a gunshot. The unmistakable flat crack of a fired rifle came from near downriver, followed by the echo of the shot bouncing back and forth across the narrow gorge, reflected loudly off the walls of rock. For a moment we straightened up, stock still, as the echoes died away, then dropped our pans as one and ran for our camp where we had left our guns.

There we stood, spaced out apart, staring up at the hill rising from behind our bench, I with my revolver strapped to my waist, carbine in hand, Fox and Harry clutching rifles ready-primed. Tension grew with the silence as we waited, watching anxiously, but neither sound nor movement came. We began to relax a little, to walk about, still alert but wondering who would have fired a shot and why. Had Hartley and Reilly been discovered? Had they been attacked, were being driven from their claim as we stood here, waiting? Was our time to work these claims alone about to be ended? Were we ourselves about to be overrun?

Tense hours passed. Nothing more happened. Harry returned to panning by the river. Fox and I hung apprehensively about the camp, still anxious, still tense. Suddenly from above came the tumbled unmistakable sound of human voices. Again we rushed for our weapons, standing in the open near our camp. I held the carbine in my left hand, took the heavy revolver from its holster with the right. We waited, uncertainly. Visions of being overwhelmed by a maddened mob swam in my mind amid memories of heedless men streaming up the road from Dunedin in that first rush long ago, of the sullen crowd that confronted Fox on the jetty on the Molyneaux.

Then into sight, down the hillside just above the bench, came a rush of men. Near running, falling down then scrambling to their feet, jostling, downward. Close. Shouting. Unaware of the three of us standing there on the bench just below them.

I glanced at Fox. Raised my revolver into the air, arm extended upward. He nodded. I fired, the Beaumont-Adams kicking back violently in my hand. The explosion startled the first of the men instantly. They grabbed at the tussock to stop their downward charge. As others piled obliviously onto them from above, I fired again. The sound of the shot died quickly away to silence. A crowd of some 40 men all bunched together stared down the hill looking wildly about to see who had been shot.

Then stopped, glaring at us. Men with wide staring eyes. Men with glazed vacant faces. Men possessed with gold madness.

Fox stepped forward across the bench toward them. Cupped a hand around his mouth.

'THIS LAND IS ALREADY PROPERLY CLAIMED!…..WE'LL SHOOT ANY MAN WHO COMES DOWN OFF THE HILL!…. YOU WILL NOT SET FOOT HERE, DIGGERS….GO BACK!'

They looked sullenly at us. Then a single voice from among the crowd: 'And who in hell are you?! You can't claim all that land - there's only three of you!'

Fox called back: 'I'm Fox, from Gabriel's Gully. My mates are the Frasers from the Molyneaux. We're working this beach we claimed weeks ago. I'll tell you now there's no gold on this bench – it's in the river gravel. We've claimed eighty feet of river frontage each. That's fair – and any man that thinks it isn't, will have to fight us first!'

We waited, tensely, for a response. There was some movement; the men lower down at the front turned back toward those above them. We could hear muttering, some angry.

The voice called again: 'We've heard of you Fox. But there's frontage down there for more claims than just your three. If you are the Fox from Gabriel's, you're known to be a fair man – so let more of us down to claim the top end of your bench and the rest of us will leave without a fight.'

Fox looked toward me. If the men now bunched together were to spread out, they could rush us easily. We might shoot the leaders but the rest would be on us before we could reload. We knew the beach we'd claimed at the downriver end was much richer ground than the upper end. More men down here on the river would help us defend our claims. I nodded.

'We'll agree,' Fox shouted back. 'Only two men chosen fairly can come down. But then you others go back up immediately, or be fired upon!'

The men huddled together amid the clumps of tussock on the hillside. Again we waited. There was a single cry of jubilation, then men began to straggle back up the hill, disappearing over the first brow until only two remained. When all the others had gone, they came slowly, carefully, apprehensively down toward us. We lowered our guns but held them ready.

They approached us cautiously, like two new dogs joining up with a pack, not sure how they would be received. They looked like any other two diggers, felted conical hats above bearded faces, heavy coarse-woven jackets over moleskin breeches, long leather boots laced up the front, swags slung on their shoulders. They introduced themselves as the Donaldson brothers. They had been chosen from among the mob by drawing the highest card from a digger's deck.

We did not converse; there would be time for that later when we wished it. Fox led them to the cairn marking our third claim, waved them off dismissively toward the upriver end of the bench and with guns still at hand, we returned to our panning at the river's edge.

The horses! In our anxiety, we had forgotten our horses in the gully up on the hillside. I ran, the revolver still strapped to my belt flapping at my side. I struggled up through the tussock, scrambling over the rock ledges, around the side of the ravine, up over the brow at the foot of the first basin, gasping for breath. That basin was already deserted, the miners had moved on.

I ran diagonally across the basin, pushing through the tall clumps of snowgrass. Over the sloping ridge to the next basin where we had last moved the horses.

But they were gone. I stood there, chest heaving for air, sweat and anger stinging my eyes. Only piles of dung showed where our horses had been; the retreating miners had stolen them both. I swore.

Our food supplies had been dwindling; oatmeal porridge in the morning and tasteless dampers of flour at night was insufficient to sustain the hard physical work of panning gravel. We were all experiencing the gnawing pangs of hunger and my thoughts during the day often drifted off to visions of huge meals of roast mutton. Securing food had become urgent, but driven more by the riches that lay waiting at our feet to be won in every hour of daylight than by the hunger growing within us, each day we had put off leaving to buy supplies from Galloway's or Fraser's stations.

We had been intending that Fox would ride to Galloway's for a sheep carcass while Harry and I guarded our gold hoard, but the theft of the horses now precluded that. Besides, the miners suddenly arriving at the gorge would quickly exacerbate an already precarious food supply in the whole area.

Vast swathes of mountain and valley in this central region were devoid of life, bare and dry, a barren rocky wasteland of wiry brown tussock and thornbush, over a hundred miles from the coastal settlements. Fox had been driven out of here months previously by starvation; now we understood why he had looked so gaunt when he had met us again at Beaumont.

While we worked together next day, we were discussing how we should now attempt to find food – meat especially – when a man suddenly appeared on the hill above the bench, climbing purposefully down toward us. Closer, we saw he was tall, dressed in black or dark-blue, bandoliers of white webbing crossed over his chest, a sword swinging at his waist, a carbine in hand, fez-cap upon his head. As I again ran for our guns, Fox called out 'It's all right JC – it's a Joe, a Trooper!'

The trooper strode directly to us, stood squarely facing us, drawn up to his fullest height, severe dark eyes between trimmed sideburns. He announced himself: 'I'm Jackson Keddell, Commissioner of Police for this district. I'm told that men have been fired upon here and I've come to investigate. Name yourselves!'

We declared who we were. Both Fox and I mentioned immediately that we were known to Sergeant Garvie and Sergeant-Major Bracken, the Troopers at Gabriel's. Keddell looked more at ease as we explained how we had come to the gorge, staking our claims weeks ago. As we showed him our claim-markers, we related how the mob of diggers had suddenly appeared, threatening to rush us off our claim, forcing us to defend ourselves. We protested the theft of our precious horses by the retreating diggers and the implications that held for our now-precarious food supplies.

Keddell well knew of my freighting business on the Molyneaux and had heard of Fox's reputation for maintaining order in the early days at Wetherston's. He was especially curious to know how we had known to find gold in the gorge. He listened avidly as Fox retold the story of recognising Hartley and Reilly returning again down the Manuherikia after they had told him they were leaving for the coast because there was no gold in the area. Then following them into the gorge and discovering the riches that lay in the river gravels. How he was driven out by hunger, walked to Beaumont to have us join him work his claim back here in the gorge, how we all returned to work secretly.

Immediately Fox's story ended, we pressed Keddell as to why he was here, why a mob of diggers had suddenly appeared in this deserted place. As the light was already beginning to fade, the Commissioner decided to stay with us overnight. He climbed back up the hill to where he had left his mount tethered, returning with his bedroll and a very welcome haunch of mutton to share with us.

We sat huddled close to the fire in the still-bitter cold, searing delicious chunks of meat in the flames as the sweet smell of burning fat drove us increasingly ravenous. After we'd assuaged our hunger, Fox produced the remains of our last precious bottle of whisky, pouring a generous dash into Keddell's mug.

Jackson Keddell was an impressive man. He was as tall as me, a little shorter than Fox, ramrod straight with broad square shoulders but a light frame. Like his troopers Sergeant Garvie and Major Bracken, he had served much of his life in the British Army and was a veteran of the recent war against the Russians on the Crimean Peninsula. Keddell was reputedly an excellent horseman, having been a member of the Light Brigade of mounted cavalry.

As Fox's whisky warmed him, he recounted for us how the Brigade a thousand strong, armed only with carbines and swords had charged straight at the guns of the Russian artillery. Grape shot and chain were fired at the charging horsemen at point blank range, scything hundreds of them to the ground in a maelstrom of tumbling bodies, screams and blood. But such was the ferocity of the charge, the remaining cavalry – Keddell included – swept over the guns, cutting the Russians down and not stopping until they had passed fully through the enemy lines. As they pulled up and wheeled into a line, Keddell saw that barely three hundred of them had survived.

We heard his brief story in silent awe, understanding more fully the reputation of the Otago Mounted Police for strength of character, endurance, integrity and dedication to duty when its members and the Commissioner himself were such men.

But we were anxious to know of the events of the past few days here in the gorge, so as Keddell drained his mug, glancing at Fox's empty bottle, I pressed him for how it happened, that diggers had suddenly arrived in this unknown and desolate place.

Keddell looked surprised that we were as yet unaware.

Apparently, as he related it, the Californians must have already left the gorge by the time we ourselves arrived, or else they had departed very shortly afterward. On a cold grey August day, Hartley and Reilly had turned up unannounced at the Dunedin offices of Gold Commissioner MacKay, declaring they had discovered a new goldfield in the remote inland of the Province. As proof of their claim, accompanied by MacKay they went directly to the Bank of New South Wales where before an incredulous Manager, they heaved 87 pounds weight of gold onto his desk.

Within an hour, word of their find had swept through the whole town. A huge agitated crowd gathered in the street outside the Gold Commission, demanding to know the location of this momentous new goldfield. The Californians had a clear legitimate right to claim the Provincial Government's reward of £2000 for any new significant gold discovery, but to do so, had to declare to the Commissioner exactly where the new field lay. Instead, they offered to lead a police and Gold Commission party back into the mountains of Central Otago that same day, directly to the site of their claim.

By a coincidence, Fraser-of-Earnscleugh had chosen that very time to visit Dunedin to purchase supplies and on hearing the surprising news of Hartley and Reilly, knew immediately that the Californians' gold find must lie somewhere close to his own homestead by the upper Molyneaux. Fearing that his station would be overrun or destroyed by hordes of gold-crazed diggers, Fraser immediately took a fresh horse from the stables and fled anxiously from the town back inland, taking the quicker – but longer – northern route.

Commissioner Keddell was called to lead the party with the Californians and return to the site of their claim. Within hours they had assembled and rode out, taking the Dunstan Trail due west from Dunedin, followed by a straggling heterogeneous army of men in a new rush of madness to be first to win their fortune.

Up into the desolate convoluted ridges of the Lammerlaw Range they rode, camping that first night in a windswept freezing gully. Around them in the snowgrass huddled hundreds upon hundreds of men, mostly ill-prepared and ill-equipped to be out there in the open country, still locked in the cold violent hands of winter.

At first light the Police Commissioner's party pressed on along the Dunstan Trail, leading a long ragged line of prospective miners. They skirted around the Great Moss Swamp, picking their way carefully to avoid the treacherous patches of frozen ground through which men following behind and unfamiliar with the terrain, crashed through shouting and yelling waist deep into the chilling muck beneath.

Passing beneath the jumble of rocky tors reaching upward on the Rock and Pillar Range, they rode directly into an increasing north-westerly wind which rapidly increased to a gale. Behind, struggled the lines of diggers, some dragging improvised sleds with supplies piled on poles, some trying to push wooden barrows in front of them over the broken ground, others stumbling about beneath enormous loads of goods piled high on their backs. A crowd of grim determined near-silent men, each withdrawn into his own private struggle against fatigue and cold, driven only by their dreams of the gold to be won.

As they headed out across the maze of swampy creeks in the vast open valley west of the Rock and Pillar Range toward the far horizon of Rough Ridge, rain came down the howling wind. Buffeted and knocked about by the fierce gusts and stung by driving rain, their horses refused to press on, fighting against the reins to turn their tails to the storm. Keddell was forced to order a stop, though such an exposed and desolate place to endure the night could not be worse. Shelterless, wet and hungry, it was impossible to erect tents in the gale, so they rolled themselves in the canvas and crawled tightly against clumps of snowgrass.

Back across the valley the hundreds of miners lay strewn on the ground, piling their supplies into makeshift walls behind which they crouched vainly trying to find respite from the driving rain and tearing wind.

As darkness fell, rain turned to sleet, then into snow. Men died there where they lay. Keddell knew not how many. Poorly clad, ill-prepared for the harshness of winter in the mountains of New Zealand, with little or no waterproof clothing to protect them from the rain and snow, with neither shelter nor adequate food, their bodies were shapeless mounds of snow in the cold morning light.

Snow showers lashed down at the Commissioner's party as they crossed westward to South Rough Ridge, all those miners who had survived the night's storm in ragged lines back across the valley, their moving greyness a contrast against the white landscape. Concerned at their plight but powerless to help, Keddell rode back down the trail calling and encouraging the haggard men to keep moving. Some, exhausted from the heavy loads they carried through snow waist-deep in drifts, wet, hungry and ill-equipped, collapsed and died along the trail. But most miners tramped on by, not stopping for these failing strangers, withdrawn into an unseeing unthinking struggle of their own endurance, heedless of others.

On South Rough Ridge they spent another vicious night trying vainly to shelter from the killing wind, hunched against or beneath broken columns and ledges of rock, hundreds of men scattered over the lee-side of the Ridge.

They traversed the swampy valley west of Rough Ridge next daylight and struggled exhaustedly over the barren ground of the Raggedy Range, swept almost clear of snow by the gale. Still a long line of men staggered behind stretching way back in the distance in an almost unbroken line onto the west face of Rough Ridge.

Eventually, as they came down from the crossing of the Raggedy Range, winding lower through the bare rocky folded hills toward Galloway's in the valley of the Manuherikia, the sky began at last to clear. Shafts of pale sun angled from patches of blue. Ahead, Keddell was amazed to see groups of diggers hurrying down the Manuherikia from the north and already well down the valley in the distance toward its junction with the Molyneaux. Behind him back up the Dunstan Trail as far as he could see, came the surviving diggers who had followed him from Dunedin. Together, from both directions he estimated he could see many hundreds, thousands even, marching toward the junction.

Later, Keddell learned that Fraser-of-Earnscleugh on leaving in haste from Dunedin, alerted his friends in the town that the Californians Hartley and Reilley had used his station as their prospecting base earlier in the year. And the rich find they had now declared must therefore be somewhere nearby. Anxious to protect his homestead and sheep flock, Fraser had left Dunedin promptly, travelling up the coast, then inland by the northern route over the Horse Range into the headwater valleys of the Taieri and Manuherikia. Although he rode hard for two days, stopping only for changes of horse at stations along the way, on reaching his friends the Galloways, Fraser was surprised to find that miners had already passed through ahead of him.

The Galloways themselves were in a siege-like state, firing their guns over the heads of any men that tried to approach the station. Some of the family had hastily driven their sheep flocks to safety out of the reach of the diggers up into the steep gullies of the Dunstan Range to the west.

Arriving by the Molyneaux at the Junction, Fraser discovered his small boat had been seized and was being used to ferry miners across the river to Earnscleugh for a fee. Several hundred were already across and spreading out over his grazing lands in a frantic search for the source of the Californians' gold. The Police Commissioner, still back on the Dunstan Trail, knew nothing of these events unfolding ahead of him.

Jackson Keddell and his party were led off to the west at Galloways by the Californians toward the formidable mountains rising starkly from the flattish plain. From here, the Dunstan and Cairnmuir Mountains though on opposite sides of the Molyneaux River appeared to be as one continuous unbroken barrier westward. Moving closer, they saw the massive slash in the mountain wall that marked the entrance to the Molyneaux Gorge.

As they climbed higher to enter the gorge above its many cliffs and bluffs, they were surrounded by diggers who had rushed to catch up with them. The group, now several hundred strong, sidled around the mountainside into the gorge, traversing for miles the ravine-ridden mountainside along the gorge, then led by the Californians, descended down a gully toward the river. Keddell and his two escorting troopers shouted at the diggers to stay well behind.

But as soon as they could see the river below, the men surged past in a heedless shouting rush. Keddell drew his carbine and fired a shot – the shot that we ourselves working on our claim upriver had heard echo through the gorge. The gold-crazed miners slowed their charge and allowed the Commissioner's party to reach the bench by the river first. Then a wave of cheering diggers surged down off the hill overwhelming all the level ground to the water's edge.

Still leading their horses, Keddell and his troopers remounted and slashing about with his drawn sword, Keddell rushed back and forth along the bench vainly trying to force the miners back. Eventually all they could succeed in doing without firing their carbines directly at the diggers was to clear Hartley and Reilly's marked claim of men. All along the bench diggers swarmed to the water's edge and were already frantically panning the gravel.

Implications of Keddell's news swirled around in our minds. Our primary concern was for food: Harry, who had always been thin all the years I had known him, was gaunt – hollow-eyed and sunken-cheeked. Fox's skin hung loosely on his huge frame like an oversize of clothes. I could guess that I probably looked similarly. Hard heavy labour daily in the cold without adequate food was draining us. Hunger was our closest companion; even Keddell's succulent meat we had just eaten was already a delicious memory.

We pressed the Commissioner, drawing on our experience of the Gabriel's rush when diggers were driven off the field by hunger within a few days. And Gabriel's was but a short journey from Dunedin by comparison – here in the Molyneaux gorge we were frighteningly far from any stocks of supplies. Keddell advised that on seeing the hordes of men marching down the Manuherikia, he had sent a trooper back to Dunedin to organise a packhorse-train of flour to be sent immediately. He had also despatched a rider to Gabriel's ordering Sergeant Garvie to Manuherikia Junction with reinforcements of troopers, to establish a Police Post at the Junction, together with a Bank for the security and safe deposit of diggers' gold.

When Keddell had left us next day and fearing for the safety of the hoard of gold we had accumulated, we quietly dug a deep hole in the middle floor of our tent. After lining it with stones, we buried the hoard enclosed in a leather pouch from the saddlebag in the bottom, then covered it with a thick layer of gravel. We blocked the half-filled hole with a large rock, then topped it up to ground-level with gravel before replacing our palliasse of snowgrass and our bedrolls.

Despite our constant hunger, we decided we must stay on our riverside claim to defend it against the rush of diggers. The Donaldson brothers also had few supplies but like us were determined to resist any encroachment on their adjoining claim. It was as well: several times each day we were forced to challenge groups of men – some large groups – who came speculatively down the hillside from above only to find us waiting on the bench by the river with our weapons clearly showing. Several times we were forced to train our guns on the diggers and threaten to fire, before they would retreat back up the hill. Fortunately, none resisted. Most, so far, seemed surprisingly law-abiding.

Diggers were quickly spreading throughout the gorge seeking workable ground.

Hearing noises from across the river, we were surprised to see a line of men picking their way across and down the almost-sheer broken-rock cliffs and bluffs of the Cairnmuir Range which plunged a thousand feet down to the river on the opposite side of the gorge. When night fell, we could see them clustered on a rocky ledge, still some hundred feet above the surging Molyneaux. Next morning, they slowly lowered one of their group on a rope down the cliff beneath to the river, only to find – as we could see from our side – that there was no bench or beach on which to work. Their man was hauled back up and they began to retrace their path further along the gorge.

Later that day we had returned to our panning when we were startled by a sudden violent shout. High on the cliffs opposite we saw the body of a man falling though the air, arms and legs flailing, his long cry reaching us. Soundlessly he struck an outcrop of rock, bounced off, body fluttering, falling into the river in a gout of water, disappearing. The scattered line of men far above who had stopped still, began again to move on.

Another day while panning, we watched as a body drifted past us in the river, rolling over and over in the surge, an arm sometimes rising lazily up as if in a final wave as the corpse tossed about before floating off downstream. Obviously there were many men through the gorge desperate to find ground that they could work. We could only imagine that every beach and bench along the entire length of the gorge must be filled with diggers.

Our hunger was ascending in priority above our zeal for more gold. Hunger touched with a fear that with hordes of diggers now above the Manuherikia Junction and so far from sources of supplies, starvation might force us to leave. It seemed an irony that the hunger, which had forced Fox to leave this gorge on his first visit here, might now force the same upon us again. For some days, our claims had not been challenged by further groups of diggers, so we resolved that Fox and I would go in search of food, leaving Harry and the Donaldsons armed with our guns to defend our ground.

Together we tramped the twelve miles down the gorge toward the

Manuherikia, encountering numerous parties of diggers moving in both directions along the hillside. We didn't encourage conversation but pressed on to the Junction, completely unprepared for the sight that awaited us there.

What had been the edge of a barren plateau above the Molyneaux on the east side of the Manuherikia, was transformed. A row of improvised shanties – mostly of canvas and kanuka brush – was surrounded by tents and bivouacs. Crowds of men surged about. Closer, pushing at times through the throng, we found armed troopers outside several large tents with cloth banners marked 'Police' and 'Bank'.

We decided to split up: Fox would cross the river to Earnscleugh Station, hoping that having stayed there previously, he would be recognised and received by Fraser who might yet have mutton to sell for gold while I would wait at Manuherikia to determine when supplies might be packed in from the east.

Fox did not return for two days.

Meantime, while I had waited for him, I had had to sleep rough in the tussock through two long bitingly cold nights. In the late earlyhours of the night, when the human spirit is always at its lowest ebb and the freezing ground beneath me seemed filled with stones at every point my bones touched it, I lay sleeplessly worrying whether Harry and the Donaldsons were still holding our claim against jumpers.

During the hungry days, I hung about with mobs of diggers around the collection of tents of the Junction. On the first day, I managed eventually to push inside the Police tent where Jackson Keddell and several of his troopers stood separated from the crowd by a log barrier on cairns of stacked stones. After a long wait I caught Keddell's eye and saw recognition spark his face. He waved me forward.

'What brings you here Fraser, some important matter for you to leave that claim of yours? We've not found your horses if that's your purpose.'

'It's not the horses I've come for, Commissioner, it's hunger! We must find food or we'll all be driven back to the coast. Any news of the supply-train you told us was coming?'

Keddell said quietly that he had expected Sergeant Garvie to have arrived by now; at any hour a rider might appear ahead of the pack-train. I should stay around and wait patiently. I moved out to the north-east that day, keeping a close watch toward Rough Ridge, but only individual diggers on foot appeared coming down off the hill, no riders.

On the second day of waiting for Fox to appear, I was loitering amongst the crowd of diggers constantly coming and going near the cluster of tents at the Junction when men suddenly stopped, pointing at a digger who ran shouting toward us from the northeast. Men closer to him began to run for him, then beyond. The shouting was taken up by others, 'The pack-train is here! The pack-train is here!' and within a moment we were all swept up into a headlong rush to follow.

I ran with the others, overtaking many, spurred by the urgency of hunger. There to the northeast coming down off the hillside came a string of packhorses escorted by riders several of whom were in the unmistakeable dark blue uniform of troopers, already surrounded at the front by a pressing group of diggers.

When I arrived, gasping, the pack-train was almost clear of the hill on the flats but brought to a stop by the quickly growing horde of diggers who surged around trying to get between the outriders to grab at the bags hanging from the pack-saddles. The troopers wheeled back and forth, shouting and slashing wildly with their swords, driving the men back. I felt the crush of diggers from behind driving me forward against the men in front falling back from the hooves of the troopers' horses. I lashed out with my elbows and arms, fighting for some space, with my height able to see over the swirling mob the anxious angry faces of the outriders. I could sense the panic of the hungry mob. At any moment they would attack the Troopers, drag them off their mounts, seize the bags off the pack-train.

A frenzied shout to my right. An outrider was being dragged from his horse and pulled down into the mob. With a roar men rushed forward. They grabbed wildly at the bags on the packhorses. Fury when they could not be freed. One bag slashed with a knife. White flour spilling in a stream, diggers catching it in their hats. Fear in the faces of the troopers at the violence of the men. Tension real in the air.

A shot rang out. Another. Men turned. The angry tumult died away. There behind us were Keddell and several more troopers on their horses, all with carbines in hand. Now in front of me, I recognised Sergeant Garvie from Gabriel's. Garvie hauled back on the reins. His horse reared up, pranced at the mob with forelegs flailing. Two rapid shots from behind. The men stilled.

Commissioner Keddell's powerful commanding voice shouted 'Get back you men! Get back or be shot! I'll have order here! Make way! Make way!' and he rode purposefully through the dividing crowd toward Garvie and the pack-train. Nobody moved. Nothing moved. Keddell and Garvie reined up together, talking, then Keddell turned back toward us again.

'This flour will be rationed! You will all get a share! One pannikin-full per man and no more! You'll pay two shillings and sixpence each, or in gold – no payment, no flour! Keep order or be arrested. I'll have no more of this!'

The crowd of diggers stood silent. Keddell's words echoed again and again in my mind…. 'One pannikin-full per man' was barely enough to feed the three of us with dampers for one meal. One meal! We would have to leave the gorge, abandon the claim and go back east for food, driven off by hunger just as Fox was previously. Damn this barren country!

I lined up dutifully with the others. When my turn at the front arrived, I looked up at Sergeant Garvie, saw recognition spark his eyes. 'Fraser! Fraser from the Molyneaux! Why… you're here with these desperate men?'

I ignored his question, impatient diggers pushing against me from behind. 'I'm here for three of us Sergeant, the others are holding our claim. Only one pannikin-full? Can I not have three for the three of us?'

'You heard the Commissioner, Fraser, I'm sorry, one per man.' He turned away. Avoided the embarrassment of denying me. I collected the flour, doled out from a bag by a trooper flanked by others. A little but better than nothing. I paid him in coin then walked slowly back toward the river, withdrawn in thought, feeling the hunger gnawing in my gut, burning now in the knowledge it would not be assuaged. One pannikin-full! Men would die here in this desolate place without food. Torn between abandoning their claims and starvation, many would not choose to give up their ground at any cost.

Back at the Junction, I milled about again listlessly, watching toward the river for Fox but he still did not return. The need for food and the precariousness of our situation totally filled my mind. To have given up the *Lady Colina* and the river-freight, to come so far, only to be driven off east again. At least Fox had been correct and true to his word: the gorge had been the richest ground imaginable, just as he had claimed it would be. We had each made a fortune in a brief time – we were not poor when we came but would be leaving as wealthy men.

I wandered back and forth, restlessly, waiting anxiously for Fox to return, hoping but not hopeful that he had been more successful in Earnscleugh than had I with the pack-train. Men, mostly sullen quiet men, gathered in groups or came and went toward the river.

'Fraser! John Fraser!'

I spun about, startled from deep thoughts at the sound of my name. A short round man, bearded, hatted, strode quickly toward me, a hand already outstretched, broad smile on his face. 'John Fraser! It's me, John Reid, from the Wetherston's! Well I'd never have expected to find you here!' He shook my hand warmly.

'Nor you either John. When you both left Gabriel's I thought you were finally cured of the gold fever. Why come back here, now, to this desolate place – and before the bitter winter's passed?'

In explanation, he said that he and his brother Peter had returned to their homes and work in Dunedin when the gold began to run out at Wetherston's and winter began to bite. When the Dunstan rush began and with the near-advent of spring, they decided to join the rush, if only for the summer period. However, drawing on their previous experience as diggers, they decided not to be swept up in the initial madness of a new gold rush, but to outfit themselves thoroughly before leaving Dunedin, so as to be able to survive and sustain themselves comfortably for at least several months.

Both on horseback and with a third horse laden with gear and supplies, they had arrived at the gorge several days ago, only to find that unlike Gabriel's, there was little or no ground left to be claimed. The savage precipitousness of the gorge, the massive bluffs and cliffs, the unexpected difficulty of trying to traverse the country on horses in search of any unclaimed ground – such as there was – had completely discouraged them. Now they had returned to Manuherikia Junction, intending to cross the river to the Earnscleugh side in hope that poor though the ground on the south side was, somewhere they might succeed in finding some payable dirt worth working.

On hearing the tumult erupt as they neared Manuherikia, Peter had remained at a safe distance while John came on foot to investigate, hoping that the noise might indicate some new ground had been discovered, only to find he was mistaken. Crestfallen, he was about to return to his brother when he had recognised me.

Briefly I related our story, seeing surprise on his face that we had joined up with Fox. As I explained my presence here at the Junction, a thought, a thread, an idea, formed in my mind. I suggested that I returned with him to his brother, knowing that our path must cross with Fox should he appear from Earnscleugh.

Out there in the empty tussock, their three horses were very obvious. A figure rose up from concealment nearby as we approached, a carbine in hand pointed toward us. Peter Reid knew the figure of his brother but was cautious of the stranger now with him. John called out: 'Don't be concerned Peter, it's Fraser from the Molyneaux.' He lowered the carbine, came toward us, shook my hand vigorously. We both told him our stories, then I turned to them.

'I can't speak for Fox, nor for my cousin Harry, but I have an idea for you to consider.' They looked at me attentively.

'Our claim in the gorge is among the richest ground here. We've worked much of it, but yet still much remains. Soon, I expect, the river will rise with the spring thaw and may flood the claim for a time. We are short of food – very short. If Fox returns empty-handed, hunger may drive us off before the thaw does.

'You have not succeeded to find good ground. What little that this wild country allows, has already been claimed. Luck may yet favour you, but I doubt that there's any rich ground here undiscovered, despite how well prepared you are for a long stay.

So, gentlemen, you have the supplies but not the ground: we have rich ground but not the supplies.

'If you are willing – and my partners agree – we could join together in this venture. You share your supplies with us and we will share our ground with you. There is no future for you in being well fed on barren ground, nor for us in working rich ground until we starve. I'll withdraw a short way off and wait your decision....'

'No need for that John', the elder Reid replied, with an acquiescing nod from his brother, 'that sounds like a generous offer and an acceptable one!'

I left them in the tussock and walked back toward the edge of the terrace overlooking the river, waiting for Fox to return.

When he did, he was a fearsome sight. Draped across his shoulders was a gutted headless carcass of a whole sheep, still covered with hide and wool, its forelegs across his chest from the right hooked through the hamstrings of its hind legs on his left. His beard, which had not been trimmed for a year, was as one with his long hair equally unkempt, both smeared with blood from the sheep. His left hand steadied the carcass, his right waved a thick length of kanuka-trunk as a cudgel. It would have been a brave or foolhardy man that tried to steal the sheep from him.

But I could see his wide grin of success well before he reached me. 'It cost us all of a day's gold JC, but if it keeps us on the claim for a week or two more, it was cheap at that price! If I'd had a few bottles of whisky, I'll swear I could've parted Fraser from another of his precious flock, but more gold was not going to do that.'

He was very surprised to find the Reid brothers with me, but despite their sometimes-testy relationship at Wetherston's, greeted them warmly.

Having a whole carcass of mutton was a saviour, but it would not last us for very long, perhaps enough time for a large quantity of supplies to reach the Junction for the hungry diggers, perhaps not. It still did not negate the proposal I had put to the Reids and which I related to Fox as we walked together back across the terrace to where they waited for us. I pointed out to him that the thaw would likely flood us from our claim very soon; having them join with us would ensure we were well-supplied and could keep digging apace until such event happened. For such a guarantee, the cost to us would be a mere two-fifths of the gold that we won meantime. He agreed.

Mindful of having had our own horses stolen from the hillside above the claim, as we loaded Fox's sheep carcass onto the Reids' packhorse we warned them that it would be a wise course to sell theirs should – with Harry's final approval – they join us.

On the journey from the Junction twelve miles up the gorge to the claim, I worried as to how Harry and the Donaldsons had fared defending it in our absence. It was a needless worry, at least in the respect that the claims were still held, but Harry was clearly relieved to have us back.

They had spent an anxious and at times tense few days, warning off several groups who had tried to frighten them into relinquishing the ground. Only by a resolute display of their willingness to resist – by demonstrated force of arms if necessary – had the challengers abandoned their quest. Gentle Harry, who had declared after the tense violence of the famine in Ireland he would never again bear arms against his fellow men, had had to fire my carbine in warning above the heads of the most truculent group of claim-jumpers before they would retreat.

I thought that the prospect of 'strength in numbers' helped bring him quickly to support our proposal for the Reids to join with us almost before I had finished explaining it to him. Now we were five.

The Reid brothers began work with the eagerness and zeal of newcomers, especially when they saw through their effort just how rewardingly rich was the ground by the river, while we three stopped frequently for the luxury of our first decent meals for weeks.

John Reid, Fox and I returned to the Junction nearly a week later, Reid to sell two of his horses which we had been constantly guarding and Fox and I to deposit some of the gold from our hidden stockpile.

At Manuherikia Junction, we were amazed at the transition that had occurred in such a short time. Where a few tents had previously clustered, a 'street' now separated facing rows of tents and improvised shelters of stone, canvas, iron and wood. Crude signs advertised stables, gambling saloons, grog shanties, a dancing hall, a fortune-teller, card rooms for poker, monte and euchre, even a wrestling-room, but as yet, no eating-houses. John Reid took his horses to the stables whilst Fox and I sought out the transformed Bank – its tent now replaced by a small solid building of stacked dry stone with a sloping roof of corrugated iron. Immediately alongside was a similar stone building with canvas roof, clearly marked 'Police'.

Inside the Bank, Fox and I were escorted by an armed bank officer through an internal wall to a small room at the rear in which we both had to stoop beneath the low roof. There on a counter of planks on gin-boxes, the gold we carried was weighed carefully on gold scales. Between us, this first part of our cache we carried, weighed nearly 900 ounces. The sum of £3388 was credited to our account; a fortune yet only part of the gold in our stockpile.

Before returning to the gorge we visited a crowded grog shanty. Behind a canvas screen open to the sky, diggers stood drinking, many obviously having already consumed too much. We pushed through to the rear where on a plank bench, whisky in small kegs and gin in bottles was dispensed into enamel mugs. Safely behind the men at the bar were stacked boxes of gin in familiar wooden cases, even loose bottles of French champagne. We each paid exorbitantly for a shot of whisky, both immediately noticing the product had already been watered down.

To our surprise, two rough-looking women, both quite fat, both near middle-aged and plastered with powder on their faces were moving amongst the men in the tent, carrying partly-filled gin bottles in their hands and urging the diggers to buy more grog. They were the first women I had seen in nearly six months. The goldfields until now had been an exclusively male domain.

A week later Fox and I, travelling together for security, again made the journey down the gorge to Manuherikia, depositing another part of our cache at the bank. A further 785 ounces worth £3022 was credited to our account. The bank officer showed no surprise at these large deposits, an indication that others too were working rich claims along the gorge.

It was now the third week of September. The hard frost had gone as the night air-temperature gradually rose. Green shoots began to appear on the snowgrass and the sun at last began to penetrate lower into the gorge. With longer hours of daylight, we were able to work more ground but divided up our labour; restless Fox prospecting the ground ahead for the best paydirt, one or other of us in turns keeping watch on the Reid's one horse grazing on the hillside above the bench, one digging the gravel, two by the river panning. The Reids both worked assiduously, still relatively fresh to their labour and neither having suffered as had we, from malnutrition and the ravages of winter in the open.

During repetitive tedium of the long days I pondered how we might retrieve gravel from deeper in the riverbed beyond our reach. I experimented, using a long pole of kanuka bound horizontally to a vertical log-post buried at the waters' edge. The pole was fixed about one-third along its length so that by levering on the shorter length, I could swing the larger length out over the water, in the manner of an oar in a rowlock. At the end of the pole I fastened a leather bag cut from a saddle-flap and fixed around a stirrup. The device looked like a large spoon.

By levering and lifting the pole on its moment, I could drive the 'spoon' to the riverbed gravel in the direction of the current, then at the end of its arc swing it from the water and back to the bank. The amount of gravel retrieved was tiny, less than a pan each time, but we were all impressed at the gold it contained. Given time, I was sure I could develop a more effective method to reach the gold-bearing sediments so enticingly near but beyond our reach. Perhaps even mounting the 'spoon' pole on a raft in the river would be more rewarding.

For two days, a warm wind from the northwest swept down the gorge, followed by rain. Gentle, dense, wetting, warm rain. The thaw was now bound to begin.

Inexorably, the river began to rise. The current became ever swifter, building up small pressure waves which we could hear surging throughout the night. Each morning, the water had crept higher. It rained again, sweeping heavy sheets of rain hissing onto the river, pouring in rivulets off the hill behind onto our bench. Rain for two days unending.

Fox and I made our third journey to Manuherikia, taking the last of our cache to the bank. Ravines along the gorge tumbled with water off the Dunstan Mountains high above. We hurriedly returned, a further £3580 richer, anxious lest the river had flooded the bench in our absence, but it was roaring past just below the level of our camp. Thankfully our gold hoard hidden in the ground was now all safely deposited, only the accumulation since the Reids joined us remaining stashed in a saddlebag.

More rain. We were woken in the night as water seeped through our tents. Frantically we groped in the dark and the lashing rain to grab and drag all our gear and supplies to higher ground. Along the bench we could hear the Donaldsons calling to each other, retreating from the rising river. The bench and our claim was abandoned.

Morning light revealed a grey torrent hurling through the gorge, already two feet over the bench where only hours before we had been sleeping. We huddled in the wet snowgrass, watching the flood surge past, any thought of further digging clearly washed away until the river subsided.

Fox looked at me, the question was in his eyes as surely as it was in mine. 'What now?'

THIRTEEN

The four of us stood there in silence for some time, each with our own thoughts, watching the tumbling water racing past where such a short time ago we had been winning gold, as sweeping grey columns of rain fell again from a heavy sky.

Obviously we could not stay there standing in the wet snowgrass on the steep hillside. As a first step, we decided to move downriver to Manuherikia and deposit the gold we had accumulated since being joined by the Reids, so we loaded the gear and supplies we had retrieved in the night onto the remaining packhorse and climbed slowly away.

The Junction was crowded with many hundreds of diggers who, like us, had been driven off their claims by the rising water of the spring thaw. Deprived of their immediate purpose, many had turned to grog for solace and to fighting for amusement. Drunken men staggered or lay about. Crowds quickly gathered wherever a fight broke out, sometimes among groups of men. The mood of the bored listless mobs was ugly and quite menacing. Troopers rushed on their horses from one disturbance to another, trying to maintain order.

Fox left us to return to Peter Reid whom we had left west of Manuherikia with our laden packhorse, to be sure it was safely guarded. John Reid, Harry and I keeping closely together, went quickly to the bank and deposited all the gold that we had won as a party of five. Surprisingly that totalled another 1270 ounces of which our share was another £2933 credited to our account.

All the while, the question of what we should do next washed around in my mind. The silence of the others indicated their preoccupation with the same thoughts. Immediately we rejoined Peter Reid and Fox, we needed to agree on our next course. But we found our little group divided.

The Reids, having each earned for themselves around £1000 from their brief period of labour on our claim, already felt well rewarded. Initially in our discussion, they were both wanting to camp on the hillside above the claim so as to be ready to reoccupy it the moment the river fell again. Harry too.

Predictably the ever-restless Fox, at heart more a prospector than a digger, shook his head as the Reids gave their opinion.

'Well I for one will not sit around on my backside watching the sky and waiting for only Christ knows how long for the damned river to go down,' said Fox. 'I'll be off on my way.' They all turned to me.

'From my experience of the thaw last spring on the river, it will be two or three weeks before the flow eases off, perhaps longer if there is more warm rain. When we began working the claim, we started at the lower end of the bench where the paydirt was richest. As we've worked our way upriver, the pickings have been leaner – not by much but less for every yard.

'If the five of us resume digging when the water goes down, we'll soon work the rest of the claim out and whilst we do, we'll be less and less rewarded for our effort. When the claim is worked out, what then?'

Harry was first to reply.

'I came here to try and stake myself. I always intended to return to the north and buy myself enough land to farm. I've already got more than a stake – I can not just buy land to farm, but land enough for a lifetime. Being a digger is not my life – just a means to a better life. I don't like this country down here, this harsh and barren nothingness, nor do I like the violence and lawlessness that's growing all the time now that thousands of men are coming here from Australia. So I think I'll stay long enough to finish the claim off, then I'm going back to the north. I'll be sorry to leave you John – and have so much to thank you for – but I'm a farmer, not a goldminer.'

Harry stared at the ground, scuffed at it with his boot. After a long silence, Peter Reid spoke next, looking at his brother as he did so.

'I agreed to join my brother again, when he asked me, just for the summer. I have a wife, a family and a business waiting for me back in Dunedin. Staying here to work the claim out, is the only option for me. By then it'll be time I returned home. Thanks to the three of you, we've been more successful already than we could ever have imagined possible. If I return home before the year is out and with the prospect of even more money in the bank, what more could a man wish for? So I'll stay to help work the claim out or to summers' end, but no longer.'

John Reid turned to Fox. 'If you're not staying here Fox, where will you go now?'

He looked at us all, eyes roving to each of us, shifting impatiently from one foot to another. 'There's a lot more gold to be found in this country yet, of that I'm sure. Perhaps more undiscovered than all that's been found already. I'm going to look for it – and I'm going to find more of it!

'I'll go west again. Far to the west. Back into the mountains, to the Wakatipu where I've been before. I'll go back to Rees's station on the shore of the lake where I can get all the supplies I need while I search for Maori Jack's gold. I've seen the stuff there in his hands. I know it's in that country somewhere, just waiting to be found. And I'll find it! Before some other bastard does!'

He faced me directly. 'What about it, JC? Are you going to sit around here on a wet arse and watch the weather? Or will you come with me?'

Another long silence. For me there were other dimensions to such a decision. Surely the claim here in the gorge would soon be worked out. Harry would return to the north. But what of me … alone?

I was already well-off financially, perhaps even wealthy. What else remained here to be done? I had mulled ideas to design and build a boat or a barge that could recover gold from out in the river but that would take time; time for the river to subside, time to get materials and equipment from Burns' in Dunedin, time to build it … a long time.

Since the fateful day that I learned of Elizabeth's betrothal to Haile, only successive circumstance had led me here. Perhaps now my time in this Colony itself was done. Should I take all my new wealth and go to South America as I had intended? What other future was there, to keep me here?

Another thought competed in my mind. There was probably nothing to lose by staying through the summer and get out of this harsh and hostile interior land before winter next set in. And meantime, at very least I'd see what lay toward the west, this wilderness of lakes and rivers, towering mountains and forests that Fox had talked of endlessly, when we sat watching the firelight deep into the night.

I felt the need for a deep breath, and took one. 'I'll go with you Fox! At least for a while, but not through another winter.'

John Reid, who had remained silent all this time, suddenly spoke. 'And I'll come too – if you'll have me with you. I came for the summer, to find gold, and as my brother said, we've already won more than we ever had imagined. I could go back east today a happy man, but the summer hasn't yet even begun. I'm all for more prospecting and if a chance to find more gold lies in it, then I'll be all the more rich for it.

'Peter, if the others agree to it, you and Harry can stay here and wait for the river to fall, then work the claim again for as long as you both wish, but for now I'll go with Fraser and Fox.'

And so we five decided to part company.

Harry and I walked off a distance to take leave of each other for the second time in our lives, not knowing when, if ever, we might meet again. Certainly the first time we had parted, all that time ago in Ireland, I could never have envisaged that we would meet again as adult men in this remote Colony on the other side of the world. Harry had always been peace-loving and gentle, wanting to be alone, self-reliant, and farming with animals. After all our time together on the river and then on the goldfield, I understood how difficult it had been for him as a young man to leave Castledawson, his family and familiar surroundings, to emigrate alone and penniless to the unknown antipodes in search of a dream. At least now that dream which had seemed impossibly far beyond his reach, could be turned to a reality.

We had been fortunate to have shared such good times; in my boat on the river, then here on the goldfields of the gorge. Now I could only wish him well, and say goodbye.

* * *

We left them – Peter and Harry – about to camp on a level ledge of a gully beneath the Leaning Rock, near to the Upper Junction where the Kawerau River and the Clutha River merged to form the Molyneaux. Travelling as light as possible, carrying only sufficient supplies to last us until we could stock up again at Rees's station on the shores of Lake Wakatipu, we three set off on foot to retrace the route followed by Fox when he had come east from Rees's in the autumn.

Rounding the steep mountainside above the gorge as we approached the Upper Junction, we were surprised to see clusters of tents on the west bank and diggers in every small ravine that led down to the water. Already the beginnings of a settlement, similar to Manuherikia and being called by some the 'Dunstan' after the mountain-range it faced, was forming on the plateau high above the river gorge.

Instead of having to trudge miles along these mountains up the Clutha river to attempt crossing at the islands (Fox had struggled to cross the river there in autumn when its water-level had been far lower than it was now), for a small fee we used a device erected by the diggers at the Junction. Here a rope had been slung across the ravine, anchored around columns of rock on each side, sagging quite deeply at its centre. A large wooden pulley-block was free to run on this rope, from which hung a thick plaited length of rope fixed to a short log, forming a T-shape. Another light rope from each bank was fixed to the pulley-block, which was used to drag the block along the rope to each side. By sitting astride the log and clinging to the section of vertical rope rising from between the legs, a man could ride the pulley across from one bank to the other, while dangling precariously some 80 feet above the torrent below.

Fox was the first to cross – appropriately, given that the diggers called this nerve-testing device a 'flying fox'. Leaving from the east bank, he had to be restrained by the lighter control-rope, lest the pulley raced downward with the sag in the main rope, then hauled from the west side upward from the mid-point until the pulley arrived at the west bank. When Fox had unloaded himself, the pulley was returned to our side.

I went next. Swung a leg across the log on either side of the vertical plaited rope. I wrapped my arms tightly around it, the weight of my swag and bedroll pulling me backwards until the plait was angled above with me dangling beneath. I stared upwards to the sky, trying not the think of the chasm opening up below me as the guide-rope was let out and the squeaking pulley-block began to ride down the main cable. As I reached the lowest point in the sag of the cable and my momentum slowed, the tension was eased off on the guide-rope. Relieved of its drag effect, I began to swing around, buffeted by a wind coming down the gorge, first twisting clockwise, then revolving back. Please God, get this journey over!

I glanced down. Not straight down, but on an angle down. The lower ravine was a deep slash into the earth, as if two mountain ranges had been pulled apart, the valley floor split open between them. Sheer walls of black rock, vertical into the river. A tumbling cascade of blue and white water hurtling down the ravine.

I looked back to the sky, begging for deliverance back to hard earth as I felt the pull of the guide-rope dragging me up the cable toward the other side.

Then new voices – and hands grabbing me. There was Fox. Grinning. I demounted the log – tried to stand up, but the ground itself seemed to be moving. I lost balance, fell sideways, other hands held me, steadied me until I could stand alone. I looked back to the east bank, the device on its way already to collect John Reid. Fox commented that crossing the Clutha ravine on a rope cable was far less-fearsome than if we had had to try to forge the river in its present state of full flood, upriver at the islands, or worse, to cross the infamous natural-arch rock bridge over the tumultuous Kawerau.

When Reid had crossed – equally shaken – we turned westward again, out across a broad grassy plain from which, about a mile distant, the Pisa Range soared abruptly upward. This forbidding chain of broken-rock capped peaks dominated the western sky, stretching north into the far distance and southward to intersect at right angles, the equally stark Carrick Mountains along the south side of the Kawerau River. Those mountains and the Pisa range as Fox had explained, were separated only by the chasm of the Kawerau River gorge.

There was a choice of routes westward. Either, we could attempt the difficult traverse of the Kawerau gorge, winding in and out of the steep ravines that plunged off the Pisa Mountains, picking our way through the maze of sheer cliffs and bluffs that marked both sides of the gorge all the way up to the natural-arch bridge beyond which the gorge was utterly impassable, then up the Kittleburn which led onto the Criffel Range. Or we could climb directly up the steep eastern face of the snow-capped Pisa Range, then down the western side into the Kittleburn. Fox chose the route by which he came out of the mountains in the autumn, the steep circuitous trail up onto the Pisa.

Closer to the foot of the Pisa Range, I could see that the valley of the Clutha first rose up in several elevated terraces – each hundreds of feet high and with flat horizontal tops – which from a distance blended with the face of the Pisa Range itself. These giant terraces ran the full length of the valley northward, even and symmetrical as if shaped from the earth by some giant's spade. Even though mid-day had just passed, the sun was already lost behind the towering height of the mountainside confronting us.

Fox angled us more northward as we trudged over stony ground mostly covered with short grasses, until I noticed the first terrace which we were approaching was itself cut by a ravine coming down off the high mountains. In the ravine, a narrow valley formed by a tumbling stream, wound back into the mountain range before rising steeply up through another ravine in the second – higher – terrace and then onto the rocky face of the Pisa Range itself. This stream, the Lowburn, was our route up and over the Pisa.

Even trail-fit as we were, climbing the Pisa Range was a daunting effort. The Column Rocks along its peak were some 6000 feet high – much higher than the Dunstan Mountains we had left behind to the east – and at this time of early spring, still deeply covered in winter snow. The short grasses on the terraces soon gave way to heavy clumps of waist-high snowgrass as we climbed slowly upward, then to clusters of impenetrable *matagouri* thornbush between which we had to weave a careful path and finally to steep broken slopes of jagged rocks, grotesque columns and short sheer walls. Narrow deep gullies cut into the mountainside were filled with savage bushes of speargrass, so tough and sharp as to pierce the leather of a careless boot.

Ever up we struggled. The mountainside loomed darkly above us, seemingly never nearer. It was the steepest and longest climb I had experienced. We each weaved about, selecting a favoured footing. In silence, as each step became an effort of will to place one foot above the other, sharply exhaled breath the only sound, faces wreathed in clouds of steam as our heated breath hit the cold air.

Despite the cold shadow air, running sweat stung my eyes and trickled irritatingly down my chest under my heavy flannel shirt. The swag, its straps now a dull pain on my shoulders, felt to have doubled its weight since we'd left the valley floor. Atop a large rock I paused to look back and down. John Reid had not kept up; I could occasionally see his miners' hat bobbing about among the rocks below.

Fox too had stopped just above me. Between deep breaths I called to him, said we needed to wait for Reid to catch up, find ourselves some ground where we could pass the night fast approaching, and before we reached the snowline.

There was no level ground for a tent. No sticks or wood for a fire. We found a narrow sloping ledge tucked beneath an overhanging buttress of layered rock, spending an uncomfortable near-sleepless night huddled together for warmth and to stop each other from sliding downhill.

We waited awake interminably for morning light, to find the valley of the Clutha from whence we'd climbed filled with fog, its smooth level surface like a layer of white wool just below our present altitude. Hungry and thirsty, we set off upward again, soon reaching the snowline not far above.

Fox and I took turns to lead, kicking steps into the snow for the others to follow. A landscape of black and white; stacked columns of rock like layered slate, great protrusions jutting out from the hillside on seemingly impossible angles as if defying gravity itself, ledges and walls of the stuff. Long snow-covered slides of shaley shingle stones plunging steeply downhill, that moved frighteningly when crossed. And all over, patches of white snow clinging to any surface not vertical, long dripping icicles of clear ice dangling from any that was.

As my body heat rose and the sweat again began to flow, I saw the ground among the rocks was not so steep and just above I could see sunlight striking bare rock on the Pisa ridge. In the lead, I picked my way ahead between irregular columns and huge tors of black rock rising starkly into the sky as if a giant's playthings were left scattered over the land. There immediately before me, the ground fell sharply away into the valley of the Kittleburn rising to its headwaters to the north on my right and on the west side of the Kittleburn, directly ahead and slightly lower than the Pisa Range we had just surmounted, the rounded ridgeline of the Criffel Range.

The others came up to me and we three stood together, gazing westward. Fox pointed out how earlier in the year after crossing the natural-arch bridge over the Kawerau River, he had followed the Kittleburn up from its junction with the Kawerau, buried deep in its gorge out of sight far down on the south side to our left, then climbed over a pass (which he indicated on the Criffel ridge-line ahead) that led directly on into the valley of the Cardrona River.

In the distance above the line of the Criffel Range, was row upon successive row of jumbled peaks and ridges glistening white in the sun, each higher than the next, stretching far off the to west and I realised that formidable as the Dunstan and Pisa Ranges we had climbed had seemed, they were but mere foothills to the stark giants of the alps ahead. For some minutes we stood gazing in silence. Broken wave upon wave of mountains, like a glittering white jumbled ocean in a tempestuous storm. I felt inconsequential and insignificant in this timeless empty wilderness, conscious that from here westward we would be beyond the reach of any human help or sustenance, over the edge of the reassurance and comfort that life itself was survivable. If for illness, injury, or whatever reason we could not make Rees's on the shore of Lake Wakatipu somewhere far off in those mountains, the meagre supplies we carried would run out; we would have well-passed the point of return and could starve to death in this barren land.

Fox – familiar with the ground ahead, took over the lead, Reid and I following him down through the valley of the Kittleburn and up the long climb onto the Criffel Range. Fox strode purposefully onward – as I had seen him do before – never stopping or glancing back. At first I had thought these forceful bursts of his were a demonstration of his strength and endurance, as if challenging us to try to keep up with him. But when I had made the effort to do so, I had found he was almost in a self-induced trance-like state, seemingly oblivious to his surroundings or the severity of the terrain, having drifted off in his mind to some faraway place. When he was like that, it took a rough physical contact or a shout to bring him back to immediate awareness, unless he himself of his own volition, suddenly returned. I understood that it was this ability to remove himself from the ardours of the present which had helped him to survive his previous journeys alone through these mountains in the last autumn.

Once over the rounded tops of the Criffel Range, we could see below us down a more gentle rolling hillside, the winding valley of the Cardrona River, in the same north-south line as the Kittleburn but rising in the reverse direction, with headwaters to the south and flowing away down toward the north. Fox headed straight down off the Criffel Range into the Cardrona Valley, sidling along the hillside to make an easier gradient.

The Cardrona was a broader slowly-winding valley, quite benign compared with the country we had so far traversed, its open slopes clothed with brown tussock and snowgrass, large stands of kanuka and matagouri thornbush on the small flats either side of the river. As we trudged gradually upward, the valley began to narrow, its sweeping turns giving way to a tighter ravine with rocky outcrops. We kept to the sunny east side, avoiding acres of savage speargrass and matagouri thickets growing over the shaded western side. As we progressed further up the ravine the more-rounded snowgrass-clothed Crown Range replaced the snow-covered Harris Mountains to the west.

Camping for the night high in the headwaters of the Cardrona River, now reduced to a small brook less than three feet across, we cut a pile of kanuka and lit the first fire we had had since leaving the Manuherikia. At this altitude and yet early spring, the frost settled before dark, so we heated river stones by the flames to warm our bedrolls until the early morning hours and each enjoyed our first good sleep in three days.

Cold drove us to set out again quickly next day, crunching through the frosty snowgrass up a steep saddle of the Crown Range at the head of the Cardrona. From the top, we could see almost sheer below to the southeast, the deep gorge of the Kawerau, a short thread of silver river visible thousands of feet down in its bed. It was obvious from the scale and precipitousness of the gorge, why our trail westward had been by a different route, following the broad direction of the natives who for centuries had travelled to the western coast in search of the prized green jade they used for weapons and ornaments. The gorge of the Kawerau we had thus avoided, was clearly impassable.

We sidled westward down off the Crown Range for a thousand feet, Fox still in the lead, until the hillside bathed in morning sunshine levelled out onto a gently-sloping plateau. This wide terrace cut from the side of the mountains now above to our east, gradually narrowed as we trudged across soft slushy ground cut by numerous small creeks.

As the sun passed its zenith, we reached the farthest corner of this terrace and stopped at its very edge from where we could look out over a wide oval basin stretching miles ahead, ringed by high mountains on all sides. Far in the distance, Fox pointed out a thin sliver of our destination, the Lake Wakatipu, a narrow finger of silver-blue squashed between towering peaks. Immediately at our feet, the terrace we were on fell nearly vertically down to the Arrow River tucked tightly along the base of the hillside at the top of which we were now sitting.

Perched on the edge of the terrace, we lay back in the tussock warmed by the sun, absorbing the sweeping view to the west and south, awed by the magnitude and serenity of this mountainous land. Sunlight glistened from peaks of snow. For the first time, I was more conscious of its beauty than its hostility. I was reminded of the sea voyage to this Colony, standing by the rail on the *Black Swan*, looking out over the blue ocean to huge white-capped waves tumbling on the horizon, Elizabeth at my side. She too, would surely have delighted in this awesome splendour of mountains, valleys and rivers; and I to have brought her to this place. Elizabeth: I didn't need a reminder – it all seemed so long ago already; almost as if in another life so much had now passed, but the pain would probably still be there deep down, waiting to return if I should let it.

In his swag, John Reid carried a brass telescoping eyeglass and whilst Fox traced for us the route we would follow out across the convoluted floor of the basin below, I tried to follow his directions more closely through this eyeglass. Unfortunately, the wide basin seen through the glass was a jumble of small hillocks, mounds of rocks, shallow gullies running off from the mountains to the north, and broad swathes of matagouri. Even through the eyeglass, no clear route was readily visible.

As Fox talked to Reid, I idly scanned back across the basin toward the ground more directly below us where our path would initially take us, then back out across the land trying to pick up features Fox was identifying. But I could recognise nothing.

I swung the glass more quickly back, then not quite aware why, suddenly stopped. In the blur of ground moving rapidly across the glass, had my eye tripped on something? Something unusual or out of place here … or did I just imagine it? Was it a shadow of light … an unusual feature … or a movement?

I slowly scanned back over the near basin, but there was nothing, just an emptiness of snowgrass, tussock, great lumpy rocks and thickets of matagouri. Imagination in an empty lonely wilderness plays strange tricks on one's mind; one can often think to see what one wants to see.

The others were silent, expectant, stilled by my sudden exclamation and quickened movement. But no, there was nothing that could have disturbed the deserted basin below. I swung the telescope quickly back toward the base of our hill and was about to take it from my eye when I was certain I saw it again. There. Yes, a movement, definitely something was moving down there in the matagouri.

'What is it JC?' urgently from Fox. 'What is it, what have you seen?'

Then right into the centre of the lens, I saw a man walk into clear space out of the brush. Then another. Far below and out in the basin, they were just tiny figures reduced by the magnitude of the landscape to the size of insects. But quite clearly they were men, and they were moving slowly in our direction.

'See what you make of this Fox' I said, handing him the eyeglass, striving to keep calm. 'Out there about a mile and to the right, I can see two men, walking this way. They're both carrying large swags or something across their shoulders. Here, take a look.'

He grabbed the glass from my hand. Scanned back and forth impatiently. 'I can't see the bastards JC, but my eyesight's not that good….' We waited, then: 'Ah,… there they are, I see them now. You're

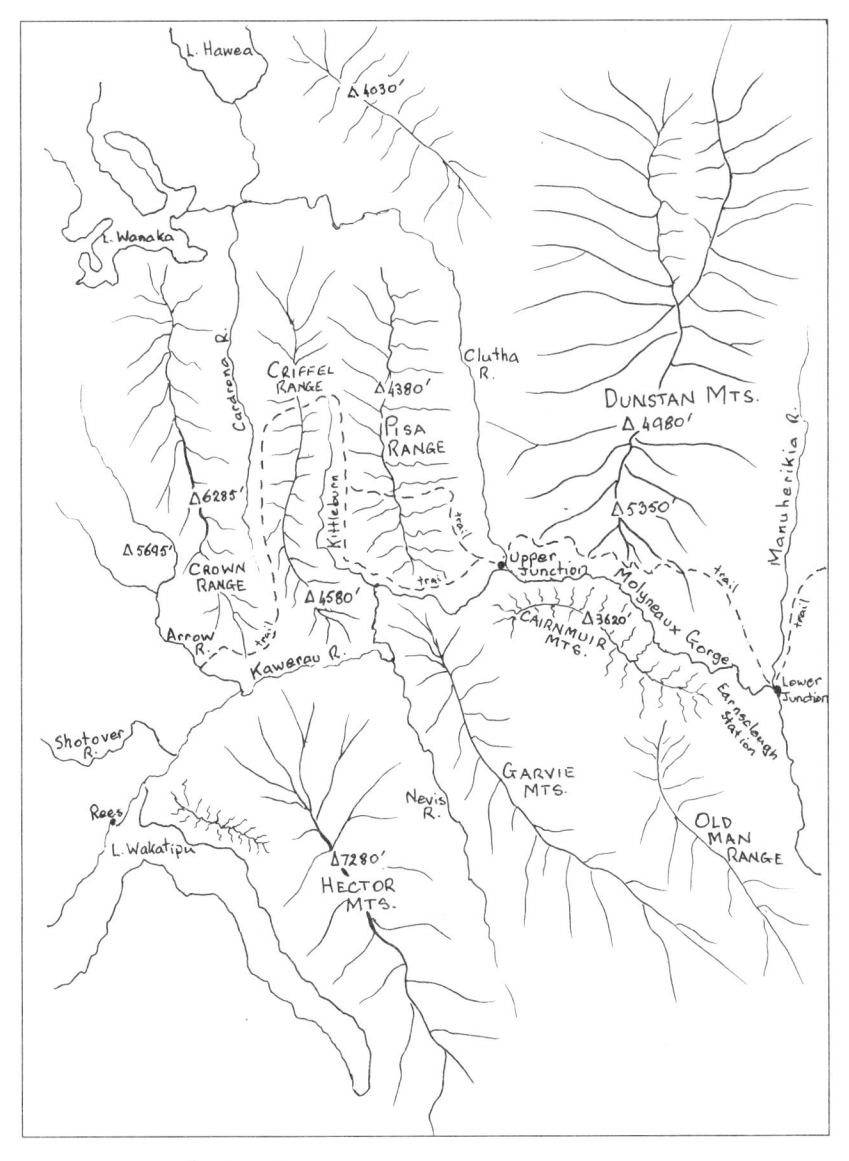

Lower Junction to the Arrow River

right, there're two of them. Not surprising really, that there should be others, probably prospectors, about in this area. Christ knows, there're a few thousand diggers back there on the Molyneaux not that far behind us. Bound to be some others who've ventured west, just like us.

'But I'd like to know why – at this time in the spring – they'd be coming back toward the east. Doesn't make sense, unless Rees has kicked them out. I suggest we sit here and wait for them to come this way, then ask them.

'While we wait here, let's keep still and out of sight, or they could see us move on the ridgeline of this terrace. Here Reid, take your glass back and keep watching them. Your eyesight'll be better than mine.'

He gave Reid back the telescope and we waited, soporific warmth from the sun helping time to pass. The two strangers were apparently making their way across the basin toward the north-east corner below us, where they would have to cross the Arrow River before climbing up the very steep face to the terrace on which we perched. When they did, we could easily move in either direction to intercept them.

Reid passed the glass back to me. 'Take another look Fraser. Those men are both carrying enormous swags on their shoulders, and neither of them have hats.'

They were much closer now, walking quite determinedly in an almost direct line toward the point below to our right where the Arrow River suddenly appeared from a rift in the northern mountainside. If they forded the river there, an angled ascent up the face would bring them out on the terrace within yards of where we were sitting.

I studied them closely as their figures bounced about within the narrow lens of the eyeglass, particularly the strange swags they both carried, protruding beyond their shoulders on either side and near level with the tops of their hatless heads. Then I remembered. I had seen such a load being carried before – it was Fox returning from across the Molyneaux after visiting Fraser-of-Earnscleugh. The men below us were each carrying a sheep slung across their shoulders, just as Fox had done!

'Those men Fox,' I said as calmly as I could, 'are not carrying swags. They're both carrying sheep!'

'The bastards! Either they're up to no good, or they're onto something. Don't lose sight of them JC,' he spoke urgently. 'They must be camped somewhere near here. We need to know just where they're going.'

I kept the glass fixed on them, my eye straining from staring down the tube of the telescope, trying to hold it steady. The men gradually closed in toward the Arrow River which, about 30 or 40 feet across with the spring thaw, flowed swiftly over a boulder-strewn bed tucked tightly along the base of the face immediately below us. Fording it should not prove too difficult and given the direction they were purposefully taking toward the huge cleft in the mountainside from which the Arrow emerged, they must already know the best place to cross.

As I watched, they eventually made the river, right at its mouth beneath the mountainside. I could see them through the glass very clearly, though they were still a third of a mile distant. Together, they waded carefully into the river, thigh then waist then almost chest deep, suddenly passing from sunlight into the dark shadow of the mountainside towering sharply above them.

Then, though I was watching their darkened shapes closely, they vanished!

Fox too scanned the river below. We waited. 'They must have a cave or a rock overhang alongside the river that we can't see from here because the face below is too steep. Whatever, to be carrying carcasses back here instead of bedrolls, they must be up to something. Let's go down that way and find out.' Though we waited for longer, the men did not reappear.

We dropped off the edge of the terrace, lowering ourselves down the vegetation-covered precipitous hillside from one clump of snowgrass to the next. The steep slope ended hard against the east bank of the Arrow River which we had to cross. The near-freezing water fired a chill up my spine as we waded in, thigh deep, angling downstream across the fast-flowing river to avoid being knocked off our feet by the strong current.

The riverbed was a mass of rounded rocks in a mixture of interesting colours – green, grey, white – interspersed with sheets of firm sandy gravel. By picking our way across at the widest point, we avoided deeper water and quickly headed off upstream to where the river emerged from a narrow ravine in the mountainside, now more clearly visible.

Though we kept close alongside the river, there were no caves or rock overhangs in the hillside where a man could hide, even in the area of deep shadow that had been difficult to see from above on the terrace. We reached the giant cleft in the mountainside from which the Arrow surged, with no trace of the sheep-carriers. We stared all around, mystified.

'They can't just vanish,' I said firmly, 'I was watching them closely until the very moment they disappeared. That leaves only one place they could have gone.' I pointed into the darkened cleft in the hill we were facing. 'And that's in there!'

From where we stood, the mouth of the river lay between two near-vertical walls of rock that soared almost 100 feet on either side before angling off slightly from the vertical. Where the cliffs ended, the hillside continued upward on a face sloping away from us northward for at least another 1000 feet. Staring into the cleft which was initially about 30 feet wide with the river running swiftly from rock to rock, we could see into the shadow for perhaps 100 yards before the cleft appeared to bend sharply to the right. From the shape of the mountains above, we could see that there was a ravine running far off back to the north, widening at its higher elevations but with very steep sides. From the shadow-lines, the Arrow River obviously twisted back and forth up this ravine. What lay immediately beyond the first 100 yards into the cleft was conjecture, but possibly the ravine widened out further upriver.

Declaring that there was only one way to know for sure where the men had gone, Fox strode into the water with Reid and I following close behind. The riverbed was firm but rocky, the water feeling not quite so cold because we were still feeling chilled from our previous crossing. As we pushed against the strong current it quickly deepened; thigh then waist then near-chest depth, just as I had seen for the two sheep-carriers.

The force of the current from the river which, in full flow with snow-melt was being channelled through the narrow cleft, made a firm footing precarious. John Reid, much shorter than Fox or me and thus even deeper in the water, was at risk of being swept off his feet and we linked our arms together for better stability. The heavy swags we carried helped to anchor our boots on the riverbed, otherwise pushing upriver against such force might not have been possible.

After successfully covering the first 100 yards, the ravine duly turned sharply to the right and as we rounded the corner keeping to the shallower outer-side of the bend, we saw that within 40 yards, it immediately cut back to the left again. There were no banks - the steeply-sloping rock walls, wet, dark and glistening rose directly up out of the river before angling away above out of sight.

Around the next sharp bend, the ravine widened slightly and the river became shallower. Fox and I now shoulder to shoulder forged onward breaking the force of the current for Reid following closely behind, all of us stumbling about on the loose rocky bottom. Ahead on the next outer curve of the river as it again turned to the right, we could see dry ground for the first time, a high steep bank of shingle and large stones above water level, against the base of the cliff.

Another 100 yards forward and we rounded the right-hand bend. Directly ahead at the top of a straight stretch of river was another rounded shingle bank at the foot of a steep slope. There on the bank at the waters' edge was a man, his back toward us. He had not yet seen us. He was panning.

We slowed instantly, more to stop the noise of our passage than in surprise. I tensed, expecting to be seen at any moment. We waded slowly on toward him.

Suddenly another man rose head and shoulders above the bank. He faced directly at us. He shouted, pointing to us. The man panning dropped it, spun around, staring.

Together now, they rushed higher onto the shingle bank. 'Get out! Go back!' waving us away furiously, 'This land's ours! Go back!'

Fox and I, shoulder to shoulder, strode steadily on, Reid close in behind. We reached the shingle bank. The two men who had come forward retreated up the bank to its highest point, obviously intimidated by the size of Fox and I and the three of us ignoring their instructions.

I saw Fox's fists clenched at his side, a sure sign he was ready to fight first, talk afterwards. I dropped my heavy bedroll to the ground, the leather holster of my revolver visibly strapped to it. I stood tall with arms down, opened my hands fully stretched, fingers fanned, in the pose of a wrestler ready for action. The two of them stared in silence at the three of us. None moved. The air between us turned almost solid with tension.

One of them spoke. 'This is our valley. We're here first and we've claimed this land as ours. Go back where you came from.'

Fox uncurled his hands, took a few steps slowly forward. 'We're not going anywhere till we know what you're doing here. I'm a prospector named Fox, and you look to be panning for gold. If there's any here, we'll claim a right to it. Or if you want to fight us, we're ready for that too!'

The same man answered. 'There's no need for that. We don't want a fight. I'm McGregor and my mate here is Low. We're just sheepherders looking for grazing land. We found our way in here and decided to do some panning on the way up river.'

'We saw you,' I replied firmly. 'We watched you. You were carrying sheep carcasses on your shoulders, not bedrolls, so it's not the first time you've been in here. You might well be sheepherders but you're diggers too.'

Whilst I spoke, Fox stooped and picked up the pan dropped at the waters' edge, swirled the gravel in it, swished the fines with the back of his fingers. 'Christ, look at this JC!' and he held it out to me. The edge of the pan was rimmed thickly with gold.

McGregor and Low looked at each other. McGregor sighed, said resignedly 'Right then, yes we have found some gold, can't deny it, but we've got miners' rights and we've properly claimed it.'

Fox and I crunched across the gravel to them, Reid following. Fox grinned at McGregor. 'I knew there was gold hidden here somewhere. I spent weeks searching for it earlier this year, but had to get out when winter came. This is one of the places I didn't think to prospect, and it was here all the time. When did you come here? How did you know where to look?'

I could feel the tension easing. I introduced Reid and myself. Low suggested we join them at their campsite and they would explain. We followed them, a short wade in the river again, around the next bend where a short bench lay at the base of a steep hillside. Amongst a few stubby matagouri bushes were two tents. The sheep carcasses we had seen them carrying dangled from a pole propped against the rock. Driftwood was piled alongside a stone fireplace. We offered tea from our meagre supplies and Low lit a fire.

Whilst we drank its welcome warmth, McGregor related their story.

He and Low were indeed sheepherders. Just as winter was ending, they came up from the south along the Mataura River, scouting for grazing land but it was all claimed. At the southern end of Lake Wakatipu they happened to meet Rees who had taken his whaleboat down the lake to collect a man at the trail-head at Kingston on the long lake's southern shore, who Rees was employing as an extra farmhand for the summer season. The intending farmhand, Thomas Arthur, had not appeared.

McGregor and Low persuaded Rees to take them north back up the lake with the intention of scouting the high valleys in the Harris Mountains further north of Wakatipu, as the winter snow receded. During their stay at Rees's station while waiting for a late snowfall to thaw, to help in passing the time, Low had produced some bottles of whisky which they all proceeded to drink.

In a spirit of friendship promoted by their inebriation, Rees's stockman Jack Tewa, 'Maori Jack' as Fox had called him, showed McGregor and Low the same fistful of gold nuggets he had shown to Fox many months prior. But this time, inexplicably, he told them where to find it.

Thinking it was just a trick, McGregor and Low set out immediately they were sober to check Maori Jack's story. Expecting only to be gone briefly, they took no equipment nor supplies. Arriving at the Arrow, facing the oppressive-looking cleft in the mountainside through which a formidable volume of water was pouring, they were even more convinced they had been despatched on a fool's errand and could imagine Maori Jack amusing himself at their expense. But having come this far in pursuit of the tale, they resolved to enter the ravine to satisfy themselves it was indeed fictitious before returning to Rees's station.

Not anxious to wade further up the river through its oppressive ravine, they stopped at the first shingle bank they reached. On sifting gravel in their bare hands from beneath some stones, they were utterly amazed to find small nuggets of gold scattered on their palms.

They hurried back to Rees's and told him of their discovery, surprised to find that Rees had also known of Jack Tewa's gold locality for some time but had not pursued it. Aware that there was gold in the area, Rees had decided not to be caught up in a goldrush with the risk of losing all his precious grazing land to squatters if he were to leave it unoccupied, even briefly. Nor would he instigate a rush by revealing Maori Jack's secret. Instead, he had decided that if and when the gold was eventually found, he would be a supplier to the diggers but would not join them.

Rees agreed to keep McGregor and Low supplied. They returned to the Arrow with their gear and a small stock of flour and salt (such that Rees could spare) to set up a camp. After a week of panning, they again visited Rees to purchase some mutton. It was on the return journey that we had spotted them from high up on the Crown Terrace. They had not seen us, nor thought to keep a lookout, somewhat unaware of the hundreds of diggers on the Molyneaux not that far off to the east. They were aghast at being discovered.

Fox had in turn described his stay at Rees's back in the autumn, his knowledge of Maori Jack's fistful of gold and his fruitless frustrating long search of the lake and rivers before being driven back east by the onset of winter. I related to the two men our experience as diggers in the Molyneaux Gorge, impressing on McGregor and Low the benefit of having worked there in secret for as long as possible.

Fox declared a proposition. We three would prospect further up the river; if we found paydirt, the five of us would continue to work the gold in secret. If there were no other paydirt, we would leave McGregor and Low in the valley alone.

Assuming there was more gold in the valley and we stayed, we would maintain a guard on the first shingle-bank inside the ravine entrance. The three of us had guns (the other two didn't), so we would provide one gun to the person keeping guard in daylight whilst the remaining four worked the gold. Any person entering the ravine would be held at gunpoint.

No fires would be lit in daylight ('Not like this one here' Fox pointed) so that smoke would not reveal us. All the food supplies would be fairly shared. Whoever went to Rees for more supplies would leave before daylight and return after dark. Nothing would be said to Rees about the paydirt or how much gold we had recovered. Fox himself would be in charge and he would enforce the rules if necessary.

McGregor and Low agreed without further discussion. We shook hands to seal it.

The three of us left immediately to prospect further up river. We waded several long reaches and rounded more tight narrow bends where the river ran hard against stark rock cliffs. The valley began to open out high above us and we could see quite some distance toward the north; a wider sprawling valley narrowing down toward its base, with many side gullies branching off on both sides. More distant, there were scattered patches of green forest high on the flanks in the gullies.

We passed several benches forming riverbanks, their exposed edges a mix of colourful large stones interspersed with gravel and coarse sand. Around another bend we came to a wider and higher terrace forming the left bank of the river and on which tussock grew among scattered low matagouri bushes. We dumped our swags and each set off to pan the gravel benches we had passed.

I found colour all along the bench I prospected, not abundantly rich but very payable. Fox, who was prospecting the lowest bench, returned upriver to me with a similar finding. We waded up to the third bench to find John Reid grinning. He showed us his pan, studded with small rough-shaped nuggets – a claim-site well worth working. When we returned to the terrace for our swags we found that that too had quite rich dirt, especially closer down to the water. We speculated that when the river level fell, the bars and bedrock beneath the shoad stone of the riverbed could be very rich findings indeed.

So we began to mine the Arrow as a party of five. We each took a turn for a half day to stand an armed guard near the ravine entrance; a cold, long, tedious and lonely time with only the river tumbling by and a narrow strip of sky above to watch. Reluctantly, I showed McGregor and Low how to load my Wesley Richards carbine, at least secure in knowing that whilst they held it on their turn at guard, we had two other guns and my revolver close at hand in our camp.

John McGregor and Thomas Low shared their mutton with us but our scanty supplies had near gone in two days. Fox set out in the dark for Lake Wakatipu to renew his acquaintance with Rees, returning at night the next day heavily laden with flour, salt and legs of fresh mutton. Until Rees could secure more supplies from the south, it was all the flour he could spare.

We had a reasonable camp on the terrace. John Reid being an experienced stonemason quickly built a wall of stacked river-stones packed with gravel which protected us from the force of the wind which swept fiercely either up or down the valley. An extension to the wall gave us a galley-space for a sheltered fireplace.

We worked steadily through the daylight hours, panning the gravel. The ground was excitingly rich but not as rich as on the Molyneaux; in the first two weeks we estimated we had accumulated over 500 ounces – McGregor and Low more than double that amount. Rich rewards for hard effort.

Fox was tireless as usual; taking his turns at guard, moving huge quantities of gravel, sharing the chores of firewood collecting and cooking. He and Low made a further trip to Rees's, returning with mutton and flour but no salt. But still he was restless, wandering off upriver frequently to prospect other sites, returning – often in darkness – either with a pouch of nuggets or nothing for his effort.

Obviously there was more payable ground along the valley and Fox was keen to find the best of it and lay claim to it before we should eventually be discovered. Every day we expected to be found, but the valley stayed undisturbed, remote and quiet, save for the bubble and tumble of the river and the hush or howl of the wind over its slopes. We wondered how long it would last.

FOURTEEN

Though we worked hard, mining in the Arrow in the Spring of 1862 was quite enjoyable compared with the rigours of the Molyneaux.

With longer daylight hours and the sun higher in the sky flooding the valley with warmth for hours each day, even the ever-present blustery winds driving down from the headwaters were not a hindrance. It was rather like a hidden world: the cleft of precipitous rock walls guarding the entrance to the ravine were a forbidding door with no indication of what, if anything better, lay beyond; up here the valley unexpectedly opened its arms to the sky, widening out into long hillsides of tussock rent by many concealed side valleys before far off to the north disappearing into a jumble of snow-covered peaks.

Our stone shelter had grown into a hut of sorts, with a doorway and a stone chimney surrounding an internal fireplace – testimony to Reid's stonemasonry skills. We had climbed to the nearest copse of green forest, to find stands of magnificent evergreen beech trees with straight black trunks and lacy-layered canopies of delicate small leaves. From there we secured long poles for the roof of our hut which when covered with tight bundles of snowgrass gave reasonable protection from the heavy showers that often swept down on us.

The worst and most ever-present difficulty was a shortage of food. Mutton, even when hung in the coolest shade, lasted but a few days before beginning to rot, attracting swarms of large flies. Though William Rees kept us stocked with flour, we had virtually no vegetables.

I took my turn to make several trips to his homestead in a sheltered bay on the shore of Lake Wakatipu. The homestead, now extended in two directions from an original stone hut, was tucked into a sheltered corner of a small deep bay. Around the southern end of Rees's bay, another bay – more a longer narrow inlet squeezed between two hills – led to the lake's only outlet, the source of the Kawerau River and itself one of the sources of the Molyneaux.

The lake was a long narrow strip of flooded valley between massive mountain ranges rising sharply up from the waters' edge, shaped in three connected equal-length long arms like a chair without its rear legs. One arm – out of sight from Rees's – led far off to the northwest into the main divide of the Alps. The second arm – at the end of which Rees had his station – lay due west-east. The third, headed due south.

When settling the station, Rees had hauled a whaleboat up the Mataura River far to the south with horses, then dragged it with bullocks overland on a carriage to the southern end of the lake. Given the great mass of steep-sided high mountains that hemmed in the lake on all sides, his boat was his only means of bringing supplies in to the station and shipping his wool out.

The voyages along the lake were totally weather-dependent. The lines of mountains funnelled the frequent winds along each arm of the lake often with ferocious force, driving huge rolling waves before them. It was impossible for Rees to take the boat against the wind; many times he had been stranded at the southern end waiting for the northwest wind to abate, swing to the south and help drive him back north to his homestead, or waiting at the homestead for a strong southerly wind to die away. In periods of calm, it was a long row for he and Jack Tewa with a heavy load aboard.

We were concerned that the gold we were paying to Rees for our supplies would attract attention if and when he took it south to a bank for security.

Meantime, we five worked the gravel as fast as we could, firstly just with pans, then with cradles made from the wood of gin boxes and tea chests which Rees obtained for us. Mostly the gold we recovered from the riverside benches was quite fine, from pea-size pieces down to sand or even a light dust. A large volume of gravel needed to be washed to secure it, but the yields rewarded our effort.

Fox continued to prospect, initially not finding any paydirt better than that we were already working. But he returned late one day in some excitement, having found strong sign in a western side gully some two miles further upriver. This gully had long sloping sides of often-exposed soft gravel up some 60 feet to terraces on both sides. Down in the gut, he found good-sized nuggets scattered in the streambed but samples of gravel from the slopes all the way up to the terraces also had good sign of finds. We decided to mark claims on this land and relocate ourselves there if and when we should be discovered.

On a warmer spring day, I lay sprawled in the sun on the first gravel-bank nearest the entrance to the ravine, watching fluffy lumps of white clouds racing across the sky from west to east above the valley, taking my turn of duty on guard. The heavy carbine which so many times I had cursed carrying as we sweated our way over the Pisa Range was at hand, the Beaumont-Adams revolver in its holster at my waist. Lazily lying there enjoying the respite from the labours of washing gravel seemed a futile waste of valuable time.

We expected that any diggers prospecting the area would come as we had, wading upriver through the forbidding cleft in the hillside, so when on guard we tried to be alert for any different sound in the gurgle, bubble and rush of the river that would foretell of a human wading up against the strong current. But well aware that we ourselves had come this way without McGregor and Low detecting us, we also kept more than an idle watch on the bend of the ravine immediately downstream.

The rattle of stones on the hillside above was not unusual – the warmth from the sun after a cold night often dislodged rocks or a rivulet of stones that would tumble downhill for a distance before coming to rest or even falling off some precipice into the river. It was the second such rattle quickly following the first that prompted me to turn and look upward.

To my surprise, three men had suddenly come over a side ridge and were scrambling down the hillside toward the gorge. They did not appear to have seen me. I grabbed the carbine and rolled quickly over the edge of the shingle-bank. Out of site crouching by the river, I peered carefully back up.

The men were coming down the near-vertical slope on their bottoms or backs, lowering themselves from clumps of snowgrass, sliding feet-first, checking their fall, the leader peering below unsure if a bluff or precipice lay in their path. A sidle sideways across the face to avoid a rockface, then downward again. Silently, except for the rattle of dislodged stones.

They were coming down directly above me. They would arrive just above the bank where I lay. I gripped the carbine and slipped a charge into the breech, hoping the river noise hid the metallic sound. I undid the tight clasp on the holster flap so the revolver was comfortably freed.

Then I waited, tensely.

I kept hidden, trying to make myself small, fighting the urge to look, to see how close they had come. Then the leader, who must be just on the bank above me, called back to the others, 'I've got to the river! Just come on down!' I waited.

The muzzle of the carbine and my eyes peered above the edge of the shingle bank together. The leader had his back to me, looking uphill. The scrabbling boots of the other two popped through some snowgrass. They arrived at the bank and stood up, rubbed dirt from their britches, grinning in relief after their dangerous descent.

At the instant they looked around, anticipating their next move, I stood up, levelled the carbine at the leader and shouted aggressively 'Stand where you are!'

All three leaped simultaneously with fright. They turned to face me. Eyes staring, mouths open in surprise. White-faced above their beards. A brief long moment passed when none of us moved. I needed to hold the initiative: 'Get down from that bank into the river! One wrong move and I'll shoot the first man!'

'Yes, all right, we will. But don't shoot – we mean you no harm.'

'Just do as I say!'

One at a time, they slid off the bank into the river just upstream of me. I kept the carbine steady, aimed directly at the leader. I didn't allow time for questions: 'Now wade together up the riverbed. Stay in the middle. Stop well before that next bend.'

They waded ahead together, glancing back to see I was following, measuring the distance. I tucked the butt of the carbine under my elbow and reached across with my left hand and removed the revolver. When a man glanced back, he could see it.

'Stop now!' I closed up toward them just before the bend. 'Go slowly round this bend. Stay together. I'm right behind.' The force of the current would hinder them from trying to rush around before me and using the rock bluff to block my line of sight.

Around the bend, into the next reach. They began to drift apart, the man on the left slowing as the others waded on ahead, each trying to separate so I couldn't cover all three of them with my guns. 'Stop there!' They turned and looked back at me balefully, but kept wading.

I waved with the revolver, 'Close up!' They didn't move. They stood still, waiting, watching me.

An instant of decision. I smoothly swung the revolver toward the man at the left and kept the carbine aimed at the leader. I fired. The revolver kicked back in my hand. A gout of water burst up close beside the man at the left. He lurched sideways in fright and threw his hands in the air. 'Don't shoot!!'

I listened to the flat crack of the .45 rolling off the hills nearby. That would bring help, and bring it quickly. It did.

Just as the three men regrouped closer together, McGregor and Low ran into sight over the next bench. Fox and Reid burst around the bend above, guns in hand, throwing a wash of white water aside in their rush. The three strangers quickly bunched together, trying to look both ways at once.

Fox was instantly in command, shouting at the men huddling together in mid-river to go to him, up on the bench. Low hurried off up river.

Fox ordered the men to sit on the gravel, back to back, hands on their heads. I explained what had happened, anxiously looking back to see if more men were following, but the hills and the river were bare.

The leader said his name was Cormack, his mates were West and a wild-looking red-haired man they called Blue. They assured us there were no others, they were alone. They had come up from the far south, stopping at Rees's where they met up again with Rees's farmhand Thomas Arthur whom they knew. Arthur, who had not long joined Rees as a farmhand, told Cormack there were diggers working in the area but he was unsure of just where. With some vague directions and Arthur's estimate of about a day's walk away, they began combing the mountains to the north of the basin starting at the farthest point, intending to work their way back westward toward the lake. Deterred by the forbidding look of the cleft from entering the ravine via the river itself, they chose to climb up and try to sidle into it from above. They had not expected to find us.

Thomas Low returned back down river, carrying a small rope Fox used to tie his swag. With the assured moves of a man with previous practise, Fox bound each man's hands at his back, then all three of them together so they were sitting face outwards. Only then did the tension ease and we discussed what to do with them.

In answer to our direct questions, the newcomers were defiant that they had no lesser right than did we to do as they wished, to stake their claims and start mining, but Fox was having none of it.

The five of us had agreed to a set of rules that not only preserved our secrecy for as long as possible but shared responsibility for the arduous effort of hauling food from Rees's, gathering firewood from up the valley and for our general security. We also acknowledged Fox as being the leader of our little group and although most issues were discussed, we accepted his final decisions. In addition, we presently had the run of the valley and had not had to restrict ourselves to specific claims. We explained our rules and reasoning to the newcomers, but – still pushing their absolute independence – they refused to agree to any of it.

We left them tied up and with one of us on guard to reflect on our explanation, whilst we returned to our diggings. 'Maybe a touch of hunger and the frustration of sitting there tied up will drive some sense into them,' Fox growled tersely as went back upriver. I hoped that would happen quickly; I would not support depriving them of their liberty for long and besides, it would be impossible for us to keep them fed.

They held out until the next day. A cold night trying to sleep tied together, sitting on hard stones, water their only sustenance, was sufficient for them to agree. Fox made each man swear aloud to us all his acceptance of the rules and the responsibilities before they were set free, knowing full well that transgression would bring collective punishment. Now we were eight.

Cormack's party decided to work the first right branch up the valley which then we named 'New Chums' Gully'. During his hurried rough prospecting, Fox had thought this creek was no richer ground than any other. He was wrong; within the first week Cormack and his mates had recovered over 500 ounces just with panning and in four weeks, they weighed out a record total of 1760 ounces.

McGregor and Low who had worked out their initial small bench of gravel, moved to a new site upriver onto a long bench beneath a higher hanging terrace. We ourselves decided to abandon our bench by the river and begin work in the western gully that Fox believed was particularly rich. Inevitably, we called this 'Fox's Creek'. John Reid quickly built us another stone hut in only one day.

Keeping ourselves supplied with food which had been a frequent problem for five of us, was now much more difficult. Two men were constantly tramping to or from Rees's because in the two days required for the journey, we would nearly eat all that had been carried on the previous journey. Though in fairness we each took our turn, it required a huge physical effort, not only to carry the heavy loads back to the river, but to negotiate part of the rough track in total darkness.

By early November, McGregor had been on the river for a month, we ourselves into our fourth week, Cormack's party two. Rees had plentiful sheep to kill from his large flock but struggled to keep us supplied with flour and particularly salt which was inexplicably scarce in the south.

Short of flour but becoming desperate for the salt without which we could not survive, Fox decided to climb out and journey back to The Junction. If successful, he would return within six days. He carried only his bedroll, a small amount of our recovered gold and my revolver for protection.

We continued working, waiting with increasing anxiety as six days became seven, seven became eight. In daylight on the eighth day Fox arrived back, escorted up the river by West who had been on guard. He looked exhausted, but he had brought some salt.

We all gathered together that night to cook our food on an open fire in the riverbed, listening to Fox's tale of his journey.

He had followed the same route back east to The Junction that we had taken for our journey west, making The Junction on the second day only to find few supplies of any description. So many diggers had poured into the Molyneaux, up to The Junction and all over the surrounding country, that the rugged tracks around and over the Dunstan Mountains from further east could not carry the huge volume of supplies now required.

Fox learned that two tracks into Manuherikia – one from the north, the other the Dunstan Trail we had followed from the east – had been improved and would soon carry coaches. A Captain Jackson was regularly bringing wagons of supplies and herding flocks of sheep into Manuherikia and a new settlement called Dunstan at the eastern end of the Molyneaux Gorge. Supplies up to there were quite plentiful, so Fox immediately set out again, crossing over above the Clutha on one of the now many 'flying foxes' that had been slung across the chasm, complete with semi-enclosed chairs.

He was surprised to find that the new settlement called Dunstan was larger than the Manuherikia we had left; the bank, police, hotels, post office, stables, and the shacks and shanties of gaming and grog houses had moved there from Manuherikia, closer to the new goldfields scattered through the gorge and beyond. Miners in their hundreds thronged the rough 'street'.

There was no need to travel further on east to the Manuherikia settlement, which was also being called 'Lower Junction'. Drovers brought sheep flocks to feed the diggers down through the Manuherikia valley to the banks of the Molyneaux where they were slaughtered in hundreds beside the river, their guts and offal feeding broiling masses of eels, blood turning the water red, the stench drifting on the wind for miles around. The diggers were calling the site on the riverbank 'Mutton Town'.

Fox bought salt in Dunstan, but he was recognised by diggers who knew him from the gorge and from Gabriel's. They were all curious to know where he was now mining, the more so when he would not tell them. He banked the small amount of gold he had carried and left to return up the gorge to The Junction. Near Leaning Rock, close by the site of our gorge claim which he presumed Peter Reid and Harry were again working, Fox suspected that he was being followed. However, so many men were moving about in both directions on the gorge trail, he could not be certain.

Immediately he dismounted from the flying fox over the Clutha, Fox headed off northwest at full stride, confident that any pursuers would now be delayed crossing the Clutha and he would be leaving them behind. He slept rough in the tussock just north of The Junction settlement, setting off in the first light of dawn for the Lowburn and the Pisa Range.

As he climbed up the eastern side he looked frequently back down to the flats below but saw no one. Climbing and walking as fast as he could sustain, Fox reached the top of the Pisa and plunged down into the valley of the Kittleburn, hoping to climb out across the lower Criffel Range and into the Cardrona valley before nightfall.

As he climbed the western side of the Kittleburn he again stopped to look back across the valley from where he had come. To his surprise and fury he saw five men had left the top of the Pisa and had already begun coming down into the Kittleburn, obviously following him. As he would be in clear view of them from across the valley when he reached the ridge-line of the Criffel Range, he decided to turn back and meet up with his pursuers, rather than let them see just where he was headed.

Fox returned back down to the Kittleburn again, reaching it before the five men, sitting nonchalantly on a rock beside the stream to await them. They were jubilant on finding him there, surprised to have finally caught up with him. They were quite open with Fox at having followed him, exultant that they had managed to track him down. They declared that he might just as well reveal his destination as he could not hope to evade them next day. But they did not know William Fox.

The men had a tent which they pitched by the Kittleburn for the night which they invited Fox to share. After a meal, Fox (with deep concealed reluctance) produced the sole bottle of whisky he had carried from Dunstan, in turn generously sharing it with his new companions but drinking little himself. Later, they settled down to sleep, cleverly placing Fox at the very back of the tent so that he could not reach the entrance at the front without crossing over their bodies.

Fox lay awake in the dark for hours, himself fighting off the urge to sleep. Eventually, some time in the very early hours when he was sure the men were deep in a whisky slumber, Fox took a knife from his swag. Working slowly, a few inches at a time, quietly and carefully he sliced a long slit in the thin canvas wall beside him. He eased his huge frame through the hole, crouching outside clutching only the precious bag of salt. Even his breathing seemed loud in the stillness of the night, but the men slept on.

Fox reached back through the hole, gently retrieved his bedroll but not his more bulky swag and took off into the night. By daylight, he was deep in the tight winding gully of the Cardrona headwaters, lost to his pursuers. It was not surprising that he looked exhausted when he finally reached us in the Arrow.

However, hidden isolated in the Arrow, we were not to know the aftermath of Fox's escape – only learning of it later.

On discovering that Fox had disappeared during the night, the five men cast about for sign of him but found nothing. They returned to The Junction where their story was quickly passed around the diggers, many of whom were without claims of their own to work. A 'Fox hunt' was declared and parties of diggers crossed over the Pisa Range, fanning out in a search for him, convinced he had again secretly made another strike.

On November 9th, a party following the Cardrona River downstream to the north, themselves discovered gold on its banks, only a mere mile north of the point where the trail came down into the valley from the Criffel Range. We ourselves – and many other previous travellers – had unknowingly passed close by this find.

A rush to the Cardrona quickly followed. Within a few days, more than 500 men from The Junction and Dunstan crowded claims along the banks of the small Cardrona River. But Fox was not there; many diggers sure that his lair was elsewhere, kept searching.

On the Arrow, we worked our ground frantically, knowing our time undiscovered was precious. But we'd had trouble keeping Cormack's party to their agreement; reluctant to give up a man when required for the supplies-journey to Rees's or wanting only to make the journey in full daylight. When McGregor caught their man Blue sneaking back to work their claim when supposedly on guard, Fox warned him of a beating.

Next day, from our claim, we noticed a long shaft of smoke spiraling into the morning daylight sky from Cormack's claim in New Chums' gully. We ran downriver and into the gully, to find Blue and West crouched by their fireplace cooking food. Reid and I rushed to kick the fire out, upending their billycan onto the embers. West scuttled off but an enraged Fox caught Blue by the shirt, then sent him flying backwards with a crunching blow to the jaw.

But we were too late. Only an hour had passed when we heard shouts from up on the hillside above New Chums'. Surging down through the snowgrass into the gully came a scattered horde of men. We were discovered.

McGregor – who as discoverer of the Arrow gold quickly acquired some status – urged the crowd of newcomers to elect Fox as the field boss. Fox declared that claims should be limited to 24 feet per man and that he, personally, would punish any claim-jumpers. The diggers dispersed quickly into the valley to find ground to lay claim.

At the very moment of our being discovered, fear for our food supplies surged uppermost in my mind. John Reid, Low and I left the Arrow immediately for Rees's, leaving Fox and McGregor to defend our claims.

I was certain that within days, the newcomers would exhaust whatever food they had carried; facing the reality that here in the western high mountains we were far beyond the fringes of human organisation, men would be torn between their hunger and their lust for gold. Such men – as I had already seen – soon lost their veneer of civility and reason.

We took all that we could carry from Rees, which included most of his stock of flour. We warned him that he could be overwhelmed by hungry diggers within days; to send his boat south down the lake for whatever supplies he could secure, before hungry men arrived at his door.

He heeded us and did so. By the time the boat returned, a restless crowd of starving diggers was already waiting on the shore. An armed

Rees had gathered his sheep flock into walled yards at the station, stood ready to shoot to protect them. Before Rees could stop the hungry mob they rushed into the water pushing and fighting, grabbing whatever they could seize, overturning the boat in their panicked frenzy, spilling precious flour into the lake, driving the empty-handed into a fury.

The foodless attacked those who were carrying supplies. Shots were fired, including Rees's. Several men were wounded, others staggered off into the tussock bleeding from injuries.

(Rees learned quickly. When next his boat returned from the south, the waiting diggers were held back at gunpoint. The flour was eked out at two shillings and sixpence per pannikin-full.)

Though so careful to ration our supplies that we were always hungry, we hoped they would last us until the amount being brought up from the south could be increased. How that might happen we were not sure; Fox and I even discussing obtaining or building a boat of our own.

More men arrived over the ridges into the Arrow, pushing far upriver in search of good ground, despite the maze of sheer bluffs, steep shingle slides and deep rocky side-gullies. Even just upriver from our claim, a large waterfall blocked passage up the riverbed, forcing men to take to near-sheer hillsides to circumvent it.

Word reached us of new discoveries in the Arrow, first a distant eight miles up the valley, then in the headwaters at twelve miles. Newcomers from the Dunstan told us that the Arrow goldfield was being called 'Fox's'. We kept working our claims, particularly the creek-bed itself where we found many curiously misshapen nuggets of gold, looking as if they had been poured as molten droplets writhing into a quenching bath.

No sooner had we heard of some new discovery or arrivals, than another event would supercede it. Just as November turned to December, men came rushing through the valley shouting news of yet a further, richer find of gold. Thomas Arthur, the shepherd employed by Rees for the summer, had 'accidentally' found gold in a river near the Wakatipu itself. Groups of men only recently arrived in the Arrow raced off in a rush to stake new claims.

We soon learned that Arthur, apparently out exploring the grazing-land on Rees's station, had his Sunday walk stopped by the steep bank of a river. Rees had called this river the 'Shotover', copying the name of favourite land from near his home in Scotland. The Shotover had its watershed in the same mountain range as the Arrow but about mid-basin, near half way between the Arrow River and Rees's homestead on Lake Wakatipu shore.

The Shotover River was more than double the size of the Arrow. Like the Arrow, it too poured from the mountainside in a racing tumbling torrent from a deep cliff-lined gorge. It was deep, fast and dangerous to cross. In order to ford it on our many trips to and from Rees's, we could only cross it safely about a mile downriver from the point where it emerged from the mountains. There, the volume of water surging toward its meeting with the Kawerau River divided into many shallower braided channels spread over a wide gravel bed. Each of these was easier and safer to cross.

Thomas Arthur was walking along the foot of the mountains bordering the north side of the basin when he came to the Shotover. It poured along a narrow channel some 60 feet below the steep bank on which he stood. Thinking he could possibly ford it, Arthur managed to climb down the near-vertical gravel bank to the river. As he dislodged stones near the bottom of the bank, he saw a lump of gold uncovered at his feet.

In minutes he found several more. Excited by his find, he rushed back to the station homestead, told Rees he was leaving his employment and returned to the Shotover next day, telling two diggers he had befriended, Pyke and Worthington, of his discovery. At the river, digging the base of the gravel bank where the Shotover emerged from the gorge, they collected nugget upon nugget of gold. In just one day, Pyke and Worthington gathered up nearly 13 lbs of gold worth more than £700.

Thomas Arthur who had arrived at Rees's in rags left only a week later in riches. His find at what was called 'Arthur's Point' in days triggered yet another heedless rush of diggers into this barren mountain vastness that near stripped the Dunstan bare and halved the diggers working the Arrow.

Though Arthur was credited with the discovery, Fox believed that Jack Tewa – Maori Jack – surely knew also of the Shotover gold; possibly the nuggets he had shown to Fox some 10 months previously had once lain in the gravel at Arthur's Point.

More and more diggers streamed into these mountains from the east enticed by tales of vast wealth lying on the ground waiting to be found. Many continued to arrive in the Arrow. Despite the rush that drew men from the Arrow over to the Shotover, we estimated that no less than 1500 men were still spread throughout the Arrow Valley. Diggers were everywhere in the maze of tributaries and gullies that fed into the Arrow.

The richest ground was also the easiest to work – the stony riverbed itself, the rocky bottoms of the tributary creeks. But all these being small, the ground was quickly being worked out by the huge number of diggers working all the daylight hours. As the thaw was passing, the water levels continued to drop encouraging diggers to divert the river in its bed with walls of piled stones, exposing new ground to work.

In our own gully, we worked the little creek down to the bedrock, recovering a lot of gold lying against the base rock itself until that part of our claims was exhausted. Then, as we had planned for, we began to move up onto the terrace above the creek where Fox's earlier prospecting had shown the dirt was payable. But for this ground to be worth the effort, we needed to wash more of it than could be achieved just with pans and cradles alone.

A group of men had set themselves up supplying the diggers with firewood cut from the stand of beech forest in one of the western gullies nearby. It was the only source of wood for cooking or heating water.

I climbed up the gully to visit the woodcutters, offering to pay them well with gold if they could saw us some timber from the beech logs. Together, we dug a pit in the ground deep enough for a man to stand upright. A log placed over the hole could then be sawn by two men using a short double-ended blade - one man above the log, one below. It was hard work for them, but successful, soon producing some rough-cut planks which we carried between us back to our claim.

I used these to make a long sluice-box. Fitted with baffles made from bundles of tussock and set up on pillars of stacked stones, we were able to wash far more dirt than was possible using just cradles and pans. It was not very effective at catching fines, but our objective was to recover all the larger pieces of gold, from nuggets to flakes, as quickly as possible. The fines we might lose in the process were not worth the extra effort – they were discharged with the tailings.

McGregor's party soon had the men up in sawpit gully cut them enough planks to copy our sluice. They too began work on the terrace above their riverside claim, stripping away all the vegetation to expose the layers of alluvial gravels beneath.

We worked in all weathers through the long daylight hours of

December. On the last day of the year, many of us gathered around fires on a calm, warm night. Some men produced cornets – others a fiddle – and as best we could, we all joined in to sing songs until midnight, with the Irish, Scots and English all competing to out-voice each other with their favourites. To hear the ringing sounds of massed voices echoing around the valley, helped to dispel the loneliness that most of us otherwise felt out here in this mountainous wilderness far from civilisation, away from families or the countries we had called home. It was a wistful memory of the goldfields that I carried with me for many years after.

The New Year brought heat and hunger. Day after day, the sun burst early over the ridges glaring down for hours from cloudless skies. The valley trapped heat, the rocks becoming too hot to touch. Waves of heat shimmered upward from the exposed gravel. At night the stone walls of our hut radiated heat back at us until we found it was cooler to sleep outside.

The supply of food was precarious and insufficient; though Rees tried his best, even continual voyages from the south with his whaleboat could not carry enough flour to feed the thousands of men now scattered throughout the high valleys. Although a three-day-long coach service had recently commenced over the Dunstan Trail, the high mountains, savage river gorges and rugged country west from Dunstan, made any form of transportation into this remote vastness impossible.

Hunger was the closest and most constant companion for the majority of diggers, many of whom had never lived in such isolation nor were equipped for it. Most of the new arrivals into the mountains had come directly from the ships berthing in Dunedin almost daily from Australia. Finding all the goldfields already crowded, they struggled on westward on foot, oblivious to the terrain and conditions they would find here in the mountains when eventually they arrived, weakened with exhaustion and hunger.

Making conditions worse for us all was the complete lack of any form of vegetables. The monotonous daily diet for all of us consisted of mutton – stewed or roasted – with dampers made from flour. Tea was the common drink – liquor unobtainable at any price. Fortunately, our party still had some salt, but most others did not.

In the hot days of January, like a curse from God, dysentery swept through the goldfields. No man was immune from the agonising, gut-twisting pains that would suddenly grip us, sending us off writhing to crouch over a latrine hole, with sweat bursting from every pore until the agony passed. Even strong men lay about for days, almost totally debilitated, unable to eat, surviving only on water.

With so many diggers upriver from us, we were afraid the water of the Arrow River itself was probably badly contaminated. A sickly stench of excrement wafted on the air because the wastes did not quickly decompose in the dry stony ground. A plague of flies – big heavy-bodied black flies – harassed us throughout the daylight.

Claim-jumping, vicious assaults and robberies increased. A violent convict from an Australian prison-hulk, Richard Burgess, preyed on isolated groups of miners further up the valley, terrorising the headwaters goldfields with a gang. The bodies of several men, savagely beaten or shot, were recovered from the river. Burgess only attacked hatters or parties of less than four, beating them with cudgels to drive them from their claims, then seizing their supplies, searching and finding their hidden stores of gold. Then he and his gang would vanish into the myriad headwater gullies until suddenly descending on another hapless group days later.

Though the area close to us was mostly peaceful and law-abiding, we began to hear of more fighting up the valley. Men came past us heading out for the Shotover with bruised and battered faces, having been driven violently from their claims or robbed of their supplies. Others were being forced to leave, desperate for food. In all the rushes that had occurred in Otago, the thousands of men had been surprisingly orderly and law-abiding – now it was clear that violent criminals were among the many new arrivals from Australia.

Although some of the recent discoveries up at the twelve-mile were rich ground, our original claims in the area just inside the ravine were as yet far the richer; indeed Fox's prospecting during our first weeks in the Arrow had found none better. If diggers were being violently dispossessed of their claims or being forced to abandon them up in the headwaters without risk of retribution to the perpetrators, then we ourselves on much richer ground were also at risk of attack. We resolved with McGregor that at the sound of any gunshot, we would all immediately rush to support each other; an attack on any one party must be met by a collective defense. We worked with our guns close to hand.

On another hot January afternoon as the sun moved westward over the head of our gully, a shout above us on the hillside suddenly cut through the still air. I looked up, dropping my shovel to shade my eyes against the bright glare. Silhouetted dark against the sunlight, I could see the figure of a man standing on a rock outcrop. He was not alone. He shouted again.

'You diggers down there! We'd be the Tipperary Men! Leave your claim now and you'll go unharmed! If you don't, we'll drive you from it!'

I cupped my hands, shouted back, saw Reid from the corner of my eye scurry across in a crouching run toward our hut: 'Hey Tipperary Men, and we'd be boys from 'Derry too! Ireland mates are all mates – just leave us be!'

A momentary silence. I could just see against the blinding sun, the shapes of men clustering together on the rock. Then he called again: 'To hell with Derry y'northern scum! Get off or get shot. We're comin' down!'

Reid came running back, threw me my carbine as he passed, then dived off into rocks off to my right. Fox was over somewhere to my left, now out of sight. I lunged desperately up the hill, threw myself to the ground under a large boulder. I heard a bullet twang beside me, chips of rock flying and the sound of the shot rolling around the gully. Men were shouting from above.

I pulled the ever-present revolver from my belt, huddled closer to the rock, peered cautiously around it to the right, down at its base at ground level. If the Tipperary Men traversed downward across the slope from the left they would all reach Fox first, then outflank us in a mob. But if they came directly from above, they'd have to overrun us all at the same time and divide themselves.

A quick look around showed no sign of Fox or Reid but I knew they were there, waiting. Others should be coming to our help, alerted by the shot. I could feel my heart thumping in my chest, silence ringing in my ears, tense and dry-mouthed. Waiting.

On the hill above I glimpsed a man weaving through the snowgrass, a pink face appearing then ducking swiftly from sight. I grabbed the carbine, sighted along it where I'd seen him last. Men were shouting off to my left.

Then I saw him. Hatless, a mass of hair, a bearded face peering above the snowgrass, staring down, knowing I was there, but unsure exactly where. Expecting me to appear over the top of the rock. He rose up higher, head darting left and right, trying to find me. He had a pistol in one hand. Tucked tightly under my rock, he hadn't yet seen me. I sighted the carbine on him, there on his exposed left shoulder, held my breath and squeezed on the trigger. The heavy Westley Richards kicked back. There was a puff of smoke from the muzzle, the sweet acrid smell of powder, and a hollow 'thwunk' of the bullet striking softness.

The man yelled loudly, spun around and upright by the force of the shot and fell backward into the snowgrass out of sight.

I knew instantly, instinctively, the shot had revealed my hiding-place. I dropped the carbine, picked up the revolver and dived to the left side of my rock. There were more shots and shouts somewhere off to the right, I thought it must be Reid or reinforcements arriving.

Somewhere close above me, there was a violent roar. Just on the uphill side of my rock. I sprang to my feet, backed away from the rock to get some space, knowing not what was coming. Over the rock above charged a man, snarling open-mouthed, wide-eyed, a huge knife in hand. He saw me and leapt at me. There was no time to aim the revolver. I crouched, then thrust violently upward at him as he landed on me, hand outstretched scrabbling at my face, knife-hand swinging wildly. My violent thrust caught him off balance. I rolled back with his momentum, then in one twisting heave, threw him off and out downhill with all my strength. His snarling roar now anguished cry, he flew downward through the air and crashed into the rocks below, the wind crushed from his lungs in a bursting moan, and then lay still. Thank God my cousins in Castledawson had taught me to wrestle!

I snatched up the carbine, revolver still in hand and backed away further from the rock, expecting another bandit to lunge from above at any moment. None came. Shouts, shots and cheers from down the gully to my right. Thank God again! Help is to hand!

Well above I could see men scrambling away uphill. I chambered another cartridge into the carbine and fired in their general direction to keep them going. More shouts from my right, then John Reid burst into sight, red-faced, wide-eyed and breathless. 'Fraser! Are you safe? I heard shots. I didn't know. What a fight! McGregor and the others arrived. I think we've chased them off!'

I pointed down to the creek-bed below where my last attacker still lay in the rocks, moving slightly. 'There's one alive down there that didn't get away, another up there somewhere in the snowgrass that's shot.'

When the Tipperary Men charged downhill, Reid had taken cover in a little gut, barely deep enough, but he was seen by two men coming down to his right. They both fired shots at him but as is common when shooting downhill, they aimed too high and he heard the bullets buzz perilously overhead. Reid fired back before they could reload and hit one of them who fell back into the snowgrass. His companion dived for cover near him. When McGregor's party arrived, they saw the wounded man being helped away uphill.

We hurried up the gully to find Fox. He was crouched by the creek washing blood flowing from a cut to the head above his right ear, extending down to the top of the lobe which was partly torn away. As I had feared, he'd had the worst of it.

Although his Enfield rifle was to hand when the Tipperary Men attacked, he only managed to fire one missing shot at a dodging figure before three of them were upon him. Fortunately the men had no guns themselves but were armed with pick-handles and knives. Fox had an ever-present knife strapped to his leg and a shovel.

Faced with three attackers, he knew the knife alone was no defence, so instantly charged at them swinging the shovel as a flail. The lethal edge of the blade caught the nearest claim-jumper in the chest, sending him reeling backward with the force but smashing the blade off the shaft. Before Fox could re-balance, the attacker on the right clubbed him hard on the head with a cudgel, splitting open his scalp. Such a blow would have killed a lesser man but Fox was not only a giant, he was hardened by all our months of labour. Oblivious to the blood pouring from his wound, a roaring enraged Fox leapt at the man thrusting the shovel shaft at him like a spear. Driven violently backward, the man stumbled and fell. A quick boot to the chest, then Fox swung and caught the hesitant third attacker with a blow to the jaw that lifted his feet from the ground. All three of them fled up the creek-bed.

McGregor's party had securely tied up the semi-conscious claim-jumper I had tossed down into the rocks. Later, he recovered sufficiently to be taken out of the ravine, where he was kept chained to a log, being kicked or stoned by every passing digger. The harsh environment alone caused us such suffering that those who had preyed violently on the hapless deserved no compassion, nor were shown any.

Having driven off the Tipperary Men and shown our determination to defend ourselves, we hoped that word would spread amongst the lawless and we would not be challenged again, although the convict Burgess continued to maraud the upper reaches of the Arrow.

News from over the ridges in the Shotover Valley reached us of new discoveries in the tributary valleys of the Moonlight and Moke rivers. Hundreds more new arrivals with the bright gleam of gold in their eyes poured into the valley. Following the industrious and adventuresome came more lawless violent vultures to prey upon them. More bodies of dead men came tumbling down the Shotover.

On a late-January night, the air again lay hot and still over the Arrow, so thinned by the day's heat as to leave us breathless. Despite it, we had been forced to take shelter inside our stone hut from the relentless swarms of mosquitoes that plagued all the dark hours, screening the doorway and window apertures with kanuka swatches to keep their pestilent buzzing at bay.

Some time in the early hours, I was suddenly awake. I lay staring up in the darkness, feeling the hard ground driving through my palliasse of dried tussock. Was it that, that had awakened me? Had I heard something, or was it just a dream? I lay still, listening to the silence.

Then it came again. A low soft voice with a touch of urgency. Clearly. Somewhere outside, just through the wall. 'Mr Fraser, are you there Mr Fraser?'

I rolled over, felt for the comforting steel of my revolver. Fox and Reid breathed on undisturbed. It came again, very close: 'Mr Fraser?' That voice, had I heard that voice before?

I crouched, eased the thatch apart in the doorway, held the revolver steadily in front of me, and peered out. Outside, in the starlight, I could sense more than see the bulk of a man. Then the whites of his eyes moved.

'Mr Fraser, it is me! Erihana!'

FIFTEEN

I moved out of the hut into the soft night. Erihana was not alone; I could sense then see the outline of another man.

'How did you know I was here and why do you come calling me in the middle of the night?' I asked.

He replied in that same deep, slow sonorous voice I knew so well: 'I have always known where you were Mr Fraser, ever since you left your boat on the river.

'This man here with me is my relative. His name is Hakaria Haeroa.' I could see the whites of this man's eyes too when he moved in the darkness at mention of his name. 'We have come here to ask you for your help Mr Fraser. Coming to ask for help does not choose between darkness or daylight.'

John Reid who had woken with our voices, emerged from the hut. We moved to the fireplace, kicked the embers into life and I explained who our visitors were. In the flickering yellow light of the flames, Erihana told us why he had come.

Together with several other natives of his group, they had earlier travelled some distance up the Shotover River to lay claim to an area which they knew from early times contained gold, but on arrival had found that miners had already taken possession of the best or most likely sandy benches. As they walked along the east bank, they passed an encampment of diggers but noticed that a wide shingle beach opposite on the west side beneath jagged bluffs appeared untouched. When they enquired of the diggers whether this beach too had been claimed, they were told that although the beach looked to be promising ground, no miner had the courage or the daring to swim the turbulent river – still bitterly cold even in hot summer – to find out.

Erihana – as I knew from our time together – was not only an excellent swimmer, but could seemingly ignore cold water. He plunged into the deep fast-flowing river and swam across. An old dog, his favourite companion, jumped into the water to follow, but was caught by the current and swept quickly downstream. While Erihana watched anxiously, his dog fortuitously managed to struggle across to land on a rocky ledge further down on the west side, beneath a vertical wall several hundred feet high. It crawled from the freezing water, shook itself vigorously, rolled on the ground and then stood looking back plaintively toward Erihana.

Without hesitation, he plunged back into the river determined to rescue the animal and easily swam downriver to the ledge on which it was perched. The dog rushed up to him immediately as he arose from the water. To his amazement, Erihana saw specks of gold clinging to the animal's wet hair. Quickly looking around the small ledge, he could see lumps of gold clearly visible, lodged in crevices in the rock.

He called and waved to Hakaria who swam across to join him. In the brief time before closing night forced them back across the river, the two men collected over 400 ounces from among the crevices and a few square yards of the ledge.

Next day, joined by others from his group including his Chief, they claimed the beach and the rocky ledge further downstream. To the diggers on the nearby reaches, their claim was quickly known as 'Maori Point'. To reach the claim more easily, the natives swam a bullock-hide rope across the river, then secured it to large rocks on both banks. Two logs lashed together, looped onto the bullock-hide, could be pulled across with a smaller rope, to carry small loads back and forth. Natives crossing the river pulled themselves hand-over-hand along the bullock-hide rope. The miners nearby called this contrivance, the 'Maori Point Ferry'.

The ground proved to be very rich. In a short time, the little band recovered a large amount of gold including some exceptionally big nuggets, each of many ounces. At night, they camped together on a tussock-covered bench on the east bank opposite their claim.

Two days ago, in the early morning as they were preparing to cross the river again to their claim, they were suddenly startled by the crash of gunfire and shouts from the hillside above. A large group of men was scattered there among the snowgrass. One called down to them. Erihana recounted his words.

'Hey you thievin' bunch of cannibals down there! We'd be the Galway Boys and we've come to take over your ground! Now get off it y'savages

– or we'll be shootin' every last one of you!'

The Maoris had no guns, were armed only with clubs or spears and were few in number compared with their attackers. As they stood together hurriedly discussing what they should do, the Galway Boys came charging down the hill, firing shots and shouting. Erihana's little group fled downriver along the bank with their Chief and escaped up the hill.

They split up. The Chief and his men set off southeast to gather reinforcements from among their tribe. Erihana and Hakaria decided to come east to the Arrow to seek my help.

'We hear that you and your friends have also been attacked by these bad men, Mr Fraser. We know there was a fight and you won. Your attackers were beaten and are gone. You are left in peace on your claim. Many people now hear of this.

'So we have come to ask for your help. Please come with us, Mr Fraser. Help us to take back our claim stolen from us by these bad people. Our Chief will return with many warriors from our tribe, but when these Pakeha also see that white men with guns have joined with us, they will be even more afraid. We will fight them. We will take back our claim. We too will win.'

Fox had emerged from the hut whilst Erihana spoke. Fox knew him – as Daniel Ellison – from his first journey up the Molyneaux to Gabriel's with us on the *Lady Colina* but now, as then, he showed no acknowledgment, nor surprise to find him here.

Briefly, I recounted the purpose of Erihana's visit.

Fox's response was immediate. 'I'll have no truck with these natives, or any other of them. They're just a traitorous bunch of warring cannibals that'll turn on us too when they want, just as they do now to each other. Let them kill each other – the less of them remaining, the better for all of us! But don't get drawn into the violent disputes of these savages JC, I most certainly won't!' and he abruptly returned into the hut.

I made no comment to Fox's outburst. Instead, I asked Erihana to wait until daylight, when I would decide what I would do. He and his companion lay down near the fire. Reid and I returned into the hut.

At first light, the four of us visited McGregor and his men. Again I explained who the Maoris with us were and why they had come to me. Already, my own decision was made.

'We diggers have all stood here together and fought off the claim-jumpers,' I told them. 'Violence and lawlessness is the same, whether it's on the Arrow or on the Shotover. Whether it's against the lawful claims of white miners or the lawful claims of native miners, is all the same to me. If we do not resist these violent gangs everywhere and deny their lawlessness to succeed against any man, then none of us will be safe, anywhere. If we don't help these Maori diggers, the claim-jumpers will take our lack of action as a signal that they can do as they wish with impunity. And more thuggery, violence and murder will rule these goldfields.

'Until we have Troopers come here to maintain the law, for our own sakes we must maintain it ourselves. Either we make a stand together, or the Galway Boys and others like the Tipperary Men will return and drive all of us from these goldfields. So I for one, am willing to go and help these Maori miners take back their rightful claim. Now who among you will come with us?'

John Reid was quick to voice his support. Cormack, with five other men stepped forward. McGregor himself wanted to join us but was urged to remain to guard their claim against any new attack, as Fox would surely stay and protect ours.

The nine of us left the Arrow gorge and set off across the basin toward the Shotover River valley, some eight miles distant. Erihana and Hakaria, both barefoot, set a pace the rest of us struggled to maintain. The Maoris, accustomed to walking long distances over rough country, were forced to stop repeatedly and wait for us to catch up with them.

Before reaching the Shotover, we turned and climbed high up onto the mountain range that formed the northern boundary of the basin, then sidled around into the long terraced gorge of the Shotover itself. By mid-afternoon, we were a long way back up the valley, following a track that the natives obviously had used in pre-European times, high above the winding gorge.

As we tramped quickly along this track, two more natives appeared silently from among rocks above us and joined Erihana. Within a few hundred yards we rounded a small ridge to find a large group of natives gathered in the snowgrass, some 30 strong. They stared curiously at us as Erihana led us toward a heavily-bearded grey-haired man seated on a large rock, closely surrounded by several younger men.

Erihana spoke briefly to grey-hair in his own language, then turning to me said: 'This man, Mr Fraser, is our Chief, 'Patu'. He is our leader. All these others are of our tribe. As you see, we are not alone.'

The natives were armed with axes, spears, long or short-handled clubs and several old flintlock fowling pieces. Together as a group of mostly big heavy men, they looked quite intimidating; wild-looking black hair, some with tattoos on their faces, many completely bare-chested, others dressed in an assortment of ill-fitting clothes. But some smiled reassuringly at us.

We all moved further up the valley, dropping down from one terrace to another, gradually getting deeper into the gorge. When Erihana advised we were getting closer to their Maori Point claim, I suggested that Reid and I should first talk with the diggers nearby, to see if we could gather more support. Ahead, I could see smoke rising from their campfires.

The two of us went down near the river. The first group we approached reacted quickly at the sight of two armed men approaching but emerged cautiously from their defensive positions to talk when we assured them we meant no harm. They too were very afraid they themselves might next be attacked by the Galway Boys and were surprised that we should have come all the way from the Arrow to help the natives.

Readily they agreed to join us, sending two of their mates off to seek more support from other diggers nearby. As the daylight was strong until near 10 pm, we had time to prepare and mount our attack on the Galway Boys before nightfall; to restrain the revengeful Maoris until next day was an impossibility.

We gathered together high on the hillside, not visible from the disputed 'Maori Point' below. Another party of miners arrived, most of them armed with guns. With Erihana's help, we discussed the imminent attack with the chief, Patu, and his men. The Maoris were clearly working themselves up for a fight and were wanting to charge downhill immediately.

Instead, we agreed on a plan that would force the Galway Boys to defend against two fronts simultaneously. The natives would move back down the valley, then when well out of sight, would descend into the gorge to the riverbank terrace. They would then proceed up-river to a bend just below their claim. From that obscured point, they would mount their charge.

Meantime, we white men would sneak down through the snowgrass above the Galway Boys, as close as we could without being discovered, and await the Maori charge. When the claim-jumpers rushed to defend themselves against the natives, they would be clearly exposed to us firing at them from above. The natives, who relished close-quarter fighting, would carry the attack whilst we with our guns, were at lesser risk up above the fray. With a line of retreat left open to them up-river, the Irish gang would be less inclined to stand and fight.

The Maoris left us. We spread out into a line along the hillside with Reid and I at its centre and began descending. We kept low, creeping on hands and knees between the yard-high bushy clumps of snowgrass. We sneaked down until – from the sound of the rushing river below – I thought we must be within effective shooting distance. Then I passed a whispered word along the line to stop, keep well hidden, and wait for the sound of the natives' charge before exposing ourselves.

We waited. I could feel the tension rising. The wait seemed interminable and I began to wonder why the impatient Maoris were taking so long. Occasionally we could hear voices from below above the steady noise from the river. I looked up the wide brown valley of the Shotover, lined with stepped successions of perfectly sculpted winding terraces. Such an incongruous place of beauty and peace to be the home of such violence.

Then in an instant I felt the hair on my neck rise and my heart leap. A blood-chilling roar such as I had never heard brought us all crouching up out of the snowgrass. Below, I saw men rushing about wildly on the riverbank bench. There were many of them – more than I expected. Across the river on a stony bank beneath a sheer cliff, another smaller group rushed to the waters' edge.

First a shot, then another, then a burst of gunfire as the natives charged along the bench, closing on the men below. I saw several natives fall. With a clash we could feel from above, the Maoris hurled themselves, screaming their war-cries, onto the first line of the Galway Boys. Immediately, we began firing down at those further back concealing themselves from the natives behind rocks or rushing to find defensive positions upriver.

Suddenly aware of being attacked from two fronts, their confusion was obvious as they scrambled for cover from our new firing. I crouched momentarily above the waist-high snowgrass, fired the carbine at any movement below or in the general direction, dropped instantly down from sight, dived sideways to a different place, lay there reloading, then leapt up for another shot. All along the line, other men did the same. Swirling swathes of sweet acrid powder-smoke drifted in the air. Unless acting in my own direct defence, I had no wish to kill or wound any man, so just fired my carbine in their general direction to intimidate.

The Maoris below were driving the Galway Boys back in close hand-to-hand fighting in which the Irishmen had no chance to use their guns. Only those concealed further back along the bank could keep firing but were also shot at by us from above the moment they showed themselves. Shouts, screams and horrible cries rose up to us from the river. Bodies of men – dead or alive – were being thrown into the river. Some flailed about, others drenched the river with blood before being swept away.

The ferocity of the natives' attack increased. A savage roar burst from them as the Galway Boys' line suddenly broke. The Irishmen scattered in a frantic panicked run along the bank upriver to escape in the only direction we had left open to them. Others leapt up from hiding behind rocks to join the flight. Only the group across the river, standing helplessly watching the natives' attack sweep through their camp, remained.

The gunfire quickly died away, overtaken by cheering from us and a rhythmic chant from the Maoris below. The surviving Galway Boys had now vanished up into the gorge. Bodies still washed about in the river shallows streaming blood off into the clear water as we climbed down from our firing-line up in the snowgrass to join the victorious natives on the riverbank.

The Maoris took no prisoners. As we arrived, a war-party was about to cross the river to seize the remaining Irishmen huddled in a frightened silent group on Maori Point. Fearing more bloodshed would result from the still wide-eyed natives, I rushed to find Erihana who, thankfully unharmed, was clustered with others around his Chief Patu.

Although he too was still agitated from the fighting, I urged him to stop the war-party and allow us to secure the surrender of the Irishmen waiting anxiously across the river. Enough men had already died, I argued; the Maoris' had won back their claim, their quest for revenge had been satisfied, their honour regained. We had restored goldfields' law. Nothing further would be achieved by attacking defenseless men.

A brief discussion among them and they agreed. Clearly showing our guns, we called the small band of Galway Boys to return to us across the river and they would be unharmed. They came, clinging their way along the ropes spanning the river. None were armed. We made each man swear to keep the peace, to leave the Shotover, and then released them.

The natives had taken no other prisoners. Every man overcome had been thrown into the river, dead or alive. Several Maoris themselves had been killed. Others that were injured – some quite severely – had their wounds bound with strips torn from the Irishmens' clothing.

In the subdued aftermath that follows the high excitement of a fight, we white miners sat quietly together exchanging our experiences. The Chief Patu, Erihana, Hakaria and others approached us in a group. They stopped, facing us. Erihana – standing tall – stepped forward from the group and spoke, softly but with stature. Even now, despite the turmoil of the attack, he projected an aura of some inner calm strength.

'Our Chief asks that we thank you Mr Fraser. You and all these men who came here to fight beside us. Now we stand together again on this – our land – wrongly taken from us. All will know that Maori too will not be forced to give up what is ours – that others will fight beside us. We will not forget what you have done here today.'

As if we were now dismissed, they turned about and walked away. Although there were later occasions when I sensed that he might strangely appear, just as he had three times before, I have never seen Erihana again.

We left, climbing slowly back up the hillside through the bracken-fern and snowgrass, parted from the Shotover diggers who had joined us and set off to return to the Arrow.

With so many diggers already on the rivers and more arriving each day, another goldfields' shantytown was growing along the side of a small hill directly opposite the entrance to the Arrow ravine. When the first shanties appeared it was known as 'Fox's', but having become considerably enlarged, it was now being called 'Arrow Town'. It was the usual goldfields' ramshackle collection of stacked riverstone and canvas huts, some with the addition of rough-sawn timber slabs brought down from sawpit gully.

Despite the constant difficulty of bringing stores so far inland along rough tracks, then up the long arm of Lake Wakatipu, there was a surprising array of goods for sale. For a lot of gold (the only currency), diggers could buy simple tools, clothes, legs of bacon, whole sides of sheep, canned fish, or potted jams and meats.

A grog shanty sold gin by the mug or by the case. In an earthen-floored dancing saloon behind the shanty were the only women to be found among the thousands of men on the goldfield. By day, these 'bar-girls' were paid to dance or touted drinks to the diggers; by night they touted their bodies at 'half-and-half' – half an ounce of gold for half an hour.

Just below the town I was surprised to see a group of Chinamen clustered together carefully washing gravel on the riverbank, ground so poor that it was ignored by diggers. These small dark men looked the same as those I had seen previously at Gabriel's; shapeless dark blue gowns, long plaited strips of hair hanging from beneath close-fitting skull-caps, crouched painstakingly picking through the washdirt in their pans. Nearby were their shelters – small cave-like holes dug into the slope of the hill with little stone walls forming the entrance to each.

Reid and I walked over, curious. The Chinamen, keeping their heads down, peered up at us from the corners of their eyes, alarmed at the approach of two white men. One of them straightened up, turned to face me. At full height he didn't reach my chest. Thin slits hid his dark eyes, a flat oval face with only a few wispy strands of hair for a beard, his hands visibly shaking.

'No harm Missa, no harm,' he said through dark-stained teeth. I held out both my hands, palms uppermost, smiled and crouched down beside them. They were all stilled, watching me cautiously, expressionless, apprehensive like a flock of birds tensed ready for flight.

I gently reached out a hand. 'Please,' I said as I looked into the pan still held by the man who had faced me, traced a finger gently through the remains of the washdirt while he held the pan steady. No sign of gold, only sand. I handed it back.

I put a hand on my chest. 'My name is Fraser.'

The faintest crinkle in the corner of his eyes. 'Ah, Missa Flaser. My name Oon, Oon Yew Gow.' A short silence. 'We no harm. No white men ground (a wave of his hand toward the riverbank). Ground no good white men, only good Flowery People, Flowery People work hard, long time, small gold.'

I nodded my understanding. Such hard work deserved better rewards. 'This ground is very poor. You should find better ground up there in the valley,' I pointed up toward the Arrow ravine.

He shook his lowered head slowly, 'White men no want Flowery People.'

He was probably correct. I stood up, waved a hand to them. Reid and I set off up the gorge back to our claim as they stared, watching us go.

We found Fox anxiously awaiting us: armed groups of men constantly wandering the Arrow valleys challenging the rights of diggers to their claims had had to be warned off, shots had been fired and all the diggers were carrying revolvers. It was a tense situation.

Fortunately within days, Mounted Police Sergeant-Major Bracken arrived in Arrow Town with a detachment of six troopers, having received news of the attacks by the two Irish gangs. With him came Lowther Broad, appointed Gold Commissioner for the Central Goldfields, who commenced a register for all miners' claims and to judge disputes.

Bracken came immediately to visit us, having known Fox at Gabriel's and me when I was running my boat on the river. We related to him the fear of starvation which had forced men to violence, the influx of enormous numbers of ill-equipped and inexperienced men into these remote mountain valleys, the lawless gangs of ex-convicts and Irish deportees from Australia who attacked and killed defenceless diligent diggers, seized their claims and stole their gold.

Appalled at the murderous mayhem, violence and general lawlessness, Bracken and several troopers headed into the labyrinth of headwaters gullies of the Arrow in search of the ruthless Australian convict Richard Burgess who was still terrorising diggers beyond the twelve mile. Other troopers patrolled the lower valley to restore order whilst several others left for the Shotover.

Bracken and his men returned days later having successfully hunted down and seized Burgess. The police were cheered as they passed down the valley with the bound convict being dragged behind them. He was securely chained to a log in Arrow Town, kicked and abused by every passing digger until he was eventually escorted back east for imprisonment.

The heat of summer was reluctant to leave us; clear cloudless days continued as the water in the river dwindled. Groups of diggers joined together to build a large rock dam, called the 'Hit or Miss' to divert the reduced riverflow and expose its dried course to be mined for several hundred yards down to the bedrock.

In our side-branch the small creek had reduced to a trickle, in places disappearing completely into the stones to emerge again at a lower level. We struggled for water, laboriously collecting and carrying buckets up the steep hillside to our sluice on the terrace. All along the east side of the Arrow opposite us, the diggers (including McGregor's party) lugged buckets of paydirt down from their terraces to wash at the riverside.

We needed water. The bench where we had sited our sluice was some fifty feet above Fox's creek in the gully below. The narrow gully itself rose quite steeply up to its westward watershed, high above the level at which we were working. If we built a small dam up the creek at a level above us and diverted the water in a channel around the hillsides, I reasoned we could bring a small flow directly down to our sluice. But building such a channel would take the three of us many weeks of hard labour; winter would surely soon arrive and every day working our present tedious method was at least recovering some gold for us. We needed men to work on such a channel whilst we continued sluicing but no digger would likely give up mining his own claim to work so arduously just for wages.

The Chinamen! At Gabriel's they were renowned for their patient tireless labour. I went to see them. At their camp outside Arrow Town, they looked up in huddled alarm at my approach. Recognition flickered on Oon Yew Gow's face as he left the group, climbed up the small bank from the river. He nervously sucked air in through his teeth in apprehension.

'Ah, Missa Flaser, why you come Flowery people again? We no harm.'

'Mr Oon Yew Gow, I come to speak with you, to ask for your help.' I squatted down on my heels – a frequent posture I had seen Chinamen at Gabriel's adopt when talking amongst themselves or eating.

His face was completely expressionless as he listened to my proposal, clearly understanding more English than he could speak. Working here as they were on such very poor ground, I commented they would have to work hard and long for very small reward. Their ground was so poor, white men would not waste effort to work it. If they were willing to come and help us on our claim, we would pay them far more in gold than they could dream of finding by their own exhausting efforts here by the river.

With a stick, I drew a diagram in the sand to explain the help we needed, the Chinaman nodding his head in understanding. When I had finished, he rejoined his group who had resumed their work by the river. I waited a long time whilst they huddled together in discussion, their strange lilting chatter like a flock of roosting birds.

Eventually, when it seemed impossible they could have anything further to discuss, Oon Yew Gow returned. Shyly but firmly, he asked how they would be paid, immediately challenging my offer as insufficient. After some gentle but persistent negotiation we were agreed upon one ounce of gold per day for his group of nine men. He beckoned for me to follow him back to the group where we all squatted while another long discussion in their language ensued.

With difficulty because of his limited vocabulary of English, Oon Yew Gow raised a further issue. The Chinese were very afraid and concerned for their security and the risk of violence from white diggers. That was the reason why they had not attempted to claim more profitable ground in the Arrow Valley itself, why they kept to themselves well away from other miners.

As Oon Yew Gow slowly explained, I understood that two years previously at Ballarat in the Australian goldfields, a huge mob of more than 1000 diggers had attacked defenceless Chinese miners. When they fled, the mob – many on horseback – hunted the Chinamen down, whipping, beating and shooting them. Many were dragged by the 'queue' – their traditional long plaited length of hair – behind horses until it was torn out by the roots. Their huts were burned down and their gold stolen. Oon Yew Gow had escaped, but among the many who were tortured and killed, was his brother Oon Yew Tong. With a small group of others, Oon Yew Gow journeyed furtively to the coast. As soon as they heard news of Gabriel's gold discovery, they paid an exorbitant price for passage to New Zealand, buried many days deep in the darkest bowels of the ship.

After such an experience, the Chinese wanted to keep away from white miners and avoid any further risk of conflict. They could only agree to come into the Arrow valley to work with us, if we would assuredly protect them during the day. They would not camp in the valley but would come and go during darkness each morning and night. I agreed, explaining that we ourselves had fought off attackers, that we had defended the natives on the Shotover and that now there were Mounted Police in Arrow Town who would help protect them from violence.

Fox was furious. Just as he had with Erihana, he refused to have any contact with or responsibility for the Chinamen. Despite the potential for much higher returns from our sluicing if we could bring water to the terrace and without losing precious time ourselves labouring to dig a channel for it, Fox did not care.

'Be it on your own head JC,' he said vehemently, 'The bloody natives were bad enough, but I'll have nothing to do with these little yellow bastards! Who knows what devil-making they're up to – when you can't see into a man's eyes you can't tell just how devious they're being, plotting and scheming. They put curses on people and have heathen gods. Besides, they stink and they talk secretly in that language of theirs. I'll not pay those slit-eyes of yours a grain of my gold! Do what you will JC – but keep them clear of me, protect them yourself and pay them from your own share!'

Fox had been showing signs of restlessness, just as he had when we worked together in the Molyneaux gorge. Always more content as a prospector roaming the empty country alone, he had now been confined to one small place for months, tediously working the claim. News of rich new gold finds came to us almost daily and Fox would rather have been their discoverer than arduously accumulating even more wealth here on the Arrow.

Reid shook his head sadly as Fox walked away. 'You can count me in John. I'll pay my share of their wages and help to guard them too. If they can get us water here to the sluice we can extract a lot more gold from this dirt in a short time.'

The Chinese quietly squatted in a huddle outside our hut when daylight came next morning. They each carried boiled rice and tools in bundles tied to the ends of a pole balanced across their shoulders. They each wore a shapeless loose robe of dark blue cotton; some had close-fitting caps, others a wide-brimmed conical hat plaited from dried flax.

Higher up our narrow gully, I marked a point with a rock from where a channel dug around the hillside would bring the water from the diverted little creek to a point just above our terrace. But the hillside itself was rent by numerous small guts, folds, shallow ravines and rocky outcrops; the channel would have to wander back and forth through and around all these obstacles whilst maintaining just sufficient a slope as to keep the water flowing. Oon Yew Gow seemed to understand instantly what I required. The Chinese set to work.

Many times during each day, either Reid or I would visit our Chinese workers. Isolated high in our branch gully away from the main river ravine, they were quite secure. They laboured tirelessly, mostly in silence. Their method was to dig into the slope of the hillside and create a level pathway about two feet wide, then using the spoil and stones dug away, to build up a small wall along the outside edge of the path, thus creating a channel.

Where narrow side-gullies were separated by the sharp spine of a small intervening ridge, I suggested that they should dig a hole through it, like a small tunnel, but Oon Yew Gow became quite agitated. I learned that the Chinamen had a fear – a superstition – of caves, mines or tunnels; instead they tediously dug a narrow cut down from above sometimes as deep as 20 feet and exactly the width of a man. To form the channel on rocky ground, they meticulously stacked tightly-packed layers of small stones, painstakingly packing the inside with a plaster of tussock and earth.

While we three daily continued to lug water up to the sluice on the terrace, the Chinese channel – or 'water race' as Reid called it – crept slowly around the hillside toward us. When the Chinese stopped briefly around midday to brew tea and eat their bowls of rice, I often joined them. Their tea, which they offered to me, aromatic and green with a clean herbal aftertaste, was more refreshing than ours.

Oon Yew Gow gave me the names of several of his men, Kwan Hay and Ye Goon I understood easily but names of others belonged only to their language. Oon Yew Gow alone spoke any English. Between sips of tea, I also learned that the Chinese were not entirely isolated; together they all belonged to some organisation, a club or society, the acknowledged leader of which was both father-figure and protector. This Chinaman, Choie Sew Hoy, was a merchant in far-off Dunedin with contacts and influence in China – the 'Flowery Land' Oon called his country.

Choie Sew Hoy supplied them with rice, their distinctive clothing, provided assistance if they should be ill or incapacitated, could even bring wives for them from the Flowery Land, banked all their gold so that the amount was known only to them and – should they die – would ship their bones back to China for burial. Oon spoke of this man with reverence.

The Chinese worked diligently day after successive day from first light until darkness. Snaking all around the hillside with such an imperceptible degree of fall it appeared to be level, the dry channel was finally dug and built some five hundred yards to our sluice on the terrace. Even Fox was grudgingly impressed with the physical tenacity of the Chinese and their ability to maintain a perfect line of sight for the channel just by their eye. At the end of the channel above the terrace we constructed a V-shaped chute from pitsawn timber which would carry the water – when it arrived – down directly into the sluice.

Watched by McGregor, Low, Cormack and his diggers from New Chum's Creek across the valley, the three of us (including a newly-enthusiastic Fox) easily damned the little creek up in the gully and diverted its flow into the head of the channel. The Chinese scrambled along it, keeping pace with the oncoming water, carefully checking for leaks; one man would stop to plug a seepage with earth whilst the others kept moving with the flow.

A whole day passed interminably until the race was sufficiently saturated for the water to stop soaking into the ground and flow to the terrace, albeit reduced to a trickle. Oon Yew Gow and his men grinned for the first time, clapping their hands excitedly as the water tumbled down the wooden chute and through the sluice to cheers from the small crowd of diggers gathered to watch. Even a no-longer sceptical Fox jubilantly offered his share of the gold Reid and I had paid to the Chinese for their labours.

Within days, our yield of gold had increased hugely as we shovelled paydirt into the sluice as fast as we could wash it with the small flow. Several times during each day we diverted the water from the sluice box, cleared away the tailings piled up at its lower end, carefully gathered up the larger obvious pieces of gold that had accumulated in the sediment behind each of the riffle-bars across the bed of the sluice, then pan-washed the remainder.

An impressed McGregor promptly contracted Oon Yew Gow and his men to dig a water-race for them, drawing water from New Chum's Creek. McGregor built a similar sluice on their terrace above the Arrow with timber from sawpit gully and, within ten days, had water flowing in the race and washed the first gravel.

New arrivals continued to come into the valley but, finding the field already crowded, moved on. We were told that in the month of March alone, tens of thousands of men arrived in Dunedin from Australia, the harbour at Port Chalmers so crammed with ships there was no spare space – as one ship cleared the port another from the fleet waiting at the entrance, took its place.

Arrow Town continued to grow along the shingle-bank opposite the mouth of the ravine. Hotels competed with each other to ply the diggers with liquor; even bottles of French champagne could be bought if a digger had enough gold. Diggers flush with gold vied to pay for drinks for every man in the grog-shop.

In May, Buckingham's' 'Provincial Hotel' at one end of the shantytown fiercely contested Bully Hayes' new 'Prince of Wales Hotel' even though Hayes had married Buckingham's daughter. Their rival groups of 'good-time girls' hurled insults at each other from the doorways. The police were needed to keep them safely apart.

Peace, order and the law had been fully established by the Mounted

Police and the Goldfields' Warden, though so many miners had so much gold it was pointless to fine transgressors, more effective to lock them on chains to logs. Every variety of food was available at a price, including tins of Russian caviar and supplies of tools and equipment were abundant. The banks provided regular armed escorts to carry diggers' gold back east.

Though the days were rapidly shortening with the approach of winter, the continuing balmy weather lulled us all into believing that winter in these high mountains must be far off – an expectation that sunshine and drought would continue. The diggers celebrated when the first frosts arrived, reasoning that the more severe the frosts, the less water would flow in the rivers, so that more rich gravels in the newly exposed bed could easily be worked.

John Reid had intended only to be a miner for the summer months, then return east to Dunedin but, like me, saw no cause to give up such rich rewards whilst the climate was still so benign. Fox seemed to have acquired a renewed sense of purpose since we began sluicing, trying new ground, ordering lengths of hose made from canvas to feed water to the sluice and devising new methods to increase our yield.

When light rain began one afternoon in late June we took little notice, not expecting it to last. Wispy strands of cloud had slowly drifted across the sky from the northwest until a white sheet was gradually drawn that shut out the blue. A faint glow of sun through the white haze was extinguished by a squeeze of growing greyness.

The first isolated raindrops that fell were so warm we were almost unaware of them. We worked on as the scattered droplets crept closer together into a sprinkling light rain that vanished without a trace into the desiccated ground. As the sky slowly turned a darker shade of grey the raindrops increased in size and fell noiselessly but more heavily to the earth, instantly sucked into the parched gravel. That evening, the light began to close early, weighed down by a darkening sky.

Throughout the first night I woke often to the unaccustomed sound of rain on the ground outside, thankful that we were in shelter and not under canvas. Even so, water seeped from the drenched hut roof through every crack and crevice until drips and trickles were unavoidable in the confined space.

In the dull morning light, Fox and I clad in oilskins plodded up to check the sluice on the terrace. Dense rain beat down without respite from clouds that looked too heavy to stay suspended in the sky, as if their weight was crushing down upon the earth itself. The long-parched ground had drunk its fill; puddles and pools appeared and rivulets ran down the track we followed up the gully from our hut.

On the terrace, a gush of water poured out of the race onto the bared gravel, spreading out into a delta before soaking into the stones or disappearing off the edge. To stem this flow, we sloshed our way up into the gully to the diversion dam at the head of the water-race, but it had already gone, swept aside by the flood now surging down the creek. The water-race collecting the runoff from the hillside above was filled to the brim, overflowing the outer wall in places. Working the claim was now impossible.

Sheets of rain bore down on us as we returned to the hut, as if displacing the very air itself. Our former creek was now a river, the river below us in the ravine a swirling racing flood. And still the rain came relentlessly crashing down.

The second night closed in even earlier. We were growing apprehensive as the rain seemed to increase in intensity rather than abate. As the water surging down the gully rose even higher towards our stone hut, its sanctuary began to feel less secure.

Much of our bedding was wet, the floor was sodden with leaks from the roof and we were having to shout to be heard above the heavy beat of the rain. Instead we huddled close to the fire, trying to doze in the dark, wondering when it would ease.

Through closed eyes, a flash of light and a crash of thunder brought me instantly awake. A long flickering flash, then another with the deep rumble and crack of thunder shaking the hut. All three were on our feet, crowding the doorway trying to see in the lightning-light how close to us the creek had risen. Flash after flash cut the darkness open, casting the valley in a sterile cold grey light.

There was another rumble, deeper than before, growing in strength. The very ground itself began to shake, a vibrating violent quiver. Above the rumble, a roar, close by. Above the roar, the shouts and screams of men. Across the Arrow ravine the sodden terrace, stripped of its vegetation by sluicing and saturated beyond capacity to a slush, could hold the bedrock no longer and in an avalanche of mud and gravel, slid into the torrent below. Huts, tents, shelters and men swept with it.

We scrambled out into the soaking night fearing our own safety from the slope above. In lightning flashes we could see an open gut, slashed from the hillside across the ravine. The terrace avalanche now dammed the swollen river, quickly banking up behind. Then with another thunderous shaking crash, the whole earth dam collapsed. A black wall of water burst away into the night. A pressure wave of spray-filled air struck us. Then only darkness, the roar of the raging torrent, and the heavy beat of rain remained.

By daylight the rain began to ease, the cloud to lift. The creek in our gully still swirled angrily past, just below the hut. Up in the gully, our sluicing terrace too had gone, replaced by a long sloping slide of gravel and stones, rent with rivulets from the water-race above. Our claim was lost. The Arrow was a seething, boiling, tumbling torrent.

Frightened diggers appeared along the Big Hill track from up the river, filled with stories of countless miners and camps washed away in the night, claims buried in slides of mud, gear gone and huts destroyed. Then horror in Arrow Town as the wall of water from the avalanche-dam collapse exploded from the mouth of the ravine onto the town, sweeping half the line of shanties away into the night. Bodies, tools and timber lay scattered on a great wide fan, a delta of rock and slushy mud spread out across the basin.

Men arrived fleeing from the Shotover. The raging river there had risen 35 feet, the Kawerau over 20 feet. None knew how many lives were lost, but hundreds were gone from where diggings lined the river only days before.

It was time to go. Anxious now to have tarried so long, Fox, Reid and I were trapped, held captive between a triangle of flooded rivers. Fox was all for taking the southern route, down Lake Wakatipu to the gentle Mataura Valley but the raging Shotover blocked that path. Across the basin the Kawerau in its gorge was normally impassable, even without the flood. Reid and I would head back east but beside us the still-turbulent Arrow could not yet be crossed.

We waited. We packed our gear, deciding what to abandon, what to carry and waited. Impatient to leave, a crowd of miners prodded and probed in the murky but quickly falling river, searching for a way across. Eventually they succeeded in finding a ford. By the time we arrived there, they were mostly gone, leaving behind a rope strung across the river to guide those who followed.

Safely across, we traced their muddy footprints through Bracken's Gully which led up onto the Crown Terrace high above the basin and from where we had first spied McGregor and Low carrying their sheep carcasses some nine months before. There were no regrets to be leaving the Arrow behind. All over the mountain goldfields men were on the move – only the foolhardy or the ignorant remained.

We made good progress across the wide Crown Terrace, following a well-worn track now made muddy by the hundreds of miners who had already headed back east. Although the rain had eased, heavy bluish-grey clouds still hung threateningly in the sky. As we reached the end of the terrace and began to climb toward the Crown Range saddle, the first snowflakes danced softly from a slowly darkening sky.

Like autumn leaves of white they trickled silently in erratic paths, lying scattered and broken on the tussock. High up on the Crown Range the snow began to become a nuisance, falling more thickly and building up a layer on the ground, covering the track which we could still see between the clumps of snowgrass.

On the descent into the Cardrona River valley, the falling snow increased, thick flakes dropping quickly, coating the ground in a deepening layer of white. We trudged on in single file, Fox leading, Reid trailing, still stepping easily in the boot-deep soft white snow. No diggers in Cardrona, the field was abandoned till the spring.

As we climbed out of the Cardrona heading due east up the Criffel Range, a wind arose. Out of the shelter of the narrow Cardrona Valley on the exposed treeless flank of the Range, the wind and driven snow soon slowed us down. With my shoulders hunched and head held low, I trudged on upward trying to keeping Fox's huge frame in sight, barely visible ahead, coated with snow in a haze of white.

Despite the exertion of climbing upward, battered by the rising wind and dragging feet through the deeper snow, I could feel the cold, the temperature dropping sharply. Breath in bursts of steam clouded in front of my face. I stopped, looked back and screened my eyes against the wind with a hand, but I couldn't see John Reid below me through the murk of swirling snow.

I turned back to find him, surprised to see how quickly my footsteps had been filled, then buried by the snow. I stopped, waited. Then slowly he came, a shapeless movement of white, plodding toward me. Up close, I shouted to him, the words being snatched away by the wind, 'You go in front! Follow Fox! I'll come behind! We must keep moving!'

We struggled upward, heads down, step by step in the deepening snow. The bulky shape of Fox loomed up, standing hunched against the wind, waiting for us. His brows and beard crusted with snow. I shouted through cupped hands: 'Let me lead. Keep Reid between us. You and I take turns!' He nodded, stepped aside.

The snow was now knee deep, being driven along in swirling streams. I lurched at every step, plunging my boot into the drift, feeling for the ground to firm up beneath. Then crushed snow clinging, holding back the other boot until I dragged it free, trying to kick a path for the others to follow.

A blizzard of wind now roared in my ears, tearing, pushing and tugging at me relentlessly. Snow raced past, near horizontal, biting at my face and hands. I could not keep going like this for long. We had to find shelter from this raging storm.

Fox came up, pressed close and with cupped hands around a snow-lined mouth shouted in my ear. 'We've got to get over this ridge JC! Down into the Kittleburn … get out of the wind! You remember the rock? We've got to find that rock!'

I did remember. The huge overhanging buttress of rock where we spent the night coming west, those many months ago, trying all night to stop from sliding off downhill.

Fox took over the lead again, kicking steps for Reid and I to follow. Methodically I plodded on, a step, a step, another, a step. I tried not to think, to stop being aware. Float my mind to other things….

Lost in thought, I almost pushed Reid over. He and Fox had stopped, standing braced against the wind. 'Take over the lead. We're at the top. Way down there we'll find the rock, across to the left.'

I plunged off down from the ridge, thankful to be out of the full force of the wind. The snow was deeper but soft, windblown drifts swirled about. We floundered downward, sidling left. I could hear the wind shrieking high overhead. We bunched together now, barely an arms-length apart, striving to see the black shape of the rock buttress come looming up through the thick haze of white.

Then there it was. We staggered in under the overhang, kicking the snow clear from the sandy ground beneath. With frozen hands we built a bank of snow up on each side, packing it into a wall, then slung a canvas fly across the rock like an awning to the ground and weighted it with stones.

Wrapped exhausted in our bedrolls, close beside each other, we spent a fitful night, listening to the roar and howl of the wind above and the jerking flap of the canvas fly.

Light returned with the cold intense. The canvas fly was stiff with ice. The wind still shrieked as we unravelled our bones, trying to get warm blood to aching joints, beating our hands and faces to dispel the cold. We could not stay here in this shelter with no food or fire. We had to reach The Junction and some habitation or we'd not survive.

Hungry and frozen, we swung our swags on our backs and set off again. Down into the Kittleburn where drifts lay deep, the burn itself buried beneath the snow. The bitter cold overnight had frozen a hard crust on the surface of the snow, polished to a glaze by the ferocious wind. But Fox and I, big men as we were, broke through at almost every step, crashing waist deep through the soft snow beneath, fearful of landing on hidden clumps of dreaded speargrass, strong sharp blades slicing through our boots and feet.

Fighting a way through the drifts, our turns in the lead were short. To struggle out onto the icy crust, only to crash back through a mere few steps further on, was despairing exhausting work. Difficult as that was for Fox and I, our pace was further slowed by Reid following our trodden path, so short a man that the snow often reached to his chest.

The wind had not abated but the snowfall had eased. Somewhere we crossed the Kittleburn, I know not where, buried in the deep drifts. Down there we had been somewhat sheltered but as we climbed out and up the Pisa Range we were again exposed to the nagging tearing wind. Wind-driven streams of snow were hurled along, snatched up by gusts and flung upon us, freezing to an icy crust on brow and beard. Shards of ice hung from our hats and dangled round our cuffs.

The cold cut through my clothes. My hands and feet were numbed, all feeling lost. Cold stung my nose and ears and hunger gnawed my gut. The constant scream of the wind drove into my brain. Doubt sneaked through my mind: would we leave these mountains alive or would winter be the winner?

We were agonisingly forging our way up, high on the Pisa Range. The snow was not so deep here, more blasted by the wind and icy glazed. We picked our way precariously among jumbled rocks, buffeted by the gale, still trapped in blizzard clouds of swirling snow. Near to the top. Shambling along, exhausted, close together. Dragging icicles dangling from beards and clothes.

I heard Fox yell above the wind then stumble forward to a rounded hump, a mound there on the snow. Another, then another, a line of frozen lumps. Fox cried out again, rushed from shape to shrouded shape, then lurched back to Reid and me, horror staring from his face.

'Jesus Christ, JC! They're dead! A line of dead men – frozen to the ground!'

The figure-shapes of men all sitting on the snow, backs to the wind among the scattered rocks. I staggered toward them and looked at the first. His staring sightless eyes peered out through darkened holes in a sculpted shroud of ice and snow. We counted thirty of them there among the rocks. Just what had happened here? Exhausted men who stopped here for a rest, hoping for shelter from the blizzard in the night? Waiting for light before the steep descent to safety at The Junction? Then overtaken by the cold, too tired to stand, the dreamy drift down to unconsciousness and death. Frozen to the ground.

Fox stood there, shaking his head slowly from side to side, horror still in his eyes, mumbling words lost to the wind. I grabbed his arm – Reids' too – and urged them on. We could do nothing here. Standing still on top of the ridge risked sharing the same fate – we must press on.

We staggered, slipped and slid down off the Pisa Range, knowing that The Junction lay somewhere down there, hidden from sight by torrents of snow streaming from the top of the range in the wind and roiling misty clouds below. Down the steep east face we went, endurance-drawn by thoughts of warmth and shelter, food and rest, heedless in our haste to the risk of falling from a cliff or bluff that scarred this eastern side of Pisa Range.

Down into the Lowburn, the ground levelled out onto the plain that led to The Junction. We desperately struggled through waist-deep drifts of snow. We had no sense of time or space. Then we had our first sight of buildings, substantial solid things in rows above the Clutha gorge. Figures of men were scurrying about between them.

We were seen. Several men rushed to our aid, seized us by the arms and dragged us willingly inside through a door. We were shocked by the warmth, the burning stinging ache as faces, feet and hands began to thaw and the uncontrollable shaking and rigours as the cold released us. Then in warm and clean dry clothes there was the taste of hot tea, the deep warm glow of brandy and the gorgeous satisfaction of mutton stew. Then we slept, luxurious blissful sleep.

SIXTEEN

How many men died in the savage snows of 1863 or in the disastrous floods that preceded them will never be known.

From the devastation we ourselves had experienced on the Arrow as whole hillsides of diggers were swept away in avalanches of slush; where a roaring wall of water overwhelmed everything in its path including half the town, there may have been hundreds whose lives were lost. Similar catastrophes had also occurred on the Shotover. When the flood-crest crashed through the Molyneaux gorge, many diggers along the banks had neither warning nor time to escape.

In the blizzard that followed, ill-equipped and unprepared miners were scattered all over the high mountains, fleeing eastward from the floods. The thirty frozen bodies staring sightless at us from the ground atop the Pisa Range were not the only men to die; buried beneath fifty feet of snow in Serpentine Gully searchers found forty more and there were many others who panicked and died in the dark. Even our good friend Sergeant Garvie, veteran of the icy wastes and bitter battles of the Crimea, froze to death while trying to find lost diggers and lead them back to safety. They found him two days later lying there in the snow.

Those men naive or foolish enough to stay on the alpine goldfields often with inadequate shelter, no heating and no food, froze and starved to death. It was too late to flee.

We waited for the heavy snow that blanketed the whole of the south all the way to the coast to dissipate so we could continue our journey. At night the cold was so intense with fierce frosts that travel was impossible. Thankfully we had sufficient wealth to pay for food and lodging in this hostelry – at least until we were required to move on.

Since we had last passed through the Upper Junction as it was now called, quite substantial buildings, most of stacked schist rock had been built in facing rows on the terrace where the Clutha and Kawerau Rivers met to form the Molyneaux. Whereas we had crossed the chasm through which the Clutha hurtled, clinging perilously to a flying-fox dangling from a rope, now several rope and wire footbridges spanned the gap. On the eastern side a rough formed track, wide enough to take a small bullock-wagon, led back through the Molyneaux Gorge past our previous claim, all the way downriver to the Dunstan and Lower Junction settlements. From there, horses could be hired and exchanged at relay-stables along the Dunstan Trail or the Northern Trail out to the coast and Dunedin.

I was uncertain as to what I would next do. Not so John Reid who had already decided to winter-over in Dunedin, rejoining his brother and then possibly returning to the Arrow again in the spring.

Having now participated in three vast rushes to newfound goldfields and watched tens of thousands of miners dissipate their energy and resources rushing about in wild stampedes from one discovery to another, I was slowly convincing myself that the days of diggers with their shovels and pans were over. If engineering and equipment were properly applied, far higher returns could surely be secured – even our rudimentary sluicing on the Arrow was proof of that. In many long days of tedium that had followed from first arriving at our claim on the Molyneaux Gorge, my thoughts had often turned to devising a boat that with some lifting or dredging device, could work the rich bed of the river that lay beyond our reach. Perhaps I could return to the house that I had built and still owned back at Molyneaux Mouth and usefully spend some of the winter designing such a machine. Perhaps....

It was Fox who again surprised us. Since our epic struggle through the blizzard to this comparative safety, he had been quiet and withdrawn, almost distant, the consequence I thought of our exhaustion. My attempts to engage him in conversation were brusquely brushed aside until, at huge expense, we obtained some whisky. Not being a drinking man, John Reid had long left us alone by the fire and retired. Late in the night as the last bottle between us dwindled, Fox decided to break his silence.

'I've decided I'm not going back, JC', he suddenly said rather vehemently as if he had at last overcome a struggle to say so. 'I've had my fill of the gold fever. It's passed ... and I'm not going back!'

I looked at him, astonished at his sudden outburst and waited as a silence grew. He took a heavy breath, lifting his shoulders, then sighed it out.

'I've known the thrill of being the first to find new gold, have more riches than I'll ever want, but now I need no more.

'I've had enough of this mining life: living rough for years in these desolate places; the endless labour from dawn to dark; unyielding mountains and sunless gorges. I've had my share of hunger and filth. I'm tired of tearing winds and chilling rain, blinding heat and freezing cold. Always there's more gravel waiting to be washed, wondering if you'll ever find gold and then when you do, worrying that it'll soon run out.'

He gave a shudder. 'I've felt the chill breath of fate blowing hard on my heels and seen enough men die. Bodies tumbling in rivers, falling screaming off cliffs, being shot and shooting them too. Ragbound bundles of starving diggers.

'I've pushed my own luck too many times. That line of frozen ghosts there on the Pisa Range, JC, their staring eyes, they haunt me still. So nearly were we looking at ourselves. And all for what? More gold?' He shook his head. Gave a shudder. 'No, not more gold! I've had enough.'

His voice trailed off. He stared into the fire. I waited, but he said no more.

'So what will you do?' I asked quietly.

He drew another long deep breath. 'I think I'll go back south. Down there along the Mataura River, on the southern plains somewhere. It's beautiful country, JC, reminds me of England – rolling, peaceful, soft and green. I'll buy a hotel, or build one. Try to find myself a wife and settle down.'

When the pale winter sun returned and the worst of the weather was passed, he left us. He took my offered hand and crushed it firmly. John Reid's too. He stared unblinking into my eyes, 'You've been a good mate JC, Reid too. If ever you venture down south, be sure to pay me a visit. Just ask around, I won't be hard to find.'

We waited at the swing bridge and watched him go. Saw him hoist his huge frame up on a hired horse…ride off toward the Leaning Rock and disappear into the Molyneaux Gorge. When he was gone, I stood there for a long time, knowing we would miss this man with whom we had endured and shared so much. What course would my life have followed had I not plucked him from the angry mob on the jetty at Molyneaux Crossing back in 1861?

Fox was an enigma: quick to anger and violence, yet imbued with a strong sense of fairness and honour; physically huge and powerful, yet fatigued by physical labour; a leader of men and friend to most, yet so utterly dismissive of the natives and the Chinese. A man of indomitable courage, yet haunted by the horror of death; a restless searching spirit, yet finally craving for a stable and quiet life.

In years that followed, whenever I met a traveller from the south, I always asked did they know of William Fox. None did. Though others and I enquired, no hotel was ever registered in his name.

Perhaps his hotel on the southern plains was just a dream, a vision of stability and calm that helped to assuage his restless spirit – a dream he knew himself he would never attain. Perhaps he changed his name – tried to escape the notoriety that pursued him from the goldfields – or he might have left the Colony for some other place. Whatever; no more was ever seen or heard again of William Fox.

When John Reid and I left The Junction, snow still lay heavy on the ground. We too rode hired horses down the rough track through the Molyneaux Gorge, high above the sites of our earlier claim and that of the Californians, but not suprisingly given the harshness of winter, there was scarcely a digger to be seen.

We took lodgings in Lower Junction which would be the parting of our respective ways; Reid to take the northern route up the Manuherikia and out to the coast to Dunedin, I to take the Dunstan Trail back to Gabriel's, thence down the Molyneaux to my house at the Mouth. Lower Junction had grown to a large settlement, soon to become the inland terminus of a coach route to be commenced by Cobb & Co when Spring came, quite crowded now with men forced to abandon the goldfields by the snow.

We were both still there together when a trooper came to our hotel, calling out above the noise in the bar, 'A man called Fraser!' The noise of voices subsided, 'I'm looking for a man named John Cameron Fraser!'

Conversation and drinking resumed as I pushed my way through the men to reach the trooper and another man standing beside him. 'I'm of that name, but why it should be I of whom you seek I do not know.'

The trooper turned to the man beside him. 'This is Mr Cooper from the office of the Gold Commissioner in Dunedin and it is he who seeks you Sir, not I.'

The other man spoke: 'If you are John Cameron Fraser, late of the Molyneaux and the Arrow, then I am the bearer of an urgent letter for you which I am instructed to deliver by hand. I was delayed by the blizzard not long after leaving Dunedin or I would have reached you earlier than now. I am not acquainted with the content of the letter Sir, but I am advised there is no need for me to await your response.'

He handed me the letter, face down so that I could see the unbroken seal of the Commissioner's Office. A parade of cold thoughts raced past my mind – such letters usually bore only unpleasant news and if such this one did, then I wanted to read it alone. I left the bar for our quiet room before breaking the seal.

It was single sheet of script, quite long, beneath the crest of the Gold Commission.

John Cameron Fraser Esquire.
Dear Fraser:
I trust that this letter will find you in appropriate time and that you are in good health.

I write to you at the request of and on the behalf of His Excellency, The Governor of this Colony, Sir George Grey with whom you may recall, I am personally acquainted. The Governor has contacted me on an urgent matter of Government business, seeking my assistance, the circumstance of which prompts me to forward his request directly to you.

As you are no doubt aware, for some considerable period there have been numerous insurrections by the natives in the North. The most recent such disturbance is by far the more serious, so serious in fact as to threaten again the security of the Capital, Auckland, being the seat of the Colonial Administration, its citizens and commerce.

Sir George is determined that not only must the present insurrection be put down but that the capacity for any further armed resistance by the natives must be extinguished. To that end, the Governor has instructed the Military Commander, General Cameron, to invest the natives in their homeland in the central North Island, overcome their resistance and to seize or destroy all those responsible.

To facilitate this impending military expedition, the Governor has commissioned the construction of a fleet of armed and armoured vessels capable of forcing the major river, the Waikato, which flows throughout the territory occupied by hostile natives. Several such vessels are presently under fabrication in New South Wales. Immediately upon the return of the naval ship transporting them to Port Waikato at the mouth of the river, the fabricated vessels must be assembled and made capable of carrying out their intended function in support of the military advance, with the greatest possible urgency.

With by far the larger population of the Colony now resident in this Province of Otago, Sir George has sought my counsel to locate any qualified Marine Engineers willing to assist the expeditious completion of the river gunboats. Knowing no person better qualified for such an endeavour than your goodself, I have therefore made haste to place the Governor's request before you.

Given that it is now winter and activities upon the goldfields are thus somewhat constrained, you may favourably consider the Governor's call to a higher duty for the short period involved. If so, I am personally confident that Sir George would ensure you would be well remunerated for such service.

Should you decide to accept the commission offered by the Governor, please attend to this Office in Dunedin without delay. There is no obligation for you to respond to this letter in writing prior to so doing. Upon making yourself known at this Office, you will be provided with documents of passage on the first available ship from Dunedin to Auckland. The writer would also take the opportunity to provide you with his personal letter for delivery by your hand to Sir George himself and by way of introduction.

With respect,
I am,
Yours Faithfully Etc,
Charles MacKay
Gold Commissioner of Otago.
10th July, 1863

In amazement, I read the letter a second time, noting in process that his language was strictly direct and impersonal. MacKay was by far the last person from whom I would have expected to receive any communication whatsoever, least of all such a letter. Nor, in all the circumstances of our previous acquaintance, would I have wished any further contact with the man. So why, then, had he taken such a liberty as to write to me?

Probably, I reasoned, through a number of officers such as Dunedin's Mr Burns, the Police Commissioner Keddell and MacKay's own network of Gold Wardens on all the major goldfields including most recently Lowther Broad at Arrow Town, he would possibly have been aware throughout all the past two years that I was still here in Otago Province. With his dislike of me so previously apparent, no doubt he would prefer

THE FAR BEYOND

that I had left the Colony for the Argentine, as I had proposed.

Now an opportunity had arisen by which, if he continued to harbour that dislike as I suspected, he could at last be rid of me from his province and from the very goldfields of his own jurisdiction. If such were the case, why then should I offer him such satisfaction?

In one respect at least he was correct – the timing was opportune. I could venture to the north, undertake the commission and return again to the south within the same passage of time as I had proposed staying in my house at Molyneaux Mouth. I could usefully occupy the coastal voyage north furthering the design of the river dredge I had thought to build and operate over the next summer in the Molyneaux Gorge.

Not that I needed the remuneration, but the Governor's commission might be worthwhile; I would see another region of the Colony with whatever opportunities it might hold and I would possibly make the acquaintance of people in the Colonial Government who could be of some future benefit. Compared with three months closeted in my little house at Molyneaux Mouth, it would at least be an interesting adventure.

I showed the letter to Reid and asked for his counsel. His comments concurred with my own conclusions. 'Rather than ask yourself "why?" I suggest you consider "why not?" There's nothing we can usefully do here on the goldfields now for several months, especially with high water in the rivers following the spring thaw – and with this huge snowfall, the thaw surge will be higher than normal, I'll be bound.

'So you have little to lose and perhaps a lot to be gained, at least as I see it. Think of it as an opportunity, not that you are accepting MacKay's bidding. All that needs doing is to overcome your justifiable rancour of the man. Meantime, I'll be waiting in Dunedin until you return.'

So I decided to go. John Reid and I travelled together back east to Dunedin along the northern route that was less snowbound than the Dunstan Trail. Up the long open valley of the Manuherikia, leading gently into the basin of the upper Taieri River, thence along the Shag River through the Horse Mountains adjoining the coast and finally south along the rugged coast itself to Dunedin.

We descended from the last northern hill down into the town I had last seen nearly two years before and had hoped when I left it, not to see again. I was quite unprepared for the change that the central goldfields had wrought on the settlement and none at first sight for the better.

Over 80,000 people had arrived here on ships in only one year, drawn by visions of fortune on the goldfields. Outfitting them and subsequently supplying such a huge population in the barren hinterlands to the west had overwhelmed the town. Buildings of every description and construction crowded in disarray everywhere. Many were perched precariously on steep raw hillsides up slippery narrow paths between other ramshackle buildings haphazardly huddling the boggy lower streets. Others could only be reached by wooden ladders laid over the mud.

The main streets paralleling the harbour shore were near-impassable quagmires. Stinking ditches of watery waste festered alongside the road joining the two areas of town still separated by a short steep hill between. I stared in disgust at cesspools of raw sewage and as we passed by, saw people throw household waste out into the filthy street. Revolting stenches wafted about.

With John Reid's help, I went directly to Burns & Co and found a surprised cousin George. He and Lucy with whom I was reunited that night had prospered and matured. Their first child, a boy named Hugh, was already more than a year old. Lucy was again expecting another child to help fill the large two-level timbered home they had built overlooking the harbour from a hill at the south end of the town.

Late into the night I recounted all that had occurred since last we had parted. They too were incredulous when I read them the letter from MacKay. Neither of them made mention of Elizabeth, probably to avoid the risk of causing me any further distress. They had also maintained a correspondence with Harry whom I was pleased to learn had purchased a large block of land for a farm near the mid-north coastal town of Gisborne.

I called at the large stone building of the Gold Commission, sited imposingly with banks and other institutions clustered around a square at the southern end of town. I gave my name to a clerk and was asked to wait.

Eventually, I was led through a passageway to a closed wooden door. The clerk knocked, opened the door and announced my name. I took a long deep breath and entered. Facing me, standing protectively behind a desk, stood MacKay.

I felt calm, confident and fully self-possessed, almost disdainful of the man before me. I looked at him impassively, waited in silence, forcing him to speak first. 'So, Mr Fraser, obviously you have received and heeded the Governor's call for assistance. I'm sure he will not be displeased, nor you to regret having done so.'

I offered no comment, allowed another brief silence to grow. He looked uncomfortable.

'I understand you have had good fortune on the goldfields since leaving your successful venture on the Molyneaux. My Commissioners and Wardens have related your name and activities many times and always in good circumstance.'

'I have indeed been fortunate, but no more so than others whose endurance, industriousness and daring have equally been well rewarded.'

To my surprise, he smiled – a capacity I had thought he did not possess. 'Such modesty does not do you justice, Mr Fraser,' then lowered his head and hastened to gather some papers from his desk. I gave no response, no smile in return but remained impassive, offering him nothing, no condescension for his touch of affability.

'If opportunity provides, I'd be obliged if you would deliver my letter to Sir George in person and convey him my respectful regards. You will find the Governor a most engaging and impressive man, I'm sure.'

I took the letter and documents from his desk where he placed them, left the office and returned to the street, thankful that our meeting had been so brief. For the first time, I had faced him not requiring anything of him, neither his acquiescence nor his approval, and confident, feeling at least his very equal. Not that I had thought it otherwise, but my enmity of the man had not diminished.

With so many ships making Dunedin their first port of call from Australia before heading north, I soon secured a passage. Before departing, accompanied by John Reid I met again with jovial Mr Burns. We arranged that the engineering works would undertake construction of dredge components should I complete designs and send them to him from the north.

The voyage up the coast was swift, with the prevailing southwest wind driving hard on the aft port quarter. Five days and four nights of rolling pitch, familiar sounds and smells before we finally stood out from the port of Auckland awaiting the harbour pilot and a tug. At least I had usefully occupied the voyage sketching designs for a gold dredge.

The colonial capital of Auckland was built on the southern side of a deep-water natural harbour, protected at its entrance from the open sea by scattered forested islands. Between two sheltered bays, the town's substantial quay ran along the shore from which projected long timbered wharves clustered with rows of bare-masted ships. Others swung at anchor in the channel. Many small boats and native canoes scurried about.

Behind the quay, a broad slope cut with several valleys and their intervening ridges rose gradually southward toward higher ground marked with a number of dominant rounded cone-like hills. Along the valleys and over the ridges were scattered the many large buildings and houses of the town.

Ashore, I was directed to the residence of the Governor and took a hired gig up a long steep road to the Government House high on a promontory overlooking the town and port. An imposing large white-painted timber villa was set back among trees and lawns surrounded by a high protective picket fence, its entrance barred by a gate-house complete with uniformed sentries bearing arms. The Imperial flag and the Governor's ensign fluttered from a tall white flagpole. It seemed an appropriate residence for a Colonial Governor.

Clutching MacKay's letter, I presented myself at the gatehouse, stated my name and business and was requested to wait. Messengers and visitors hurried continually in both directions along the driveway. Eventually I myself was called and escorted by a uniformed messenger through the grounds, up steps, across a broad verandah, through two wide-opened doors and asked by a reception clerk to join several other visitors seated in a furnished foyer.

My turn arrived. 'His Excellency will see you now.' I followed the uniformed usher through a wide passageway to a half-opened door, a knock, my name announced and I was shown in.

Across a large, ornately furnished room the Governor stood, with a dark velvet smoking jacket over his white shirt with stiffened collar and cuffs, and a wide bow tie at the neck. He was a tall strait-backed man with wide-spaced eyes set in an oblong face, wavy well-cut hair, a long forehead, prominent cheekbones, kindly-looking and clean-shaven except for a closely-trimmed moustache. Glass-paned windows from ceiling to floor cast a shaft of light across his shoulder. I remained in silence by the door as the white-gloved usher took MacKay's letter from me opened on a silver tray, crossed the room and presented it to the Governor. He glanced at me, then turned away to read it.

'Come, Fraser,' he eventually beckoned me over, 'my friend MacKay writes here most highly of you.' The thud of my boots on the polished wood floor rang embarrassingly loud as I crossed the room.

'We are obliged to you for abandoning the goldfields, where MacKay tells me, your endeavours there have met with remarkable success. He apparently has some high regard for your skills as an engineer.' His eyes stared into mine intently.

'I thank you Sir, for such kind words. This present southern winter has begun most severely and the goldfields will lie fallow until late Spring. The timing of your call Sir was therefore quite opportune. I hope that I can be of some help, temporary though that may be.'

'Well Fraser, my naval architect Mr Stewart who is presently in Sydney, will no doubt be delighted to have another experienced assistant upon his imminent return. General Cameron himself is anxiously awaiting the riverboats before continuing his Waikato campaign against these warring natives. The fire's now blazing in the fern – so to speak – and I want it put out, quickly, before the flames of insurrection rise and engulf us all.

'When you leave here, please proceed to the Government dockyard and stores depot at Putataka, the port at the mouth of the Waikato River. There you will find Mr Stewart's Assistant, another young engineer called Steedman. I will ensure that he knows you are coming to join him and that you carry my commission. Steedman will fix your stipend and take care of you until Stewart returns from Sydney.'

A knock at the door and a Clerk appeared again. 'Well enough of that for now, Fraser. Unfortunately my time this afternoon is being quite pressed but perhaps you would care to accept an invitation to return again this evening? My friends and colleagues will gather here tonight and some, I know, would be most interested to share your immediate knowledge of the goldfields.'

How could I not accept? I assured him with thanks that I'd be honoured to return and took my leave.

That night, appropriately attired in evening clothes hurriedly purchased in the town, I went back up the hill. Once past the guards at the gate, this time I was met at the door and escorted to another wing of the vast rambling house.

At the entrance of a large room already filled with people, a footman announced my name in a loud voice. The crowd of men in the room ignored me, but the Governor himself stood near the door, receiving us all as we arrived. He seemed to greet me again quite warmly.

'Ah, Fraser, I'm pleased to see you've been able to return. There are several men here whom I would like you to meet; they will be keen to learn the latest of news and opinion from the south. Come, follow me!'

We crossed the crowded room past men in groups, some of whose heads now turned to stare curiously at us. Another cluster of men opened up instantly at the Governor's approach. I took several quick breaths, feeling ill at ease among so many well-dressed men whom I did not know. The Governor himself introduced me.

'Gentlemen, we have a visitor from the south who's just arrived today. Meet Mr Fraser, an engineer fresh from the Otago goldfields who's come to help us build the river fleet'. With a waving hand, he indicated each of the men, 'the Premier, Mr Dommett … Sir John Logan Campbell – a distinguished leader of this town … our recent Waikato Magistrate, Mr Gorst…' he carried on around the group, other names that trailed off from my conscious mind. They all seemed to stare at me expectantly.

The Governor himself turned to join another group close by, leaving me standing there alone. The Premier was the first to speak: 'What news do you bring us from the south Mr Fraser. What are the people saying about this war here in the north?' All their eyes were upon me.

I drew a deep breath. 'It's not a matter for frequent discussion Sir, at least among the people I've been with. It seems very remote to most, I daresay, as if it were happening in a different country. Their real concern of the war that I've heard most often voiced, is about the price of gold.'

The Premier raised his eyes quizzically. 'What so, Fraser? The price of gold…?'

I had already taken the first step – I could only continue the journey. 'Yes, Mr Dommet. The miners are saying they alone are paying for the war. They complain that the Government profits from the fixed price of gold by buying at that price and on-selling at another. The difference is being used by the Government to finance its war – they would rather that the difference was residing in their own pockets.'

'But that's preposterous!' the Premier said, looking around at the group for agreement, 'it isn't "this Government's" war. The whole Colony itself is at war and the whole Colony is at risk until we prevail. The General's army may report to the Governor, but its paymaster is my Ministry. Imperial Sovereignty is being challenged by these rebellious natives and the uprising will be crushed, no matter at what cost or whoever must pay!'

Heads nodded in agreement. I plunged on. 'That may well be so Sir, from where the Government sits, but you must surely be already aware that many in the south do not feel part of the Colony and therefore not bound to support what is happening up here.'

Before the Premier could comment, Mr Gorst interjected: 'How can they conceivably hold to such views, Fraser? We may be two islands but we are all the one country – the fates of us all are inextricably bound.'

'I can only express Sir, what I commonly hear, and read in the press. The population of Otago alone exceeds that of all the rest of this Colony combined. Most of those people are men who are recently arrived from Australia, California even. Their knowledge and affinity resides with their origin. They know nothing of the north nor have any interest in what happens up here. There's no war in the south or the remotest possibility of such – the number of natives is negligible and their situation is mostly quite pitiable.

'It's been voiced for some time – as surely you have heard – that the south should secede from the Colony and join with the State of Victoria. The Governor of Victoria I understand, himself speaks in support of such union. With such prevalent opinion being frequently voiced, is it not therefore surprising that the miners are aggrieved over the fixed price for their gold? Or that they pay for a war in the north that is not of their making?'

My questions were greeted with uncomfortable silence.

'Yes Mr Fraser,' the Premier commented resignedly, 'we are all quite aware there is strong feeling in the south. For some obscure reason, Sir George himself is not popular there, despite his visits and the efforts he's made on behalf of the people. But dissolution of this Colony will not be supported by the Crown, no matter how much it may be desired by the south.

'And although they may feel far removed, this war is a threat to us all. White settlers here are being savagely killed and forced to abandon the land they legitimately own. The natives have vowed to attack this Capital itself and drive us all into the sea. If that were to pass, do the southerners think they would then still be immune? It's not many years since tribes from the north invaded the south and attacked and slaughtered all the natives they found. It's one reason (some smiles) why you've so few of them left down there today.

'So the people must understand their security depends absolutely on what happens up here. The British Army has been sent to defend us but it's my Ministry that must pay for the privilege of having them here; and when most of our wealth is down in the south, the fixed price of gold Mr Fraser, is not really much pain to be borne.'

He nodded his head to emphasise his point and turned away to another group as the remaining men looked in silence at their feet. Fortunately, Sir John Logan Campbell seized the moment, stepped forward and, taking me gently by the elbow, steered me slightly away until we were alone.

'Come now, Fraser' he said as we stepped away. 'all this talk about war with the Maoris. As you've just heard, this settlement is convulsed with the fear of it, which, I'm convinced, is truly worse than the threat itself. And thousands of soldiers marching through town brings the reality of war visibly to their doorstep which just heightens their fears.

'But it's not fighting the natives I want to discuss with you, I want to know more about gold. So tell me Fraser, what do you think, have the fields all now been found or do you believe there will be more?'

Sir John proved to be an avid listener as we discussed the current state of the Otago goldfields, the extent of the discoveries and the tens of thousands of miners who now smothered the south. Whilst there could yet be new discoveries, I proffered that that was less likely now with so many men having prospected so much of the ground.

Instead, I ventured, there was probably more gold yet to be taken from the existing known fields than the 40-odd tons that had been recovered so far.

'There's only so much that can be worked economically by men with shovels and pans. There's probably not much really rich ground remaining to be dug by hand and that will quickly be cut out during the next summer. But on each of the known fields there are still many thousands of acres of lesser-grade auriferous spoil as yet untouched, but it will take machinery and investment to work them profitably.'

From an engineering perspective, I thought that either some large-scale sluicing operations or new types of dredges would probably be the only mechanical method of recovering gold from such vast tonnages of lower-yielding gravel.

Sir John assured me that if a suitable venture were proposed from the south, it would not lack for northern investors should capital be needed. He revealed that with others, he had held mining rights to large areas of auriferous quartz rock on a coastal peninsula not far from Auckland itself but the terrain was precipitous and the easily-reached surface deposits had now all been worked. If a new southern opportunity arose, he and his partners would all be very keen to be involved.

We resolved to be in mutual contact should any future prospect arise and on that encouraging note, I sought out the Governor, thanked him effusively for his kind invitation, and took my leave.

The Capital settlement of Auckland was sited on a narrow isthmus between two large harbours to both east and to west. Between the two, the land undulated upward to a north-south spine, its flanks dotted with the many prominent protrusions of conical cones of long-dead volcanoes that I had seen on my arrival. The deep eastern harbour – its entrance protected by forested islands – was favoured by shipping. The broad shallow western harbour lay exposed to prevailing winds, its entrance made hazardous with fierce rip-tides and shifting sandbars pounded by huge waves.

Most of the settlement was spread over the slopes facing east, sheltered from westerly winds and facing the sun. A large population of natives lived scattered among bays of the harbour and amid terraced gardens on the volcanic hills. Their canoes plied the harbour and their labour worked the port.

The whole town was most obviously on a footing for war. Quite near Government House, a large military post, Fort Britomart, stood on a promontory bluff overlooking the town and dominating the port. A high parapet topped with a stockade was cut with embrasures through which protruded the large guns of a Royal Artillery Regiment.

Just inland from the fort and crowning a nearby hill, a massive high wall of grey stone some 12 feet high, loop-holed for rifles and stepped with enflanking bastions, enclosed Albert Barracks. The Barracks not only garrisoned some 1000 men, but was built to provide a refuge for women and children of the town in the event of an attack.

All able-bodied men between the ages of 16 and 55 were bearing arms and on active service in the Auckland Militia. All over town, groups of militia were marching about, being drilled by officers of the Imperial Regular Army. The complete militarisation of the town was omnipotent and in such stark contrast to the absolute peace I had left in the south.

I had intended to remain independent of the military, hire a horse and ride to Paerata alone but was advised at the stables that all travel beyond the immediate boundary of town was under army control. Until very recently, the only road south had been a narrow track to carry supplies between clusters of settlers cutting small farms from the bush on an irregular rough forested plain that extended south and southeast from the isthmus. To protect these isolated and vulnerable farms, General Cameron had established a chain of redoubts like beads on a necklace along 40 miles of the newly rebuilt road to the farthest southern army post at the junction of the Mangatawhiri and Waikato Rivers. Each stockade was strategically sited within 30 minutes' march of the next.

To the rebellious natives of the Waikato basin, these redoubts were seen as an obvious preparation by the army for an invasion of their lands in their vast valley which stretched south into the very centre of the island itself. They had responded by sending raiding war-parties north, concealed by the jungle-like forest. Bursting out of the dense bush without warning, the natives attacked settlers on their farms, shot and tomahawked whomsoever they found, then vanished back into the forest. By the time the army arrived, they were mostly gone.

These pitiless gruesome murders of settlers, including women and children, had ignited hot flames of vengeance among the soldiers of the army and militia. Travel in the area was only permitted under escort by cavalry of the militia.

In early September, just prior to my arrival in the north, a raiding party had crept upon the Resident Magistrate at Waikato Mouth who was unloading stores from a ship at the small port. In an ambush volley from the bush-lined riverbank, Mr Armitage the Magistrate and two others were cut down. The natives then sacked the stockade, seized whatever could be carried and destroyed all that remained.

When the heavy firing was heard at the Alexandra redoubt upriver, two officers and fifty soldiers rushed to intercept the native war-party. The two sides met in dense bush and the soldiers found themselves heavily outnumbered. Fighting and skirmishing lasted until dark, during which the senior officer Captain Swift was killed and his next-in-command Lieutenant Butler was severely wounded. After fending off the Maori attackers during the night, the survivors struggled from the forest to the redoubt next morning. Two men had been recommended for the Victoria Cross for their courage and daring during the fight.

In a swift response, General Cameron set the army to building a new fort at Putataka, atop a high bluff overlooking a wide sweep of the Waikato River. A large garrison of troops was positioned there to patrol and protect the lower reaches of the waterway that was the army's route into the native heartland. A dockyard for the naval river-fleet was established on the riverbank below the fort and to provide a secure base for the assembly of the gunboats being fabricated in Sydney, Australia.

In the early morning following the Governor's function, I was directed to a coach service that daily went south from the town. We rode with an escort of mounted militia some fifty men strong.

Slowly we made our way along the rough military track they called the Great South Road, stopping at each of the army redoubts in turn. Mostly, the land either side of the road was heavily forested with a thick profusion of evergreen trees, some tall and stately, others gracefully drooping, festooned with creepers and vines and covered with moss. It was what I had imagined from reading as being a jungle – dense, dark and foreboding. Alongside much of the road meandered swampy creeks, their beds marked by impenetrable thickets of tall flax clumps. It looked the most perfect country from which the natives could launch an ambush and retreat into the wilderness. Pursuit would be futile. I was thankful to have an armed escort and understood why travel alone was not permitted.

The land off to the east was marked by an irregular range of high bush-covered hills which, as we travelled some 20 miles south, then swung westward to lie as a barrier directly across our path. At a large military encampment and redoubt called Drury, headquarters of the 65th Regiment, the road divided.

One branch carried on directly south from post to post, surmounting the range of hills and descending steeply on the south side until blocked by the Mangatawhiri River at its junction with the Waikato. The other, which my coach now followed, headed southwest through more heavy forest, past more redoubts to the fort at Putataka above the lower Waikato River. I arrived there very late in the day and made my way on foot down the steep track to the riverside dockyard where I found Mr Steedman, the engineer to whom I had been instructed to report.

James Steedman was a Scots engineer of about my own age. He too was tall, with a very high forehead, widely-spaced eyes and pronounced cheekbones above an enormous moustache that drooped either side of his mouth.

Since arriving in Auckland in 1859 he had established a business maintaining the engines and mechanical equipment of visiting ships. On the outbreak of war he had quickly been engaged by the Governor's naval architect Mr James Stewart, as his assistant for the construction of the river fleet. Steedman had already been advised of my coming and hastened to tell me his knowledge of ship-building was far less than mine, but having served his Articles with the Scottish Central Railway Company, he was very experienced in steam engines.

It was thankfully very quiet at Paerata. Apart from two small coastal sailers that brought supplies to the garrison and equipment to the dockyard, the small port near the mouth of the Waikato River was empty. The garrison drilled daily and mounted patrols around the overlooking hills to protect us against any further native attack.

Steedman was waiting for the first purpose-built gunboat to arrive from Australia. The New Zealand Government had contracted the Australian Steam Navigation Company in Sydney to build this initial ship to Mr Stewart's designs. A large naval ship, *HMS Eclipse,* was to tow the near-complete gunboat on the two-week journey east to New Zealand and on arrival at Putataka, we would complete her fit-out.

Whilst we waited, I usefully occupied time to further my designs for a pontoon-boat to dredge gold on the Molyneaux on my return south. The completed drawings I despatched to Burns & Co with the next coach.

It rained. Almost every day it rained, with heavy drops plunking into the river from sullen grey skies or sudden squally showers racing in from the sea to the west. Low cloud and mist swirled round the hills and the darkened bush dripped with menace. Out in the rain, the troops trudged about along trails churned into soft sticky mud.

The gloomy wet weather was apparently encouragement for attacks by the natives, so we turned out in the dark every morning, tensely awaiting first light and the time the Maori most favoured for a surprise assault. We crouched with the garrison, clutching our guns and straining to hear any unusual sounds through the constant hissing of the falling rain as the light slowly grew to the east.

Just as my patience was waning and my thoughts turned more frequently southward, aware that advancing spring would soon be warming the Otago valleys and thawing the snows, the *Eclipse* arrived.

It was a calm still morning. The early fog had mostly lifted off the river, to hang suspended in rafts above the silvered surface of the water, when the boom of a signal gun from up at the redoubt rolled around the valley. Startled, we looked about to see if an attack was imminent, then saw the silhouette of the *Eclipse* loom into view, her bare poles drifting

THE FAR BEYOND

in and out of the swirling mist.

Riding the flood tide upriver, she was an impressive sight, the first vessel of the British navy ever to cross the bar at Waikato Heads and enter the river. As she came closer, I could see she was a barque-rigged steamer of around 750 tons, her twin raked funnels amidships trailing wisps of

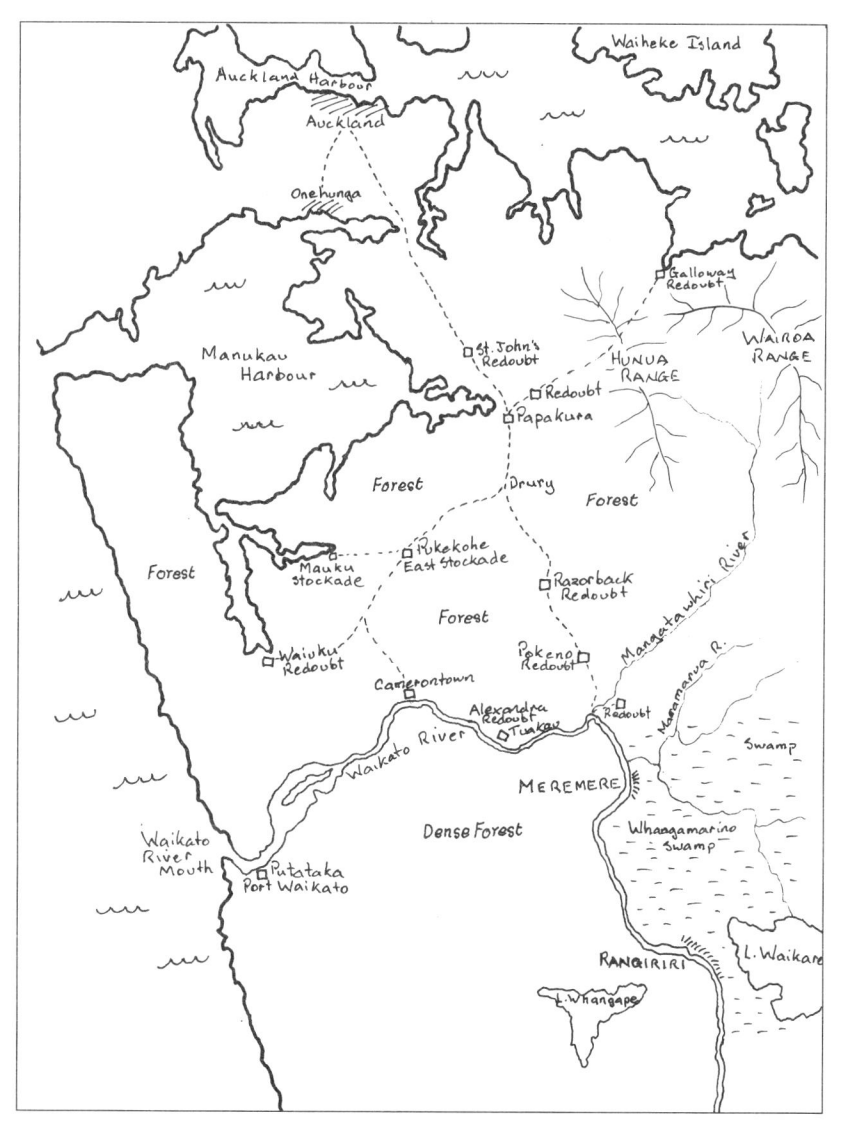

South Auckland and the Waikato River

coal-smoke in the still air. Sleek, low and lean, she looked far more of a steamer than a sailer, her three bare masts showing no furled canvas and scant rigging.

Well behind, attached by a thick hawser, she towed a squat ugly hull, like a long narrow barge except for a thick stubby funnel sprouting from the flat deck and a large prominent paddlewheel across the stern. This was the already-named *Pioneer*, the first such vessel for which I had been summoned north.

When *H.M.S. Eclipse* had anchored and the *Pioneer* towed dockside, I saw she was indeed quite barge-like, an iron flat-bottomed stern-wheel paddle steamer some 140 feet long but only 20 feet wide, flat-sided and with a short bow. Designed by Mr Stewart specifically for river use, she appeared to rest almost on the surface, with little draught. I could imagine she would be most difficult to manouvre, but would easily negotiate the sandy shallows of the muddy Waikato or nose into tight narrow creeks.

James Steedman was almost the first aboard, going below to inspect the engine while I wandered about on the flat deck, surprised to see two steel masts lying against the heavy protective plating of the gunwhales – surely masts and sails would be an encumbrance on a river gunboat.

The *Eclipse* was brought alongside and immediately her heavy derricks had swung fabrications and steel plate aboard we set to work. Our task was to assemble and erect two large heavily armoured iron turrets, like cupolas or rounded towers, each to house a 12-pounder gun and pierced for rifle-fire. Steedman and I respectively took charge of one.

On shore, I set up a coal-fired forge with a set of bellows to provide a forced draft to heat rivets that would hold together the large rolled plates of the turrets that had been fabricated in Australia. Soon the hillside echoed the ring of hammers flattening the white-hot rivets, the men working inside the turret swathed to protect their hearing. When complete and rivetted to the deck, each heavily-armoured turret was 12 feet in diameter and eight feet in height. A sliding door on an internal rail was wide enough for a 12-pound Armstrong howitzer to be slid inside with its barrel menacingly protruding through a gun-slot. Racks were fastened to the internal walls for the artillery shells.

While I fitted and raised the fore and aft masts in place, Steedman connected the drive-shafts from the armoured engineroom to the paddlewheel, then fired up the steam engine for a trial.

We were visited for an inspection by the Commander-in-Chief,

Lieutenant-General Sir Duncan Cameron himself and the river-fleet commander, Commodore Sir William Wiseman accompanied by their respective staffs. They came down river on board another small gunboat, a 60-feet long paddle steamer called the *Avon* which had previously been used on the South Island coastal trade and which I had once seen in Dunedin. Since coming north, the little *Avon* had had steel plates added to her bulwarks and around the wheelhouse, then was towed around to the Waikato entrance by *Eclipse* where she entered the river under her own power to become the first steam-powered vessel on the river.

This little steamer, armed with a 12-pound Armstrong in the bow and a rocket-launcher had ventured up the river into hostile territory twice in August. The first time, she was fired upon by natives hiding in bush on the riverbank but their bullets twanged harmlessly on her armoured plates. A little further upriver her commander Captain Hunt saw a large fortification of pallisades and earthworks high on an escarpment overlooking the river at a place the Maori called Meremere.

A week later with General Cameron on board for a reconnaissance, *Avon* returned to Meremere. The natives again began firing at her from the bush and the gunboat replied with a barrage of shells and rockets onto the fortifications. When General Cameron moved close to the escarpment, the air was shattered by the crash of a heavy gun fired by the Maori but their aim was too low and the charge ploughed up the water alongside the steamer. *Avon* quickly retreated and since then had been moored beside the General's headquarters at the Mangatawhiri River junction with the Waikato, waiting the arrival of *Pioneer*.

Steedman and I were introduced to the two Commanders. General Cameron, a heavy thickset man with graying hair and an enormous moustache dominating his red face, was clearly anxious for *Pioneer*'s trial to be completed. With both officers on board, a senior naval officer Captain Sullivan at the helm and Steedman supervising the engine room, we took her out from the berth and slowly up river. With the huge paddlewheel at the stern relentlessly thrashing the water, we progressed several miles against the gentle current. As I had expected, turning about even in this broad stretch of the river was difficult. At the first arc of the turn, Captain Sullivan disengaged the engine, then waited for the current to swing the bow around through ninety degrees, before re-engaging and returning to the dockyard where the wider estuary allowed for a full turn under power.

Commodore Wiseman, his eyes smiling from a genial full face, sought us out, personally thanked Steedman and I for our work and pronounced the ship ready for service.

H.M.S. Eclipse was about to depart to Australia to collect two additional gunboats being built in Sydney by P.N. Russell & Co. James Steedman was anxious to sail with her and help Mr Stewart complete the fabrication of these vessels expeditiously. Until they arrived back in New Zealand for assembly, there was little for either of us to do. For my part, I was impatient with the thought of having to wait the many weeks for this to occur, knowing that Spring was advancing in the south and the river levels would soon fall on the goldfields.

Steedman took these matters into his own hands and sought a meeting with Commodore Wiseman, to which I too was summoned. It appeared some decisions had already been made.

'Ah, Mr Fraser,' the friendly Commodore beckoned when I entered, 'just the man we need!' I stood waiting, expectantly.

'Mr Steedman – with my support – is about to embark for Sydney on *Eclipse*, where his additional presence could help speed the completion of fabricating my next two gunboats and their prompt return here.

'General Cameron has advised me he intends advancing upon the enemy immediately, without the further delay of waiting for my full fleet to be complete. I am in agreement for Steedman to leave us, but I also want to be assured that an engineer is aboard *Pioneer* for this expedition, especially given her as-yet-unproven situation.

'I well-understand Fraser that you are one of Governor Grey's men and therefore not mine to command, but I would strongly request you to accompany us in prosecuting the war until Mr Steedman brings his two gunboats back here for assembly.' The Commodore paused, his eyes swung from Steedman back to me.

'So Fraser, what say you?'

SEVENTEEN

A smooth furrow of muddy water curled off the bow of the *Pioneer* as she thrashed her way steadily upriver against the fast-flowing current.

Dark grey clouds hung suspended low overhead, heavily pregnant with even more rain, patches of damp mist still swirled over the silvered surface of the river and water dripped off the branches of the bush overhanging the banks.

It had rained for days before *Eclipse* slipped silently away on a full tide, carrying James Steedman back to Australia to collect the remaining two gunboats. Then rain continued as preparations were completed for the departure of *Pioneer* up the river, now risen by four feet, its placid steady flow transformed to a dark torrent pouring toward the sea.

I had reflected for barely a moment before given an answer to Commodore Wiseman's request; given that I had come here north for this very purpose, how could I deny him my further time just because the expedition was taking longer than expected. Whilst I knew that soon the melt-fed rivers in the south would be falling and the gold workings would begin anew, I had accepted the Governor's commission to serve and this brief passage of time was not sufficient reason alone to absolve myself from it. So I accepted, at least until *Pioneer* had proven herself on this maiden voyage, if not much longer.

The Commander of *Eclipse*, Captain Mayne, had remained ashore when his ship departed, keen to join Commodore Wiseman and experience whatever military action may be about to take place. Together with a contingent of marines from his ship, the Captain was aboard *Pioneer* with us as we forged our way on this late-October day against the flood toward the headquarters of General Cameron at Queen's Redoubt high above the river at Camerontown, also known as Tuakau.

The General, whom I had met during his earlier visit to Putataka to inspect *Pioneer* under completion, came down from the redoubt high on a bluff overlooking the river at Camerontown and together with his staff, came aboard. Apart from checking boiler pressures on the ship and the temperature of glands on the shaft in case of misalignment causing frictional heat to build up, I had little else to occupy me as we headed off upriver.

As best I could, I kept apart from the military officers but, mingling about on deck, I learned that our present voyage was to be of short duration, a reconnoitre of native fortifications threatening passage upriver, after which we would return to embark the army for an assault. Not much further upriver, we passed beside a large military encampment on the left bank at Whangamarino, which marked the most southern advance the army had taken before their path was blocked by vast swamps stretching far off to the east. From there on the last hard ground on the riverbank, the only way south into native territory was by the river itself or by retreating north and casting a wide arc far to the east around the morass of the impassable Whangamarino swamps.

Moored to the bank beside the encampment was a fleet of four large barges for troop transport, equipped with steel plating for armour along their sides and a steel foredeck gun platform on which a 12-pound Armstrong gun had been mounted. These barges had been hauled up the river many months earlier in August by the little steam paddle-wheeler, the *Avon*.

The Waikato River stretched before us in wide sweeping curves and long broad reaches, some 600-800 yards across from bank to bank. The right bank was shrouded right to the waters' edge by a thick dark forest of drab olive-green totara trees interspersed with the drooping fronds of tree ferns. There was no discernible left bank, with a phalanx of huge flax bushes, spindly swamp-trees topped with bushy clumps of flax-like leaves and dense groves of manuka scrub-bush marking the river's edge, now flooded back into the foliage to merge with the great swamp.

A spreading silence among the officers on deck indicated we were nearing our first objective and all were gathered along the port rail, staring intently ahead as we slowly beat our way around a westward curve into another long broad reach. Rising out of the swamp on the left about a mile upriver was a long broken ridge several hundred feet high, devoid of forest but covered with brown scrub. Clearly visible above its highest and steepest point was a redoubt or fort of some construction, topped with a flagpole complete with drooping flag.

As we closed with this feature, it was possible to see several lines of embrasures of stakes or pallisading traversing across the face of the ridge, the first low down near the river at the base of the hill, then several more at intervals up the slope toward the redoubt at the top. This, I was told, was the first native entrenchment, a place called 'Meremere' by the Maori. It was strategically placed to prevent further access either by land or river south into the heart of the vast Waikato Valley held by their King, from whence their war-parties had launched attacks on the colonial settlements. Friendly natives had warned General Cameron that over 1000 warriors had come together to garrison this fortified position.

Pioneer was slowed and crept closer. At about 300 yards from the shore whilst we were still underway a billow of white smoke burst suddenly from all along the lowest entrenchment. Officers dived below the armoured bulwarks. I leapt behind the aft gun cupola as the sound of the enemy gunfire rolled over us. But no shot reached the ship.

Pioneer was still moving slowly when a huge burst of smoke appeared higher up on the hillside and almost instantly a ragged fountain of water erupted up, midway between us and the shore. The boom of a heavy cannon echoed off the hills.

We stopped. Anchor chain rattled out from the bow. The ship swung slowly broadside to the shore. More anchor chain jumbled off the aft quarter. There was a violent hiss of steam as the valves were opened and the boiler-pressure was released.

Another burst of smoke came from the lowest position at the base of the hillside and immediately a huge jet of water spouted hard alongside us. Shrapnel thumped and rattled against the armour. A lump of steel tube hurtled across the deck, crashing and spinning wildly inside the starboard bulwark. I clung protectively against the cold steel of the cupola as a cascade of water from the shot splashed over us. Men were shouting and running. A whistle blew and orders were calmly called.

The ship lurched as both our Armstrong guns fired together. The concussion crushed against my chest, forcing air from my lungs as their boom set my ears ringing. I peered cautiously around the cupola, only a dozen feet from the muzzle of the cannon, smoke still dribbling from the gun-slot. Across on the shoreline the shells burst, throwing gouts of earth skyward. I thought I could see sticks flying about in the explosions – perhaps it was human limbs. Officers crouched below the rail, peering over.

Our for'ard gun fired again. I dived back behind the cupola to avoid the blast as the aft gun fired a second time.

Several officers came aft, stood with me behind the cupola. There was a sharp crack from somewhere downriver, a long hissing sound overhead, then an enormous boom thundered out across on the native fortifications. 'That's the Artillery Battery back at Mangatawhiri joining in,' an officer told me. 'They have 40-pound Armstrong guns there.'

We peered around the cupola again. A jagged cloud of black smoke hung drifting in the air above the Meremere ridge. 'Damned if it didn't burst in the air,' the Officer said, 'their fuses are just too short.' Then 'Take Cover!!' he shouted and we all dived back. A fusillade of shot pinged and whined off the ship's steelwork all around us, then the rattle of the musketry that fired it from the native entrenchment reached us. They seemed to be well-armed and well-supplied with ammunition.

The ship's guns kept firing alternately, their exploding shells sending fountains of earth into the air from the native's hillside, whilst the heavy artillery at Whangamarino maintained a steady barrage of short-fused missiles that burst above the ridge in clouds of black and white smoke. From all levels of the Maori fortifications, a fusillade of musketry sent balls rattling and pinging against the plates of the *Pioneer*, but at this range they were mostly spent and harmless.

Several more shots were fired by the native's heavy guns but the charges only ploughed up torrents of water in the river. An officer explained to me that the Maoris had neither ball nor shells for their artillery, having instead to use a charge called 'langridge' made of iron scraps, nails and bolts held together in a bag or section of pipe or rocket-tube. Without ball or shell, the charge would not carry to our ship and the range varied hugely each time they fired.

All the while, I noticed the General's Staff peering cautiously from behind the bulwarks and through the rifle-slits of the cupolas, making careful notes and sketches of the native defences as their firing revealed them. An order was called and our guns fell silent, but still we stayed at anchor for another half-hour, General Cameron quite happy to see the Maori expending their powder, harmlessly trying to reach us where we lay safely beyond their range.

Captain Sullivan called for steam. I went below to see the stokers hurling shovels of coal into the furnace and watched the boiler pressures rise.

Back on deck the funnel belched sooty smoke. The bow anchor chain was hauled up, the ship swung around with the current, the aft chain was drawn and with a sudden thresh of the paddlewheel at the stern, we headed off back downriver. Pushed along by the surging current, we soon reached Camerontown where the General and his Staff disembarked.

I remained on board ship next day, supervising the naval ratings lubricating all the glands and seals on the drive-shaft and the large bearings of the paddlewheel with a mixture of lard and whale-oil. I carefully checked all the topside plating, pleased to find that our hundreds of rivets were all tightly held.

Early on October 31st with General Cameron back aboard, we again set off upriver, this time to attack the Meremere entrenchments. At Mangatawhiri, some 600 men of the 40th and 65th Regiments, together with a two-gun detachment of Royal Artillery were embarked on the armoured barges, the little paddlesteamer *Avon* and on the *Pioneer*. The soldiers were silent, grimfaced, purposeful.

With two barges of men in tow and our decks crowded, we were soon underway, followed by *Avon* towing a third barge. I could not help but reflect upon the irony of my present situation: not so long ago, I had fought in support of Erihana and his fellow natives against white claim-jumpers, yet now here I was supporting the Colonial army to fight against the natives. If these northern Maoris were rightfully defending their own land, were they in fact any different from Erihana's tribe rightfully reclaiming their goldfield? The only difference I could reason, was that these northern Maoris had chosen to attack defenceless settlers and threaten to destroy the Colonial Capital, whereas the Otago natives had only asked us to uphold our own laws.

After making a slow journey of the short distance because of the flood-current and our towed loads, the Meremere ridge again eventually appeared out of the swamps on the east bank. We gave the fortification a wide berth by keeping close to the west side of the river, but the natives still fired at us with both their low and upper artillery and a ripple of musketry from their rifle-pits. We sailed harmlessly past without returning fire.

Beyond, the Meremere heights turned eastward into a general line of rough broken hills and ridges, replaced along the river's edge by another morass of swamp which extended away for at least a mile. It was now obvious why the natives had chosen to fortify the Meremere heights – they were the only high ground in this area of the lower-Waikato basin from which traffic on the river could be fired upon and an attempt made to prevent the Colonial army from penetrating deeper into the domain of the Maori King.

Some eight miles upriver, the broken high ground to the east swung back toward the river and appeared to continue closer along the east bank as far as was visible to the south. At this point, our two ships made fast to the hard ground and landed the entire force. An entrenchment was promptly thrown up and the artillery positioned.

Leaving one armoured barge with the land force, *Avon* returned downriver with us, towing the remainder of the barges. We headed back to the army headquarters at Whangamarino to embark a further contingent of 600 men. The General's purpose was clear; the force we had landed upriver would march back next day to attack the Meremere fortification on the eastern landward flank, while we would land the new force upriver to assault the fortification simultaneously from the rear. With the two ships bombarding the hillside with their heavy guns and the long-range battery at Whangamarino weighing in, Meremere could be taken.

As troops were filing aboard the barges in the pale grey light of dawn next day, an army scout arrived downriver in a native dugout canoe. We watched in surprise as he leapt from the canoe the instant it grounded and ran off toward the headquarters tents. Within minutes, an army Captain appeared and the loading of men on our barges was halted. We waited.

General Cameron and his staff suddenly arrived on the bank, hurried aboard the *Avon* and departed upriver. Only as *Avon* disappeared from sight did we learn that the scout had reported the natives were in retreat, fleeing eastward in large numbers in canoes across the flooded lagoon adjoining Meremere. The General had departed in haste on the *Avon* to reconnoitre; we were to take 250 men on board *Pioneer* and follow.

When we arrived at Meremere, the fortifications lay silent, apparently deserted. We were instructed to land our contingent at the first line of embrasures. We crept close to the bank, sheltering in a crush of sweating nervous soldiers behind the armoured bulwarks and the cupolas, tensely expecting at any moment to be swept by a hail of musket balls.

But only silence greeted us. Our troops swarmed ashore and rushed cheering and waving up the deserted hillside. A Union flag was raised on the heights. The first engagement in this river war was over without a fight.

But as the army officers clustered on *Pioneer*'s deck exchanging congratulations on their success, I noticed Commodore Sir William Wiseman standing alone at the rail, staring at the hills. He maintained his gaze shoreward as I joined him.

'So, Mr Fraser,' he said reflectively, 'we celebrate a victory without loss … though I'd rather their thousand warriors now lay dead or captured on these hills than live to fight us again another day.'

The soldiers searching the abandoned fortifications seized two of the natives' three large guns, one broken musket and one small canoe but a 6-pound swivel-gun and all their firearms had vanished. It seemed a hollow victory.

We returned to Putataka to await the return of *Eclipse* bringing the two newly constructed gunboats from Australia. As soon as James Steedman and his senior, Mr Stewart arrived, I could take my leave and return to the south. It was now November and I could imagine longer days and warmer sun had banished the last vestiges of winter from the alpine valleys of Otago.

Everywhere the goldfields would be swarming with renewed activity, yet here I was still, far from the majestic high mountains, the wide valleys filled with rippling snowgrass and the rushing blue rivers of the south. Instead, we sat in a dull sense of anti-climax, watching sheets of rain cascade from heavy clouds, pocking the surface of the muddy swirling river, hemmed in by broken hills clothed in drab olive bush and drifting mist, surrounded by the stench of damp and rot and swamp. If the natives wanted this sodden seemingly-useless sprawling valley, why not let them keep it.

But having assembled his army and the river fleet, the General was impatient to press on with his campaign, reluctant to delay longer, waiting for *Eclipse* to return. Only the extremely flooded state of the river was preventing the next advance. And so we waited.

Meantime, General Cameron took the *Avon* on another reconnoitre deeper upriver into the interior. Above the point where the Meremere attacking force had been landed, more swamps bordered the east side of the river until, several miles beyond, a long broken spine of hills meandered back and forth before withering out in yet another morass of swamp and lagoon.

However, not far beyond its southern-most end, a long steep-sided ridge rose up lying parallel to the river, hard against it and forming its eastern bank for more than a mile. At the northern end, the ridge grew from a strip of flat land bordered on both sides by a marsh of flax; the southern end fell off into another maze of swamp. A small lake flanked the eastern side and the steep western side fell directly into the river that at this point was more than half a mile across. The natives had chosen this long ridge as their next stronghold to block passage by either land or water into the heart of the river system and their King's domain. They named this place Rangiriri.

The General came down to Putataka to consult with Commodore Wiseman. We learned that this next Maori fortification was a formidable obstacle which would require a major assault by all the forces under the General's command; delaying such an assault would allow the natives time to strengthen their position even further. Time was of the essence. The General intended an immediate attack.

Sir William gathered together all the Royal Naval forces from around the region – a brigade of 100 men and officers under command of Naval Lieutenant Alexander. With these men on board, we set out upriver once again for Camerontown and the headquarters of the 40th Regiment to collect the General, then onward to the army encampment at Mangatawhiri.

The army camp there had been transformed by the addition of four Regiments who had marched overland from Auckland, together with a three-gun battery of artillery. An almost continual canopy of white bell-tents covered every piece of available ground, like a field of mushrooms in rows.

The 12th, 14th and 65th Regiments embarked. All four of the armoured barges were filled with soldiers and the decks of *Avon* and *Pioneer* crowded with men, munitions and stores. Towing such heavy loads against the swift current of the flooded river reduced our progress to walking pace as we again headed off upriver.

We landed this entire force, together with the artillery battery and including the naval contingent, at the Takapau redoubt eight miles upriver from Meremere – the same place we had landed the rear army prior to that engagement. This force was to begin a march immediately, hauling the guns over the meandering trail that roughly followed the river, to take up a position at the northern end of the Rangiriri ridge.

Meantime, swept quickly by the flood-current, we returned downriver to collect the 320 men of the 40th Regiment waiting at Mangatawhiri. It was clear that General Cameron proposed to repeat the strategy he had used successfully in the Meremere engagement, employing the force we had already landed to attack from the northern end of the Rangiriri position while the 40th Regiment now embarked, would launch a simultaneous assault from the south.

With our decks crowded with soldiers and two of the barges in tow, we set out again at daybreak on November 20th. As one of few civilians involved in this expedition, I felt superfluous to the enterprise, quite insignificant. Everywhere I looked around *Pioneer*, I saw officers of varying ranks talking together in clusters or standing along the rails glassing the bush-clad shorelines.

I kept aft near the wheelhouse where Sir William Wiseman, Commander of the whole river fleet, Captain Mayne from *Eclipse* and other naval officers had gathered. I was joined there by another civilian, a correspondent from the newspaper in Auckland. He passed the time by recounting for me the latest reports from the civil war that was raging in the United States of America, causing me to conjecture on the fate of my good friends among the crew of the *Black Swan*.

With the river still in flood, the swirling, roiling current slowed the heavily-laden ship to a crawl. A crewman was taking soundings at the bow with others calling the depth back to the wheelhouse as we tried to avoid banks of shifting sand invisible in the heavily muddied water.

By the time the dark feature of the Rangiriri ridge hove into sight it was already afternoon. As we closed, we could see the land force had arrived at the end of their long march and a great mass of men were already in place, crowded onto a narrow strip of land with swamp on both sides. Officers on board *Pioneer* lined the port rail to glass the fortifications while we crept upriver close by the western bank, expecting a barrage from native guns at any moment, but not a shot was fired.

The Rangiriri ridge lay alongside the river like the body of a large animal at rest. At the northern end, an initial broad strip of land sloped up to form a sharper ridge, its eastern side falling away to a lake edge and the western side dropping steeply down to the river. The ridge continued steadily upward, then levelled off to form a hill. The feature had been covered by low scrub or brush, but now clearly visible across the northern face was a huge scar of bare earth.

Through a telescope, I could see this scar was an enormous earthwork that spanned the ridge completely, starting from the eastern lake, up over the broad slope and back down to the river. It appeared to be a steep wall of earth, perhaps 15 feet high, with a flat top. It was at least 1000 yards long. Immediately behind and above was a second earth wall of about the same height.

Toward the western end, on the steep hillside dropping down to the river, two more earthworks extended off at right angles, parallel to the river, spaced across the face of the hillside and even higher and steeper than the principal earthwork. There was no sign of any pallisading anywhere along the whole system, but as the parapet of the earth ramparts appeared to stand out from the land, it was probable that a trench or deep ditch lay hidden behind the earth wall.

The fortification was a work of impressive magnitude, taking a very large force to have dug and formed it with picks and shovels. It was also cleverly designed for defence, with large buttresses protruding at intervals along the face of the rampart to enable an enfilading fire to be directed in both directions. The main feature across the northern slope of the ridge was placed to resist an assault by land from that direction; the contiguous twin ramparts along the steep slope facing the river to resist any flanking assault by a river-borne force.

The officers along the rail were awed to a silence. From where the land-army had taken up their positions, a pinnace appeared and we slowed for it to come alongside. Two officers came aboard, conferred hurriedly with the General while *Pioneer* held steady against the current, then returned swiftly ashore.

As we resumed our advance upriver, I saw that the first height on the ridge was only the lesser of two. Beyond the first height, the ridge widened, dipped gently lower to a broad near-flat saddle crossed by a transverse fence of stakes, then rose again in a long upward slope to the second – and greater – height. Very prominent on this greater height was yet another massive earthwork.

It was the shape of the whole Rangiriri feature, rising as it did from the flat swamps all around, that reminded one of some large animal at rest. The northern slope up to the lesser height was like the animal's hindquarters, from which the spine then dropped lower across its gut, then rose up again to the apex – the greater height – as being the animal's heavier and higher forequarters. The similarity continued as now we could see the southern end, as if the neck of the animal stretched down to the final hump of the head against a short bend in the river.

The fortification crowning the summit of the greater height was formidable. It appeared to be a large rectangular citadel, a trench of unknown depth along the outer perimeter from which rose a near-vertical rampart at least some 20 feet high, topped with a parapet. We could not see what lay immediately behind this wall, but set further behind rose a second defensive line, yet another sheer rampart even higher than the first. Any attacking force surmounting the first outer wall would be directly exposed to fire from close and above by defenders atop the inner higher wall.

How many warriors were defending Rangiriri was not known, but the fortifications could obviously conceal several thousand. Only an occasional movement just above a parapet revealed that there was a garrison. Otherwise, the whole dark feature lay silent and still, threatening in its unknowns.

Progressing slowly further upriver, we rounded the sharp eastward bend to find *Avon* at anchor directly opposite from an obvious landing-place – a long slope forming the southern extremity of the ridge, flattening out as it reached the riverbank. Higher on the slope but still well below the citadel on the greater height and some 100 yards apart, were two smaller L-shaped earthwork fortifications, insufficient to prevent a landing but capable of some resistance to delay any advance up the hill.

Attempts were made to anchor *Pioneer* in mid-river on the sweep of the bend some 100 yards aft of Avon, but the drag of the barges still crowded with men and the thrust of the flood-current prevented the anchors from gripping in the soft sand of the riverbed. We swung nearly broadside to the river, the paddlewheel flailing at full speed, as Captain Sullivan at the helm struggled to regain headway, *Pioneer* almost uncontrollable. Suddenly we were swung fully round, the barges crashing against us on the aft quarter.

The Captain waited as we charged off downriver until we had reached full speed, then swung the ship hard around and held her head against the flow. Control was regained but valuable time was being lost as we thrashed our way back toward the still-anchored *Avon*.

It was now mid-afternoon with only some five hours of daylight remaining. Nevertheless, General Cameron decided to commence the engagement. A flare soared skyward from the for'ard deck and immediately the artillery battery out of our sight at the north end of Rangiriri responded, the heavy boom of its guns rolling up the river. Our guns opened fire, joined by the single Armstrong on *Avon*, the shells bursting together in a fusillade on the two fortifications above the landing-place.

For nearly an hour the violent explosive barrage continued. Although our constant shelling sent gouts of earth showering into the air, there was no sign of any defenders and eventually at a signal, both *Avon* and *Pioneer* ceased firing. We moved close to the shore, expecting at any moment to be met by a hail of muskets, but the remains of the two small earthworks opposite stayed silent. Unopposed, the two barges carrying the 320 troops of the 40th Regiment were landed on the flat land at the bend of the river to the south, beneath the redoubt some 500 yards away up on the greater height.

Leaving *Avon* anchored in the river and the 40th Regiment now waiting ashore, we moved back down river to join the artillery battery in directing fire onto the first line of defensive earthworks. With our two Armstrongs joining the three of the artillery battery ashore and all firing at a range of about 700 yards, the bursting of shells on the line of fortification was almost continuous. Fountains of earth were being blown into the air and bursts of smoke from the explosions drifted over the hillside. If the natives were sheltering in trenches behind the ramparts, there surely could be few left alive.

After the bombardment had been sustained for two hours, at 5 pm General Cameron ordered a halt, while sufficient daylight still remained for an assault. The big guns stopped firing.

More orders were called. More flares roared up from the foredeck. More silence. Then a roar from 450 throats of the soldiers ashore as the ground assault was launched. I watched at the rail through a glass.

A Company of the 65th led the charge, closely followed by two more Companies spread out in a wave, then another line of the 14th behind in support. Out of our sight around the east side of the hill, the 12th was also on attack.

The first Company of the 65th in the van carried ladders and planks as they surged up the manuka-strewn slope to the first rampart. Immediately, a solid line of dark heads appeared above the top of the first earthwork as the natives swarmed to defend their position. The 65th were almost at the base of the embankment. Light flashed on fixed bayonets.

The Maoris opened fire. The top of the wall disappeared in a gush of smoke. I saw men fall, topple forward, others twist around and drop to their knees, overtaken by the rush of others. The crackling sound of massed muskets reached us. A dark blue wave of soldiers charged the line. The storming party threw ladders against the wall, men scrambled upward from the mass of soldiers at the base of the rampart.

There was a roar of continuous fire and explosions as grenades were hurled over into the defenders. Figures rose up from above and below, on top of the wall, fighting together, hand to hand. Bodies flew backward, soldiers swarmed up the rampart, defenders fell back, the 65th poured over the wall, a wave of cheering men followed close behind.

Another surge of defenders were atop the second line of defence. There was another burst of musket-smoke and screams and shouts above the roar of battle. More ladders, more crump of grenades, another wave of the 65th in assault up the second rampart. Natives appeared on top of the wall, firing down, being shot from below. Attackers and defenders clashed together. The assaulting wave swept the defenders back. Screams and shouts and gunfire and explosions were all mixed together.

Suddenly the defenders broke. Soldiers of the 65th poured over the wall. I could see natives running away still carrying their guns, over and around the lesser summit, fleeing back along the ridge and then up the long slope toward their final citadel. More natives surged from the earthworks facing the river, their line broken, now flanked by the fall of the main defences. Soldiers appeared in the open beyond the fortifications, kneeling, firing at the retreating warriors.

From around the slope of the ridge to the east came a roar of cheering. The line there must be broken too. More Maoris appeared running up the longer and higher slope of the ridge to their redoubt beyond, disappearing into its refuge.

The sound of firing slowly died down. There was jubilation amongst the staff officers clustered on the deck of *Pioneer*, grinning and handshaking, exhulting in the success of the troops ashore, safe here from the dangers of the battle, congratulating the General.

On the hillside, the still forms of bodies were scattered everywhere, some lifting their arms in the air, others moving slowly away supported by their comrades. Parties of soldiers with stretchers carried the wounded and the dead.

Pioneer was quickly moved further upriver until we lay directly opposite the highest point of the ridge, crowned by the forbidding ramparts of the rectangular central redoubt, the scarp of its earthen walls rising almost sheer. A throng of natives danced about along the top, waving their weapons amid chants of defiance, as the main body of the 65th and

14th advanced steadily toward them along the spine of the ridge and up the long slope of the northern face.

A flare was fired from *Pioneer*, a signal to the 40th to advance from the south where they had waited on the flat by the river.

As we watched, the assaulting force charged on up the long slope to the base of the redoubt. A host of ladders were thrown up onto the wall, but I could clearly see they were too short for this huge new scarp - some four to six feet too short. The storming party swarmed upward, standing atop the ladders, hoisting other men above them onto the near-sheer earthen wall, scrabbling and kicking for a footing. But the few who barely reached the parapet were flung back by a wave of defenders.

There was a huge burst of gunfire and clouds of swirling smoke. Another wave of soldiers surged up, many to tumble back down the wall. The blue figures of soldiers appeared from the drifting clouds of smoke, cresting the parapet of the high rampart, then a rush of natives at them and the soldiers were shot down, hurled back off the wall.

The solid sound of shooting began to fade. Natives appeared, clustered on the parapets, chanting and waving their weapons in the air. The ragged line of soldiers fell slowly back down the slope, their storming charge broken, dragging the dead and the wounded with them. Desultory shots were fired back up the hill. The assault had faltered.

On board *Pioneer*, the staff officers were silenced, chastened by what they had just seen, the failure of the 65th to storm the redoubt and the many casualties that they could see had been sustained. A lull in the engagement developed as the ship was maneuvered gently to the riverbank and made fast. We waited while reports were gathered for the General.

The 40th assaulting from the south had quickly overcome the two defensive works close to the river without resistance, then charged up the steep hill toward the redoubt. They clustered beneath the rampart without ladders to scale it, were fired upon by a massive volley of shot from above, retreated back downhill with their wounded and some dead, knowing not what next to do.

I was still at the rail, transfixed by all I had seen unfold, the enormity of the violence, the dead and the wounded. Surely now, General Cameron would order the combined artillery to pound the redoubt until the remaining natives, overwhelmed by the firepower hurled upon them, finally sought to surrender.

But it was not to be.

The General – seemingly more determined than ever in the face of this defeat of his arms – ordered the ninety sailors of the Naval Brigade to take the redoubt. Captain Mayne, the Commander of *Eclipse* who had voluntarily joined this expedition for adventure, was ordered to lead the assault. There on the deck beside me, he shook hands wordlessly with his commanding officer Sir William Wiseman and departed ashore.

Pioneer was moved out from the bank into the channel, from where we had a better view of the battlefield. We waited apprehensively at the rail while the little force wended its way slowly up the long hill, their blue jackets clearly visible as they passed through the darkened line of soldiers of the 65th.

They gathered there near the base of the redoubt, clustered together, rifles and cutlasses at the ready, Mayne and his Lieutenants slightly out in front. Then a bugle sounded and they charged.

We watched them plunge into the trench along the foot of the wall, then swarm upward together in a mass, cheering and shouting. Like the surge of a breaking wave they swept up the near-sheer scarp, their momentum slowing and numbers thinning as they neared the top.

The Maoris on the parapet kneeled and fired. Some blue jackets just reached the top but there was a rush of natives at them, with bodies flung in the air, falling downhill. Then there were more natives along the top, another massed volley of shot and more bodies falling. The stormers had been thrown back leaving more dead and dying men strewn about in the ditch.

The firing faded away until only the shock and silence of the failed assault remained.

The General was furious. Red-faced, he stamped about the deck, a dwindling coterie of anxious staff officers milling behind. Reports were brought quickly from ashore. Captain Mayne severely wounded may not live. Lieutenants Alexander and Downes shot in the chest, Lieutenant Hotham in the leg. Cameron swore, smashing his fist on the rail.

I leaned against the cupola, stunned and sickened and scarcely believing what I had seen. Aghast at the loss of so many good men. Surely now this General would see some sense and use the massed artillery to bury the defenders in a crescendo of exploding shells.

A pinnace was being swiftly rowed to us from shore. Jubilant natives pranced around atop their walls. The General stamped about, more angry than before, smacking one fist against the other palm, muttering to himself, kicking a boot against the plating of the bulwark.

I could not stand here and do nothing. This slaughter had to be stopped. I crossed the deck toward the only officer on the ship to whom I could appeal. 'Commodore Wiseman, Sir!' Sir William turned his head, eyebrows raised in surprise.

'Sir William, Sir, surely you can you speak with the General to stop this madness? It takes no skill to see that assaulting infantry cannot take that citadel, only cause more needless waste of life. Can you not intercede Sir and bring the General to some sense?'

He looked at me as does an adult to a child. 'Your sentiment may be rightly placed Mr Fraser, but you do not understand. This is a military matter and General Cameron is in command. I too must go, if so the General orders.'

'But Sir, your own best officers lie dead or wounded on that field – and to what end? The natives still easily hold the day. Must more lives be lost to further prove the redoubt can not be taken by assault? Yet only an hours' shelling from all the heavy guns would surely bring the natives to their end.'

'Cameron alone will decide what next to do. His military authority is absolute and we are his to command, without question. I cannot do what you request!'

For seconds I pondered his reply. 'Well I'm a civilian and not the General's to command. If you Sir William cannot bring the General to some sense, then I will try myself!'

The Commodore shrugged his shoulders. 'Then be warned Mr Fraser if you do. He will not thank you for it!'

The pinnace had pulled alongside and disappeared beneath the starboard rail while we spoke. I looked landward, suddenly aware this day was nearly gone, the light about to fade. My mind made up, I headed directly for the General. From the pinnace below an officer appeared at the rail, climbed over and stood spendidly tall on the deck. I glanced across and found myself staring into the cool grey eyes of Lieutenant Oliver Haile.

For the briefest moment we both stopped. Haile gave a small dip of his head. 'Well Mr Fraser, we meet again and in this strangest of circumstance.'

'Indeed we do.'

We continued walking for'ard. I saw he was now a Captain, no longer a Lieutenant. Coming from opposite sides of the ship, we both reached the General at the same time. Haile came to attention, saluted. For me, the moment had come. In a loud voice I called out: 'General Cameron Sir !'

Many pairs of eyes turned toward me. Cameron looked up from beneath his heavy eyebrows. His moustache pulled with frustration from side to side. His red face glared, twitching at the interruption.

'General, Sir, I implore you! Make no more frontal assaults on this redoubt! It'll only cause more needless loss of life!'

His face seemed to swell with his anger. 'What….impudence! How dare you! This is a military matter of which you know nothing! Your counsel is not required!' He began to turn away.

I raised my voice: 'But General, you have the Maoris surrounded. They must either surrender or starve. To assault their redoubt yet again would be futile – why risk the lives of good men?'

He swung around, apoplectic, as if his face would burst and raised a hand, pointing his finger at me. 'Dammit man! Hold your tongue, or I'll have you arrested!'

'Sir, you have artillery, mortars even. All you need do is stand off and pulverise their earthworks until nothing remains….'

His anger burst. He almost screamed: 'Sergeant-At-Arms! Arrest this man and get him off my deck!'

He turned his back. Some officer stepped up and took me firmly by the arm. I stood my ground. 'Come Sir,' he said quietly, 'nothing can be further served by your remaining here. Come aft with me please.'

He was right. I had tried, I could do no more. I turned to go. I glanced across at Haile as I went. He dipped his head in acknowledgement. I thought I saw a trace of smile.

I allowed the officer to lead me away. As we went I heard the General raise his voice, call an order, 'Now Mr Haile! Go ashore! Get Mercer and his artillerymen, and drive that native rabble off that hill!'

We passed Commander Wiseman by the aft cupola, but he looked firmly away. The officer still gripped me by the arm but said calmly: 'Mr Fraser Sir, I can't remove you from this ship, there are no means to do that. If you'll give your bond to remain silent and cause no further trouble, we'll just stay here together aft, out of the General's sight. If not, I'll have to escort you below.'

At least on deck I could watch what would unfold. I acquiesced –

provided that the officer would get me a glass – and gave my bond. In a moment he returned with one apiece. We stood side by side at the rail and looked at the hill. The sun was long set, the light about to fade.

The pinnace had already reached the shore. The men of the 65th had regrouped, and formed a line across the ridge, in the saddle between the lesser height and the redoubt above, then flanked along the face of the steep slope parallel to the river. I saw a small knot of men come striding along the ridge, a little group perhaps 40 strong, two officers in the van. Were they Mercer and Haile?

They stopped for a moment at the 65th line, stood clustered together. The line opened and let them through. They all walked on up the slope together then stopped just short of the ditch beneath the ramparts of earth raised above. The men appeared to have no guns.

The officers – one tall, one short – turned their backs to the redoubt, faced the little group close, huddled together. Then as one they turned and looked up. I took a deep breath, sighed it out. I heard the officer beside me, softly, 'Oh no! The poor bastards! They've only got pistols and swords!'

Across the evening light came a small cry. I stared down the glass, scarce believing what I saw. The two captains were out in front, swords raised forward in the air, catching the light. The little group charged over the shadowed ditch and up onto the wall. Scrambling, scrabbling, spreading out, some climbing the remains of ladders, reaching down to drag others up.

Faint cheers rose from the wall. I could just see Haile as he half turned to his men below, reaching back with his sword arm, sweeping it pointing upward at the top, exhorting the men on.

Natives with guns surged out onto the parapet. Some stood, some knelt. Bursts of smoke and the ragged rattle of shots. I could see men falling, sliding down hill. Smoke drifting across the face. More shouts and shots. Rising from out of the smoke itself, several men crested the parapet.

Mercer and a group were on the left, Haile and others to the right. They charged at the natives from both sides. I could see Mercer's hands clutch at his head, fall backwards and tumble down the slope. Others fell, some natives too. Haile in front of his men charged again at the Maoris, hurling himself forward, lashing out with his sword. Hit, he fell to his knees. The natives lunged at him, rushed over him on the ground. His body was flung out in the air, bounced once on the slope and tumbled into the darkened ditch.

Two men staggered back, throwing themselves down off the parapet. Others retreated, diving and rolling down the face of the wall. Some natives were still firing, others were prancing about, waving their weapons. The remnants of the artillerymen scrambled to escape. So few, so very few! So futile.

I lowered the glass and stared out at the hill, sickened by what I had seen.

The *Pioneer* moved slowly to the shore. Darkness lowered its shroud on the battlefield and no more assaults could be launched. The wounded and the dying were carried aboard and laid all round the deck, moaning and calling in the night. I went below and slept fitfully, haunted by visions of bodies lying carelessly discarded on the hill, the night punctuated by shouts and war-chants from the natives and bursts of firing as others attempted escape across Lake Kopuwera on the eastern flank.

As the grey light of dawn returned and combat would somehow be resumed, the Maoris raised a white flag above their redoubt. An interpreter and an officer were dispatched to negotiate the surrender, but quickly returned. The white flag was gone. They had a message for General Cameron.

When they had reached the redoubt, the Maoris highest chief had come forward over the parapet. He shouted down to the General's emissaries: 'Peace shall not be made! We will fight on! Give us more gunpowder!'

The General exploded into another violent rage. Even from where I remained still aft, I could hear his shouting, could see his feet stamping, his fist smashing down on the railing. Relieved of his temper, the General calmed down and gathering his staff about him went ashore, determined to address the chief of the natives directly himself.

Although we were out of line of sight, news quickly arrived that the natives' had agreed to a peace and would give up their arms. From all over the hill cheering came from the regiments – were they the cheers of victory, or perhaps cheers of relief?

More wounded were carried aboard and laid closely in military rows. The stiff bodies of the dead were stacked into a barge like so many cords of wood.

The natives who surrendered were escorted down to the river. They walked together, 183 of them, not slumped and sullen as the vanquished, but proudly upright, like victors. They had surrendered their arms – 175 old flintlock muskets, fowling pieces and double-barrelled shotguns with which they had kept a modern army at bay. Inside their redoubt were the bodies of 36 defenders, including five women and children, and some 14 others had died on the hill.

We fired our boilers and set off down river, leaving the army behind. The decks were a mass of the suffering and dying, some with hideous wounds to the head, many with multiple shots to their chests and arms, the deck smeared with their blood. Captain Mayne lay near me, a serious wound to his hip.

I looked out at the rows of the 85 wounded, more sickened than ever by the sight of so many good men now struggling to live. Behind was the barge, carrying the 47 dead. Somewhere among them lay Mercer and Haile, with valour alone in exchange for their lives.

In sombre and darkened mood, I moved further aft, leaned at the rail, the beat of the paddlewheel smothering the moans of the wounded. I stared down at the murky river swirling quickly past, my mind filled with visions and flooded with questions.

The General had four regiments of regular soldiers, some 800 men trained in ground assault and carrying repeating rifles and grenades, regrouped and expecting to renew their attack. Batteries of Armstrong guns and mortars ashore and afloat, firing explosive shells, all waiting unused. He even had Royal-Engineers with tunnellers and charges to blow up the walls.

Yet he sent only 90 sailors of the naval contingent with muskets and cutlasses to attack a defended fortress, strategically crowning the top of a hill. And then when that failed, he tried yet again – with just 34 artillerymen, pitifully armed with pistols and swords. And for what? A muddied and blood-soaked lump of a hill, surrounded by swamp? Stupidity or madness? Or was it just both?

Suddenly aware I was not alone at the rail, I turned, surprised to find Commodore Wiseman there standing beside me. He didn't face me, but too looked down at the river.

Together we stood there as the silence grew heavy, waiting for each other to speak. He started, uncomfortably, 'I'm sorry Mr Fraser, that the General would not…' then stopped, seemingly changing his mind, unwilling to continue. The silence grew again. I took a long breath.

'Since I came to this Colony, Sir William, I have seen too many men die. They fell off cliffs, drowned in rivers, died of hunger, disease and cold; some in defending their claims. But those men died in pursuit of their dreams.

'So now look about you Sir William and tell me: just for what have all these men lost their lives, and these others lie around us, shattered with pain? If this is the cost of a victory, then what be the price of defeat?'

Wiseman turned toward me. 'You are civilian, Fraser, and I don't expect you to understand. We who have made our careers in the military would see an engagement like this in a quite different light.

'We do not question our orders, nor those in command who give them. It's their inalienable right to make their decisions, to give their orders and expect them to be carried out, without hesitation nor question. If we ourselves were in command, we perhaps may make different decisions, or give different orders. But we are not in command, it is not our right – and we would not even think to doubt the decisions of those who are.

'History will record General Cameron has won a great victory and the names and the number of those that died there will soon be forgotten. With the day nearly gone, the General had to press his assault, no matter how or at what cost. He could not risk the enemy escaping in the night – as they did at Meremere – only to fight us again. So he demonstrated resolve – and coming the dawn, he secured their surrender.

'You may not be aware Mr Fraser, that at the time of surrender, a large party of warriors arrived from the south to stand with their fellows against us. They confronted the 14th and prepared to attack, but on hearing of the General's victory, immediately gave up their arms and went peacefully away.

'So do not be aggrieved, Fraser. We are at war here, a war that we will win, and with casualties sustained no less than what is expected in war.'

I allowed some moment to pass in silence. 'Thank you Sir William, for what you explain. But I can't comprehend why a commander would not use the formidable weapons available in his force, to achieve this result with the least loss of life. But instead, he would choose to send such brave men to their certain death, not once, or twice, but do so thrice, accountable to none and beyond any question. That, Sir William, for a civilian, is quite difficult to understand.'

He made no response, but stayed there at the rail beside me, watching the river slide past. After a moment, I spoke again.

'I should tell you now, Sir William, my mind is made up and my time here is ended. I will take no further part in this war. Already a month has passed since I intended to return to the south. Whether *Eclipse* and Steedman have arrived back or not, when we reach Putataka I will depart from this expedition, take my leave from the Governor, and go back to the goldfield from whence I came.'

The kindly Commodore Sir William Wiseman stepped back from the rail. He reached out and shook me firmly by the hand, saying nothing, nodded his head several times as if in assent and walked away.

EIGHTEEN

Flowers flourished in the Governor's garden as I walked up the sweeping drive toward the big house in the warmth of this late spring day.

I had come to the gatehouse the previous day, immediately on arriving in the town from the south, seeking a time when the Governor might receive me and reluctant to depart without formally taking my leave.

We had come downriver to Putataka, only to find the dockyard was bare and *Eclipse* had not yet returned. The urgency that had greeted me when I had come north in the winter had passed with the defeat of the natives at Rangiriri; General Cameron would now regroup, re-arm and await the new gunboats from Australia before renewing the advance on the upper Waikato. I would wait no longer and took the first coach back to the capital, anxious to depart and relieved to be doing so.

A reception-clerk met me in the foyer of Government House. After a brief delay, I was ushered down the hall, announced at the door and shown into the room. Governor Grey rose from his desk. Again I was struck by his upright tall figure – almost as tall as me – a neat moustache on an otherwise shaven face and his bright intense eyes.

He thrust out his hand. 'Ah, Mr Fraser, just recently returned from the war?'

'Yes, Sir George, I have come directly since the fighting at Rangiriri was ended.'

'And a splendid victory, I'm delighted to say!'

'A victory indeed, Sir, but not without cost.'

'Yes, yes, yes.' The Governor said hurriedly, 'I would wish that this confrontation would soon all be ended. The loss of life is deplorable – and on both sides.'

'I have to say, Sir George, I believe that many of those lives were lost there quite needlessly.' He stared at me quizzically from beneath raised eyebrows. 'General Cameron gave some extraordinary orders that day that astounded many who were there. Brave men died who should still be alive, had the General only used the full force he commanded.'

'Well Fraser,' he replied with rather brusquely, 'we're fighting a war, and all wars have a cost. It's not for either of us to be critical of how the General succeeds to wage war. However he did it, Cameron has won us a notable victory. The threat to this town and the lives of its people is now receding. For that we are grateful and the casualties suffered – dismaying as they are – but a small price to be paid.'

'Including among many good officers, Sir George, Captain Oliver Haile, whom I understand was a relation of yours.'

'Yes, very regrettable, a somewhat distant relation but a relation no less.'

'I knew him briefly, Sir, we came out on the same ship. I saw him die, leading his men in a most futile assault. He disdained his own safety – a very brave man – in an act of great courage.'

We stood facing each other. An uncomfortable silence lay heavily between us.

'Surely you have not called upon me at a busy time Mr Fraser, just to voice your criticism of my General's conduct of the war?'

'Indeed not Sir George, though what I saw at Rangiriri concerned me greatly. I have come to request of you, the relief of my commission. Now that summer is at hand, I wish to return to the south. The expedition was late; at Commodore Wiseman's request, I have already delayed my departure for more than a month. If you would grant me my leave Sir, I am now anxious to go.'

'Of course, Mr Fraser, I'm grateful you came and that you answered my call. I'm sure that your skill and your time have been most usefully applied. The *Pioneer* gunboat was essential to launching the campaign and the haste to complete it quite vital. I must thank you for your help.'

'Such little as it was, Sir George.'

'And now Mr Fraser if you could wait a short while; I should write a brief note to Commissioner MacKay in the circumstances and would ask that you carry it south and deliver it by hand.'

Without waiting for a response, the Governor strode back to his desk. While Sir George began writing I turned to the windows overlooking the lawn. The park-like grounds and serene gardens all enclosed by a high fence seemed far distant from the mud, the mists, the swamps, the thunder of guns, the blood and death I had just left behind.

The quiet was broken by the scrape of a chair. The Governor escorted me across to the door, handed over his letter. A brief shake of hands, a murmur of thanks and the waiting clerk led me away. I walked down the hill to the port, the wax seal on the letter still hot on my palm.

Several days later, we passed out of the port heading south on the *Olive Peake*, a small steamer that reminded me of the *Queen* that plied the Otago coast when I worked from Port Molyneaux. This wooden vessel was about the same size, but fitted amidships with paddles. She carried a full rig like a brigantine – square rigged on the foremast and schooner-rigged on the mizzenmast aft.

Now heading south, her sails were all furled and we drove steadily along to the beat of the paddles, a long tongue of coal-smoke trailing back from her stack. The prevailing wind in New Zealand comes up from southwest, so voyages north can be driven by sail, but to travel back south under sails alone is otherwise a long and a hazardous venture, beating far out to sea on long reaches against the wind. Equipped with both steam and sail, the *Olive Peake* was an ideal coastal vessel in this situation, using sails to come north and steam to go south. She was much in demand.

We rode the long swells with a gentle pitch, watching dolphins and seabirds by day and gazing up at the night as the Captain displayed his wide knowledge of the astronomy of the southern sky. We soon crossed the straits separating the northern and southern islands and two days later arrived in the morning at the headlands standing astride the entrance to the long arm of Otago Harbour.

The *Olive Peake* turned inshore and manoeuvred up the long channel to berth at Port Chalmers. Bare-masted ships lay rafted together in rows and the quay was crowded with horse-drawn vehicles and goods. We made fast to a jetty and I clambered ashore, dodging through the throng to the road where cabbies sat waiting for fares to Dunedin.

After obtaining a room at one of the many hotels that now lined the streets of Dunedin town and before attending to my own business, I decided to deliver the Governor's letter to the Gold Commissioner.

If the town had been filthy when last I visited, with the onset of warmer weather it was now quite disgusting. A foetid stench hung over the streets as refuse lay where it had been discarded in festering rotting piles; liquid wastes with abominable smells flowed in open drains into the same streams from which the inhabitants drew their water supplies.

In the lower southern section of town near a large marshy lagoon of slime-green septic water, rows of dancing and drinking saloons, theatres and cafes crammed the narrow streets.

Carefully, I picked my way along busy Princes St, jostled by crowds of idle men, horses and wheeled vehicles of every description. Gold had transformed Dunedin from a quiet, drab and cheerless colonial settlement into a disorderly, rough and booming frontier-town.

When eventually I had waited my turn to reach the desk-clerk at the busy office of the Gold Commission, I was asked to wait as soon as I made known the purpose of my visit. Within moments I was advised that Commissioner MacKay was present and would see me. Without further delay, I once again walked the familiar wood-panelled corridor to his rear office, anxious to present the Governor's letter and promptly leave.

MacKay rose from his chair as I entered, eyebrows raised, clearly surprised to see me again.

'Well Mr Fraser … you've chosen to return from the north, and so soon? '

'I had every intention to do so and am already a month later than expected, but I have come to this office only at the request of Governor Grey himself. Sir George has asked me to convey to you a letter, to be delivered by hand.'

I held it out…passed it over with the prominent seal uppermost. To my surprise, MacKay asked would I wait for a moment while he perused it. He stood near a window, partly turned away from me, opened the letter and began to read. A clock ticking loudly on the wall was the only sound.

There was sudden sharp intake of breath, a short studied silence and then he swung about, facing me. 'Are you aware of the content of this letter, Mr Fraser?'

'No, not directly Sir, but I was present as the Governor wrote it and can somewhat presume as to its tenor.'

'So you would be aware that Mr Haile has been killed while on active service?'

'That I am. Unfortunately, I was present when it happened.'

'Really? Please can you tell me more?'

'As you wish.'

I related how the army had begun its advance into the interior, to put down the natives' insurrection. I described the Rangiriri scene; the valley, the river, swamp and lake, the long ridge curled along the riverside like the spine of a sleeping dog, seeing it again so vividly in my mind. The rising ground where the 65th charged, then the stark steep ramparts of earth, rising up to the crest of the natives' redoubt; all the assaults that were launched with such confidence, which gradually turned to despair. My anguish with the mounting loss of life; the appeal to an officer to counsel the General; my decision to approach him directly myself to urge an artillery barrage instead of more futile and costly assaults; of my being shouted down and arrested. Our mutual surprise when Captain Haile appeared on board *Pioneer*.

'Captain Haile and another officer led the last assault. He must have known the attack would be futile, that none of them could survive. But courageously he rallied his men and led them forth. It was the bravest thing I have ever seen. They were all cut down as we watched.'

MacKay stared silently at me, serious faced, a deep frown creasing his brow as I continued.

'I'm sorry that I could do no more. The General's conduct was a disgrace; such needless loss of brave men's lives. The whole engagement left me sickened. I chose to take no further part and left. I asked for Governor Grey to grant me my leave. He did.'

'He has written highly of you,' - indicating the letter.

'I really did very little.' I shuffled my feet and turned to the door, wanting to bring the interview to an end.

'Please Mr Fraser, a moment longer if you would…' MacKay turned away. He paced back and forth in the office, head bowed, stroking his beard with one hand then the other, while I watched and waited in silence. As if suddenly taking hold of himself, he stopped squarely before me.

'This is much to ask of you Fraser, I know. But could I avail you to visit my home and repeat for my daughter, what you've just told to me?'

A thousand thoughts crashed together in my mind. I struggled to know how first to respond. The clock ticked loudly on the wall. I needed to choose my words with care.

'Thank you, but I need no repeat of my last invited visit to your home.'

'Indeed yes, it was somewhat unpleasant.'

'Unpleasant? You impugned my character, you insulted me grievously, then ordered me to leave.'

'Strong words were said by us both ... it was a rather difficult moment.'

We were standing quite close together. I turned squarely to him and stared face to face.

'As I unwillingly recall MacKay, you contemptuously dismissed me as 'the abandoned son of a Highland blacksmith'. Only your age protected you – such words from a younger man would not have passed unchallenged, would have demanded some redress.'

He lowered his gaze, dipping his head and spoke softly, 'I made a harsh and hasty judgement of you Fraser, that I've been given much cause to regret.'

His contrition and sudden change of tone surprised me. I barely believed I had heard him correctly. We looked at each other as a lengthening pause hung in the air.

'If now Mr Fraser, I extend you my apology – belated as it may be – would you be gracious enough to accept it and put the matter behind us?'

I looked at this man, who from the time of our very first meeting aboard the *Black Swan*, had shown me only hostility. For the first time, I saw he was looking tired and old.

'Very well MacKay, I will accept your apology. But putting it behind us, is not a thing I can so lightly do.' I turned to leave.

'But Mr Fraser ... what about my invitation ... I would be most gratified if you would agree to attend?'

It was a moment of decision I'd being trying to avoid. A door being opened that I'd long kept closed. Would I regret it, if now I left it so?

'Could we expect you tomorrow afternoon, say around 3 pm, if that was convenient?'

He seemed rather pressing, rather anxious to please. I gave an involuntary sigh, as if some new weight had been draped on my shoulders.

'Very well MacKay. As you wish, but I will not stay for long, my time here is necessarily brief. I have much yet to do.'

To my further surprise, he proffered his hand which I could not avoid but to take, then walked with me from his office through the long passageway to the reception desk, where we parted. I stepped into the street, relieved that this meeting of which I'd been so apprehensive, was now at an end.

There was indeed much to be done. I called first at Burns' Engineering Works where I was warmly greeted by my cousin George Bruce and then in turn by Mr Burns himself. The shipping business up the Molyneaux had continued with Arthur Denniston for long after I had sold the *Lady Colina,* surviving the subsequent rushes to the Central Otago goldfields and the building of new roads into the interior. Though the most profitable period was long passed, the venture had provided much wealth for the Dunedin businessmen involved, for which Mr Burns remained most grateful for our efforts together.

I inspected the construction of the current-wheel dredge that had followed from the drawings I had sent from the north. Two large tubular pontoons lay ready in the yard, each 20 feet long, their rivetted joins all sealed with pitch.

A rectangular frame of bolted steel beams was loosely assembled on the ground, diagonally braced and short-decked with light plates. An A-frame midway on each side supported brass bearings through which ran a shaft some two inches in diameter.

Inside the works, I was shown a stack of small odd-shaped buckets. These had been rolled from plate into a half-circle, so as to resemble a half-bucket with several raised teeth on its curved rim. Of even more interest to me was a driving gypsy wheel I'd designed, to drive a long chain on which the buckets would be fastened.

My next call was to the wheelwright business of Peter Reid. There I was told that when I had not returned as expected at the beginning of spring, my partner John Reid had departed some six weeks prior, off to the Arrow to work again on our old claim. He intended to stay there until I returned.

Peter showed me two huge paddlewheels he had built to my design. The paddlewheels when driven by the fast current would drive the chain and buckets to and from the riverbed. Each bucket lowered to the riverbed on the chain, would drag on the bottom, then hopefully be raised filled with gravel as the paddlewheels and the gypsy wheel drove the chain around. When the bucket passed over the wheel it would spill all its content into a waiting sluice-box; any gold would be riddled and the tailings would empty back into the river. If it worked as I planned, a dream from long ago in the Molyneaux gorge with Fox when the presumed riches of the riverbed lay frustratingly beyond our reach, would at last be realised.

That evening I dined with George and Lucy. The Burns' engineering business had grown substantially with all the development that had occurred in the region and George's responsibilities had increased commensurately; he now filled a broad management role and was being well rewarded. They had heard once from my other cousin Harry, who with his gold from the Molyneaux, had successfully purchased a large block of land in the northeast which was already becoming a productive farm.

Next morning I was fully preoccupied with arranging for a bullock-team from Cobb & Co to convey all my new equipment – including large coils of hemp rope and several ships' anchors – on the long slow journey inland, such that I gave scant thought to my visiting the MacKays. The day thus passed quickly and the time to set forth to the MacKay's arrived.

I reluctantly retraced my steps of two years ago to the big house on McLaggan St, never having thought that I would do so again, feeling only apprehension in place of the anticipation of that previous time. I had avoided all thoughts of that event; it was not a memory I could revisit without anguish – thoughts that I'd repressed to avoid the pain.

When I knocked on the large front door, it was opened by the same Miss Robertson who had escorted me off these same premises at the order of MacKay; wearing the same dark dress with the same white collar and cuffs. She showed neither surprise nor emotion to be greeting me again. I stated my name and business, was led down the hallway and announced at the door of the drawing-room.

MacKay, who had obviously been waiting, came across the room from the windows and greeted me in a friendly manner, thanking me again for coming. 'My daughter will join us shortly – Miss Robertson if you will, please advise her that Mr Fraser is here with us now.'

We stood together beside the French doors overlooking a small level lawn with a steep hillside of bush rising up from its edge, making idle talk about the growth that had taken place in the town. I felt a sense of misgiving, uncertain if I should have come here at all. I heard footsteps coming lightly on the wooden floor.

Elizabeth MacKay walked purposefully into the room. She was dressed, appropriately, in mourning black but her head and face were not covered. When last I was in her company, Elizabeth had been a young lady: this Miss Elizabeth standing before me was a mature woman; her head erect, shoulders back, with poise and self-possession. The fair hair that previously tumbled to her shoulders was now gathered and drawn tightly back, accentuating the prominence of her high cheekbones, but the pale blue magnetic eyes were just the same, locked on to mine.

'Pleased to meet you again, Mr Fraser. I'm very grateful you agreed to come and visit us – and I thank my father for inviting you.' Her voice like lilting music spilled through my ears to someplace deep inside.

I slightly dipped my head in greeting. 'Miss MacKay.' Her eyebrows rose perceptibly at my use of the honorific. 'I regret the circumstances that have brought me here – and my most sincere sympathy in your loss.'

MacKay suggested we be seated and awkwardly we each found places on the chairs, Elizabeth directly opposite me, her father to the side.

'Father has already related, Mr Fraser, that you were present when poor Captain Haile lost his life.'

'By chance, yes I was – a chance that in retrospect, I'd rather not have had.'

MacKay interrupted quickly: 'I've acquainted my daughter with the circumstance which placed you there, Mr Fraser, but I did not recount the details of the engagement, nor what happened to you subsequently. I'd rather my daughter heard tell of that in your own words, not mine. If you would be so inclined….' He motioned his hand toward her.

Gently I recounted all that I had described to her father the previous day.

Much as I tried to keep calm, the memory and frustration flooded back. 'Miss MacKay, I assure you I did all I could to prevent it, but the Commander just would not listen. He appeared consumed with his rage, quite beyond the capacity for reason. He had me arrested, and I was forcibly taken away.'

They both looked at me in serious silence and more resignedly I continued. 'Haile – and another young officer – was then ordered to lead yet another attack. Pitifully armed with only pistols and swords, this mere handful of men was expected to take the redoubt, when hundreds before them had already failed.

'I'm sure they all knew – the moment the order was given – that none of them stood a chance. Haile set an admirable example, leading his men out in the front, encouraging and urging them on, heedless of his own safety. The whole army stood and cheered at their courage as the little group pressed on under fire. They struggled to surmount the steep rampart but barely made to the top. Men fell all around, but still

Haile charged on, still leading the way, waving his sword forward as they charged.

'He was the first of only a few to get there, but they were instantly overwhelmed. I stood there, watching, sickened, as they were all quickly cut down. It was the bravest thing I've ever seen – nor would ever wish to see again.'

I paused to give them a moment of reflection, took a breath and continued.

'Having seen how their war was conducted – such stubbornly stupid decisions, the Commander's detached disregard for his men, the deplorable death and injury that resulted – I would not continue to stay. I sought a meeting with the Governor who agreed to revoke my commission and I quickly returned to the south.'

We sat for a longer moment in silence, my story ended. Elizabeth, head bowed, spoke at the floor: 'Poor Oliver, I would have expected no less of him. Honour and service were everything. The army was his life and he had scant concern for anything else.'

She took a long breath, sat up and looked to me. 'And tell us now of you, Mr Fraser, you're back to the goldfields again I presume?'

Before I answered, her father suddenly rose from his chair. 'Please excuse me a moment Fraser … some urgent work that demands I attend….' He glanced at his daughter, as if undecided what to do, then vaguely walked from the room. Immediately, I was conscious we were now left there alone.

'Yes I am, Miss MacKay. I have much planned to do there and now less time remaining before next winter to achieve it.'

'Will your business require your return to Dunedin?'

'Certainly not Miss MacKay. At least not before the winter comes, and I've given no thought about then. I still own a small house at Port Molyneux. Perhaps I will go back there again.'

She glanced to the door, then turned to me quizzically – a gesture I remembered – and said softly, 'You once called me "Miss Elizabeth".'

'A different time – a different circumstance.'

We lapsed into a taught silence. So much I could say … but couldn't. Elizabeth sat there looking at me, her lips squeezed closed, an almost pained expression on her face. Both of us hesitated to begin new conversation. Mr MacKay re-entered the room. I stood up, indicating I was ready to depart.

'Are you leaving us so soon? Well thank you, Mr Fraser, for graciously giving us your time. If your business should require your return to this town, I would be obliged if you would call upon us again.'

'I very much doubt that will happen, MacKay. I have a great deal waiting to do.'

He responded almost obsequiously. 'But please remember if for any reason you should return here, be sure to come and visit us again.'

I walked to the door. Elizabeth stood still, visibly quite ill at ease, her earlier assurance and poise now seemingly lost. I quite firmly took my leave and Miss Robertson showed me to the door.

Out in the street, I glanced back at the house, somewhat relieved it was over. Almost imperceptibly, I thought I saw a curtain move, a flash of a face at the window.

As I walked away, I pondered why the conversation had been so stilted, why I had been so strained, how differently the visit unfolded from what I had expected. There had been some kind of tension there no doubt – a brittleness apparent in the air, as before an electrical storm breaks out.

I reminded myself quite firmly, that whatever had once gone between us had long passed. That door had been well shut – and so it would remain.

* * *

I took a small coastal steamer a short way up the coast, to land at a new coach station, the eastern terminus of the northern route inland. I rode the long hours, lurching over the rugged coastal hills aboard a Cobb & Co coach, then watching the miles of tussock slide past in the valley plains where once we had trudged on the trail, struggling along with our loads, driven on by our dreams. How quickly those times had gone by, replaced now by such relative comfort and ease.

My thoughts flickered back and forth: forward to building the dredge on the river; back to my stilted meeting with Elizabeth. I rethought through every moment, recollecting her expressions, recalling the words. Had I imagined it – or just wished it so – that she had seemed wistful or hurt, that she'd struggled to contain things she wanted to say.

Well, quite understandable, having so recently lost her betrothed. She had even said 'Oliver' – an expression of endearment – just like she had once called me 'John'. I had certainly been rather abrupt, had made no effort for a friendly conversation, nor invited any openings for one. Perhaps I should have done so, but the memories of my earlier visit to that house still kept me prisoner – memories that were still too fresh, too strong, too painful. Oh if only we could forget: forget old love, old hate, remorse, regrets and shattered dreams.

We changed horses in the Maniototo, came down the long valley of the Manuherikia and arrived at the Lower Junction, now a large bustling town. While I waited for the bullock-train to haul my huge load over the Dunstan Trail, I hired a messenger to cross the mountains further west to the Arrow with directions to locate John Reid on our claim. Should he now wish to join me, I wrote, our venture was at long last to hand.

Every day, amid the bustle of men, vehicles and horses in the town I watched for the arrival of the bullock-train dragging all my equipment in from the coast. Such was the profusion of activity that it was almost in the town before I saw it – a six-ox team heavily yoked, plodding slowly but with relentless strength, the waggoneer seated behind them on the front of a long narrow dray loaded high with gear. I hastened to greet him and direct the team down off the escarpment toward the riverbank itself.

John Reid arrived from the Arrow just as I was organising a group of men to unload the equipment; pleased to have a new prospect just as the paydirt on our Arrow claim was dwindling away, the yield almost reduced to tucker-ground. Together, we set to work with the band of labourers and soon had all the gear off the dray, laid out on flat ground by the bank.

Keeping a few of the stronger labourers with us to help, we bolted the frame together on top of the two large pontoons, covering it fore and aft with rough-sawn planks. The gypsy wheel was fitted to the shaft between triangle-supports above the pontoon on each side. An otherwise listless crowd that had gathered to watch, helped us slide the raft-like vessel into the river where it floated high on its pontoons. Carefully with many hands, we lifted Peter Reid's two large paddlewheels into place on either end of the drive-shaft.

At the stern, we fastened a long wooden contrivance built like a ladder which would be lowered deep into the water when the dredge was positioned in the river; the 'ladder' would separate the upcoming chain from the downward chain so as to avoid entanglement. The remaining gear – chain, buckets, timber and coir matting for the sluicebox, mooring ropes and anchors – were loaded aboard and stacked on the platform.

Four of us positioned ourselves along the side of the vessel closest to the riverbank, equipped with long poles to fend her off from grounding. The team of labourers took up a long mooring rope hitched at the front of the vessel and began the long slow haul to drag the vessel upriver into the gorge as far as the precipitous banks could be traversed.

When we eventually reached that point four exhausting days later, we were at the head of a long reach immediately below a narrow passage of fast swirling water tumbled about with pressure waves. If gold lay out in the riverbed as we surmised, much of it should have deposited in just such a reach after being swept by the force of current through the narrows immediately upriver.

By rigging a baffle-board angled at the bow and using a steering oar at the stern, we hoped to swing the vessel out across the river sufficiently far to drop an anchor. The labourers slowly paid out the mooring rope through the eye of another anchor buried on the bank as we inched the vessel further and further out into the river.

With all the mooring line paid out, we reached a point where the current against the baffle-board held the vessel almost stationary, disappointingly less than halfway across the river. Desperate heaves on the steering oar gained merely another two yards. Until we could get a rope across from the far bank, we could not reach further out into the river. We dropped the second anchor and eased back.

Peter Reid released the tethers on the paddlewheels and immediately the current swirling past under the vessel drove them around, rotating the shaft and the gypsy wheel. Together, Reid and I slowly lowered the chain with its small buckets down the 'ladder' into the river. The sluice-box was hastily assembled across the platform and propped onto a frame. Though still improvised, all was now ready for a trial.

Tense with anticipation, we hoisted the slack chain above the gypsy wheel and lowered it down into place over the face of the wheel. Quickly the links dropped into the recesses in the rotating wheel and the chain began to drive. The manifestation of my dreams – to prospect the riches of the very riverbed itself – was almost at hand.

We crouched aft, peering anxiously into the river as bucket after bucket came up from the blue depths empty. Perhaps, we questioned, the dragline was too long, the buckets slewing and emptying their contents before the chain lifted them from the riverbed. But suddenly, there it was - the first bucket grey with gravel. It appeared from below, clanked up over the edge of the ladder, wobbled with its weight to the gypsy, then as it followed the circumference around, spilled its burden into the sluice and plunged back down into the blueness of the river.

The rising chain crawled with the weight of so many filled buckets but still the current was sufficiently strong to drive the paddlewheels slowly around. Reid shouted for help as gravel began to pile high in the sluicebox and together we shovelled the heavier stones through the box into the river, peering intently for any sign of gold. Water sloshing from the emptying buckets washed the pea-gravel and fines along the angled bed of the sluice, over the choir matting, pouring in a grey stream out the end into the fast-flowing water.

Within only minutes, a thick vein of heavy sediment had accumulated in the bed of the sluice, burying the choir matting in the base. Reid and I could not be patient. We delved our hands into the sediment, staring as it poured in a slurry through our fingers. And there it was – a rich mixture of dull gold amid the flickering silica sand; not the irregular nuggets of gold that we found on our claim in the Arrow, but a profitable stream of fines, misshapen flakes and grains. Paydirt. Gold at last!

We kept on for several hours, slightly adjusting the mooring lines, until the approach of twilight brought our first day of operation to an end.

We raised the ladder and eased off the port mooring rope, letting the platform drift gradually back across the river until we were fast to the bank. Together we carefully removed every vestige of sediment from the sluice into buckets and in the failing light, gave most of it a rudimentary wash with pans. Although further work remained to clean the gold fully from the coir mat, we estimated our first few hours dredging had yielded us at least 40 ounces.

So began the pattern of subsequent days. Word of the success of our venture quickly spread – each day men would arrive at the bank, staring out to us on the river or gathering in a crowd in the evening to see what riches we had dredged up from our day's work.

Positioning the dredge each morning was arduous and time-consuming work, especially when we needed to move the anchor buried far out in the riverbed. The river was also now in full flow with the early-summer thaw, making hauling the dredge difficult and dangerous work.

John Reid decided to attempt a traverse of the precipitous southern side of the gorge, to establish a mooring line to that bank, with which we could more easily and rapidly manoeuvre the dredge over all the span of the turbulent river. He gathered a small group of men together and set off, crossing to Earnscleugh Station downriver then working their way along the south bank until several days later they reappeared, climbing down a steep broken rockface opposite.

I had the dredge hauled across to its extremity above the anchor in the river. Reid attached a stone securely to a long length of light twine, twirling it furiously in an arc around his head and hurled it out into the river toward us. On the fifth attempt, the rock flew low overhead, draping the attached cord over the dredge. I attached a heavier line to the cord, which Reid hauled back to his bank further upriver. Next we fixed a section of thin rope to the cord which in turn he reeled in, then a heavy mooring line tied to that rope was finally dragged across and made securely fast to an outcrop of rock. At last we had lines fixed at equal points to each bank and could position ourselves around the river at will.

Our daily yields were sometimes hugely rewarding but varied greatly. When the dredge was positioned in the swiftest current so that the paddlewheels were driven fastest – thus bringing up more buckets from riverbed for each hour – the river gravels were larger stones and contained little gold. If we positioned in slacker water, the paddlewheels revolved very slowly, but the riverbed sediments were far the richer. We quickly learned to best compromise one with the other.

We built stone huts on the shore, thatching their roofs with thick bundles of snowgrass. Men we employed to work with us on the dredge put up tents or assembled rough shelters, until quite a collection of housing sat clustered on the terrace above the river. With food and firewood being brought to us daily from Manuherikia and a steady stream of the curious coming down off the gorge road to visit, our little settlement was quite busy. Even armed officers from the Cobb & Co Gold Transport Service arrived regularly to collect our gold, checking the assay and weighing it there on the riverbank before transporting it to the bank at Manuherikia.

With the season well advanced, we were working in daylight some eighteen hours each day. The tally of our accumulated yield was growing to a quite spectacular sum and my thoughts were filled with ideas to build an even larger dredge for next summer season; a power-dredge driven by steam-engine that could work anywhere at will, including the still waters where we believed could lie the richest ground.

At the close of such a long dreamy hot day, we slowly hauled our way wearily back toward the shore. As we approached, I saw a tall uniformed figure standing on the bank, apparently waiting for us. As we neared the river's edge, I could see he wore the dark blue serge uniform and peaked cap of the Postal Service. The Messenger approached us as we clambered ashore, one hand on the flap of the leather pouch at his waist.

'Which of you gentlemen is Mr John Cameron Fraser?' he enquired, glancing from one to another. With a pang of apprehension I identified myself. The Messenger passed over a letter which I tucked into my jacket, reluctant to open it immediately.

When I later did so, in the relaxing firelight of early evening, I discovered it was from Lucy in Dunedin:

To our Dear John:
I hope that this letter reaches you wherever you may be, that you are well and that your new venture is meeting with the success for which you hoped.

I must forthwith request you please to forgive my temerity in writing to you so, but I have just had the unexpected pleasure of being called upon at home by Miss Elizabeth MacKay. Miss Elizabeth, whose acquaintance I was delighted to renew, eventually disclosed the reason for her visit, which prompts me now to send to you this letter.

Miss Elizabeth it appears, though extremely grateful to you for your recent visit to their home, has been left discomforted and unhappy by the events of that occasion. Whilst the circumstances of your visit were of themselves unfortunate and distressing, Miss Elizabeth revealed that she was left the moreso by the brevity of your departure and by what she has interpreted as some harshness of your manner toward herself. Furthermore, despite her invitation to you to visit them again and even, to my surprise, the entreatment of her father to you to do so, she gave me to understand that you were somewhat dismissive in your response and displayed no intention of ever calling upon them again.

Miss Elizabeth believes that you may harbour some ill-feeling or resentment toward herself relating to the past and if so, understands why that may rightfully be. However, due to the unfortunate circumstances of your visit, Miss Elizabeth is aggrieved that she was thus denied the opportunity to converse with you alone, to acquaint you of a matter of which you are not aware. It distresses her greatly that because such an opportunity is not now likely to present itself, you will therefore, forever more, continue to bear some ill-will toward her.

Unable to affect this situation herself directly, Miss Elizabeth decided, somewhat courageously, to call upon me and seek such assistance as I may be willing to offer, even though we have not seen each other for a very long period. All that she has asked of me was that, if I should at any time be in contact with you, I might acquaint you with what she has disclosed to me, that you might therefore reconsider and avail her the opportunity to speak with you again which otherwise she will be denied.

I truly believe, dear John, that Miss Elizabeth is indeed sorely troubled and distressed by some matter which she did not reveal to me but quite fervently wishes to do so to you. Accordingly I would implore you, if any reason should arise whereby it may be advantageous for you so to do, that you consider returning again to Dunedin and however difficult as it may be for you, that you do indeed revisit the MacKays.

Meanwhile, on a personal note, the arrival of our new child comes ever close, being due to join us some four weeks following Christmas. With our cherished little Hugh already so actively demanding our attention, I wonder as to how I will cope with yet another to attend.

George joins with me in sending you our warmest of regards.
Yours affectionately,
Your cousin-in law,
Lucy Bruce

I read the letter again. What, if anything, should I do? I sat there alone on the bank, reflecting, watching the restless river racing past as the last pink touch of fading light brushed the perpetual snows of the high mountains off to the west and deepening shadows crept down the ragged ravines into the gorge. Against such sureties, my own indecisions seemed such trifles.

NINETEEN

It was in Ireland in the big house at Castledawson that I had last enjoyed Christmas with my own family. So I decided to return to Dunedin and celebrate the day with George and Lucy, my closest family.

Peter Reid was quite willing to remain with the dredge while I set off on the three-day coach ride back out to the coast and the steamer on to Dunedin.

A light westerly wind wafted the stench of the town down the harbour toward us as I approached, reminding me that the warmer summer temperatures had only exacerbated the foetid wastes washing through the streets. I could well understand the reports we had received in the Dunedin newspaper that deadly fevers were rampant in the community, with many deaths particularly among children and the elderly.

I had arrived several days before Christmas, so I made use of the time by visiting Burns' Engineering several times to discuss the next development of the gold dredge. Before next summer, I planned to lengthen the pontoons and extend the deck, then power the drive with a steam engine, either by purchasing a new engine from England or by exercising the Bill of Sale I still held over the engine of the *Lady Colina*.

If we changed the standard ship-chain for a flat-link chain driven by sprockets instead of the gypsy-wheel, we could fit much larger and more stable buckets, which would need to be cast in the Burns' foundry. To control the heavier flat-link chain and to dig deeper into the riverbed gravels toward the bedrock where the richest gold would be found, would require a new 'ladder' for the chain to ride on. Such a ladder needed to be raised or lowered by chains on winches.

We agreed that Burns would commence the purchase of a new steam engine and flat-link chain from England; after all we had been through together, I could not bring myself to wreck the *Lady Colina* by tearing the engine from her. I also resolved to produce the drawings for the new buckets, the ladder proposal, the drive-sprockets and the pontoon extensions shortly after returning inland.

On one afternoon as I returned to my hotel along Princes Street, carefully picking my way to avoid the roughest ground and deeper holes in the roadway, or the cesspools alongside, I noticed among the many people walking to and fro, a Chinaman was approaching, distinctive in his long dark gown and wide-brimmed hat. He was avoiding the main part of the street, clinging to the shopfronts and doorways, well out of the way of the milling throng. He looked almost furtive – unsurprisingly, as chinamen were poorly regarded in the town – his hat lowered to obscure his face, arms tucked in close to his sides, shuffling along erratically, slowly coming toward me.

As our paths closed, about to cross, the Chinaman suddenly stepped out directly in front of me. He raised his head, tipped back the brim of his hat. His oriental face was familiar. It was Oon Yew Gow. He showed no surprise at seeing me again.

'Ah, my flend Missa Flazer! I know you here … now I find you.'

So this was not a meeting by chance. I was aware that people passing by were watching us.

'Oon Yew Gow! Why are you here in this town and not on the goldfield? How did you know I was here and why have you found me?' I asked as I led him quickly to the side of the road, away from the curious passers-by.

Standing there in the street, he slowly explained. The Chinese miners near Manuherikia had heard of the early success of the current-wheel gold dredge. Word of this new development had been passed back to Dunedin, had caught the attention of the merchant Choie Siew Hoy. Being well aware that Oon had worked for me on the Arrow, Siew Hoy had called him to come to Dunedin. Once there, Siew Hoy had briefed Oon on his interest in dredging and sent him to find me, with a proposal. By coincidence, before Oon had set out again for Manuherikia to deliver the message, I myself had arrived in the town. Siew Hoy who seemed cleverly well-informed as to everything happening in the town, soon heard of my visit to Burns' Engineering Works. Oon Yew Gow had sought me out.

The explanation – in halting and broken English – was difficult to follow; the proposal itself was simple. If I wanted to build more dredges, or even a larger dredge perhaps, I would possibly need much money.

Although his 'master' Siew Hoy was 'certain I was already a rich man', he would be very willing to provide such money as I may need, in return for a share of the venture. It would be a private arrangement between us, with no need for others to know. Should I wish to avail myself of Siew Hoy's proposal, all I need do was visit him at his warehouse on the south side of town whenever I so wished.

With multiple thanks to each other, smiles and much head nodding from Oon, he scuttled off between some buildings and disappeared.

The two days of Christmas celebrations, including attending services at the new stone church together with George and Lucy, passed quickly and most pleasantly. I waited impatiently for the first Sunday following before making my visit to the MacKay's, anxious to have it over and return to the gold dredge.

I chose a Sunday, in the afternoon, to be reasonably sure that MacKay himself was likely to be there and Elizabeth would not be alone in their home. Given the man's previous antipathy toward me, there was little point in my acceding to Elizabeth's wish to meet with me again if her father's hostility was renewed.

I walked slowly in the hot afternoon sun along McLaggan Street, my apprehension rising as I approached the house. Miss Robertson answered at the door with an agreeable smile as I announced myself and without keeping me waiting there, immediately ushered me down the familiar hallway to the large drawing-room.

Loud footsteps presaged the arrival of MacKay, who strode briskly into the room.

'Mr Fraser! I'm so pleased that you have indeed returned to Dunedin. I heard from my friend Burns that you were back in town, so we were rather hoping that you might call upon us.'

I could not judge whether his joviality was genuine or contrived. I assumed a neutrality.

'Some pressing business and the arrival of Christmas happily coincided to induce me to return here briefly MacKay. On my last visit you kindly extended me an invitation and having a day or two to spare before the next coach departs for Central, I thought to call …. I would hope it is not inconvenient?'

'Not at all, no not at all. Very good of you to do so Fraser. But no doubt it is not me you have called to see, but my daughter, who momentarily will join us.'

We stood side by side near open doors leading out to a small sunlit lawn flanked with trees, while I answered his several questions about the gold-dredging operation. Almost abruptly, he interrupted the line of conversation.

'Before my daughter arrives Mr Fraser, may I for your benefit offer you a word of advice?' It seemed more a statement than a question.

'Why surely....'

'When they are so few, you may not have had much social contact with the women of this Colony, Fraser. If not, I should advise you that their behaviour can be somewhat disconcerting, inappropriate even.

'It would seem when they journey out here to this Colony, their social mores and conventions get left behind. Here, the women forget their station, the proper conventions of society don't prevail. They become quite outspoken, even aggressively assertive in fact. My daughter no less than any others I'm sorry to say, as I myself have experienced.

'Perhaps in this harsher life here, they must need shed some graces, assume more responsibilities. Or they're influenced by women arriving from Australia who are of a much lower social class. Whatever, it is certainly to their detriment, much less becoming and indeed can be quite disconcerting.

'So I apologise for my daughter, Fraser, should you find her manner to now be so. I have attempted to counsel her on the matter, but to no avail. At the least, you are now forewarned.'

I did not know how to respond to this unexpected advice. Fortunately, before I needed to do so, a far door opened and Elizabeth herself entered the room. I was struck immediately again by the presence she radiated; standing tall, her blue eyes catching the light, a slight blush to her cheeks, even white teeth in her wide mouth opened in a smile.

'Oh Mr Fraser, what a surprise and a pleasure that you should call upon us again!'

Even before I could reply, MacKay himself spoke quickly. 'Well Fraser, if I may excuse myself. And rather than keep Mr Fraser standing here indoors Elizabeth, may I suggest you both take a walk in the garden....' He excused himself again and left the room.

Elizabeth held out her hand toward the open doors. 'Would that be agreeable to you Mr Fraser?'

'Of course Miss MacKay, whatever you wish....'

I followed her closely as she walked outside, watching the swish and sway of her dress, my mind filled with a confusion of MacKay's unexpected pleasantness, Elizabeth's appearance, being alone with her and hearing again the musical sound of her voice.

We crossed the small lawn together toward the shade of the border trees beneath which was a large wooden seat. As neither of us spoke whilst we walked, I could feel a certain tension arise. Elizabeth seated herself at one end, half turned and faced me. I remained standing, looked down to her upturned face.

'Thank you for coming Mr Fraser. I hoped that you would, some day.'

'I received a letter from Lucy, my cousin-in-law. She advised you had visited her. Lucy said you were apparently somewhat distressed when last I was here, that you wished to discuss some matter with me, but in the circumstances of that occasion, you were denied. She conveyed to me your wish that I might call upon you again, though I know not what the matter might be that has distressed you so – other than understandably, the unfortunate loss of your intended husband.

'I had business reasons to return to Dunedin at Christmas. I have some days to spare before departing, so I have come.'

'You are kind to do so, Mr Fraser, and I thank you. Indeed I was upset when last you visited, beyond having learned that Mr Haile had lost his life. I may have misunderstood you at the time, but your manner toward me was quite unexpected. It distressed me greatly, that you seemed to bear some ill-will, some resentment toward me. Perhaps that's a misjudgment on my part, but I have been grieved you may continue to carry such feeling toward me unjustly, because of circumstances of which you are unaware.

'When last you visited – and I sensed your displeasure – I was unable to speak with you. The time was not opportune. Since then, it has been much on my mind, distressing me greatly, especially not knowing what, if anything, I could do in mitigation. Then I thought to seek the intercession of your cousin Lucy. I hope you can forgive my presumption in so doing....'

Her voice trailed off as she visibly struggled to contain some emotion. I decided this was no longer time for me to remain circumspect.

'If there is misunderstanding, Miss Elizabeth, it's perhaps moreso on your part than on mine. If there's reason for either of us to be aggrieved, then surely such reason is mine.'

She looked up at me, her face composed and serious, her eyes wide with surprise at my words. I took a long breath.

'Whether you were aware of it or not on the ship, Miss Elizabeth, I was in love with you. I probably was from the moment I first saw you … when our eyes first caught each other as you came aboard the *Black Swan*.

'It was then a favour of fate that I managed to meet you. I was fortunate to spend such happy times with you on the ship, which only increased the affection that I held for you. I thought – mistakenly so it would subsequently seem – my feelings toward you were reciprocated, at least in some measure.

'Then as we entered the southern ocean, you no longer came on deck. Each day, I longed to see you, but sought you in vain.

'So in some desperation, I wrote to you. I know you received my letter, because Nathaniel delivered it into your hand as I asked – he told me had. But you did not reply.

'I waited expectantly, every day that followed, for weeks, but nothing came. I could not understand. I did not see you again for the all the remainder of the voyage.

'When we arrived in Dunedin, you left the ship so hurriedly, without even saying goodbye.

'I remembered your invitation to visit and waited a respectable time, impatient and anxious though I was just to see you again.

'Then at last when I came – and filled with expectation – your father refused me permission to see you. Then he told me you were bethrothed to Haile.

'I could not believe what I heard. My hopes and my dreams that we might share a life together, all now destroyed.

'I realised then, why you had stopped coming on deck, why you didn't respond to my letter. But I could not understand how such a thing happened. Especially after all that had passed between us. How could you have changed – and in so brief a time? It was vexatious in the extreme. Almost more than I could bear.

'When I tried to question him, your father spoke to me quite severely. He insulted me greviously. We exchanged more words. He ordered me from your house….'

I paused; the emotion of recounting those events that I had tried so hard to forget, constricting my chest. I took several deep breaths. Elizabeth stared at me, open mouthed and silent. I continued.

'I left from this town, never wishing to return. I could not bear that I might encounter you here, as Mrs Haile on the arm of the Lieutenant … even that thought itself was too much. For two years I was gone and I tried to my utmost, to forget.'

I stopped. Elizabeth's eyes had welled up as I spoke. Tears suddenly spilled over her cheeks. Her hands, clenched white in her lap, screwed restlessly together in anguish.

She rose quickly from the seat. I was afraid she would run to the house. But she stood and faced me. I'd never before seen a woman cry and knew not what I should do.

In consternation, I held out a kerchief. 'Miss Elizabeth, I'm sorry if that story upset you, but it is true.'

'No, no Mr Fraser, I'm not crying because of you. I cry for myself. Oh dear, I just must explain, you must listen to me, please!'

I waited while she became more composed, concerned that MacKay would observe her distress and come rushing to intercede, furious I had upset his daughter, but Elizabeth had turned away from the house and faced to the trees.

After a few moments, she turned back to me, her hands clasped at her waist, her face quite crestfallen but fortunately now free of tears.

'Please Mr Fraser, can we be seated while I relate you my story….'

She held an upturned hand out toward the seat and resumed her place at one end. I accepted the other, very conscious how close together that placed us.

'You were not wrong, in what you believed. We shared such good times together aboard the *Black Swan* and I enjoyed your company as much as you said that you enjoyed mine.

'The night of the dance, when we were alone, I tried to convey my growing affection for you. If – as you say – that you then felt love for me, it was no less than the love that I too, had for you.

'But I grievously wronged you then by revealing how I felt. As I learned only later, I did not have the right to encourage you so. I was soon to discover that what I might want, was not what I might have.

'As best that I could at the time, I did try to explain. I recall that I warned you my father would not react kindly to any man showing an interest in me – regardless of whom that might be.

'I'd lost my mother – my father, his wife. All he had left was his daughter, who – because mother and I were so alike – daily reminded him of what he had lost. He was disconsolate for her – and fiercely protective of me.

'His decision to leave home and come to this Colony was to try and assuage his unbearable grief. I remember I told that to you, and asked for you not to judge him severely.

'I was very young – I'd never before left my home. All I had learned I'd been taught by a governess. I knew almost nothing of the ways of the world. I looked to my father in all that I did. I respected his word and always did what he said.

'When Mother had died and I was left all alone, my father was forced to decide what to do. His family all urged I should then live with them – it was not right for a man who was widowed to remain there in the home with only his daughter, alone.

'He would not part with me, but he could not just remain, so he decided we should leave and travel abroad. By good fortune, he was offered the post in this Colony that he came here to take.

'Having rejected the advice of his family and friends, father was now doubly responsible for me. And our travelling abroad made him increasingly so.

'On board the ship, when we encountered the first storm, he realised then that he had placed me at great risk. If anything should happen to him, I would be abandoned, alone. It weighed on him greatly. He would say so to me, 'Oh Elizabeth, my dear, how could I have done this to you?'

'Then such a surprise … Captain King invited you to dine. I did not know who was joining us and scarcely believed when I saw who had come. I recognised you immediately – the man I had seen as I boarded the ship – among all that were there amid the hustle and bustle that day, I had seen only you. For me too, it was as if I had met you before.

'I tried to contain my excitement that night, but father understood me quite well. I'm sure he could sense there was something between us. That's why he reacted in the way that he did – being so very unpleasant to you. Especially in front of the company, trying to shame you for being who you are. I was deeply embarrassed, but I tried not to show.

'I did not think that I could meet with you again. I knew you were not permitted on our deck, nor even to converse with us unless we spoke to you first. Though we were allowed to go down to your deck, to do so I needed my father's – and the Captain's – permission. He would deny it – and of course, he did.

'It took all my courage to ask for I knew he'd say 'no'. So I responded by staying in my cabin and displaying my displeasure, hoping that on seeing how unhappy I was, he'd relent.

'You could know nothing of this Mr Fraser, just how difficult it was for me. But it worked; he relented – and I met you again.

'After each time I was with you, I had to conceal how joyful I was. Despite that, my father would constantly remind me of my responsibility to him – and of his to me – and to warn how careful I must be, not to show friendship to those who were not of our station.

'After the night of the dance, I stopped asking permission to come to your deck. I just came. I think then that father was finally aware my feelings toward you had grown and could no longer be disguised.

'He took me to task: it had been wrong of me to have gone from our quarters without securing his approval first. I was sternly forbidden to visit your deck again. He said how concerned he'd become, that I was forming a friendship with you and your relatives. He was my father, and responsible for all that I did. I was a minor, with no rights of my own — only those that in his wisdom, he might choose to extend.

'Father flatly declared that nothing could come of my friendship with you. He'd been too permissive, and I'd been unwise. He was implacably opposed to you and I must not visit you again.

'I was confined to our quarters and remained there, distraught. I could not believe we might not meet again. I thought then how I'd wronged you. I felt so guilty that I'd encouraged your company and your friendship without having a right so to do. Despite that I wanted to keep seeing you, I was being forced to accept I could not. I was deeply upset and I cried till I ran out of tears. None of this could you have known, Mr Fraser, nor till this day, could you be told.

'By then we had sailed much further south. The weather had changed – it was too cold and too dangerous to venture on deck.

'And then – yes – your letter arrived. Mr Greene was correct – he delivered it to my hand – and said that had been your specific request. Though I tried quickly to conceal it, unfortunately my father had seen. Before I could retire to my cabin where I could read your letter in private, my father demanded that I surrender it.

'It was very unpleasant. Never before had I seen him so vexed. He sternly commanded 'Give me that letter! I'll have no more of this!' And having always been an obedient dutiful daughter, I meekly obeyed him. To my utter dismay, in front of me there, he just tore it up.

'What was I to do? I did not know what you had written. I could not reply, unless I did so in secret. I could not disclose to you what had happened. I was forbidden to visit you. You were not permitted to come on our deck.

'I was disconsolate and in anguish. Father was right – without his consent, nothing could come of my friendship with you. He'd seen to that, and I'd been remiss to have encouraged you so, wrongly believing I could do as I pleased.

'When we entered the southern ocean, my father became unwell. He stayed in his cabin on a number of days and I mixed with the passengers, alone.

'Mr Haile had always been attentive, courteous and pleasant. With my father absent and unwell, he became more so, but all his increased attention concerned me, made me uncomfortable. There was little choice to avoid him – I could only remain in my cabin – and I could not stay there indefinitely. Confined by the weather in the saloon, we were in close proximity together each day and we all dined at the same table each night.

'I was assiduously careful not to encourage Mr Haile. I was polite as was needed, but no more. He sought to involve me in games and discussion, but I kept to myself – at least as much as I could. I endeavoured to remain with the Doctor's wife but the Lieutenant kept trying to draw me away.

'Father's illness grew worse. Dr Carrington made him a tonic but it had no effect. As his health waned, he began to worry about me. The thought that he might not survive the journey and that I could be left all alone, troubled him greatly

'One day he was sufficiently well to join with the men in the saloon. He returned to our cabins that evening and gave me alarming news.

'Lieutenant Haile had approached him and had asked for my hand in marriage. Furthermore, Father had given his consent, provided that I did too.

'I was aghast. Marriage to Lieutenant Haile was quite beyond contemplation. I had shown not the slightest interest in the Lieutenant – on the contrary – I had avoided him as much as I could. His persistence had upset me. I felt sure I had shown by my manner, that his attention had not been desired.

'But despite my very obvious feelings, Father would not be dissuaded. He urged me to consider the proposal very carefully. His paramount concern for my security and safety weighed heavily upon his mind.

'As if fulfilling his worst fear, Father's health then continued to fail. Dr Carrington was perplexed and could not determine what ailed him. Father was confined to his bed with the doctor attending him daily.

'I too began to worry ... I had never before been alone. My mother was gone, now my father so ill. I was there on the ship far from home, voyaging for the farthest place on the earth. What if I arrived there alone? What would I do? Who could I turn to? And having apparently spurned you, Mr Fraser, how could I find you and ask for your help?

'The more ill that Father became, the more his anxiety grew. Several times every day he would murmur to me 'What will become of you dear Elizabeth? Why did I bring you to this?'

'He begged me to consider Mr Haile's proposal. "The Lieutenant comes from a very good family, well connected and with considerable wealth; your security and wellbeing would be assured".'

'Each day whilst I sat there beside him, he would plead with me to agree. His fear for my future security preyed constantly upon him. Certain himself he would die, he would have peace of mind for my future, if only I'd agree to accept. "Please Elizabeth," he would beg me, "you must follow my advice".'

Elizabeth's voice slowly rose as she related her story. She stood up, pacing agitatedly, clasping and unclasping her hands continually. She paused...and bit her top lip...her eyes tensed up as if in pain.

'I was there all alone, Mr Fraser. I was fearful. My upbringing had been so protected. I was yet only young, probably Father knew best. If the worst was to happen and father did not survive, I was being foolhardy to think I could manage in a strange new Colony – and alone. It was like standing at the edge of an abyss.

'I was faced with no choice but to accept.' Elizabeth gave a shrug of her shoulders...a shake of her head. She looked up at me, as if in appeal: 'What else could I do?' The question unanswered. 'So – though I was sure, and I knew it was wrong – I agreed.'

'Father passed a note to Mr Haile – I could not bear to face him myself. And that night the Lieutenant announced to the table, that he and I were betrothed.'

Elizabeth paused and looked at the ground. I waited, my mind reeling with all I had heard. She took several long breaths then lifted her head and continued.

'Then that huge wave struck the ship. The water smashed through the saloon. Our cabins were flooded. We thought we were lost. For a moment, I even wished it were true. But for father it achieved a small miracle – from that very night he began to improve.

'Quite quickly, he recovered. But the more he regained his own health, the more disconsolate I became. I felt trapped and deceived. I had accepted a marriage proposal believing it certain my father would die. The security that the marriage would have given, I now no longer required. But I was bound.'

The words caught in her throat. She swallowed and breathed deeply, regaining composure.

'No doubt Mr Haile would have been a good husband – and I, a dutiful wife. But I had no love for him, Mr Fraser, for my heart belonged to another. I want to say now, it belonged just to you…'

She turned and looked at me wistfully, small tears squeezed again from her eyes.

'I pleaded for my father's intercession, to ask the Lieutenant to withdraw. He refused even to listen, said I must not even think such thoughts. It was quite beyond any question. He said Mr Haile and I were a good match, that I would be happy, that our marriage would be for the best and I must stop harbouring doubts.

'When we arrived here in Dunedin, I wanted to leave the ship quickly. I could not bear the thought I might see you and have to say goodbye, especially when you were unaware of all that had transpired.'

Elizabeth stared at me sadly, her face now turned quite pale.

'Fortunately, within a few days, Mr Haile embarked for the north to take up his army commission. We had not set a date to be married; the army needed his services and for how long that would be, was unknown. He expected the campaign could last for up to a year and then he would be given leave to return. I would remain here with father and when Oliver came back, we'd be married.

'Within a few days of his departure, you came and called at our house. I only learned of it later – Father said not a word – but Miss Robertson, curious as to who you were, told me what had occurred.

'I was devastated. I could only think of how grievous it must have been for you and the reality of my own situation upset me again. I was deeply unhappy; each month that passed made me worse. I just had to do something.

'I decided to confront my father. I had never done that before. I had always been the respectful and obedient daughter.

'I told him I must break off the engagement. I did not love Mr Haile and had no wish to marry him. Father had pressed me to agree to the engagement and in the most stressful of circumstances. Now he must help to release me from it.

'To my horror, he declared that was impossible: Mr Haile could call me to the Court for breaching my promise. Father could be ordered to pay a large sum in damages – and I would be embarrassed and shamed. Father would do nothing. He refused. I despaired.

'A rift arose between us and we, who had been so close, were driven quite apart. Though in his wisdom he had done what he thought was best for me, his actions had only brought me misery and my future now likely ruined. Unless I myself took charge of my life – and he could secure my release – the rift between us would grow.

'When at last father realised how much my unhappiness was driving us apart, he became quite contrite, overcome with anguish and remorse. Though he apologised to me, over and again, I would not be consoled.

'Oliver wrote to me regularly, every few months or so. His letters were quite formal – about life with the army and descriptions of the land in the north – they were factual, impersonal and dutiful. I answered him each time and in kind.

'I decided I must wait. Though I was certain you were lost to me, Mr Fraser, I was determined I'd not become Mrs Haile. More time would pass before Oliver could return – time that would separate us even more. I would wait, and one day I would write and plead him for my release.

'A year passed, and one year stretched toward two. The time between Oliver's letters had grown. Eventually one came and I sat down and wrote my reply. I told him we'd been apart for two years; I had changed and was no longer the person that he'd known. I didn't want to be married. It was better for us to part now as friends than it would be to live an unhappy life together. Please, I begged him, for the sake of us both, would he agree to release me.'

Elizabeth paused, as if exhausted by the stress of reliving her tale. I waited, then softly encouraged her to continue. 'And what did he say in response?'

She took a deep breath and looked at me, shaking her head side to side. 'I'll never know. He died without ever replying.'

Thoughts and questions suddenly crashed through my mind. Haile's face when he saw me as he came on the *Pioneer* with that faint, almost mystical smile. He knew what I didn't. Then that last enigmatic look as he swung over the rail toward the longboat waiting below, saying nothing but conveying his farewell, and both of us knowing then that he'd probably not survive. Did he carry her letter, as he charged up the hill? When he threw himself at the enemy, did he care if he lived or if he died? Honour to die but dishonour to live?

Elizabeth interrupted my thoughts as she resumed her story: 'Though I learned of this only recently – my father had sought to make some amends with you, for both his sake and mine.

'He had known of your riverboat business and later heard of your activities on the goldfields from his commissioners. When his friend Governor Grey wrote that engineers were needed in the north, father asked his commissioners to find you. He thought if he encouraged you to take up a post with the Governor, it might later result in your being offered a senior position in the Government. He told me recently that before you departed, he met you and sent you off with his personal introduction to the Governor. I knew nothing of this.

'When you unexpectedly returned – and conveying such astonishing news – father said that he had apologised to you for his misjudgments of the past and invited you to visit us here at our home. Then when you came – and were about to depart – he implored you to visit us again.

'I am thankful he has apologized and I hope you can accept now, that he bears you only goodwill.'

Elizabeth took another long breath. She came close and stood directly before me. She looked up at me intently.

'But none of that is of much comfort to me. After father announced you were coming here, I could barely wait. Sad though it was for Mr Haile to have lost his life, his death had set me free. I could scarcely believe you were still here, in the Colony – and I was about to meet you again. I counted the days, then the hours, until you arrived.

'It was unthinking and naive of me, to expect that nothing between us had changed....'

I interrupted: 'But it all changed for me, as I said, on the very day I came to this house long ago and was told you were betrothed to Haile....'

'Yes, I understand that now. But for all that time since, I did not forget you. You have always been in my thoughts, though I knew not where you were, nor what had become of you.'

'And ever since that day, Miss Elizabeth, I've tried to drive you from my mind.'

'Now I know that too, but I did not when I met you again. I had built up such an expectation of a chance to begin anew. Your remoteness was so strange, so unexpected. I was bewildered and upset. I didn't know what to say to you. I desperately wanted you to know this entire story, but the time and the circumstance prevented.

'Then suddenly you were gone. Though both of us tried to persuade you, you said you would not return. I could not bear the thought that I had lost you again, without your knowing my feelings and all that I had endured. I just had to find some way for you to know, so I called on Lucy and begged for her help.'

Tears welled in her eyes and rolled down over her cheeks. 'If now that you know all this, you still cannot forgive me, I'll try to understand.'

I reached out toward her and took her forearms in my hands, wanting to draw her close but yet holding us apart, feeling myself being drawn deep into the blueness of her eyes.

'Elizabeth, dear Elizabeth, there is nothing for me to forgive. But neither of us will ever forget. Forgetting is different. Scars on the skin fade and heal with time: but scars on the heart, we carry forever.'

EPILOGUE

Though it defied convention – only two months had passed since the death of Oliver Haile – Elizabeth and I were engaged. Elizabeth declared that we had already lost two years without being together and she was not going to lose any more.

I barely even needed to ask Elizabeth if she would accept me – she said that if, on the ship, I had asked her then for her hand, she would readily have agreed and if I were to ask her now, she would willingly do so again. So I did.

We did not ask for her father's permission to marry and together announced plans for our wedding in Spring. I reluctantly left Elizabeth in Dunedin and returned to the goldfields.

In late March I received an urgent message from Elizabeth recalling me back to Dunedin: MacKay had contracted one of the fevers that were rampant in the town. Though I set out immediately and rode hard, MacKay had died from typhus before I arrived.

In April of 1865, we were married in the new stone Presbyterian Church in Dunedin. John Reid was my Best Man and Lucy Bruce was Elizabeth's Matron of Honour.

After the wedding, we embarked on our honeymoon; first to the Molyneaux Mouth to my small cottage.

We voyaged up the river on the *Lady Colina* to Beaumont, camping ashore at night, sitting beyond the firelight and staring at the maze of stars. We toured the goldfields at Gabriel's and Weatherston's, then travelled the Dunstan Road aboard a Cobb & Co coach.

We didn't tarry when we reached Manuherikia and the Molyneaux Gorge, but continued on to Lake Wakatipu, for I was anxious to show Elizabeth the majestic mountains, lakes and rivers that had become so much part of my life. After visiting the Arrow and Shotover, we returned to Manuherikia and the dredge. Though winter would soon be sweeping the goldfields, there was still time to win more gold from the riverbed, but living rough by the river was not what I had ever wanted for my bride. Nor with fever running rife in Dunedin, did I want her to return there. I was in a quandary.

Fortunately, to my surprise, I received an interesting letter from the north. I was invited by Sir John Logan Campbell (and others) to join a new partnership venture, to mine auriferous quartz on a rich claim they held at Coromandel – a peninsula across a gulf east of the colonial capital, Auckland. It was proposed that a new company would be formed to establish a mine and build a machine to crush the auriferous quartz. I was offered a share and asked to manage the venture.

Though reluctant to leave the lucrative dredge on the river, my concern for Elizabeth and the harsh and primitive life I had brought her to on the goldfields was overriding: I decided to accept. John Reid asked to accompany us.

John and I sold the gold dredge to Choie Siew Hoy – the first of several built and owned by the Chinese merchant – and departed for a new life in the north.

In the remote tip of the Coromandel Peninsula we set up the new mine. I designed and built a giant stamper, driven by steam, to crush the quartz into powder and release the riches of gold from seams that ran through the rock.

It was the first of many such mines that were set up all along the rugged and forest-clothed peninsula. I met again my fellow engineer from the river-fleet Maori war days, James Steedman, who later managed another mine company at Thames, 50 miles south, where the peninsula joined to the mainland.

Elizabeth and I had four children, two boys and then two girls. With so many men employed in the mine, Coromandel grew into a small village by the sea. Elizabeth established a school for the children of Coromandel and taught them there herself.

When the gold seam in the Coromandel quartz was eventually worked out, I purchased a large tract of mountainous forested peninsula land from the natives. With my partner John Reid still at my side, we established a logging and sawmilling venture, felling the mighty kauri trees that dominated the forest.

But that is all another story....

AUTHOR'S NOTE

By definition, this story is fiction. However, much of it is true, or is based upon actual places, real characters and historical events as best they are known.

John Cameron Fraser was my maternal great-grandfather.

He was born near Melvich on the north coast of Scotland in Sutherlandshire. The Fraser families were millers, having fled north from Inverness in the persecutions and ethnic-cleansing that followed the Battle of Culloden. At Port Skerra, Hugh Fraser (John's father) owned a mill.

Hugh Fraser's sister (John's aunt) married an Irishman named Bruce and went to live at Tullamore in Ireland. The house that I have described as the Bruces' is in fact my historical Thompson family home near Castledawson in Northern Ireland, still owned by the family ever since they built it in 1754.

When John Fraser was a youth, my family antecedents lived through the potato failure in Ireland and the horrible famine which followed; their experiences and responses being much as I've described.

John Fraser qualified as a marine engineer and, at that time, there were few locations for both engineering and shipbuilding; Belfast in Ireland, Liverpool and the Mersey in England, were both prominent. I have placed him on the Mersey, where many famine-refugees from Ireland had resettled.

The ships that were built at the time, their builders – Page & Grantham and the Laird Bros. – and the evolutions taking place in materials and design were much as I've described. Alfred Holt was indeed trying to perfect higher pressures in steam engines and constrained by the quality of iron and steel. The quite dramatic changes that occurred – Lloyd's Rules being revised, steel in place of wood, steam in place of sail, the screw propeller in place of the paddlewheel – all happened in the few years' period while John Fraser was learning his trade as a marine engineer.

Like many others in those difficult years, he sought adventure and a new life in the colonies. He sailed to New Zealand aboard the American ship *Black Swan* just as the northern and southern States of America went to war. A passenger aboard that ship kept a journal of the voyage that I was fortunate to locate. Thus the description of the ship and all the events of that voyage are much as described: she was indeed one of the first vessels to pioneer the non-stop route, was nearly lost in a storm in the Southern Ocean, and experienced the first recorded earthquake at sea.

For the period, it was an exceptionally long journey to undertake non-stop and out of sight of land. Though the *Black Swan* was a large, well-provisioned ship carrying many less passengers than she was fitted for, the anxiety and fatigue of the voyage was extreme.

His record states that John Fraser built the first steam-powered vessel on the Molyneaux River, now known as the Clutha, in the South Island, proposing to use it to service the settlers establishing farms throughout the long valley. Just as he commenced business, gold was discovered far inland on the river and he quickly had a thriving business transporting men and supplies. He built a small house at Port Molyneaux using bricks which he hand-made and fired himself.

The rush of men to the first major southern goldfield at Gabriel's Gully took place as I've described. At some point in the flush of Gabriel's Gully, John Fraser forsook the riverboat business and instead of supplying the gold miners, became a miner himself.

Subsequent to the years of my researching and writing about the characters and events that took place on the rich goldfields of southern New Zealand, contemporary historians have updated our knowledge in some minor respects, but most of the events match the known facts. John Fraser was a miner during all the events and in the places I've described. The southern goldfields of New Zealand were among the richest and largest ever discovered in the world. In the short period from the spring of 1861 to the autumn of 1863, more than forty-two tons of gold were recovered by men labouring only with shovels, pans and cradles. That it was a turbulent and violent time, that huge fortunes were made and in the most beautiful but inhospitable of regions, under the most arduous conditions, is indisputable.

The Californians Hartley and Reilly discovered the second major field in New Zealand. They did in fact conceal their discovery, leave to re-equip and later return to mine their new claim in secret. It was at the same time that John Fraser gave up the boat to try his hand at mining. Fraser was on the Hartley & Reilly discovery at some early point.

William Fox came to the Otago goldfields from the south. Little is known of him but he was, by all accounts, a resourceful, independent, questing, physically strong character with a strong sense of self-imposed rough justice. Whether John Fraser knew him or not, they were on the same diggings in the same region at the very same time.

William Fox arrived on the third major gold discovery in the remote gorge of the Arrow River shortly after gold had secretly been found there by McGregor and Low. The names of Fox's party of four have never been identified. John Fraser also arrived very early at the Arrow. Whether he was with Fox and was one of the un-named men of his party is not known, but quite possible. A large body of men subsequently worked the Arrow in secret enforced by Fox himself, much in the sequence and circumstance I've described, until Fox was eventually followed and their rich discovery revealed.

The Tipperary Men, the Galway Boys, the claim-jumping, robberies, bandits such as Burgess and the violence were real. So too was the imposition of order by the indomitable Mounted Police. John Fraser was a man of striking physique with a strong sense of fairness and social justice forged in his younger life. His leadership among the men on the goldfield was noted; he was there in those events.

In the description of his life it is recorded that John Fraser built the first powered boat on Lake Whakatipu. I have been unable to verify that claim: John Rees owned a boat and a second was later obtained by the police; how and from where that second boat was obtained is not known – perhaps it was Fraser's, perhaps not.

The fourth major gold discovery at the Shotover River occurred as described. Erihana (Daniel Ellison) and others uniquely discovered one of the richest deposits of gold in the region as described, only to be forced from it by claim-jumpers. Surprisingly for the time (the native Maori being poorly regarded by the white ex-Australian miners), a group of diggers supported Erihana and his chief in forcibly regaining their claim. Erihana, well-known as a strong swimmer, was a deckhand aboard the Otago Harbour pilot boat at the time the *Black Swan* entered the port. Whether John Fraser ever knew him is not known; it is possible.

The 1863 floods and snows in southern New Zealand are the worst ever recorded in that region. They followed an extremely hot summer. The men I've described as having frozen to death on the Pisa Range actually died within visible distance on the Old Man Range where today a plaque records that 30 bodies were found together in one place.

John Fraser next mined at another local discovery on the river Nevis. He did build a paddlewheel dredge of sorts on the Molyneaux but did not remain south to work it. He invented a special pan for washing gold from the quartz which became widely used and was known as the 'Fraser Pan'.

Choie Siew Hoy of Dunedin was an early investor in mechanical dredges.

Today, the fearsome Molyneaux Gorge and the Upper Junction (Cromwell) lie deep beneath the still waters of Lake Dunstan. The rock bridge arching over the turbulent Kawerau River by the Kittleburn (Roaring Meg) eventually collapsed in the 1920s.

It was my other maternal great-grandfather, James Bramwell Steedman, also a marine engineer, who was seconded to the Government naval architect Mr J.J. Stewart and charged with building gunboats for a river fleet in the north. Steedman travelled with Stewart to Sydney and returned on HMS *Eclipse* with the gunboat *Pioneer*.

It was Steedman who completed her construction on the Waikato River and was on board at the bloody battle of Rangiriri. It was Captain Mercer alone who courageously led the final fatal charge of a handful of ill-armed men up onto the walls of the redoubt. The futile assaults, wanton disregard for the lives of his men and the extraordinary decisions made by General Cameron were heavily criticised by those present on that day at Rangiriri.

Today, a major highway passes close by the earthworks that still visibly remain at Rangiriri. A large steel gun cupola from the *Pioneer*, assembled by my great grandfather, still stands on the bank of the river at Mercer (near Rangiriri), where it is used once a year as a memorial to the world wars of the 20th century.

Elizabeth Mary MacKay, also from Scotland, married John Cameron Fraser after an engagement that endured for the astounding period of twelve years. Until her widowed father eventually died, she would not leave him alone. Her father was not the Gold Commissioner whose name was also McKay.

John and Elizabeth Fraser

John and Elizabeth Fraser then lived at Coromandel, which became the location of the second richest gold-bearing region of New Zealand. Fraser and his long-standing companion from the south, John Reid, established a mine and a rock-stamping machine to crush quartz rock and recover its gold. James Steedman later set up a similar venture some thirty miles south at the base of the same peninsula in which Sir John Logan Campbell, was a partner.

John and Elizabeth had five children of whom four survived.

Their eldest daughter, Catherine Elizabeth, married the eldest son of James Bramwell Steedman. Catherine was my grandmother and in turn, her eldest daughter, my mother, was also named Elizabeth.

When the gold in the mine at Coromandel was exhausted, John Fraser purchased the mountainous Waiau block, containing heavy forest, from the Maori owners. He set up a logging operation, felling the giant kauri trees and built a large sawmill, cutting the kauri into timber which was shipped across the gulf to the growing town of Auckland. He continued the timber business for many years, into his old age.

He retained his interest in engineering, designing and building a laundry washing-machine for domestic use which was sold extensively throughout New Zealand and Australia. He was regarded as an authority on mining and revisited Otago many times, advising Sir John Logan Campbell and other investors on various dredging proposals.

He died in 1915 at the age of 81. He lies buried with Elizabeth in the grounds of the small white-painted Presbyterian Church on a hillside above the present-day town of Coromandel – the church he built himself, with timber from his own mill.

A number of people and organisations have helped me by providing information and material used in this book, for which I am extremely grateful. Among them, in particular, I would like to thank and acknowledge the following for their assistance: James Horne of the Stone Store, Port Skerra, Scotland, who on his own initiative voluntarily researched my Fraser family in Sutherlandshire; A.E. Train of Forsinard, Scotland, who provided family genealogy of my Fraser family back to Inverness; The late Esther Thompson of Leitrim, Castledawson, Ireland, for family history; The Scotsman whose name was lost when my computer crashed, who gave advice on transport and access in 1830s Scotland; The Librarians of the New Zealand Maritime Museum, Auckland, for locating a chronicle of the voyage of the *Black Swan* from England to New Zealand; Master Sergeant Joe Evans of the New Zealand Army Museum, Waiouru, for advice on the armaments current in New Zealand in 1860, those used by the Otago Mounted Police and by the Waikato War combatants of 1863-64; The Otago Goldfields Heritage Trust and Roberta Lariman; The Alexandra Museum (Alexandra) and the Lakes District Museum (Arrowtown), Central Otago, NZ.

References and material have been drawn from the following publications: *Boats, Ships & Rafts* by Wolfgang Rudolph; *The Blackwall Frigates* by Basil Lubbock; 'Voyage of the Black Swan', passenger-author unknown; *The History of Otago* by A.H.McLintock; *The Story of Otago* by A.H. Reed; *Early Days in Central Otago* by Robert Gilkison; *The Goldrushes* by Kevin Boon; *Gabriel's Gully Jubilee*, Government Publications; *Prospecting for Gold* by William Heinz; *History of Goldmining in New Zealand* by J.H.Salmon; *Goldmining In New Zealand*, Government Publications; *Gold Quartz & Cyanide* by John Ingram; *The Shotover River* by A.J. de la Mare; *Maori and Pakeha* by Shrimpton & Mulgan, 1921; *The New Zealand Wars and the Pioneering Period* (Vol 1) by James Cowan, 1922; Archives of the *New Zealand Herald*, November 13, 1863; Published obituaries of John Cameron Fraser and James Bramwell Steedman.